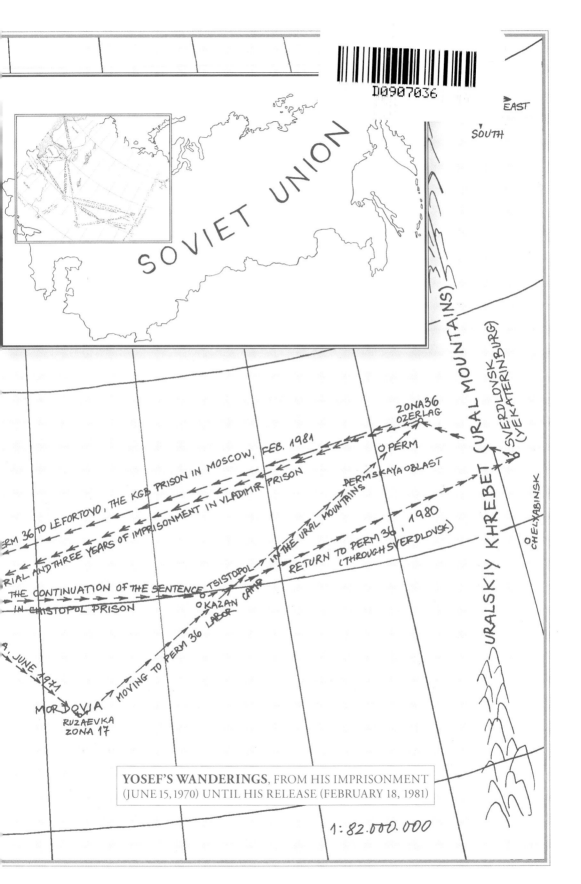

EAST

SOUTH

SOVIET UNION

ZONA 36
OZERLAG

O PERM

PERMSKAYA OBLAST

URALSKIY KHREBET (URAL MOUNTAINS)

SVERDLOVSK
(YEKATERINBURG)

O CHELYABINSK

ERM 36 TO LEFORTOVO, THE KGB PRISON IN MOSCOW, FEB. 1981

RIAL AND THREE YEARS OF IMPRISONMENT IN VLADIMIR PRISON

RETURN TO PERM 36, 1980
(THROUGH SVERDLOVSK)

IN THE URAL MOUNTAINS

THE CONTINUATION OF THE SENTENCE TSISTOPOL

IN CHISTOPOL PRISON

O KAZAN

O KAZAN LABOR CAMP

A. JUNE 1971

MOVING TO PERM 36

MORDOVIA
RUZAEVKA
ZONA 17

YOSEF'S WANDERINGS, FROM HIS IMPRISONMENT
(JUNE 15, 1970) UNTIL HIS RELEASE (FEBRUARY 18, 1981)

1 : 82.000.000

UNBROKEN SPIRIT

Yosef Mendelevich

UNBROKEN SPIRIT

A Heroic Story of Faith, Courage, and Survival

Translated from the Hebrew by Benjamin Balint

gefen גפן
publishing house הוצאת ספרים
JERUSALEM ◆ NEW YORK   Est. 1981

Translations from *The Living Torah* used by permission of
Moznaim Publishing Company.

COVER DESIGN: Michal Cohen
TYPESETTING: Benjie Herskowitz, Etc. Studios

ISBN: 978-965-229-563-7

7 9 8

Gefen Publishing House Ltd.
6 Hatzvi Street
Jerusalem 94386, Israel
972-2-538-0247
orders@gefenpublishing.com

Gefen Books
11 Edison Place
Springfield, NJ 07081
516-593-1234
orders@gefenpublishing.com

www.gefenpublishing.com

Printed in Israel   *Send for our free catalogue*

Library of Congress Cataloging-in-Publication Data

Mendelevich, Iosif.
  [Mivtsa' hatunah (Operation wedding). English]
  Unbroken spirit: a heroic story of faith, courage and survival; translated from the
  Hebrew by Benjamin Balint / Yosef Mendelevich.
     p. cm.
  ISBN 978-965-229-563-7
  1. Mendelevich, Iosif. 2. Refuseniks – Soviet Union –Biography. 3. Political
  prisoners – Soviet Union – Biography. 4. Immigrants – Israel – Biography. 5. Jews –
  Soviet Union – Biography.
  I. Balint, Benjamin, 1976- II. Title.
  DS135.R95M4561413 2012
  365'.45092—dc23
  [B]
                    2012004694

This book is dedicated to the memory of
US Senator Henry M. "Scoop" Jackson.

We Jews of Russia are grateful to him – and to the entire American people – for the great efforts he made to free us from the darkness of modern-day Egyptian enslavement. This taught us how powerfully a man can aid another man, and another nation, if he truly loves his fellow man and humanity at large.

God rest his soul.

– Yosef Mendelevich

In Memoriam

We remember those who selflessly volunteered their time and resources and often sacrificed their personal lives to secure freedom of emigration from the USSR. Their commitment and dedication will never be forgotten.

Micah Naftalin, national director, Union of Councils for Soviet Jews, 1987–2009.

Lynn Singer, executive director, Long Island Committee for Soviet Jews, 1970–2007; national president, Union of Councils for Soviet Jews, 1981–1984.

Hal Light, San Francisco Bay Area for Soviet Jews; national president, Union of Councils for Soviet Jews.

Selma Light, San Francisco Bay Area for Soviet Jews.

Irene Manekofsky, Washington Committee for Soviet Jews, 1977–1978; National President, Union of Councils for Soviet Jews, 1978–1980.

Lil Hoffman, Colorado Committee of Concern, 1960–1996.

Ally Milder, Omaha Committee for Soviet Jews.

Si Frumkin, Southern California Council for Soviet Jews, 1969–2009.

Donna Arzt, Boston Action for Soviet Jewry; Legal Advocacy for Soviet Jews.

Genya Intrator, 35s Women's Campaign for Soviet Jewry, Canada, 1971–2008; Canadian Committee for Soviet Jewry.

Delysia Jayson, 35s Women's Campaign for Soviet Jewry, UK; Keren Klita, Israel.

Rabbi Meir Kahane, founder, Jewish Defense League, 1970–1984.

Yuri Shtern, co-founder, Soviet Jewry Education and Information Center, Jerusalem, 1983–1989.

Contents

Chapter One: "Go Forth from Your Country" 1

Chapter Two: Arrest, Interrogation, and Trial 55

Chapter Three: Gulag 113

Chapter Four: "And Joseph Was Brought Down to Egypt" 165

Chapter Five: The Lord's Day 251

Epilogue 333

About the Author 337

Foreword

The fall of the USSR has receded with astonishing speed into a distant foggy past, dragging with it the clarity of our image of an empire that was governed by fear. The Kremlin's war on opposition, real or imagined, reached a climax under Stalin, who murdered millions of Soviet citizens, many of whom were swallowed up in the vast network of labor and prison camps, never to be seen again. Stalin's legacy of persecution, anti-Semitism, and terror was cultivated by his successors to stamp out flickering embers of individualism, resistance, and dissidence. The product was to be a new man: "Homo Sovieticus," a Soviet android, a mindless puppet controlled by Soviet propaganda.

Kremlin leaders made one fatal error. They failed to anticipate the determination of those who made the decision to be guided by the compass of principle and truth. The refuseniks – Jews who were refused permission to emigrate – were determined to live life as free men even in a totalitarian country. They cast off the protective armor of adherence to the Soviet lie and began a path of self-discovery that led to their identification with universal moral values, God, and a sense of Jewish peoplehood – which often set them on the long, treacherous road to prison.

The Soviets understood that they could break a person physically, but failed to realize that they could not also break a person's will. They failed to comprehend that there were voices that could not be silenced by terror; from the most remote and isolated regions of Siberia, even from the depths of a prison's isolation cells, those voices would be heard in the West.

The message of those who broke with the Soviet system never wavered: Life without principles was life without meaning. Truth demanded sacrifice.

The English edition of *Unbroken Spirit*, published originally in Russian and subsequently in Hebrew as *Operation Wedding*, has been a dream since the fall of the Soviet Union. Though it is impossible to assess the magnitude of a single event in history, the audaciously conceived Leningrad hijacking plot to take a plane out of the Soviet Union in order to attract world attention to the plight of Soviet Jews was the sonic boom that ultimately broke through the silence of the West. The trial and sentencing of Yosef Mendelevich and the other Leningrad trial defendants in 1970 inspired millions of Jews who had previously cherished no hope of leaving the USSR. Mendelevich was among the first who led the revival of religious Judaism in the USSR, inspiring refuseniks in the Soviet Union and Jews throughout the world with his unyielding determination to observe the Torah's commandments even within the iron crucible of Soviet prisons and labor camps.

The Leningrad trials ignited Jews in England, France, Canada, and the United States, and the grassroots movement they mobilized became the first line of defense for the Leningrad trial defendants and subsequently for the tens of thousands of refuseniks who were consistently denied the right to emigrate over the next quarter of a century. Through this grassroots underground network, the Leningrad defendants, along with thousands of fellow prisoners and other refuseniks, were given an international voice in the free world's press and governments.

We welded our will to theirs and we were changed in the process.

Those of us who made Yosef's struggle our struggle, fighting for his release from prison and ultimate emigration to Israel, are grateful for the opportunity to have immersed ourselves into the current of Jewish history and to have been transformed in the process.

Unbroken Spirit owes its appearance in English to many. My deep appreciation to Judy Lash Balint for shepherding this work and to Ilan Greenfield of Gefen Publishing House, who instinctively recognized the significance of this book for English-speaking readers. Benjamin Balint's translation brought the text to life in English. We want to thank the artist, Luba Bar Menachem, for her fine graphic rendering of the map detailing Yosef's deportations and transits. Rabbi Pinchas Stolper's wisdom, experience, and practical counsel were of tremendous help and encouragement and to him Yosef and I are most grateful.

It is impossible to overstate our gratitude to Dr. Irving and Cherna Moskowitz, for their generous support for this important project.

Thank you to Moznaim Press for permission to use the very fine translations of *pesukim* by Rabbi Aryeh Kaplan of blessed memory, from their publication of *The Living Torah*.

My profound gratitude to my colleagues and family who were on the frontline of the battlefield in the struggle to secure the release of the prisoners of conscience and enable the emigration of Soviet Jewry. Their generous contribution toward the English-language publication of *Unbroken Spirit* is but the most recent of a long history of commitment to the ideals and principles that this book represents.

Special thanks to the following people, whose support made this book possible:

Michael and Jackie Abels
Harvey and Jackie Barnett
Scott and Kathy Cohen
Leonard Cohen
Ron and June Daniels
Hans and Donna Sternberg
Jerome L. Stern
Bob and Susan Mednick
Lessa Roskin
Action for Post-Soviet Jewry
Bob and Doris Gordon
Judy Patkin
David and Brooke Warso
Joshua and Elizabeth Cohen
Anonymous, in memory of Naphtali Ben Mordechai and
      Erika Augusta Bas Emil
Boris and Amelia Dragunsky
Glenn and Lenore Richter
Rae Sharfman
Henry Gerber
Morey and Barbara Schapira
Howard and Hinda Canter
Howard and Brenda Goffen
A.W. and Barbara Karchmer

May you, your families, and all of Israel be blessed with life and health, peace, and security.

I am profoundly grateful to the Almighty for allowing me and so many of us to have witnessed and to have played a role in the miracle of this modern exodus.

Pamela Braun Cohen
President, Union of Councils for Soviet Jews, 1986–1996
Pesach 5772

Chapter One

"Go Forth from Your Country"

"God said to Abram, 'Go away from your land, from your birthplace, and from your father's house, to the land that I will show you." (Genesis 12:1)

Iawoke first. The sun had just risen. In a lot drawn the day before, luck, as usual, had not been kind to me: I had drawn the short stick, which entailed a night on the cold ground without the comfort of a sleeping bag. Zev had lent me a coat to bundle up in, and I had sunk into a deep, dreamless slumber, giving no thought to the likelihood that the day drawing to a close would be my last as a free man, perhaps even the last day of my life.

We arose and began our preparations. Zev went to the station to greet Eduard and Mark, who was coming with his family. Yisrael, Tolya, and I began to fill the backpacks: each got a rubber-coated club, and mine also got gags, ropes, a small ax, and a hunting knife.

We turned toward the airfield. It was an astonishingly beautiful morning; beautiful but alien. A strange morning in a strange land. And though *my* land, the land that God had ordained for Abraham and his descendants, was then a thousand miles distant, her memory had never left my heart. And now I was marching, striding toward her, fulfilling the commandment given to Abraham: "Go away from your land." To walk, to return home – or to die.

At the airfield we saw several sheds scattered about, and not far from them some small planes. We'd intended to have a quick bite to eat, but changed our minds. Not worth it. The guys told me that my glasses, cap, and Polish raincoat gave me a foreign and suspicious look. I knew I had to avoid standing out, so

I removed the coat and glasses, but left the beret – a Jew, after all, must not go bareheaded.

In the end, these precautions only belied our naïveté, for it seemed that somehow we had been tracked down and followed. The day before, Yura and Alec had managed only with great difficulty to elude our pursuers, and when at six that evening we had gotten off the streetcar at the Smolny station, Mark had noticed two men dashing after us, immediately disappearing into the bushes next to the station. Could this be mere chance?

In a forest clearing, we had been rehearsing the details of the operation ahead when suddenly a black Volga, of the type favored by the KGB, had stopped nearby. Two men had gotten out, fixed their gaze on us for some time, and then started to urinate in unison. Could this, too, be chalked up to mere chance?

It seemed to me almost as though we were taking part in some kind of film noir. The most reasonable course of action would have been to abort the operation. It was clear as day that we had been caught and set up, and that we would not succeed in escaping to Israel. Why, then, did we fail to call it off? A difficult question… But we felt ourselves on the verge of realizing our highest ambitions, our most passionate desires, of achieving what we had so long yearned for, and so it was hard to simply turn back. Besides, what alternative was there? To stay in the country? For what? So our inner compulsions overcame logic and common sense. In fact, I'd never felt so at peace with myself, so joyful. I believed I was at last fulfilling this divine commandment. I felt serene, prepared for anything.

· · · · ·

And so, all of us are present, prepared to go all the way. We split up in the departures hall, pretending not to know one another. I sit next to Yisrael and tell him about my ten-month-old nephew. Someone in a pilot's uniform sits next to us, and eavesdrops. So be it: in a louder voice, I continue talking about little Yankele. The "pilot" grins to himself, as if to say, "I can't be tricked by such idiotic ruses."

Meanwhile, a large crowd has gathered at the entrance to the airport. Bus after bus arrives. I hadn't imagined so many passengers would fly out of this tiny airfield.

They announce that our flight is boarding: 8:15 a.m., June 15, 1970.

We pretend to be innocent tourists, each of us approaching the boarding platform separately. But because we move toward the platform hurriedly, we end up walking in a single column, with me last. I look at my colleagues ahead of me with pride, but also with worry: with pride because they look like heroic soldiers determined to fight for the freedom of our people; the cause for worry, on the other hand, reveals itself soon enough. I notice that my friends are shooting anxious glances my way. At first I take the glances as the sequel of an argument we'd had earlier, when they'd asked me to remove my beret to make me appear less suspicious. I had replied that as a religious Jew I preferred not to go bareheaded. And so now I begin to feel angry: don't they have bigger worries at the moment than my beret? Then I notice that the glances aren't directed at me at all, but behind me. The leader of our operation, the Jewish pilot Mark, is missing. What has happened to him? Has he already been apprehended? Or betrayed us at the last moment? Who will pilot the plane after the hijacking?

Such are the thoughts racing through my mind, and I realize that the fate of the operation rests in my hands. No time for hesitation. I sprint back toward the pavilion where I saw him not a quarter of an hour before. Did he not hear the boarding call?

As I run, several people block my path and tell me that it's forbidden to exit this way. I charge through them, and continue running wildly.

Lo and behold, I discover our pilot sitting placidly with his wife and two daughters, eating breakfast, a guitar at his side. Nearly choked with rage, I scream: "What are you doing just sitting here? We're about to board our flight toward freedom and you're munching on sandwiches?"

Mark, startled, glances at his watch. "It's only 8:15. The flight was scheduled to board at 8:45. They're early. I don't like this."

"Nonsense. This isn't the army. Schedules change. Come!"

"Fine," he says. "I'll get everything together. Tell the others I'm coming."

I run back, nearly floating on air, filled with pride that I've saved the mission. Back on the platform, my path is again blocked, this time by passengers from a different flight, whom I overhear saying: "Look, look, soldiers are beating them." I do not see what they have seen. I hear, but cannot absorb what they have said. As I try to push through, I am tackled to the ground, my head hitting the concrete tarmac. I put up no resistance.

"You're under arrest."

My wrists are cuffed. Now I understand what the other passengers have been talking about. We've been captured. I'd been prepared for this – even for this, and when I am put back on my feet, though my glasses have fallen off, I see before me a tragic sight: swarms of soldiers, policemen, canine teams, and border police, and amid all of them my colleagues, cuffed and bound, one of them still struggling with our apprehenders. Not a moment after registering this mental image, I hear shots. As I turn toward the sound, I see that Mark, our pilot, has been shot, a severed sheet of his scalp covering his entire face. His wife, Alevtina, is screaming with fear, his daughters sobbing. Tragedy. I've never seen such an awful sight.

All is lost. They're already taking us to be interrogated on the spot. On the way, these idiots take my backpack, with the weapons inside. Fine, let them search me. They bring me to a small room, packed with high-ranking officers and special investigators, one of whom proffers an arrest warrant. "Read it and sign!"

I read it with disbelief. They know everything: "District prosecutor's office… According to the report of the operations department of the security services, a cell of Jewish terrorists has been active in the area of the airfield with the intent of betraying the motherland and fleeing to the imperialist state of Israel, thus violating Article 15-64 of the criminal code. I hereby order the arrest and interrogation of the criminal gang, and warn that if the charges prove true, its members will face the death penalty."

Death penalty? For me? How will I able to stand this – the KGB interrogations, the trial, the death sentence? These require heroic fortitude, like Judah Maccabee, or Joseph Trumpeldor, the hero of Tel Hai, whose famous last words were, "Never mind, it is good to die for our country," or Mordechai Anielewicz, leader of the Warsaw ghetto uprising. But I'm no hero, just a miserable Jewish student.

But this is no time for ruminations.

"You've read it? Sign here!"

"At least uncuff me, or else I can't sign anything." The KGB, lacking cuffs, had bound my hands with laundry cord, which was exceedingly painful.

"Unbind him."

My hands are numb. As they awaken, I pretend to read the warrant again. "No, I will not sign."

"Why not?"

"This is complete falsehood."

"Ah, you don't yet take us seriously. Bind his hands so he won't feel them and take him to the KGB interrogations facility. There he'll tell us everything. And be warned: if you're stubborn, your punishment will be severe."

As I am taken to the KGB car, I catch a glimpse of one of my colleagues, Izzy, with his cuffed hands raised above his head, a hint of a smile on his lips. Where have I seen such a vision? Ah, yes, in an album we had at home of the

Warsaw ghetto uprising, a photograph of a fighter just then being led out of his bunker by Nazis, holding his arms in the same kind of triumphal gesture. I remember thinking: he's happy to go to his death this way, in battle, rather than as a sheep to the slaughter. And so it is with us.

In the car, disguised as a civilian vehicle, I glance outside at the free world, perhaps for the last time. Though it is Russia, the very country I have been trying to flee, here too, under the blue morning skies, people are going to work, mothers are pushing carriages. Life. My life, I think, might be coming to an end.

I ask myself a piercing question: *Nu, what do you have to say for yourself? Do you regret your decisions?*

There are moments in a man's life when he cannot deceive himself, when there is no one to deceive. I think to myself: *No, I regret nothing*. So deep is my love for my people and my homeland that had I passed up this chance to escape this foreign land I would have despised myself for the rest of my days. For something of the highest importance you must be prepared to pay the highest price. I was willing to sacrifice even my love of life, and now I feel content.

The next moment, I am taken from the car and admitted, for the first time in my life, into prison, a cold, ugly place. The warden, Colonel Kruglov, is in a celebratory mood, for many new Jewish prisoners have arrived, and he smells blood. Next comes a humiliating, probing body search, conducted as though I am no longer human.

"Do you have weapons? Money?" I smile to myself. Everything is in the backpack they mistakenly cast aside at the airfield. Let them try to prove it belonged to me.

"I have nothing."

My belt and shoelaces are removed, and I am taken to my cell, a tiny hovel: a board, a small table, a barred window affording barely a glimpse of sky, loneliness. No clock, no hour, no time. Silence like a grave. I gradually lose all sense of time and place. The interrogators wish to instill the feeling that for all intents and purposes I am already dead, that no one needs me or cares about me. In the meantime, they're interrogating those whom they've already broken down. Alone, I sink into my memories of how it all began.

· · · · ·

First memory picture: I am five. The year is 1953. I'm playing with other children in the courtyard, and, as usual, fighting. An older child compliments me on my courage: "You'll be a brave officer one day." I return home to find my mother sitting on the floor in the dark, holding a newspaper, crying.

"Mama, what happened?"

"Stalin, the father of the Soviet people, has died," she said. "What will we do without him?"

My beloved father and mother, like most Soviet citizens, fervently believed in "the Sun of Nations," as Stalin was sometimes called. Such was our education.

A second image, this one from 1954. In our school, the principal would wear his military uniform, as though the war had not ended, as though we students served as little Soviet soldiers. In first grade, our teacher asked us, each in our turn, to announce our nationality. Among the forty students – Russians, Ukrainians, Latvians – I was the only Jew. The rest were Soviet children, well aware that to be Russian was the highest blessing. To be born Ukrainian was half-tragic; to be a "Chochmek," as they derogatorily and indiscriminately called anyone with roots in Asia Minor, was worse; but nothing could equal the infamy of being Jewish. "You don't look at all Jewish" – this was the highest compliment one could be paid by a Russian acquaintance. But the God-given shape of my nose and face left no doubt as to my origins. And so I waited in dread like a hunted animal for my turn to answer the "nationality" question.

"Mendelevich?"

"Jew," I replied, breathing with difficulty. The class giggled. Today, my adult heart pities the kid I was then, standing alone before an entire mocking class. Maybe it would have been better to lie, to remain silent, but I couldn't possibly have denied my Jewishness.

Yet there ended my powers of endurance. When the teacher asked, "Where does your father work?" I replied, "I don't know," and indeed in my case it was better not to know. While the fathers of my classmates served as officers or pilots, mine was a junkman, a scrap collector – work suited not for Russians, but for Jews. The teacher nodded her head in sarcastic admonishment: "Such a big child and he doesn't know…" Once more, peals of laughter burst out.

No wonder, then, that I withdrew into myself, becoming an introvert who disliked venturing out to the street. From then on, I did not grow up as an upstanding Soviet citizen, I did not love the Soviet Union, and I lived my life within our four walls. No birch trees populated my dreams, and no posters of Russian landscapes graced my walls. So when the time came I didn't have to forcibly detach myself from Russia in order to emigrate to Israel.

• • • • •

In those days I read a great deal of Soviet children's books, but somehow their propaganda failed to penetrate into my heart. Perhaps it was a mark of God's will that I would remember nothing of what I read. Naturally, I also got my hands on classic children's books like those of Hans Christian Andersen and the Brothers Grimm, but my shelves (unlike those of my young nephews here in Israel) did not include a Chumash or *Kitzur Shulchan Aruch*. My father had learned in a cheder, but although the rebbe vouched for his talents, the pupil could not continue on to the yeshiva. Instead, he had to work to support the family. Years later, however, when I was eight years old (an age when, I knew, Israeli students were already reading Genesis), my father gathered his children together to teach us the letters of the *aleph-bet*. It would be only many years later, as an adult, that I would go on further to actually learn Hebrew, the language of my people.

I realized that success at school brought my parents pride, and so I became a diligent student. No doubt my first teacher was amazed, fifteen years later, to read in the papers that the obedient child she had once known had become a "dangerous criminal."

Love and affection permeated our home. The purity of family life was surely among the values that preserved the Jews in our long exile; my home was a perfect example of the power of this ideal. Never did I hear my parents fight, and even among the children warmth prevailed. Sensing ourselves part of a family, we never felt alone. The serenity and love that characterized our Jewish home stood out in even higher relief against the backdrop of the simple Russian family, with the drunk father beating his wife, neglecting his children, or abandoning his family altogether.

How then does a Jewish child, brought up in this bosom of love and goodwill, manage to survive such a cruel environment? How does he continue to love the good, all the while hating the enemy and longing for his downfall? The inclination to "live and let live," after all, could yield only disaster. One convict I later came to know, Leib Lodinsky, sought to stay on good terms both with other prisoners and with the wardens. But life, often cruel, compels us to choose. Leib chose to take the side of the strong, the side of the KGB, and informed on Tverdochlibov, the editor of *Chronicles*, with the result that the informant ended up a broken man, suffering severe pangs of conscience. A man – in jail or on the outside – who tries to be friends with everyone usually ends up submitting to the oppressor. I always feared losing my powers of resistance, and so I steeled myself for each interrogation session the way one might before confronting an enemy. This is essential, for after the first month or so of imprisonment, the initial tension erodes and your guard is lowered. Your interrogator, often the only man you get to know within the prison, becomes like an old acquaintance (in fact he is specially trained to earn your confidence), and you must remind yourself of his true nature.

This split between the realities of home life and outside life drew me, as a child, ever further into myself. To avoid becoming a hypocrite, dutifully murmuring slogans while keeping my true opinions to himself, I sealed myself off from the threatening outside world. This was true from very early on.

I remember, for instance, playing with friends in the courtyard once when some drunken hooligans appeared, cursing and smashing empty vodka bottles against the wall. In our home, we took good care of things, and nothing was thrown away for no reason. Seeing that taboo violated, witnessing the crass expression of the will to destruction, shocked me and sent me scurrying home, and from that moment I avoided stepping into that courtyard.

Before the Second World War, drunkenness in Latvia had been a rare sight, but by the late fifties the Latvians would get drunk as often as Russians. On payday, masses of workers would congregate around the liquor stores, blowing a month's salary in the space of a few hours, even though their wives had begged them to set aside some money to feed the children. On the adjacent streets, one would see swaying drunks accosting passersby.

A Latvian once approached me and said, "Spare me some change for a little vodka, and I, a true Latvian, will bend my knee before you!" I gave him a coin and hurried off. Nor were Jews immune. I knew a Jew who after his release from labor camp used to beg – in Yiddish! – for money to buy vodka. Truly a disgrace.

I've never in my life tasted cognac or vodka. We had wine in our home only on Jewish holidays. Many in Russia got drunk in hopeless and joyless despair. It's no wonder, then, that I distanced myself from that world of emptiness and fear. But the world did not long let me ignore it.

· · · · ·

Winter vacation, January 1957. I am ten years old. As I return home with my sisters after a New Year's performance, my mother opens the door with trembling hands. Our home is being searched. Two men rummage in the closet. My mother's eyes fill with tears; my father turns pale as a ghost. The search is part of Khrushchev's much-praised war on crime. The premier has announced that by 1980 we will watch the last criminal in the Soviet Union on television. Fortunately, he died before then; otherwise he would have had to show on screen the giant Soviet factories and construction sites that employed some four million criminals.

When the Soviets searched for criminals, they habitually began with the Jews. In a grove next to our city two men were arrested for unlawful hunting, and were discovered to have homemade bullets. During the investigation, they revealed that to make the bullets they had purchased lead from a certain scrap dealer, and offered to take investigators to her store. They then lead the police to my father's workplace, and though the woman in question was of course nowhere to be found, the officers were only too happy to arrest a Jew. Hence that day's search of our home, its purpose to confiscate my father's property and gold – for surely, they believed, every Jew must have a case full of gold. In the end, they were stunned by our home's modesty.

My father's trial took place in April. We children did not accompany him to court. "My God," I prayed, "I do not want my father to be imprisoned. Do not let a tragedy befall us." It was the first time in my life I was aware of turning to God. I had no religious upbringing, and knew nothing about the Creator of heaven and earth. And yet, though I didn't even know if He existed, still I prayed to Him. I suppose this happens frequently. Unless your ears are deaf to your heart's entreaties, if in a time of crisis you find yourself asking for divine help, ultimately you will come to acknowledge God.

Because his alleged black-market profit from the imagined sale of a few grams of lead had been five rubles, my father was sentenced to five years in prison.

My father's life had been wide ranging. Like my mother, he was born in Dvinsk, in southern Latvia. Orphaned as a child, he joined a Zionist youth organization and in the 1920s he assisted pioneers from Latvia who were emigrating to Palestine. At age sixteen he joined Latvia's Communist Party, entranced by its concern for the impoverished classes. By eighteen, he was responsible for providing medical services to an entire district, and at twenty-two he was named by the Party as a candidate for election to the Latvian council.

But his Communist ideology did not distance him from a sentimental attachment to Judaism. My father told me that during those years he observed the Jewish holidays and fasted on Yom Kippur. When the Nazis took power in Germany and began to persecute Jews, he once planted an explosives-laden bottle in a window of the German consulate in Dvinsk. Hitler personally asked Latvian president Kārlis Ulmanis to launch an investigation, and my father, fearing a death sentence, went into hiding. In 1938, with the wave of mass arrests in the Soviet Union cresting, he left the Communist Party, but continued his union activities. When the Germans entered Dvinsk, not long after the war began, my father crossed the border into the USSR on a horse-drawn wagon, and encountered the Soviet reality: devastation, filth, famine, unemployment. In fact, the Soviet reality was worse than anything anti-Soviet propaganda could have imagined.

At the conclusion of the trial, my father was sent to work at a labor camp brick factory, leaving my mother alone with their three children. I've no doubt that we could not have survived without the Jewish tradition of mutual assistance: every month, my father's friends would each send us a small sum of money.

I vividly remember the trip to the camp to see him. Mother brought delicacies: chicken, candy, cake. The camp was on land so forlorn and parched that I had to wonder how they found such a desolate spot in all the forested Latvian landscape. You can imagine the horror that afflicted an eleven-year-old upon seeing his father in a tattered uniform marching in a long column surrounded by soldiers and guard dogs. My mother could not help crying aloud.

Our meeting lasted an hour. Although he appeared slimmer and his hair had been cropped, he seemed to my eyes somewhat younger than before. But my mother, unable to stand the shock of it all, suffered a nervous collapse and had to be hospitalized. My younger sister and I were sent out of town to a summer camp.

• • • • •

There, for the first time, I found myself in a "pure" Soviet reality: kicks, insults, abuse, curses, and all manner of vulgarity characteristic of children that age. I couldn't bear it. Even today, after all my years in the labor camp, I can't bear Russian cursing. But God protected my soul from corruption.

Rather than succumb to all this, I resolved to run away. On one excursion, I hid behind a tree trunk and waited for everyone else to pass by. My aim was to reach the city, some forty kilometers away. I walked along the train tracks, only to reach a military bridge. A guard trained his weapon on me. I dove to the ground, and crawled back. Eventually I boarded a train, without a ticket, and of course was soon caught. Rather than invent an explanation, I told the truth: I had run away from summer camp because I hated it there. Other passengers took my side, and the ticket inspector pitied me and let me off rather than drag me to the police station. Somehow, a compassionate Jew volunteered to take me home. Who can harden his heart in the face of a suffering child?

Yet despite my escape from the summer camp, and despite my antisocial tendencies, I felt no hatred in those days for the Soviet regime. A kind of paradox was at play: Soviet citizens combined a clear-eyed recognition of the fact that the regime was based on a lie with a complete submission to that same regime. My own self-imposed isolation had at that time not yet fully matured: outwardly, I behaved like everyone. I joined the Komsomol, the Communist youth union. I read a great deal, remained dutiful, and in school they pronounced themselves pleased with my "political consciousness."

I was especially good at reading aloud and declaiming passages in front of the class. Once, I was cast in the lead role as the famous pilot Maresyev, who parachuted behind enemy lines, injuring both legs. The partisans who found him asked, "Who are you?" to which he replied, "A Russian I am, a Russian!" The moment I pronounced these words, the class burst into laughter. Though I could recite Russian better than any of them, they would not let me forget that I did not belong to the "master race." So be it: I felt no need to belong to them.

· · · · ·

At the time when Israeli children my age were celebrating their bar mitzvahs, my life felt empty and bare. No one bothered to induct me into a life of Torah, and only the smallest spark of Jewishness, inherited from my father, glowed like an ember in my heart. At home a kind of duality prevailed: outward acceptance of the Soviet regime, inward observance of some semblance of Jewish tradition.

My father managed to bring us some matzah for Passover, and during the seder he would chronicle the history of the Jews, starting with the creation of the world and (around midnight) reaching our own era. In many Jewish families in the Soviet Union, children grew up knowing nothing of this. At least I knew I belonged to a people with its own heritage. I don't imagine that my father consciously attempted to raise us as Jews; he was simply incapable of acting otherwise. For him it was a kind of inner spiritual necessity. And as I review my own life, I realize that the same holds true for me: I simply could not have behaved otherwise. I was a Jew, and could be nothing else.

As I child I especially loved the lights and latkes of Chanukah. To help my mother fry latkes, we would be willing to peel a bucketful of potatoes, if need be. Not that food is the most significant part of Jewish holidays, but in my view it's important that the more exalted parts of a holiday be mixed with sensual delights – the very kind of pleasures that make childhood memories so vivid. Abstract symbols may be easily lost, but our symbols are preserved precisely because they are so indelibly stamped on our daily lives. And so in my child-hood memories a warm corner is reserved in my heart not just for the joy of celebrating the holidays, but the joy of preparing for these holidays, which seemed no less exciting than the holidays themselves. I can still remember how I ground up matzah to make matzah meal for kneidlach, or how I stuffed hamentaschen with poppy, or crushed potatoes for latkes. These preparations involved arduous effort. We stood in line for hours to buy chicken or fish. Buying such products in a Soviet city suffering from shortages was far from easy. To this day I'm something of an expert in Jewish food. Israeli children today seem to me spoiled and coddled in this regard. Perhaps I had an exilic kind of upbringing, but in retrospect it turns out that the strained circum-stances of growing up in the Soviet Union might have afforded me the best preparation of all.

· · · · ·

Thanks to his Jewish colleagues, who demonstrated his innocence, my father was released before his full prison term was up. Most of all this was due to senior engineer A. M. Vishniyevsky, who volunteered, unbidden, to come to the aid of another Jew. This was my first lesson in national solidarity. When my father returned home, however, he had noticeably aged, and his health had weakened. On the day of his release, he suffered a heart attack, which would affect him for the rest of his days. Several months later, my mother died.

I celebrated my bar mitzvah by reading Feuchtwanger's *Jew Suss* in Yid-dish translation, and it was a pivotal point, for it awakened within me a sense of Jewishness. I felt the first stirrings of an urge to return to my people. I found a copy of the book of Judges, which had belonged to my grandfather, a Lubavitcher Chasid. At the time, I knew not a word of Hebrew, and though I could barely string two letters together, I read a bit each day with growing excitement. My father also taught me to say Modeh Ani every morning. These discoveries were the first steps on the path I have followed to this day. Every Jewish child's heart is open to the word of God, and if he but listens to his own heart, and not merely to the dry dictates of reason, such first steps are sure to be followed by others.

Another fateful step on my journey was the aliyah of a relative of ours. Even though I didn't yet know their meaning, the words of God to Abraham, "*Lech lecha* – Go forth," echoed in my ears as Aunt Fania boarded the bus that would take her to the airport. This was 1961.

In those years very few were granted permission to emigrate to Israel, but this woman, old and infirm, managed successfully to make the journey. Aunt Fania went on to send us letters and a postcard from Kfar Giladi – my first geographic reference point in Israel. In her letters she wrote of Tel Hai and Joseph Trumpeldor. And that colorful postcard, depicting a swimming pool, opened my first small window onto the country. I gazed through a magnifying glass at the postcard's every tree and counted all the people it depicted, astonished to see so many Jews gathered in a single place. My imagination sought some foothold in reality, and from that day forward I knew that my life would not be a chain of random actions but would be dedicated to a single purpose.

Anti-Israel propaganda appeared in the press accompanied by a spirit of anti-Semitism that wafted through Russian streets. One day I was assaulted at school by Kostya Borov, the son of an officer. "Save Russia, strike the Jews!" he screamed. My shyness may have aroused my adversaries to hit me, but I was physically strong and had no problem returning blows. During one fight, I was nearly run over by a streetcar. In another, I was hit in the head with a rock. I took pride in my bandaged skull, as though I were a soldier wounded in battle. But all this only buttressed the walls of my burgeoning faith. If you ask why other Jewish youths did not feel the same way, I'd reply that God apportions to each of us differently; there is no mathematical equality among men.

In 1961, other Jewish children joined the class; those who came from Russia showed no sign of interest in Judaism, and were foreign to me. The other Latvian Jewish students, however, seemed to share my worldview. Like me, they spent evenings listening to Kol Israel, and we would compare notes the next morning about what we'd heard. Things were made easier for me by my father's habit of listening to all the broadcasts on a shortwave radio set that had cost him two months' salary. He was an expert in history and geography, and politically well informed. In the evenings, he would share his analysis of the day's events with us. Even after I was grown, I couldn't give up his daily commentary, and my friends in the Zionist youth movement would likewise listen to him with rapt attention.

Aliyah became a main subject of these conversations: what we would take with us, how we would live at first, how we would find employment. Because emigration visas were so rare, such discussions took on a surreal air and acted as a kind of hopeful escapism. Yet they were nonetheless significant. I began firmly to believe that aliyah lay in my future. Jews tend to plan their futures with great care; how wonderful that when it comes time to fulfill those plans they discover the strength to transform dream into reality.

In class I used to argue with my friends Aron and Phinia about which was better: to finish university studies and then make aliyah, or to emigrate at the first opportunity. Despite our independence of mind, something of the abundant Soviet propaganda had penetrated: we imagined that higher education was harder to come by in Israel than in the Soviet Union.

Once during a geography lesson, in the course of answering a question about the Middle East, Phinia called the Israelis "aggressive." He got an A from the teacher, and, after class, a scolding from us. It's not always easy to ignore propaganda. Here in Israel I once met a young soldier from the former Soviet Union who remarked that he was serving in the "occupied territories." I had learned from my father that these territories were ours from time immemorial.

We often could get at the truth only with the utmost difficulty. My sister Rivka and I used to visit the library to read Simon Dubnow's multivolume *History of the Jews*, which had been published in Russian before Latvia had joined the Soviet Union. I came across a map of biblical Israel in a textbook, and I hung on my bedroom wall a Soviet map of the 1947 UN partition plan for Israel, although those borders were never implemented – a characteristically Soviet gesture of wishful thinking.

At sixteen, to help support the family, I began an apprenticeship in carpentry. I felt more comfortable among my Latvian fellow workers than among the Russians, though I kept my distance from all of them, and categorically refused to take part in their conversations or habitual drunkenness. The man responsible for political activities at the factory was a retired officer who liked to read newspapers aloud. On one occasion I mentioned to him that I regarded Israel as the homeland of all Jews. He promised to "make sure" I'd be sent there, and I said I'd be most grateful if he did so. Several days later I was transferred to a more taxing and dangerous job. Then again, I've never feared hard work.

While nothing very unusual happened at the factory, a series of miracles occurred at the night school where I had continued my studies. Some three-quarters of the student body and faculty was Jewish. Although the scholastic level was quite high, had the KGB known that Public School 25 would become a hothouse of Zionism they would most certainly have closed it. Part of the miracle had to do with the fact that at that time a cousin, a doctor by profession, had come to live with us. Mendel Gordin was a man of great distinction, and he exerted a formative influence on me. Educated in the Jewish tradition, a Zionist virtually from birth, he was even then engaged in illegal Zionist activities. But life in the Soviet Union teaches a man to tread cautiously, and Mendel was in no hurry to open up to me. His mysterious personality exercised my imagination. In the Ethics of the Fathers it is said: "Make yourself a teacher and acquire yourself a friend." I chose Mendel as both teacher and friend. It was from him that I received my first taste of illegal books: essays by the Odessa-born founder of Revisionist Zionism Vladimir Jabotinsky and proponent of cultural Zionism Achad Ha'am, the poems of Hayim Nahman Bialik, all translated into Russian. Such books were mimeographed from prewar editions, or even from pre-revolutionary editions, and then hand bound. I hid them even from my father; I feared he would tell me that the risk of reading them was too high. I learned the Russian translations of Bialik's poems by heart.

Not everyone else was able to keep the flame of his youth burning bright. Take, for example, my classmate Lieva. Back in the day, he bravely appeared in class with a briefcase full of samizdat literature and Democratic Movement material mixed with Zionist publications. But when I invited him a few years later to a Jewish gathering, he explained that there were aspects of life, like work and family – "private life" – that were not worth jeopardizing.

In the upper classes, however, we were all idealists. We used to post a note on the board: "Jewish holiday – no classes today," and then run off to synagogue for services. I had occasionally visited the synagogue with my father, but in the early 1960s a new phenomenon appeared: young Jews began to gather next to the synagogue on holidays, not necessarily in order to pray, but to network and converse in the adjacent streets. Just the very idea that everyone was Jewish gave the assembly excitement enough. Here it was also possible to meet a colleague whom one hadn't known was Jewish. Every holiday, then, our joy redoubled, for these gatherings demonstrated that the Jewish people were indeed alive and flourishing, and that they retained their own distinct holidays. On Simchat Torah, Purim, or Chanukah, we would come out of the synagogue dancing, many enjoying their first opportunity to hear a Hebrew song or learn to dance the Horah.

Although it seemed at first glance that the dances and songs erupted spontaneously, when I later became involved in Zionist circles in Riga I met the young men whose job it had been to create that atmosphere: Mark Blum, Eliyahu Valk, the Eliashevitz brothers, the Greenman brothers, and others.

My benchmate at school was a somewhat confused kid named Garik. One day he told me that the next afternoon a group of young Jews would be cleaning up Rumbuli, the cemetery just outside of Riga containing the graves of twenty-five thousand Jews who had been massacred by the Nazis. I knew that Garik was a member of the Jewish choir and was connected to Zionist groups in Riga, but I didn't particularly trust him. Nevertheless, although most of my friends decided not to go, and after much hesitation, my friend Shmuel and I went.

We were greeted there by an inspiring sight: dozens of Jews – young and old, carrying clumps of dirt in homemade containers, using shovels, rakes, and bare hands. At the center of all this stood a stark obelisk memorial. Pitching in, we began shoveling with our bare hands. One particularly tall middle-aged man stood out, looking to me like a typical Israeli. This was Ezra Rusinek, a prominent figure in the Zionist movement in Riga. (Our acquaintance began a long time after I first spotted him that day in Rumbuli.) We worked feverishly, joining in common cause to build a memorial to the dead and to strengthen the sense of fraternity among the living. The sacred ground of Rumbuli, the very place where Amalek sought to wipe us out, aroused our nationalist feelings.

Shmuel and I gathered pieces of broken shovels that we planned to fix and put to use the following week. But this was to be his last time with us. He worked as an engraver at our factory, and several days later was killed when an iron bar struck his head. I continued to go alone to Rumbuli every Sunday, and the number of volunteers there only increased.

I also conversed often with Mendel, who had become like a brother to me; I read the books I got from him and others; I volunteered at Rumbuli. It was impossible in all this not to sense the hand of an organization guiding us. I dreamed of joining it, but my dream was not fulfilled – at least not in the way I'd imagined. There was no secret cabal with a hierarchy or set procedures. In those days the Zionist movement of Riga was not coherently defined. It included members of diverse backgrounds who before the war had belonged to various Zionist organizations, each of whom had kept his distinct approach. The most influential among them were those who had belonged to Betar, which had been very active in Latvia before the war, and their style was particularly well suited to conducting secret activities under a totalitarian regime. Among them was Ezra Rusinek, whom I met in Rumbuli in 1963 (he had then recently returned from exile in Siberia), but there were also younger men who had been inspired for the most part by the Sinai campaign of 1956: Lea Brenner, Boris Slovin, Dov Sperling, Yosef Schneider, Mark Blum, Yosef Yankelevich, A. "Bubby" Zeitlin – all of them unusual, well-respected men. We, the youngsters, regarded them as our leaders.

Thanks to their efforts, we were able to obtain illegal Jewish materials, and they were the ones who had persuaded the authorities to allow the ongoing work at Rumbuli cemetery, where some fifty thousand Jews were buried in five mass graves (including one that held the corpses of children). The victims had been murdered by the Nazis between November 7 and November 9, 1941. The authorities hadn't bothered to erect a memorial, in fact had entirely neglected the place, and even after granting permission for its renovation and landscaping they made our every step difficult. Yet Garber, Zeitlin, and others were unceasing in their efforts. Paths were marked, roads paved. The authorities did not permit us to put up signs marking this as a place where Jews were exterminated. Instead, they preferred the neutral phrase "Soviet citizens of various nationalities." Still, we managed to inscribe one of the memorials in Yiddish: "victims of fascism."

A very special atmosphere pervaded those Sundays at Rumbuli. All week, I would wait with impatient anticipation for those hours in our "Little Israel," as we called it. On our way back in the bus, we would sing Israeli songs, my first experience with the fraternal feeling that develops among comrades in arms. The sight of young Jews singing together was in fact so unusual that the other passengers sometimes simply got off the bus. One driver asked, "Where are you from, behaving like this?" "Like this" meant "unabashed and proud," rather than weak and intimidated. And this was Rumbuli's lesson: in unity, in joining together, we could feel a newfound surge of strength.

• • • • •

Hundreds of young Jews in Riga during the 1960s dreamed of Israel, read *Exodus* by Leon Uris in Russian translation, sang the songs of the Palmach and the Warsaw ghetto fighters. I secretly dreamed of meeting Israelis. Lo and behold, in 1964, I happened to see a car on a Riga street bearing an Israeli pennant. In the back seat was a magazine. I managed to decipher its title: *Ba-Machaneh*. Soon a crowd surrounded the car, until we were dispersed by police on motorbikes.

That day, I took my entrance exam for medical school, but my composition on "Communists in literature" earned a low score, and I was not admitted. At the time, I felt grievously disappointed. Today I know that we must accept what God gives us, for better or for worse. Had I been admitted, my passion for medicine might have eclipsed my energies for Zionist activism. Perhaps what seemed to me then a failure in fact kept me on the right path.

A year later, the Hapoel soccer team came to Riga. By the time I arrived at the sports center, throngs of young Jews had already packed in to see the Israeli athletes for themselves. As the players boarded the bus after practice, we sang "The Land of Milk and Honey." They were moved to tears. Tickets to the match itself were distributed at work, mostly to Party members, and of course I wasn't able to get one. My sister Rivka and I decided to visit the hotel where the footballers were staying. This was a most daring and rash action for a Soviet citizen to take, for in the not-so-distant past, in the days of Stalin, meeting a foreigner could cost you years of prison. I still keenly felt such fears, and my natural shyness did not make it easy to connect with strangers, but the desire to meet "real Israelis" won the day.

As I climbed the hotel's stairs, a reception clerk gave me a long stare. A tan man approached me, and by some sixth sense I knew he was Israeli. As I walked toward him, he said something and offered me two packets. I glanced into the first, and became mute with joy. Inside was a Star of David. I nearly forgot to stammer my thanks before rushing home. From then on, I wore it even to work, despite my father's pleadings not to draw undue attention to myself. (In the Soviet Union, many Jews hammered out improvised Stars of David from old copper or silver coins. In the 1970s, this became something of a fashion.) Could I have imagined then that one day I would be an Israeli citizen myself and speak a fluent Hebrew? For Israel's Independence Day 5725 (1965), Mendel presented me with a watch engraved with a Hebrew blessing. *How will I be living my life in fifteen years?* I wondered. I sensed that something important – yet difficult and perilous – awaited me, and that it rested entirely outside my will.

In 1965, Mendel brought me a kind of self-help Hebrew primer published in Israel by Shlomo Kodesh. From it I learned some five hundred Hebrew words, and all the songs it featured, but I could not master Hebrew grammar. I had no one to tell me how these words were pronounced, and I was sure I was pronouncing them wrong. Mendel gave me other reading material, too: *Six Million Accusers* by Gideon Hausner; David Ben-Gurion's Knesset address on the results of the Sinai campaign. I imagined some of these publications had been supplied by the Israeli embassy, where one of the activists, Yosef Schneider, used to visit. In my mind's eye I saw the Jews of Riga bound up in a global Zionist struggle, but of course the matter wasn't so simple: Israeli embassy staff made contact with Riga's Jews only with great caution and hesitation.

• • • • •

I longed to take part in Zionist activities, but as before I remained on the sidelines. At Mendel's request, I hid his books, some in a niche above the oven; in the basement I kept manuscripts and a photocopy of *Exodus*. I concealed lists of refuseniks in a lightbulb socket. These were the individuals who, in order to emigrate, had tried to obtain formal invitations from people in Israel, often to no avail. In 1966, when Soviet authorities announced that it was possible to request exit visas, we wrote to Aunt Fania in Kfar Giladi and asked her to send such an invitation. Her reply astonished us: "Stay where you are." I began to look for other ways of obtaining an invitation.

In those days I devoted considerable commitment to the Rumbuli cemetery. All enthusiasms wax and wane, but it is up to us to keep the flame bright. I became close with Kalman, who oversaw the cemetery, and I organized various renovations and an orderly system of keeping track of our tools there. I took great satisfaction in feeling that by such efforts I was taking part in a larger Jewish mission, being integrated into Zionist circles with young men and women like Eliyahu Valk, Ruth Alexanderovich, Yosef Schneider, and Yosef Rusinek. I participated, too, in the first memorial services to mark the tragedy at Rumbuli.

At the memorial service of the winter of 1965, we read poems and talked about those who would wish to destroy the Jewish people. All of us were moved, sensing the urgent need not merely to remember, but also to act to ensure the continuity of the Jewish people. Afterwards, participants gathered at my home, and I felt I should say something. "During World War II," I declared, "our people suffered innumerable losses. Today, however, our fate is in our hands. Here in the Soviet Union, it is we who must act to enable Jews to resist the forces of assimilation and oppression and emigrate to Israel. I therefore propose that we establish a Zionist organization. All those in favor, raise your hands."

Everyone raised his hands high, in a state of excitement; just a year before, no one could have imagined founding an underground organization. But the next day, as the first blush of exhilaration wore off and I could think rationally, I realized that we had no idea what to do, and that many members of this fledgling "organization" were not yet ripe for it. The most reliable member was my sister Rivka, and together with her I devised a "purge." These terms – purge, bylaws, "filtering out," membership cards – came to us from reading Soviet literature about underground movements. So ingrained were these concepts, we knew nothing else.

After this purge, four of us were left: My friend Avraham and I, Rivka and her friend Genia. Once a week, we met at Genia's home, outside of town, and read Zionist literature: an Israeli Russian-language magazine called *Shalom*, a biography of Chaim Weizmann, and a full translation of *Exodus*. Of course we could have read these things by ourselves, but we preferred to discuss them together.

Genia mentioned our group to Yosef Schneider, who in turn offered to put us in touch with similar groups, his own and one coordinated by Eliyahu Valk. Avraham and I, flush with romantic notions of underground activity, walked separately to one meeting on opposite sides of the street, the better to "confuse the enemy." Their groups were larger and more established, and they invited us to meet with others. One especially delightful evening, two groups competed with one another on their knowledge of Israeli history. Although I had never been one for parties, I recognized then their utility in attracting young people to Jewish activism. For myself, I was looking for ways to act, not for entertainment and levity.

In 1966, a new group assembled that included Chaim Drori, Boris Maftser, David Shriftailik, Sender Barkan, myself, Rivka, Genia, and Avraham. This was no longer mere youthful enthusiasm. In our platform I wrote: "Out of a love for our people and a sense of responsibility, we have concluded that we must join together to deepen the national awareness of the Jewish people in preparation for the future aliyah. Our central focus is the promotion of Jewish culture." Some in the West may have regarded the possibility of Soviet aliyah with skepticism, but we harbored no doubts. In fact, we saw preparing for aliyah as a matter of obligation. Avraham and I served as the group's security men (our bylaws called for the strictest caution). Boris Maftser was appointed treasurer, and soon proved that the man determines the significance of a position, and not vice versa. Though we were then still students, we taxed ourselves onerously; activism requires funds, after all. Since I was giving all the money I earned to my father, and had nothing to spare, I took on additional work.

One dark evening, as I returned home after collecting membership fees from the others, several young men suddenly blocked my way, demanding money. A glance confirmed that more of them stood behind me. I kept my wits about me, and gave them what I had in my pocket. They made me hop in place to listen for the telltale jingles of hidden coins. Nothing jingled, fortunately; I had hidden the bills I had collected for membership fees on my chest. The thugs fled, and I offered thanks to God that I had emerged unscathed. With the money we had collected, we bought a typewriter and the twelve-volume Russian set of the 1912 *Encyclopedia Judaica*.

• • • • •

The stronger one's faith, the more likely it is to be realized; a forceful will can forge a new reality, and an effort properly directed can exert an influence on events. In other words, the Lord helps those who help themselves.

Just as our group was coming together, two profoundly significant events occurred. First, several local families received exit visas, and the Jews of Riga, made newly aware of the possibility, increasingly began to think of emigrating. The second event, demonstrating the power of Jewish national feeling, was connected to the performances of Israeli singer Geula Gill and pantomimist Yaakov "Juki" Arkin, both of whom came to Riga in 1966. Their arrival had been announced on Kol Israel broadcasts, but not a single poster advertised them. By the time I got to the ticket desk of the Riga Municipal Sports Stadium at five o'clock the morning of the concert, I found a line of 350 people. After arranging a place in line, I rushed to the university to take a physics exam, but my mind was elsewhere. In those days I was studying electrical engineering, but all my thoughts revolved around Israel. I had neither the time nor the inclination to study. There was no one to converse with in my class, not a single Jew, and I felt scant motivation to attend lectures. Somehow I got through the exam, accepted without protest a mark of "average," and rushed back to the line.

By then, thousands were thronging the cashier. A sight like this I hadn't seen even at the synagogue on holidays. As always, many tried to cut in line, and we arranged ourselves into groups of ushers. Chaim Drori and I found ourselves in one such group. Gauging by the urgency of the pressing crowd, you might have thought the performance had already started. An Israeli singer performing in Riga! The very idea had attracted a crowd of thousands of Jews in a city in which a gathering of five or six Jews was rare. The unusual feeling of unity, of belonging, of joining such a multitude, intoxicated us with celebratory joy. I've no doubt that many in the throng on that day remembered that experience when they decided to make aliyah.

Each person was permitted to buy only two tickets. To trick the cashier, I repeatedly changed my appearance: I took off my glasses, pulled my cap down over my forehead, took my jacket on and off, and ultimately managed to get tickets for my whole family.

As the hour of the performance drew near, police roadblocked every access to the theater, and masses of people outside hoped to scalp an extra ticket. A pilot in an Aeroflot uniform told me he'd traveled especially from the Ukraine for the concert; I gave him one of my tickets.

At last I sat in the auditorium, finding it hard to believe I was really hearing Hebrew songs. Wonder of wonders; I felt almost as though I were in Israel myself. "Encore!" I shouted in Hebrew, having found the word in a dictionary, my lips and body trembling with emotion. "Encore!" With that word I expressed all my pain, all my longing for an unattainable dream.

The program was accompanied throughout by incessant rounds of applause. As Geula began to sing the anthem of the Palmach, she must have been stunned to hear half of the thousand-strong audience singing along:

From Metulla to the Negev

From the sea to the desert

Every fine young man to arms

Every young man on guard.

Standing, we sang the entire repertoire of those bus rides to Rumbuli. It was a festive day.

After the concert we wanted to give Geula a rousing farewell, but the police, too, stood ready. One of the ushers wished to confiscate the bouquet Rivka and I had brought, and when I refused he called a police officer over and alleged that I had pushed him. As we were arguing, Rivka passed the bouquet forward through the audience and the cops relented and retreated.

Going outside to see Geula off, we noticed police buses blocking the road, and officers in riot gear blocking the exits. The authorities had decided not to allow us to accompany her, but we were great in number and resolved in spirit, and we surged through the police lines. At that moment, the driver of Geula's bus began to speed away, pursued by her fans. Chaim reached through a window and Geula pressed one of her albums into his hand. As the police tried to disperse them, hundreds of Jews filled the immense square. Taunting the police, someone swiped the hat from an officer's head, and the policeman turned and fled.

The Soviet Union did not permit public demonstrations, making the events of that night all the more unprecedented. We were suddenly freed of our fear of the state and its security apparatus – the police, the KGB – a fear that had been nourished by our awareness of Soviet history. Mark Blum and Lea "Lydia" Slovin stood next to a streetcar stop and called on the crowd to march to the police station and demand that Naomi Garber be freed. Naomi, daughter of David Garber, had been arrested during the police dispersions.

At the police station we insisted that she had not resisted the police, but we were almost forcibly removed. I announced that I would complain directly to the chairman of the ministerial council of the Soviet Union. "I defecate on your chairman!" the commanding officer screamed. The Soviet institutions of oppression stood outside the law – and above it. Ultimately, Naomi was freed, but fell ill in the wake of her arrest. Several other friends were also charged with resisting the authorities, among them Mark Blum, a prominent figure in Zionist circles. The KGB had long looked for a way to be rid of him. Lea Slovin passed a report on the night's events to a foreign tourist, with the idea of getting it into Israeli hands, but for some unknown reason the report never saw the light of day.

• • • • •

As is well known, the Six-Day War heightened national awareness among Soviet Jewry. I often meet people who remark that they became patriots of Israel in 1967, and I ask them whether the shift came before or after the war. From their replies, I can tell whether they discovered this newfound love in their hearts when Israel was in grave peril, or whether they felt moved by the country's military triumphs and hoped that they too might take part in battles in the Sinai or the Golan. Either way, all of them, without exception, reacted angrily to the unbridled anti-Israel and anti-Semitic propaganda let loose in the Soviet press in the war's aftermath.

I lived with and befriended people who identified with Israel. I remember in particular a conversation with Mendel and Fima Zell several weeks before the war. "If only I could be patrolling the border with a submachine gun rather than sitting here in miserable Riga," Fima said. We listened to the radio, and without hesitation toasted our nation's victory; we were sorry only that we couldn't join the battle with our Israeli brethren. Even the Latvians at work expressed support for Israel, although the Soviet papers during the war were full of reports of Arab gains. At the end of the hostilities, of course, editors and correspondents were compelled to admit that the result was not exactly in the Arabs' favor, and then to fudge the contrast between what they'd published and what became apparent upon Israel's historic victory.

Several Riga Jews who had received exit visas before the war traveled to Moscow in hopes of being allowed to leave with the staff of the Israeli embassy, shut down in the wake of the USSR's decision to cut diplomatic ties. We asked them to send back greetings from Israel. But our own hopes for leaving were slim at best. Anti-Semitism was on the rise, and the rupture of diplomatic ties with Israel was widely felt. In Dvinsk, authorities closed down a Jewish choir "as a result of the international situation." (Overcoming considerable obstacles, Aryeh and Pinchas Hanoch had founded the choir just a short time before the war.)

In the summer of 1967, we rented a small house in a forest near Riga, where, tapping away furiously on our typewriter, I copied out *David vs. Goliath*, a book about Israel's War of Independence. No one sent us the fundamental books we needed by means of tourists from abroad, so additional copies of these works had to be produced by hand. I slaved over the typewriter fourteen hours a day, pausing only to eat or study a bit of Hebrew – my modest contribution to the Six-Day War. I was young, and didn't suffer too much from uncomfortable conditions. Rather than prepare food, I picked wild raspberries behind the house. When this rather limited menu began to nauseate me and I began to miss the taste of bread, I walked three kilometers to the grocery and wolfed down an entire loaf. There is nothing quite like the fiery enthusiasm of youth and its indifference to the mundane cares of life.

· · · · ·

In Boris Maftser's apartment, members of our group used the typewriter to copy out (in Russian) Zionist works such as Jabotinsky's feuilletons and Bialik's poems. Chaim Drori's father got in touch with several of his colleagues who had studied at the Hebrew high school, and together with them organized Hebrew lessons. Chaim and Rivka traveled to Lithuania to sell used clothing, bringing back sufficient funds to keep our "publishing house" afloat. We multiplied books by photocopying them. One evening I stumbled on Rivka and Chaim developing photos of the poems of Yitzchak Katznelson, who had been murdered by the Nazis in 1944. We had to hide the materials until morning, but had nowhere to dry the photos that had been developed. I had no alternative but to spread them out under the blanket and dry them with the warmth of my body.

In the meantime, we celebrated the Jewish holidays. Before Purim, we had children make noisemakers and rattles from hammered pieces of metal. The generation following ours had received next to no Jewish education at home, and were therefore in dire need of our help. We organized balls and celebrations, we told of the historic occasions each holiday marked, and we taught Hebrew songs.

One Passover night, I was reluctant to join the seder to which I had been assigned, with a group of people I hardly knew, but I decided, as usual, to fulfill my obligations. I brought with me matzah and a Haggadah. The hostess, an elderly woman, had prepared holiday dishes. I led the seder in the traditional way, but quickly noticed that I was boring the young guests, who could not understand a word of Hebrew. They enjoyed going to the movies and dressing fashionably, but neither Israel nor Passover much interested them. I cut short the Haggadah, and began explaining, in Russian, the significance of the holiday and of the Exodus from Egypt. They listened, but had a hard time sitting still, and the moment dinner was over they got up from the table and began to dance and play cards. With a heavy heart I finished the Haggadah myself, and left in a gloomy mood.

Several days later, however, one of the young men told me that the seder had made an indelible impression on many members of the group, with the result that some of them had decide to emigrate to Israel. This came as a total, if pleasant, surprise. I realized then that words spoken from the heart penetrate hearts, even if they may take time to reach their target.

On Chanukah, our group joined with another to light candles at Rumbuli. The appointed evening was so bitterly cold (-25°F) that I doubted whether anyone would show up. To my amazement, however, we were joined by many other people, including several I had not previously met. I called upon them to light candles in memory of the victims, and to pledge that the fire first kindled by the Maccabees would never be extinguished.

In the summer of 1968, after a printed copy of a biography of Chaim Weizmann was discovered in Riga, the police began a series of searches of suspected Zionists' homes. On August 21, the day the Soviet Union invaded Czechoslovakia, Mendel Gordin was summoned to an interrogation by the KGB. For the interrogators, this was the hour of reckoning. For his part, Mendel refused to give testimony.

The searches and the invasion made a keen impression on me. We all knew that given the chance, the USSR wouldn't mind carrying out a similar reprisal against Israel. To signal my protest against Soviet aggression, I resigned from the labor union. Oppression sometimes toughens people, arousing them to open resistance.

So it was that the more I became acquainted with the true face of Soviet rule, the more tragic the situation of Soviet Jewry seemed, and I felt ready to go to any lengths to save my people. I came to be a dissident through such nationalist sentiments, whereas some other "aliyah activists" were attracted first by the democratic opposition to totalitarian rule (in which Jews played a prominent role), and only secondarily to nationalist views.

• • • • •

Over time, we decided to turn the Rumbuli meetings into larger and higher-profile gatherings. To support the initiative, David Zilberman, who had spent years researching the Riga ghetto, prepared a comprehensive speech. Since his voice was soft and we had no megaphones, it was suggested that I read it aloud on his behalf. I chose to add a Yiddish poem by Katznelson. Gesia Kamyeski helped me rehearse, and I learned the speech by heart. Still, so excited was I by the occasion that I feared forgetting it.

Though the gathering met without a permit, a great many people came. After the recitation of the Kaddish, I approached the memorial, feeling that the place was sacred, the subject of the address holy. I wasn't sure I was worthy of the stirring words I spoke. When I finished, I turned away from my audience without looking up, too moved to speak. My colleagues perhaps took this silence as a sign of aloofness, but I was simply reflecting on what the memory of the dead required of us. I felt called upon to make a radical change in my life. From that moment, I resolved to determine my own course rather than, as before, to let my beliefs be determined by others.

At birth, I had been inducted into the covenant of Abraham. I had inherited from my father Jewish habits of thought, a Jewish worldview, a recognition of my national duty. But it was only at that moment that I heard the voice of God, summoning me to go forward. The hour had arrived to accept His commandments. By sheer personal example, Mendel had shown me the way. I still felt distant from being fully and truly Jewish, but I chose then, with fullest awareness, the path I would take. By suddenly grasping my attachment to the Jewish people, I understood my attachment to God.

I ceased to eat non-kosher food and to work on Shabbat. I began to observe fast days and holidays. I did not yet pray or study Torah, but in conversations with Mendel, an awareness increasingly crystallized within me that without faith in God neither the people Israel nor the State of Israel could exist; that the most exalted ideal, toward which every Jew must strive, is a return to a life of Torah and commandments. There is in my mind no distinction between secular and religious Jews. Although not every Jew can fulfill all the commandments, in reality no Jew is entirely bereft of belief. God speaks to the hearts of all men, and each man is capable of fathoming what He asks of him.

• • • • •

In September 1968, the visa department of the interior ministry revisited the question of applications for emigration to Israel. I sent a telegram to a young woman from Riga who had succeeded in making aliyah: "My uncle, have you forgotten us? Send necessary documents as soon as possible." Two months later, a formal invitation arrived from Yakov Mendelevich (a fictitious relative) in Bat Yam. We could hardly believe our eyes. An invitation from Israel for the entire family!

In order to file a request for a visa, it was necessary to assemble certain documents – not an easy matter. The interior ministry, which endeavored to put every obstacle before applicants for emigration, required a letter of recommendation from one's workplace in which superiors testified to one's good behavior and political loyalty. In certain factories, a special workers' meeting was held to disparage and humiliate a colleague who sought to go to Israel. If that man bravely and openly declared his support for Israel and rejection of the Soviet policy of compelling Jews to assimilate, he would likely be charged with "anti-Soviet propaganda." This happened in Kiev in 1969, for example, to Boris Kochubievsky.

I was more fortunate. My manager, a Latvian, supported me and gave me a letter of recommendation without difficulty, asking only that if I succeeded in making aliyah I would tell him as much as possible about Israel. This I pledged with great pleasure. The superiors of my younger sister Meri, however, refused to give her the required recommendation. I turned to the general prosecutor, who upon hearing my complaint picked up the telephone and ordered a recommendation to be granted. For this he was later reprimanded by the Party.

The interior ministry also required Jews applying for exit visas to relinquish their Soviet citizenship, which had the effect of discouraging those who didn't want to end up suspended in statelessness. The entire process, in fact, aimed to deter Jews from applying for visas.

Still, in December 1968, hundreds of Riga's Jews, Mark Blum among them, received exit visas. I'll never forget the evening he took his leave. After a concert by Nechama Lifshitz, he and I went to meet the singer and to bid each other goodbye. We expressed the hope of a reunion in Israel soon. That reunion did come to pass – thirteen years later, in Kibbutz Yavne, just after my release. The day after the concert, I brought our family's documents to the interior ministry, and in a state of great tension we awaited reply.

There were those who adopted the theory that the KGB granted the first wave of visas in order to rid itself of some bothersome activists – not believing that great numbers of Jews would wish to leave – thereby finishing off the Zionist movement with one stroke. If that was indeed their motivation, things turned out rather differently than they had planned. Once the first visas showed that the dream of emigration could be realized, the flow of applications only increased in volume. The visa department of the interior ministry began to resemble a kind of Jewish salon in which the merits of aliyah were heatedly discussed. Its staff was astonished by the sheer number of those who expressed a wish to leave, and began rejecting all applications – without exception. Our applications, too, were turned down on absurd grounds: "We are of the opinion that you can live just as well here in the Soviet Union." As if we cared about their opinion. Feeling deceived, many refuseniks, as we began to be called, became embittered but also emboldened to act courageously to obtain exit visas.

As summer drew near, Riga's most prominent activists, including Dov Sperling, Lea Slovin, Yosef Yankelevich and Yosef Schneider left for Israel. And then something remarkable happened: a large number of young people, all aflame with Jewish passion, announced their intention to emigrate to Israel. It became obvious that in their attempt to head off the Zionist movement, the authorities had succeeded only in invigorating it.

On the other side of the barricades, in the West, new people had appeared who were familiar with the predicament of Soviet Jewry, who could – and would – help. They began to send us invitations and literature, to raise the world's consciousness of our plight, to send visitors to refuseniks, even to find channels through which to offer financial aid. But it is important to note that the assistance from the outside came only after the revitalization of the Zionist movement from within. Help arrives when you are capable of helping yourself.

The refusal of my exit visa hit me hard. For a time I could not summon the will to work or study. To study meant nothing less than to deceive myself; rather than struggling for freedom I would be fighting for a diploma, a degree that in any case would only make matters worse because it might block the possibility of aliyah. I decided to end the pretense, to take off the mask, and to begin to be me. I dropped out of the university, the better to devote myself wholeheartedly to the movement.

But this entailed losing my draft deferment, and I was soon summoned to the army enlistment office. This meant trouble. Being drafted would end any chances of receiving an exit visa, for it would be claimed that I somehow had knowledge of military secrets.

The night before my appointment at the enlistment office, sleep eluded me. My mind fixated on the idea of sacrifice as a solution to my dilemma. And then, all of a sudden, I realized what I could sacrifice. "If I wish to live in the Jewish state," I said to myself, "I must begin living like a Jew, like our forefathers Abraham, Isaac, and Jacob; in other words, to observe the commandments. So why haven't I? Only because it is a rigorous life, and I'm not entirely sure I can abide all the restrictions."

At that very moment I realized what kind of sacrifice I felt called upon to make. I would give up my comfort and complacency. I rose to my feet and swore an oath: "Master of the world, if You save me from military induction, I will observe Your commandments."

The next day, I found myself before a draft officer. Thumbing through my file, he said, "Tell me, why did you choose to end your studies?"

Of course I could not tell him that I did so under the sway of my dreams of Israel. Not knowing what to reply, I glanced through the window and noticed a small bird perched on a tree. "You see that bird?" I asked the officer. "He is free: here today, somewhere else tomorrow. But I am unfree. Here I was born and here I must live. I long to be free, like that bird."

I was sent for psychiatric evaluation in a mental hospital.

I decided not to pretend to be insane; I wasn't familiar enough with the symptoms. I would behave normally, and trust in God. I avoided the other patients; they fought, screamed, and laughed uncontrollably. One had deluded himself that he was a great poet; another attempted to give lectures on some indiscernible subject. I had brought along Homer's *Iliad*, and spent my time reading it in a corner, which must itself have presented a rather strange spectacle.

"Do you feel that someone is following you?" a shrink asked. Having been an underground activist, pursued in fact by undercover security officials, I answered in the affirmative.

After several suffering-filled weeks of this, the psychiatric board notified me that I had been exempted from military duties, and would be required to begin treatment with psychiatric medicines. Faced with the prospect of being drugged to the point of insanity in a psychiatric ward, I begged to return home, where I promised to take the prescribed pills.

Finally I was released. Feeling that God had miraculously saved me, I rushed straight from the hospital to the synagogue, ready to fulfill my vow. My appearance in the synagogue caused a sensation. Synagogue goers were old pensioners. The young, fearing the loss of employment or place in university, never dared to show their faces there. Suddenly seeing a young man announcing he wished to observe the commandments, they must have thought I was a police informant or provocateur.

No one was willing to mentor me, to teach me how to keep the commandments, except one courageous soul, Rabbi Mordechai Dinur, who opened a siddur (prayer book) and began to explain its inner workings. To tell the truth, after several days I stopped going to prayers; they felt foreign to me. But in other respects I became religious: I didn't work on Shabbat, refrained from pork, and wore a beret to cover my head. Still, in my innermost heart, I felt the pricks of conscience for not fully fulfilling my promise. But it seemed that becoming religious took time, and could not be accomplished with a single leap.

· · · · ·

In the wake of the departure of many of our leading activists, we sent Dov Riger to Moscow to bolster our ties with activists in other cities. He met there with David Chabkin and Vitaly Svechinski, and returned to Riga with a proposal: a conference of activists from many cities to be held in Moscow, code-named Telephone. The plan was risky: too tight a connection between groups could endanger all of them. We also feared the plan could disguise a push for leadership by certain activists, or that it might inhibit the initiative of smaller, isolated groups. Ultimately we decided to support the idea of a conference, but to limit our contact to networking and the exchange of ideas without forging more formal organizational ties. In order to recruit other groups in Riga to the idea, we met with Eliyahu Valk, who was well connected among Riga's aliyah activists.

On August 16–17, Dov and Eliyahu met in Moscow with activists from Leningrad, Moscow, Tbilisi, Kiev, and Minsk, where it was decided to join in common cause, both to arouse Jewish awareness and to broaden the rights of Soviet Jews. Thus was founded the National Coordinating Committee, as well as a publication council to oversee a samizdat Zionist organ and to develop a plan for reproducing the scant literature we had.

We were surprised that the Moscow Zionists were not well organized, but were impressed by the wondrous Leningrad organization, founded in 1966. It included activists like Mogilver, Butman, Chernoglaz, Kaminski, and Shpilberg. Leningrad had developed a chain of ulpans, where students could learn Hebrew and Jewish history. Anyone who knew a few hundred Hebrew words taught those who knew not a word. The ulpans also functioned as cultural centers. In 1968, Aharon Shpilberg moved to Riga and shared the rich experience of the Leningrad activists with all of us in that area. We set up an administrative committee, which included Ezra Rusinek, Bubby Zeitlin, Aharon Shpilberg and Eliyahu Valk. By the fall of 1969 we had a centralized organization, though its activities were not terribly well defined; a rigidly defined organization structure, we felt, could dangerously undermine the secrecy under which circumstances compelled us to work.

· · · · ·

It had come time to take real action. We were prepared to fight for our right to emigrate "with a powerful hand and an outstretched arm," to borrow a phrase from the story of Exodus. As for how exactly to fight, this I did not know, but I was prepared for anything. I tried personally explaining to the head of the visa department that our family – four women, an ill father who had suffered two heart attacks, and a college dropout son exempted from military service – was worthless to the Soviet state, and should be allowed to leave. Regrettably, such reasoning made little impression on Colonel Kaiya, the grey-haired middle-aged lord of the visas. His nerves had been worn down by the endless requests from Jews wishing to emigrate, and on this particular day he poured out his wrath on me. "This is no market or synagogue. You can forget about your Israel. You'll die and rot here in Mother Russia."

I was going to synagogue more often. The only one left in Riga, it had been built in the seventeenth or eighteenth century in the old quarter. Mendel had found me a Bible in Russian translation, and I regularly brought together a few friends in the synagogue to study it. It would of course have been possible to meet in an apartment, but we chose to do so in the open and conduct at least some of our activities in a legal fashion.

The synagogue had no rabbi. The authorities had instead given the reins to a certain Jew about whom it was rumored that in order to escape imprisonment on charges of fraud he had agreed to turn informant. The man used to appear in the middle of Shabbat services and shamelessly boast that he had arrived by car, and then start an argument about unimportant things, like the synagogue's heating. I have no doubt he reported on us to the KGB. It was no accident that Rabbi Dinur, who secretly acted as a mohel (circumciser) and shochet (ritual slaughterer), kept his distance. Incidentally, Dinur later caught a stroke of luck. On the very day he left the country, officers came to his apartment with a search warrant. In their incompetence, they arrived too late.

Given our ignorance of Hebrew, it wasn't easy to study Torah. Still, we made efforts to create ulpans, in the hope of turning them into centers of Jewish education. Chaim Drori was particularly instrumental in this. When he would learn of young Jews who had expressed interest in studying Hebrew, he would find them a teacher (usually someone who had himself studied at the Hebrew high school before 1940, like Chaim's father Boris), follow up with them, and, for some, invite them to work at Rumbuli, to participate in "Zionist Q & A" sessions, or to help distribute printed material.

Chaim once introduced me to an eighteen-year-old student at a technological college who told me about a brawl that had broken out there between Jewish and Russian students. During the fight, a Jewish student had been seriously injured. It occurred to me that confrontations like this must take place every day, and that data on such incidents ought to be collected and made public. Such a list would only arouse the fury of the authorities, of course, who did everything possible to keep Jews isolated from one another and to make them despair of the aspiration to leave. But awareness of such incidents, I thought, would be of paramount importance both for Soviet Jews and for the West, to shine a light on our struggle. In due course I prepared a questionnaire designed to gauge the state of Soviet Jewry, with 120 questions on the following subjects: manifestations of anti-Semitism, forcible assimilation as a matter of state policy, anti-Semitic propaganda from the highest echelons, and anti-Jewish activities engaged in by the Soviet apparatus. The questionnaire was code-named Pushkin, and it was put on the agenda for the next meeting of the National Coordinating Committee.

Chaim raised for discussion a declaration calling on Jews to list Yiddish as their mother tongue on the next census (set to take place in 1970). We approved the text.

The National Coordinating Committee had scheduled a conference in Kiev in the fall of 1969, but after the arrest of Boris Kochubievsky, there was widespread worry that the KGB was tracking activists there. Instead, we decided, the publication council would meet in Riga in January 1970. An ex-Betar man was elected by Riga to serve as editor, but at the last moment he withdrew his candidacy, and I was nominated for a post that seemed too weighty for a twenty-two-year-old. There was no choice, however, and I was compelled to agree.

The underground Zionist movement of Latvia came to full flower in the years 1969–1970. Thanks to Ruth Alexanderovich, dozens of Hebrew books came to Riga from the northern city of Novosibirsk. Ezra Rusinek raised funds for printing and found a typewriter. Thanks to him, too, it was possible in Riga to watch a slide show of Israeli postcards. At one such slide show I attended, Zuka Mintz offered a running commentary. By then I'd seen many postcards from Israel, but this was something else. It was hard to believe Mintz had never set foot in that country. I felt as I had in 1961 upon seeing that postcard from Kfar Giladi, my heart once more stilled by thoughts of Israel. In its boundless affection for the country I considered my true homeland, I felt pained for the Jews who remained in exile, whose mundane worries distracted them from the true essence of their people. I found such sentiments echoed in the poems of Bialik, especially his 1897 poem "Achen chatzir ha'am" (Truly, the people is as grass).

• • • • •

On June 1, 1969, Mendel sent his identity card to the Supreme Soviet and renounced his Soviet citizenship. In so doing he was following in the footsteps of Yasha Kazakov, who had announced he would no longer work on Yom Kippur. Yasha was promptly fired from his job, badgered for a year for lacking an identity card, and finally permitted to emigrate only in December 1970.

In the fall of 1969, on the anniversary of the beginning of the annihilation of the Jews of the Riga ghetto, an unprecedented crowd of three thousand gathered in Rumbuli. Zionism had once more become a movement of the people. I delivered a speech. It is not enough, I said, to mourn our dead. Despite the Holocaust, our people endures, and the graves of Rumbuli obligate us to learn from the past a lesson for the present. To conclude, I recited Alterman's poem "Magash hakesef" (Silver platter) in Hebrew. I don't know whether many in the audience understood the Hebrew words, but I hoped they fathomed its meaning, its call for struggle rather than surrender. As I finished, a profound silence descended on the crowd. Perhaps they expected me to continue. But any continuation could only be expressed in concrete steps, not mere words.

On Chanukah, we took turns lighting candles at Rumbuli so that they would stay lit for the duration of the holiday. My turn came on the eighth day. It was a stormy night, and I plowed through shoulder-high snowdrifts. With frozen fingers I lit the candles and recited Al Hanissim. My intention wasn't to reproach the dead for going to the slaughter without resisting. I did not ask why they hadn't resisted, but why *I* was not resisting.

That November, another meeting of the National Coordinating Committee took place in an abandoned summer home outside of Riga. On the agenda: cooperative activities, publishing, and contacts with independent groups of activists. Aharon Shpilberg and Boris Maftser represented Riga. The committee decided to send out open letters – addressed both to Soviet authorities and to public bodies in the West – insisting on our right to emigrate.

In those days friction between members showed its face for the first time. Perhaps this was the inevitable result of the growing numbers in the movement and the strong personalities it tended to attract. Conflicts arose, especially in those cases in which the line between public interest and private ambition was blurred. At the same time it must be said that the Riga group, being comparatively small, afforded a wide latitude of freedom.

Apart from the problem of strong personalities there also arose the matter of our relationship with activists outside our organization. It would have been unthinkable to say to prominent activists like Ruth Alexanderovich or Aryeh Khnokh: "The organization has decided such and such." The reply would have been wide-eyed disbelief: "What organization?"

We conducted ourselves with utmost secrecy, taking pains not to draw attention to ourselves. We considered covert activism to be most efficient. We distinguished between two groups of activists: those who operated openly and were known to the KGB, and those who operated under the cloak of secrecy. The organization strictly forbade the latter to reveal their identities or in any way attract attention. Thus, for instance, we decided not to participate in the large Chanukah party, where many Zionists came from various cities at the invitation of Ruth Alexanderovich. I was part of the covert group, all the more so given my membership in the publications council.

· · · · ·

Obviously, covert activists could not sign the open letters that were prepared in Moscow, Leningrad, and Riga. The so-called "Letter of the 22" – the first letter of the Riga refuseniks – was published in the fall of 1969. It was addressed to U Thant, then UN Secretary-General, and included the demand to be allowed to leave the Soviet Union. The first signatory was Aryeh Khnokh, and below him Ruth Alexanderovich, Sylva Zalmanson, Grigory Feigman, and my sister Meri. Another letter, appearing over the signatures of twenty-seven refuseniks, was addressed to Soviet leader Alexei Kosygin. I heard the text of both letters broadcast on Kol Israel, and was seized with trembling. These people were embarking on the path of open defiance, while I considered myself to be occupied with tasks anyone could perform. Their open defiance of the Soviet regime was without precedent, and for the signatories there was now no turning back. I was ashamed of myself that I was not in the company of these brave colleagues.

On one occasion I met Sylva, who was in a state of great tension. She said that if they did not receive a reply to their letter from the authorities, they would demonstrate on Red Square, inscribing their demands in blood, and refuse to leave until they had received visas. I agreed wholeheartedly, and informed my friends that the time for covert activity had passed, and the time for open defiance had arrived. Aharon Shpilberg agreed, but Boris stressed the continued importance of underground activity. We could reach no consensus, and ultimately I decided to try the impossible: I would attempt both open and covert activity simultaneously.

On January 7, 1970, I went to Leningrad for the first meeting of the publications council. I had received ticket fare from the organization, but knowing how dire our finances were I bought a student ticket at half price with the help of a foreign student card, and proudly returned half of the money. In order to save money, I also did not indulge in a berth in a sleeper coach.

The journey took ten hours. For the first time in my life I left the borders of Latvia. I regarded the other passengers with suspicion, as though they were all would-be thieves, and I fingered my manuscript pages anxiously. They were intended for the first issue of our journal. One manuscript was dedicated to the Warsaw ghetto uprising. The second concerned the holidays of Passover and Purim, arguing that while Passover commemorated freedom, Purim marked miracles that had transpired in exile.

Leningrad is considered the most beautiful of Russian cities, but to me it seemed cold and unwelcoming. I dialed a number I had memorized. "Rome has arrived," I said. Each of our code names began with the first letter of the city we represented, and I represented Riga. I was given an address, and soon found myself in the apartment of Viktor Boguslavsky chatting with Moscow representative Karl Malkin and Leningrad representative Leib Korn. We were then driven to an apartment on the outskirts of town where we were expected to work for a day without venturing outside. My colleagues were surprised by my young age; the truth was that even in my own mind I felt too young to be taking part in a mission of this kind.

In the course of discussion I contended that Israel must be prepared to absorb Jews from all over the world. In their view, this was too radical a position. The influence of Jewish communities in America and Europe ought to be preserved, they argued. I replied that if all the Jews gathered in Israel and built a truly strong country, the influence of Diaspora communities would no longer be necessary. They made some allowance for my youthful rashness, but when we turned to discussing the material for the journal it turned out that I sided with the moderate parts of each article. In Riga we shared the opinion that it was unwise to couch our demands within criticisms of the Soviet regime, but in Russia many had come to Zionism though the "Democratic Movement" (a group working to democratize – or at least reduce the oppression of – the national government), maintaining both the network and the style of that movement. Despite the esteem in which I held the "Democrats," I espoused a clear distinction between the two realms. Besides, the Democratic Movement included many diverse impulses, and did not always act in unison, and I thought it would be best not to follow in its footsteps. I finally succeeded in getting them to agree that our journal should take a neutral tone. Still, I wasn't satisfied by the product, which seemed to me to lack useful, concrete information.

Meanwhile, throughout the day's discussions we had not once left the apartment, consuming only preserved food out of cans, too focused on the imperative of our mission even to notice what we ate. But when we finished, I asked, despite the late hour, to go see the Leningrad synagogue. I brought along the prayer book I now used, a Chassidic siddur that had belonged to fellow Jewish activist Karl Malkin. The building, though beautiful in its interior, had been sorely neglected. Seeing it, I recited the verse "How goodly are your tents, Jacob, your sanctuaries, Israel." But the building's appearance made me reflect that our sanctuaries could only be truly "goodly" in Israel.

I returned to Riga with material for the first issue of our journal, and delivered a report about the trip. We printed our first issue of *Ha-Iton* on a typewriter, using thin paper to make eleven copies at a time. We had purchased this paper in small quantities at different stores and at different times so as not to draw undue attention. Nor was obtaining a typewriter without difficulty. Rumor had it that the KGB could trace and track every typewriter on the market by means of the unique "letter signature" each machine had. Then, our printing was laborious, and poor in quality: typists we could trust were both expensive to hire and hard to find. Finally, the printing completed, we bound the issues and distributed them – in small numbers, of course. We also had to obtain reproduction equipment. Boris suggested photographing the issue, and for this purpose Misha Shepshlowitz's room was turned into a photo lab. Misha, a physicist, was the technician of the group, and combined a Jewish mind with golden hands. He had dropped out of school in order to increase his chances of emigrating.

Several days later, I was informed that it had proved impossible to find the necessary screws to build a photo developing device. I was then working as an engineer at Riga's largest telephone manufacturer, and I told someone at the company's storeroom that I needed a certain type of screw. I succeeded in obtaining a large number of the screws, but feared walking past the guard at the factory gate carrying such a quantity. I tied bags filled with screws onto my back, and over the course of several days managed to smuggle out three kilograms.

Soon the developer was built at Misha's home, and we had to transport it to the place where we intended to develop the photos of the issue. One night, we started transporting it at 1:00 a.m. "Have you gone out of your minds?" Misha's alarmed mother said. "Who does things like this in the middle of the night?" She was right. It was sheer foolishness. On the deserted streets we stuck out like a sore thumb. As we dragged the cursed crate containing the machine, a handle broke off, making our task even more arduous. We had almost arrived at our destination when a police cruiser appeared around the corner and headed straight for us. An officer jumped out and ran toward us. We stood still, not attempting to escape. The film with the complete issue of the magazine lay on the bottom of the crate. The officer rudely demanded to know who we were, and what we were dragging. Misha replied, managing a calm and even voice, as he explained that we were carrying a developing machine. The policeman thrust his hand into the crate, and I feared he would momentarily find the incriminating film. But Misha grabbed his arm. "I told you, this is a developing machine. If you break it, you pay."

The officer suspended his search, but demanded our ID papers. If we refused to produce them, we would be taken down to the police station. Seeing no alternative, I presented my papers, and my name was taken down. Misha's particulars, for some reason, were not recorded.

Finally we arrived at the apartment where Boris had been anxiously waiting. Usually he lived in dread of arrest, but this time he listened to our story with relative equanimity.

The next morning, we began the work of reproduction. This being my first experience with developing, most pages turned out grey. I'd bought the right chemicals and measured them out myself, but it seems I hadn't been precise enough. In buying up large quantities of photo paper number 7, I must have aroused the curiosity of the suppliers. One took a look at my fingers, bleached brown by the developing agents, and quipped, "What's the matter? You've been producing samizdat or something?" Indeed, a joke that hit its mark.

We worked in a rotation of our group of four: one remaining in the bathroom next to the developing machine, a second developing the film, and the other two drying prints. In the dim light we looked like ghostly devils. Almost right away, a mishap: something broke in the drying machine, which we had acquired at such risk, and the prints floated in their own chemicals. Misha made the radical suggestion that we lay the prints out to dry on the floor, and we did so until there wasn't an inch of floor available to step on. When we finished the job, we felt a sense of satisfaction with our pioneering work, work that had made maximal use of our time and energies.

· · · · ·

Although we forgot about our little midnight misadventure, the police had not, and two weeks later I was summoned to the district police station. I couldn't bring myself to tell my parents the truth, but my account wasn't too far off: I told them that I had been carrying a suitcase bursting with samizdat literature when the police stopped me and asked for my papers. My father knew of my activities in distributing "illegal" literature, and it was clear to him that sooner or later I'd be apprehended. He asked me only to take precautions. The fact that my entire family was in some way engaged in Zionist activism offered some comfort: My sisters had been printing samizdat material, study-ing Hebrew, and befriending activists. Often full families joined the effort, the Zalmanson, Greenman, Valk, Rusinek, Kamyeski, and Khnokh families among them. In such a family one could imagine himself as some felt in Israel: that Zionism was not a matter of individuals but was the collective project of an entire people.

In honor of my visit to the police station I wore my best suit, and resolved to project an air of calm self-confidence. The interrogator's room was stuffed with spare radio parts stolen from factories. When it became apparent that Misha and I were suspected of involvement in stealing such parts I calmed down a bit, and presented my account of events: I had just been approached by a stranger on the street who asked me to help him carry a crate when we were stopped by an officer. I gave my particulars, I said, but the stranger did not. As soon as the officer left, I went on, I myself walked away from the suspicious stranger, and so could not say who he was, what he was lugging about, or even where he was going. The interrogator called my story "an old wives' tale," and demanded I tell the truth. I stood my ground, insisting that I had told the full truth. I had rehearsed my story, of course, and had carefully considered each detail. The interrogator was forced to release me.

· · · · ·

Many young couples came together in the Zionist movement, and many young families were forged. But I myself never imagined I could meet a girl, or take her out to restaurants and the movies. I was far too immersed in my activism. I would get up every morning excited to be alive at such a wonderful, even joyful time. We often remarked to one another on how elated we felt. We had a passionate dream, and in contrast to millions of others living under Soviet rule, we filled our lives with purpose. Each day felt like a link in a chain of miracles, and we felt blessed.

During my last spring in Riga, Boris Penson suggested that we stage a Purim play in the synagogue to attract youngsters. I took it upon myself to write the Purim story in rhyming verse, and Boris set about preparing the costumes and stage set. Chaim's ulpan students were the actors. In composing the script I embedded hints about Jews who surrender to or collaborate with oppressive authorities . The papers in those days were full of groveling letters by "Soviet workers of Jewish nationality" claiming that they had no need of Israel, that the Soviet Union was their only homeland. And so I wrote a sarcastic ditty:

> *It seems only sensible to admit,*
>
> *That even among our people, so loosely knit,*
>
> *Are strange types, following some evil muse,*
>
> *Who want – but why? – to be Jews.*

The actors rehearsed with great enthusiasm, and all went well until "King Achashverosh" slipped up. He told his grandmother of the interesting poems he was rehearsing, of the exciting rehearsals with Gesia Kamyeski, of secretive whisperings, of precautions against eavesdropping. The grandmother, a veteran staunch Communist, was appalled by what she had heard, and threatened Gesia that if the play were not canceled she would have no choice but to inform "those who need to know" (a euphemism for the local KGB). We canceled the play, but the grandmother alerted the "appropriate authorities" anyway, and on Purim the synagogue was visited by a squad of police. In the middle of the reading of the book of Esther, the commanding officer interrupted: "Is anyone here misbehaving?" No one was, and so there was no one to arrest. So the Purim play failed; life in the Soviet Union habituated us to such disappointments.

At that time, Aryeh Khnokh introduced me to a high school student named Misha, whose vocal and declamatory talents made me consider him as my replacement for the next commemoration at Rumbuli. I went to his house, and met other young people. We discussed Israel; I recited some Bialik poems I'd committed to memory.

Several days later, however, Misha announced that he could not speak at the Rumbuli memorial. Perhaps he felt frightened, or his parents had nixed the idea. Escorting him out, I showed him the quarter that during the war had been turned into the Jewish ghetto. As we stood next to the former Judenrat building, I said, "As Jews were being massacred at Rumbuli, the Jews sitting in this building hoped they themselves would be spared. In the end, they met the same fate. If you hope your fate today will be different from ours, I'm afraid you will be bitterly disappointed." He could only mutter something in reply about Lenin and the birth of Communism.

· · · · ·

A year after one's application for a visa was refused, one could re-apply. There was no chance of a positive verdict, but the common view was that we should re-apply anyway, if for no other reason than to remind the authorities of the plight of Soviet Jews.

After my second application, in late February 1970, I and another young woman who had applied for a visa were summarily fired. Having dedicated my energies elsewhere, I didn't take it too hard. I dictated the second issue of *Ha-Iton* to Sylva Zalmanson (with whom I was becoming increasingly friendly), after which she printed it up, and Dov Riger photographed it. I discovered that the publication had already generated reader interest, and took great pleasure in hearing from one reader that *Ha-Iton* had become the voice of Soviet Jewry, and that its publication testified to high levels of Zionist awareness.

"Eduard wishes to speak with you," Sylva told me one day in mid-February. I had met Eduard Kuznetsov on the eve of Chanukah at Sylva's home. Ruth Alexanderovich had told me then that he was a former political prisoner who wanted to move to Riga, and thence to Israel. I knew he had served for seven years for his political views, and he seemed to me a man of great courage.

I admired Eduard – a man of simple ways, intelligent, and knowledgeable – and I did my best to visit him often. On our very first meeting he told me that while still in the labor camp he had decided to tie his fate with Israel's. This time, he turned the radio up full blast, to thwart eavesdroppers, and asked, "Would you be willing to attempt to escape the Soviet Union even if the attempt could cost you your life?"

I answered at once. "Certainly."

He hadn't expected such a swift reply. "Don't rush. This is a grave matter. Think it over, and answer me in a couple days."

"Listen," I said, "I've thought about this all my life. Another couple of days won't change anything."

And so Eduard disclosed the details of an escape plan. It began with a Jewish pilot, a former air force major. We would buy tickets on a Leningrad-Murmansk flight. If detained, we would say we were traveling to a wedding, and two of us would act the roles of bride and groom. Hence the name of the plan: Operation Wedding. During the flight, our pilot would hijack the plane, take the controls, and chart a course for Sweden.

I sat down, and said I was in.

As I left the Zalmanson's, I felt almost as though I had sprouted wings. At last, a way to flee this imprisonment! I told Boris Maftser that I had agreed to take part in an escape mission. I passed on my roles in the organization to others, and notified my friends so that they wouldn't be hurt after I'd left. Meanwhile, we members of the escape operation spread out a map and charted a route. A deep faith in the justness of the course I'd chosen seized me. I recognized that without Israel I would have no life.

The question arises: did I have in mind to sacrifice myself in order to break open the gates of aliyah for others? I realized, of course, that such a desperate step would draw the world's attention to the struggle of Soviet Jewry – and to the denial of their human rights. On the other hand, I also knew the operation's chances of success were slim; we could be arrested on the way to the plane, shot on the plane, or shot down out of the sky. Yet I felt I could wait no longer; I had to act decisively.

Our pilot, Mark Dymshits, was a Jew from Kharkov who, after flight school, had served in the air force, rising rapidly in the ranks. At thirty-five, he was vice squadron leader, and had he agreed to study political science in the military academy he would have risen still further. But a Party career failed to entice him. He loved the skies too much. As I boy I had read about people who couldn't live without flying, but I had never imagined I'd meet such a character myself. Mark's military service had sharpened his natural proclivities: his punctuality, decisiveness, toughness, impatience with chitchat, and his commitment to his word.

Mark hadn't had any Jewish education to speak of, nor did he know a single Yiddish word. He only remembered that his mother used to sing Yiddish songs. But somehow the heritage of his forefathers – a love of truth and justice – still beat in his breast.

Because Jews could rise in rank only so far, Mark was discharged from active service in 1963, and had to leave flying behind. He had moved to

Bukhara to try to resume flying, but missed his family and returned to Leningrad. Because of a quota, he could not get work at the Leningrad airport. And then the Six-Day War broke out. Mark followed the events in *Pravda*, the official Communist Party newspaper. I was in a better position, and knew that the Israeli army was far more formidable than was being portrayed in Soviet propaganda, but Mark, fearing that all might be lost, came to an urgent sense of how precious the imperiled Jewish state was. Not to mention that in Israel he would be able once more to take to the skies. And why not? He was a healthy man of forty, an experienced fighter pilot. The two dreams intermingled: to return to the skies and to live in Israel.

Consistency and determination are what separate idle fantasy from realizable dream. Mark began to study Hebrew, despite an almost complete absence of Hebrew textbooks. A Russian-Hebrew dictionary came out in 1965, but even this was difficult to make use of. It was impossible to buy, though one could peruse it in a library, copying down words in the unfamiliar language in order to study them later.

So Mark visited the library and copied down words. Another reader noticed his snail's pace and asked him what he was doing. "I want to learn Hebrew," Mark said. "Then come with me," the young man replied. And this is how he miraculously met someone who happened to be a teacher at one of Leningrad's home-ulpans. As they got to know one another, Mark appraised his new acquaintance at great length, and finally decided to share his hijacking idea. The teacher, Hillel Butman, was excited by what he heard, and together they began to plan an operation that would make waves internationally. It would be best, they thought, to find fifty Jews – all of them already engaged in Zionist activism and Hebrew study – who would be ready to take part. Hillel, a member of the Zionist committee in Leningrad, set out to activate his networks in Zionist circles there.

The Leningrad Zionists had, as a matter of principle, chosen to engage only in legal activities, like promoting Jewish education. The notion of hijacking a plane upset a number of committee members, and Misha Korn convened a special session to discuss the matter. Meanwhile, Hillel had met in Riga with Sylva Zalmanson to inform her of the plan and assure her of Eduard Kuznetsov's participation in it.

The three of us met to decide whom we could recruit from Riga for the mission. Through Boris Maftser, I recommended several names to the Leningrad committee: Mendel Gordin, Alec Soboliev, Leib Eliashevitz, Boris

Penson, and Aryeh Khnokh. We knew and trusted these men; even if they turned down the offer to join the mission, they would not reveal its existence.

My conversation with Mendel was particularly meaningful. As in the past, he was for me the very paragon of trustworthiness. Apart from the possibility that he might take part in the escape, I wanted to hear his opinion of the mission as a whole. Mendel worked in those days in a clinic for sexually transmitted diseases. After he gave up his Soviet citizenship and insisted on not working on Jewish holidays, the health ministry could offer him no better job. I telephoned him at work, and he came immediately; apparently he understood from my tone a sense of the gravity of the matter. I posed three questions to him: Would he himself be prepared to take part in the escape plot? Did he think the mission could succeed? And could it damage the Zionist cause?

He answered the first two questions in the negative. Too many people already knew of the plan, he said, and it must be assumed that the KGB did too. For himself, he had chosen the form of struggle appropriate for him by renouncing his Soviet citizenship, and he would continue in that path. But he also argued that the operation might very well benefit the Jewish people. If we acted with requisite care, we could insulate the legal activists from our mission, and not cause too much harm to the Hebrew and Jewish history classes, or to the Jewish choirs. I decided we should go ahead.

Aryeh Khnokh and Boris Penson immediately agreed to take part. Leib Eliashevitz said he would weigh the proposal. Leib was an aliyah activist who had, like Mendel, renounced his citizenship, and was now in danger of being drafted into the Red Army. Alec Soboliev raised a rather original objection to participating: he was working on an academic critique of Marxism, and since he would not be able to bring his manuscripts and literature on the subject out of the country, he could not join our escape. The refusals surprised but did not trouble me. There were certainly no lack of people who wished to flee the Soviet Union.

At the time, a well-known group of so-called "tamed" Jews – prominent academics and public figures – declared to the nation (this was broadcast on television) that they had no connection to the Jewish people and that they denounced Zionism. The Zionist underground in Russia responded with open letters, all of them even-tempered and persuasive, signed by aliyah activists in Moscow, Leningrad, and Riga. I signed each of them without considering the risks. In light of what I was planning, everything else paled into insignificance.

At the same time I made a request to the Israeli ambassador to the UN to fight on my behalf and insist on my right to emigrate. My letter to him was smuggled to the West through tourists and foreign journalists. Eliyahu Valk claimed that my letter had been too harshly phrased. He had no idea I was about to take a far riskier step. But many others were prepared to risk everything for the chance to emigrate to Israel. Aharon Shpilberg and I once collected signatures for an open letter demanding legalization of emigration to Israel. We knocked on the door of an elderly Jew who signed first and then asked, "Nu, so now show me what I just signed." Such was the general readiness to act – even at the cost of personal risk.

Towards April, I received a reply through Maftser from the Leningrad committee, which recommended against the hijacking plan. Despite the unfavorable view of the operation, however, the committee granted fifty rubles to Mark to carry out a kind of test run. Mark bought a ticket on a TU-124, and during the flight entered the cockpit carrying a bottle of cognac, thereby showing that it might be possible to get to the pilot without resorting to violence.

The continued debate in the Leningrad committee was exceedingly heated. David Chernoglaz resigned in protest of Butman's conducting conversations with movement members without the committee's consent. Vladimir Mogilever, one of the committee's leaders, proposed a compromise: sending a request to officials in Israel for their approval of the operation. Butman sent an encoded letter to Asher Blank, who had emigrated to Israel from Leningrad in 1969. Mogilever gave the letter to two Israeli tourists who entered the USSR on their foreign passports: Rami Arnzur held a Norwegian passport, and Karl Millman had arrived on a Swedish passport. The letter was discovered at customs, confiscated, photocopied, and then returned to the two passengers.

It was clear to us in Riga that the Leningrad activists, having for whatever reason decided to withdraw support from the plan, were merely looking for a plausible excuse to pull out. It would be inconceivable, after all, for an official Israeli body to approve a hijacking. On April 10, Asher Blank called Butman: "The medicine is likely to do harm." In other words, as expected, the Mossad opposed the operation. On April 20, Hillel Butman and Misha Korn pulled out of Dymshits's plan.

Without the cooperation of the Leningrad people, we had to abandon the idea of hijacking a large plane, but told Mark that those of us in Riga were still in. I had no idea how complicated relations between the Leningrad activists had become.

In late April, I went to Sylva's and found Eduard in conversation with a man I didn't know. "This is our 'driver,'" Eduard said. At first glance, I didn't like this pilot. He seemed too glum, too taciturn. We went out for a walk. Though it was warm, I kept on my beret, explaining to Mark that wearing it was no mere eccentricity, but a religious custom. The moment I mentioned religion, I sensed the "driver" begin to treat me suspiciously. Perhaps he didn't believe a religious man could take part in a perilous operation; Soviet propaganda used to drill into citizens' heads the idea that a religious man cannot be a man of integrity.

Asked to show Mark around Riga, I took him to the synagogue, the old ghetto district, and the Rumbuli cemetery. On the way it became clear that Mark had never stepped foot in a synagogue and was going now only with the greatest reluctance. At the door, I almost had to force him to put a yarmulke on his head. He stepped inside with trepidation, as though entering a minefield. The moment I opened my mouth to say something about the building, the synagogue's old beadle approached. "You're not a local," he said. Mark nodded. The old man wouldn't let him alone. "Are you from Leningrad?" This was too much, and Mark ran toward the exit. "You're dragging me to so many places, the KGB is sure to be on to us," he said angrily.

A long time later, when we were in prison, Mark would remember the incident and observe wryly that I had taken him to the synagogue to guarantee us God's help. At the time, however, I realized I had better change my approach, and rather than take him to Riga's Jewish sites I took him to a forest so that we could discuss the logistics of our operation in peace and quiet.

According to the new plan, we would steal a small plane, an AN-2, at the Smolny airfield near Leningrad. Because these smaller planes weren't guarded, we would carry out the hijacking at night. We agreed that Eduard and Sylva would reconnoiter the area in mid-May.

· · · · ·

Passover, the holiday of freedom, was drawing near, as was the onset of our own personal Exodus. Passover began that year on the hundredth anniversary of Lenin's birth. Our apartment building was on the historical registry because in 1903 Lenin had met there with Latvian Social Democrats. Accordingly, the building had been renovated and repainted and installed with hot water pipes. In order to restore the building to the way it looked in Lenin's day, a second entrance to the courtyard was opened. This was an extraordinary development for my purposes, because it allowed me to cross three courtyards and arrive on another street, making it very hard to tail me. In this way I brought home "fresh stock" of samizdat literature: Solzhenitsyn's *The First Circle*, photocopied on thick paper, and weighing several kilograms. I gleaned a great deal from the book about prisons and gulag camps, about interrogations and interrogators. I prepared myself with utmost seriousness for prison. I memorized the Hebrew calendar so that I would know when to mark Jewish holidays behind bars.

In the meantime I took full part in family life. Each year on Passover, we were able to recite the Haggadah more fully, and this year my father led the seder flawlessly. In the synagogue, the head of the Jewish community, a man appointed by the authorities, greeted the worshippers with a paean to the Soviet state. Two young American Jews prayed with us, and Mendel Gordin and I offered to meet with them after services. We conversed in Hebrew. It turns out they were teachers at a large Jewish school in New York. Apparently someone had warned them that they were likely to be followed; they glanced around anxiously, and feared that every policeman was a disguised KGB agent. I handed them photos of the site of the mass murder of Jews in Rumbuli, and they gave me a pendant inscribed with the symbols of the twelve tribes of Israel. Five years earlier, receiving a gift like this would have made me the happiest man alive, but now I had higher things on my mind. I asked them to send books on Hebrew and Jewish history to Riga, in the hope that they would not be confiscated.

I took them through the neighborhood of the former ghetto, an area of dilapidated buildings today housing Russian families no doubt ignorant of the murders that had been perpetrated there. No memorial plaque commemorated the suffering and death that had been our people's lot. We passed through the municipal park that occupied the land that had once housed a synagogue burned by Latvian police during the war. In the inferno, many Jewish refugees sheltering there were burned to death. I showed my guests the building where my uncle had hidden the family jewelry inside an oven. His wife perished in Auschwitz, but he survived and managed to make it to America. After the war, my father searched for but never did find the stash.

One of the Americans, whose parents had come from Eastern Europe, wanted to know how samizdat books were prepared. We, in turn, asked him to publicize the fact that Mendel Gordin had renounced his Soviet citizenship. As we took our leave, Mendel asked them: "Why haven't you made aliyah?"

"When it's difficult, it's easy," was the cryptic reply, "and when it's easy, it's difficult."

That night I arranged a second seder for fifty guests from various cities in Shpilberg's apartment. We improvised tables from planks stolen from a military storehouse, an act for which Yisrael Zalmanson was nearly apprehended. My sister Eva cooked tzimmes and gefilte fish, but the food turned out to be the only successful part of the evening. For most of the guests, who had never participated in a seder before, the Haggadah was superfluous and dull. Most didn't bother waiting for the reading of the Haggadah before ravenously attacking the food. And these were Jewish activists! Such was the spiritual destruction the state had wrought upon its citizens.

I instructed Maftser to find a replacement for me, but in the meantime I continued to work as usual, despite being utterly immersed in the escape plan. Korn, Boguslavsky, and Malkin came to Riga to prepare the third issue of *Ha-Iton*, the identity of which had started to take shape. It contained concrete information about the state of Soviet Jewry, as well as letters and declarations on the subject of aliyah. A similar magazine had started to come out in Moscow, but its editors had come to Zionism through their human rights activism, and thus they wrote in the characteristic "going to the limits of the permissible" style of the Democratic Movement. We, in contrast, called a spade a spade and struggled openly for our rights, under the assumption that the Soviet state and Western public alike must finally acknowledge that the Jewish nation in the Soviet Union still endured, even as it suffered. I had faith that God would not abandon us: "The Israelites were still groaning because of their subjugation. When they cried out because of their slavery, their pleas went up before God. God heard their cries, and He remembered His covenant with Abraham, Isaac, and Jacob" (Exodus 2:23–24).

On May 2, we gathered at Rumbuli to commemorate the Warsaw ghetto uprising. This time, in order to keep a low profile, I did not give a speech. At the suggestion of Boris Penson, we prepared several hundred Stars of David from yellow paper, but those in attendance were reluctant to put them on until we did so ourselves – the power of personal example. Soon it was clear that the number of stars wouldn't suffice.

Something similar happened when we began collecting signatures for a petition to allow Jewish artistic activities in Riga. The Jewish choirs that had flourished in the early 1950s had been shut down. We now decided to fight for their reinstitution, something that would make possible the recruitment to legal Jewish activities. Most, however, refused to sign. So I persuaded my family to sign first. People are less hesitant to sign a petition that already has signatures above their own. My sister Meri alone collected hundreds of signatures.

This time, one Jewish man requested we erase his signature. He hadn't slept a night since affixing his signature, and asked his wife what to do. So great was the fearfulness of the Soviet citizen that it took courage even to ask the authorities for permission to sing in Yiddish.

Meanwhile, Meri's fate preoccupied me. Her fiancé, Aryeh Khnokh, had decided to take part in the escape operation and wanted her to come with him. I tried to talk him out of it; the risk was too great. Ultimately we decided that they would be officially married so that if the plan worked he could request that she be released to join him abroad.

On Lag B'Omer, we held the chuppah in the synagogue. My parents were unpleasantly surprised by the unexplained haste. For me this was the last holiday I'd celebrate at home, and I raised a toast to the hope of reaching Israel safely. Chana, the wedding guest sitting next to me, stared at me in alarm. She had no way of knowing that I knew that she and her husband Zvi had agreed to take part in the hijacking. Tolya Altman and Mendel Bodnya were also expected to join, but not Ruth Alexanderovich. The KGB had taken too much interest in her Zionist activities. Before he dropped out, Butman advised Dymshits to recruit non-Jews to camouflage our designs. I argued that the operation should carry a wholly Jewish character, and so I objected to the participation of former political prisoners Yuri Fedorov and Alexei Marchenko, friends of Eduard Kuznetsov.

At the wedding of Meri and Aryeh I felt the profoundest joy. I even sang aloud, which I almost never do. Only Eduard and Sylva were missing, conspicuously so; they had gone to Leningrad to reconnoiter. Their report was not encouraging. The planes on the tarmac, they said, were chained together, and were heavily guarded at night with dog patrols. Our plan seemed unfeasible.

I was crushed. I turned up the tape recorder to full volume and listened to songs of the Six-Day War recorded on Kol Israel, feeling as though I had been physically dragged from a plane about to take off for Israel. To stay in the Soviet Union? To see my hopes once more dashed? This was more than I could bear.

When Mark arrived several days later, we tried to think of alternatives, but could find none. We agreed to wait until the time was ripe. Aryeh declared that as Meri's husband he could insist that she join the operation. Eduard supported him; after all, Mark would be taking his wife and daughters. Thinking about my parent's heartbreak should anything happen to my eighteen-year-old sister Meri, I adamantly refused to include my other sisters, Rivka and Eva, though they had been active in the Zionist movement for some time. But they were family, and as much as I was willing to risk my own skin, I could never imperil their lives.

• • • • •

In the beginning of June, Mark announced that he had found a possible solution. Hope blossomed again in my heart. It seemed that AN-2 planes had resumed flying from the Smolny airfield to Priozersk, a small town near the Finnish border. Eduard Kuznetsov flew to Leningrad to learn more.

The resulting plan was this: We would buy all the tickets for the twelve-seater plane. When the plane landed in Priozersk, and the pilot left the cockpit to open the hatch to let passengers disembark, two of us sitting next to the door would apprehend him and tie his hands. By the time the second pilot, with his back to the cabin, would realize something was wrong, we would bind his hands too, thus preventing him from reaching the gun he would likely be toting in his bag. We would bundle up both men in sleeping bags and leave them in the forest under a sign that read: Air Force Freight. We would then gather the rest of our men, for whom there hadn't been room on board before, and Dymshits would fly toward the Finnish border at an altitude of 25 meters, under the radar. We would pass over Finland and the Gulf of Bothnia and land in Boden, Sweden. At 180 kilometers per hour, the flight would last three hours, but the flight from Priozersk to the border would take only ten minutes, not long enough time for fighter jets to be scrambled. If we would be pursued, to avoid radar detection, we planned to touch down on a road in Finland and take off again. If contacted on the air traffic control frequency, we would say we'd been hijacked by terrorists, and that the pilot had no choice but to give in to their demands, since women and children were on board. (Incidentally, this part would be true.)

We began to believe that we might actually pull this off. Discussing the details made the operation seem feasible. I insisted that we take along Dymshits's homemade pistol, together with clubs and brass knuckles, in case of protracted struggle with the pilots. To be authorized to fly near the border, Soviet pilots had to pledge in writing never to cross the border, and they were always armed. I thought we had the right to defend ourselves and our freedom, all the more so because there would be no innocent bystanders on the plane who might be harmed.

The preamble to the Universal Declaration of Human Rights states that it is essential to protect those rights "if man is not to be compelled to have recourse, as a last resort, to rebellion against tyranny and oppression." We had been forced to that last resort, and therefore our actions had nothing to do with air piracy of a merely criminal kind.

On June 8, we gathered in the Shmerly forest to go through the plan one last time. I insisted that Meri and her husband not be among the group that would hijack the plane, but would wait for us in Priozersk. Sylva Zalmanson and Boris Penson would go with them to Priozersk. The others would board the plane at the Smolny airfield. My role would be to help Mendel Bodnya, an amateur wrestler, to tackle the first pilot; Yisrael Zalmanson and Eduard Kuznetsov would take care of the copilot. I read aloud the manifesto in which we spelled out the reasons we were compelled to take this desperate measure. The text – to be published in the event we were killed or captured – began with the words of the prophet Zechariah: Come! Come! Flee from the land of the north," declares the Lord…. "Come, Zion! Escape, you who live in Daughter Babylon!" (2:10–11). I felt with every fiber of my being that I was fulfilling the commandment of God.

Meanwhile, passersby were milling about in the vicinity of our gathering, and we joked with one another that our plan had been compromised. That's how impossible it seemed. Meri and Aryeh even hitched a ride home in a police car. Everything seemed like a joke, like a form of play – but it was playing with fire.

On the way home, Zvi said, "Doesn't it seem to you that we haven't entirely planned things thoroughly?"

"Yes, but that may be a good thing," I replied.

Zvi looked at me in astonishment. "What could be good about not nailing down every last detail?"

"It's quite simple," I said. "Our decision is based on our will. If our decision had waited for us to think everything through rationally, if might never have been made. In this case, our will dictates to our reason, not vice versa."

He was silent the rest of the drive, and after that never returned to Riga.

I told Maftser that we should forewarn our colleagues in Riga and transfer all the samizdat material to hiding places; but I wasn't allowed to tell him the date of our operation.

On June 13, the first group left for Priozersk. Whatever would happen, my apartment would likely be subject to search, so I began removing anything that could cast suspicion. I threw away on the street the parts of the megaphone we had used at Rumbuli. When the parts immediately vanished, I worried I was being followed. I hid behind a wooden fence, but seeing no one, I calmed down a bit.

After Aryeh took the liberty of telling Chaim Drori of our plan, Chaim and I went to Aryeh's place to check whether it was "clean." He had promised that everything would be out by the time of our operation. Far from it. We removed buckets of dust, and burned stacks of samizdat papers that had been scattered on his floor. At Sylva's, things weren't much better. In every drawer I opened were proclamations, drafts of open letters, and samizdat publications of every kind. I was shocked: any single paper of this type could lead investigators to implicate others.

Such complacency was the result, it seemed, of a certain confidence in the operation's success. I, however, felt doubtful. I hauled out all the samizdat material from my home in two suitcases and concealed it in a designated apartment. Through Leib Eliashevitz I passed to Ezra Rusinek the farewell letters of the operation's participants, two copies of the manifesto, and a letter that listed the details of the plan and the names of those who knew of it. Only I knew of the existence of this last document. It was a final precaution, one that would allow our colleagues to determine the cause of failure – in the event of failure.

I reflected on the two types of impulse that would drive a man to take a desperate act like ours. The first is faith, the most profound bond of Jewishness. The second: the personal failures of antisocial, damaged individuals. In my case, I had succeeded in school, advanced in my career like anyone else, and cultivated meaningful friendships. Thus I acted foremost as a Jew, as a loyal son of his people. As for the others on the mission – each to his own impulse, in many cases an admixture of the two.

• • • • •

On the morning of June 14, I woke up early. Everything seemed as though it were for the last time: the last bread-and-cheese breakfast at home; the last sight of my father, relaxing at the table. I didn't dare reveal to him, in hints or otherwise, that we might not see one another again. I left without looking back.

It happened to be election day for the Council of People's Commissars. According to Soviet "democratic" procedures, only one candidate was allowed to run. Although it was a certainty he would win, everyone nonetheless was compelled to vote. Each district polling station was under the supervision of an official responsible for ensuring that everyone in his district fulfilled this obligation. Since this official could not go home before every last resident had voted, toward evening it was a common sight to see election officials running from house to house, urging people to cast their vote. Those who refused were threatened with police involvement. The day before, I had gone to the polling station to receive permission for an absentee ballot; I explained I would be traveling to a friend's wedding on Election Day.

I then bought toasted bread, chocolate, and a bottle of a sour fermented milk drink called Kefir. Finland had an extradition treaty with the Soviet Union, and if we had to land in Finland we would have to walk a great distance to the Swedish border.

Zev and Yisrael waited for me at the Zalmansons. Zev left a farewell letter for his father in the transistor radio; his father was meant to discover it the next time he replaced the batteries. In fact, it was discovered the very next day by KGB agents.

The brothers could not resist mocking me for bringing along Kefir, but I defended my favorite drink. We ordered a taxi that would take us to the airport.

From the window of the taxi, I looked around suspiciously, almost as though I were playing a detective game, only to notice a car following us. At the wheel was a man in a blue suit who looked like the classic KGB agent. As we stopped at a rail crossing, this man left his car, and entered the crossing guard's booth. The gate rose, and he continued to drive behind us all the way to the airport. My colleagues made fun of my suspicions, but when we boarded the plane, I noticed the man with the blue suit sitting directly in front of me.

As we landed in Leningrad, it seemed there was a malfunction; the engines continued to whine at full power. After an hour, the pilot came out to explain that a technical problem prevented him from turning off the engines, and that in the meantime we would not be able to disembark. Strange, I thought, it should be easy to simply shut off the engines' fuel supply. Too many strange coincidences for one day made for an uneasy feeling.

At last we were allowed to leave the plane. I rushed to get a taxi. We were supposed to meet our colleagues at 5:00 p.m., and were already running late. At the entrance to the waiting hall I ran into Boris Maftser, on his way to Riga after a meeting of the National Coordinating Committee. I said, "good-bye," hoping he might guess what I was doing here, and where I was heading, but he did not. An endless line at the taxi station. More delay. A Volga picked up the man in the blue suit, and he sailed off on his way, looking like a man who had done his duty.

Now in a taxi cruising through the streets of Leningrad, we passed a tall grey building. "KGB headquarters," the driver says. "I should visit one day," I quipped. Some jokes are more fateful than others. The next day, I found myself in the bowels of that very building, and even stayed there a while.

The first link in the chain of miracles had clasped shut. From now on, I would be beset by events that had seemed impossible from the perspective of my life until then. I was about to enter a world of prisons, gulag camps, and bizarre meetings, but the most significant and emboldening meeting of my new life in that world would be the encounter with myself, a meeting of self-recognition, and as a result, a recognition of the will of God.

Chapter Two

Arrest, Interrogation, and Trial

Atrembling shudder of surprise came over me. On the other side of Herzl Boulevard in the center of Jerusalem, on October 20, 1981, there he was, surveying his surroundings: my old friend Lyosha Safronov. But there's no way he can be here, I said to myself; he is twenty thousand kilometers away, at a political prisoners' camp in the Urals. On the other hand, I was well acquainted with Lyosha's chameleon-like ability to shift shapes, to be everywhere and nowhere at once. The last time this had happened was two years earlier in the camp we shared, as I returned from covertly saying the morning prayers and thought I noticed Lyosha in a faded undershirt next to the fence. On second glance, it turned out to be Vasily, the camp welder, who for some reason had temporarily let Lyosha use his form. It could be, of course, that in the dimness of dawn, and without my glasses, I had simply mistaken one for the other; but why would Lyosha appear here and now, in Jerusalem?

Lyosha had been my cellmate; for the ten years of our wanderings in the gulag, I had exhausted many an attempt to decipher his Russian-Tatar soul. I suppose it was no coincidence that our Father in heaven had stuck us in the same cell; perhaps He intended to show me how difficult it is to prevent oneself from becoming an "almost man." It is not enough to decide, "I will be good," nor even to possess sufficient willpower to enact that decision. You must know precisely how to edify yourself; your soul must contain a detailed plan of the temple you wish to build within.

· · · · ·

In prison, I invoke with all my heart the help of my predecessors who survived Stalin's gulag. If they endured, so can I.

I wake up in the afternoon, the sunbeams flickering on the black asphalt floor and stained straw mattress. At school we learned about the tortured sufferings of prisoners under the czar. The Great Leader himself, Lenin, occupied the cell adjacent to mine in the years 1895–96. At least he had a desk, books, chess set, and the right to talk to the prisoner next door.

But the socialist era has brought great advancement to the penitentiary system. My cell features neither books nor desk, only a small cabinet and metal toilet. Living conditions are cramped, just as they are outside of prison, with two or three cots crammed into a cell designed for one. Unlike in czarist days, we cannot leave the cell, the door of which is bolted all day. I would like to pick the brains of other prisoners, but am kept in isolation, the better to ratchet up psychological pressure. As in novels, I decide to try tapping on the wall. Immediately a voice from the slot in the door: "Get away from there. No tapping. Anyway, there's no one on the other side."

"I wasn't tapping," I say, "just thinking."

"You were tapping, but even if you break your head against the wall it will do you no good. Sit in silence. Lunch is coming soon."

Everything seems empty, exposed, gloomy. The tiny window, just below the ceiling, is blocked by three rows of bars: the first from the days of the czar, the second installed in Stalin's time, and the third by Khrushchev – a little gift from each tyrant. I can glimpse a small stretch of sky, a corner of a rooftop, and cooing doves. It seems that the faculty of watching doesn't come naturally to me; while other prisoners can watch the doves for hours, I look away after a while. I want food for thought, not mere images for my eyes.

It is very difficult to feel that you are outside the stream of time. The warden has confiscated my watch, Mendel's gift: "Made in Kursk? I haven't seen one of these lately." I would get it back eleven years later. It proves impossible to mark the passage of time by the sun; my cell gets sunlight only in the morning. I put a cup under the dripping faucet, and count to sixty, estimating a minute. I repeat this sixty times and measure the water, spilling it out to mark the next hour. In principle this method should work fine, but in practice the faucet drips inconsistently, and I weary of emptying the cup every hour. In my laziness I soon lose track of time.

Utter silence prevails, as though everyone, prisoner and guard alike, is in hiding. Time begins to flow ever more quickly. The silence, the interrogators' attempts to fashion for me a different time, a world with different concepts of space, dignity, and loyalty – all of this is nothing but a cunning trick. In effect, the prison is an experimental laboratory, and I am the lab rat. There is no physical torture or beatings; I have simply been transported into a different and inhumane universe, different in every aspect from the one I had hitherto known. The silence here is the silence of a scientific research lab in which each detail has been carefully designed: the yellow-painted walls and ceiling, the door with its slot, the total isolation. Without a strong internal world capable of withstanding this inhumane and artificial environment, you will literally go mad.

But you must not hesitate, or doubt for a moment that you can endure this. You must at once tell yourself: "Of course I can get through this. Anything else is unthinkable." But this secret wisdom discloses itself only after many years. To hesitate means to lose your resolve; to believe that you can endure is to endure. You can overcome fear only when you have faith that God will rescue you from the pit of the shadow of death. How much I regret not having a Torah or a prayer book with me. But I had feared that if such books were to be found on me during a search they would be used as further evidence against me. In my pack I had brought a yarmulke, but because I did not admit that it was my pack I cannot now ask for it. During the search, they had also confiscated my old map of Jerusalem, and now I am left with nothing. I had also packed five hundred grams of chocolate and two packets of biscuits. The others by now have certainly got their packs back, and are probably sharing their food, and here I am alone and hungry. What's with this prison? Has everyone gone nuts?

I pound the door. A guard's head appears in the slot (known as an "abus"). "No knocking on the door. If you need something, press the button."

There is indeed a button. I press it, and it sends an inaudible signal to the guard.

"What do you want?" he whispers.

"Books."

"Which books?"

"A Talmud, Tanach, siddur…" He is hearing these words for the first time. "Or perhaps you have a Hebrew textbook?"

"There's nothing like that here," he says. "Anyway, the librarian will come around in a couple of days."

They bring me soup, potatoes, a tiny fifty-gram slice of fish. I eye the soup suspiciously; it might have been made with pork. The potatoes seem okay; no visible signs of lard. I eat, and feel slightly relieved. I pace in the cell and brood…but it's better not to brood.

Still, I cannot help imagining the scene at home in Riga. The strip search I endured is nothing compared with the horrible things that must have happened there: An early morning knock on the door. Father opening it to find two plain-clothed officers presenting KGB badges and a search warrant. "Your son has been arrested and charged with the gravest of all crimes against the state: treason by means of attempted escape abroad." I am helpless to protect my father and his weak heart from such horrors. I wish he would love me less so that his pain would be less sharp.

If I had only known what strength God had granted my father in those trying hours, how relieved I would have felt! For despite his own spell in jail and his heart attacks, his rejuvenated strength surged; our struggle, animated as it was by a love and belief in God, transformed him into an experienced warrior. Meanwhile, however, knowing nothing of what was transpiring, I succumbed to despair. I did not then realize God's mysterious ways.

All my thoughts turn toward home, but now I am distracted by a tapping on the "abus," and the barking of commands: "To sleep! To sleep!" They never turn off the lights here. I lie down on the sleeping board, enfold myself in the blanket. "No covering your head!" the guard orders.

"Then shut off the lights so I can sleep."

"Not allowed. What will happen if you escape during the night?" Fatigue overcomes all; despite the harsh light, eventually I fall asleep.

In the morning, they hand me back my glasses, together with four hundred grams of bread and a pinch of sugar. Next, my first walk in the prison "courtyard," which is nothing more than a narrow cell with bars on top. There are no other prisoners to be seen. Each prisoner is in his own "courtyard." A guard looks down to make sure inmates do not talk or pass notes between them. Disobeying the rules means the walk is canceled. I strip to the waist and begin to jog, twenty paces forward, twenty back, twenty forward, twenty back…the purposeless scampering of a caged animal. I think about breaking through the barriers in my head, escaping to Israel… I run faster and faster.

"Stop! Sit still!"

I sink onto the bench. Where are my friends? How might I contact them? If I could only hear someone's voice. I listen, but there is only silence. I sing our favorite tune from Riga: "Heveinu shalom aleichem" (we have brought peace upon you). No answer. Every day of my stay in the Leningrad prison I would wait for an answer in vain. Only once did I imagine I heard Sylva's voice. I sang louder, but the guard whisked me away. Four walls of an immense prison, and not a single living thing to warm the heart.

• • • • •

Now it's time for some entertainment. The guards lead me down a series of long hallways to an interrogation room. The interrogator is there, sitting behind a large desk, behind him a portrait of Felix Edmundovich Dzerzhinsky, founder of the Bolshevik secret police, the Cheka. I am seated at a small table in the corner. Both table and chair are bolted to the floor, presumably to prevent me from bringing them down on the interrogator's head.

Major Popov, a special investigator from Riga, looks like an unremarkable, middle-aged man. Unlike the energetic young interrogator who had fervently believed in his own slogans, the one I had earlier refused to talk with, Popov appears jaded and cynical. His gestures and voice are restrained – in short, he isn't repulsive. But I soon noticed the malicious expression of his thin lips, the cold look in his eyes behind the cracked frames of his glasses. Was the crack in the frame intended to soften the heart of the prisoner? In any case, he apparently enjoyed enough leisure to go hunting; he chatted on the phone with his hunting buddies a number of times in my presence.

Major Popov is not unique in this choice of pastime. In the USSR, hunting is an upper-class hobby. KGB investigators can generally not be counted among the poor: they earn high salaries and shop at exclusive stores stocked with goods long absent from the shelves of public shops.

Captain Mamliga, for instance, who interrogated Yakov Suslensky, will call his Jewish acquaintances and say, "Nahum, I'll send someone to pick up the sausages." Or "Moshe, have you got some caviar?" Naturally, Nahum and Moshe provide him these goods gratis. When he goes on vacation, he stays for free at a house owned by a certain Jew he saved from a charge of speculation in foreign currency. In the course of interrogating Suslensky, this scoundrel Mamliga said, "Look, you've suffered all your life in the pursuit of justice, and what have you got to show for it? Me – I've got a good position, a nice salary, and I enjoy life."

Hearing this, Yakov went red with fury. This gave his interrogator a double pleasure: telling the unvarnished truth, for once, and ratcheting up the psychological pressure on his stubborn prisoner. This is a tried-and-true interrogation technique: to undermine the prisoner's faith in his own moral principles and to erode the sources of his will.

In our first interrogation session, Popov says, "You're hiding the names of your co-conspirators because you fear taking responsibility." Now of course, well before we were caught, we talked a great deal about how to conduct ourselves under interrogation. We passed around Alexander Esenin-Volpin's "Memo for those who expect to be interrogated." The son of well-known poet

Sergei Esenin, Alexander was a prominent mathematician, and his writing is characterized by both scientific precision and a deep-seated knowledge of contemporary Soviet history, knowledge that he earned the hard way through years as a dissident. Eduard Kuznetsov told us that they don't resort to physical torture with political prisoners. In that case, I declared at the time, the simplest technique if arrested will be to refuse to give any testimony whatsoever. The mention of anyone, after all, even someone wholly unconnected to our operation, will likely bring them harm.

The ancient legal principle that a man is innocent until proven guilty would be a revelation to me when I later learned of it. The concept was entirely foreign to Soviet citizens, who were habitually ready to find themselves guilty in the judgment of the state. Every modern system of law, including Soviet jurisprudence, puts the burden of proof on the prosecution to show guilt rather than on the accused to prove his innocence. But Soviet interrogators force the accused to confess by threatening to punish him for refusing to cooperate, thereby persuading the accused to testify, even against himself.

"Mendelevich. Why do you refuse to give testimony?"

"As far as is known to me, as one not yet proven guilty, I have a right not to testify."

"It seems you've done some useful reading on legal strategy before your arrest, which just shows you were planning to engage in illegal activity. It seems you're acquainted with Esenin-Volpin's illegal pamphlet, which proves your connection to illegal elements. Your refusal to tell the truth is likely only to make the court's sentence more severe because it demonstrates your disloyalty to the state."

The criminal code expressly denies that a refusal to testify could constitute grounds for imposing a harsher sentence, but which average citizen could be expected to know the code in detail?

"Mendelevich, according to your indictment, the court could impose a death sentence. You must understand that your refusal to testify endangers your life."

The possibility that I could face execution for attempted escape from the Soviet Union is not pleasant to contemplate. Raising it, of course, is part of the interrogator's cruel pressure. It was in exactly this way that the KGB broke the members of Leningrad's Zionist committee – none of whom knew of our operation – and forced them to talk.

"If, as you say, I face the death penalty, then I have even less reason to give testimony," I say.

But the interrogator's job is to make you talk. He will let you spout total nonsense, and might even pretend to believe it, just so long as you're talking. In this way you gradually play into his hands. At first you talk just to be rid of his annoying questions. Then you add a truthful detail or two to make your camouflage more plausible. But one day, the interrogator, wearing his official smile, will say, "Yosef the son of Moshe: Your testimony includes some details that strain belief. Let's clarify things a bit." He lets you hang on to the hope that you can continue playing the game; you just have to "adjust" your story a bit to the stories of the others. But the game always favors the interrogator. Happy is the prisoner who can find the strength at this point to stop, to say, "No, I will no longer play your games. Do with me as you will."

Strange things happen to people under interrogation. The most hardened soldier can sometimes reveal a talkative side, even when he ordinarily clams up without too much trouble. Later, in the labor camp, we often discussed this phenomenon. Some went so far as to suggest that prisoner food was tainted with certain chemicals that inhibited the power of resistance. But I think the explanation is simpler. Ever since childhood, we heard horror stories about KGB cruelty. The anticipatory fear can break a prisoner even before interrogation begins. That which is mandated for the prisoner under interrogation is not performance of a heroic act, but a prosaic process that will demand of him indescribable inner fortitude, which he must maintain in a state of almost total seclusion. It requires great wisdom not to succumb, not to forget the purpose of his determination.

A man without faith soon loses his sense of reality in prison. No newspapers, no letters, no word from home. You are alone all the time, except when you're facing the interrogator. You wonder whether everyone has forgotten you. You are startled awake in the morning with a shout: "Get up!" You hurry to rise; any delay may be cause for punishment. Your stone cell is cold even in July. The glasses that were confiscated for the night are returned to you (a prisoner once killed himself by swallowing shards of his lenses). The prohibition against covering your head with a blanket derives from a similar reason: they want to prevent you from choking yourself with a towel under cover of the blanket. The bright lights, too, stay on all night to deter suicide attempts.

Today they mistakenly give me another inmate's glasses. This is important information: another prisoner in my bloc wears glasses too. I try to remember if I've seen a fellow prisoner wearing this pair, but all of us wear the same generic Soviet-made frames. In another minute, the guard will take them back.

Next they give out sugar, boiling water, and coarse, coal-black bread. The distribution is a reminder, at least, that you are still on the list of the living, that they haven't entirely forgotten your existence.

Even a summons to the interrogator or the arrival of a hostile guard can gladden the prisoner's heart. These events momentarily dispel the silence – a silence of the grave – and the sensory deprivation. They are living people, who come from the world that was taken from me. It has been a long time since I hated the walls of my cell, or since I regarded them as a symbol of my tragic fate. Now they are my friends: I made a pact with the metal door and the stone floor, with the windowsill and the bare wall. With a piece of brick I broke off from under the window I scratched the word "silence" into the wall in Hebrew to remind me to keep quiet under interrogation. That single word sustains me.

What else comforts me? Reflections on the history of the Jewish people. Prayer. I have no prayer book, but I compose my own liturgy in my mind – prayers for the peace of the Jewish people, for my father, for my release from prison. Since I don't know the direction of Jerusalem, I pray facing the window, toward our Father in heaven. I sing as the psalmist sang, "Out of the depths I cry to you, Lord" (130:1). Into this prayer I pour all of my aching, all of my love for my people, the full force of my faith. The more fervently I pray, the stronger my faith becomes, and the more fully it becomes embodied, in turn, by prayer. I feel as innocent as a child standing before his master and speaking straightforwardly, without intermediaries.

Since I haven't studied Torah I can't mentally call up concepts the way a more learned person might. I know that the sages learned Talmud by heart – in some cases during the course of their own imprisonment – but regrettably I cannot do likewise. Had I studied from childhood, my mind would have been furnished, even in prison, with an invulnerable Jewish consciousness. How I long to feel completely foreign to the Soviet reality, even to the point of incomprehension of their thoughts and customs. Yet the same layer of consciousness that contains the experience of my life in the Soviet Union – experience I cannot simply uproot or erase – not only understands their language but also their ways of thinking. I pray that I will be able to vomit out all this abominable foreignness.

In my view, the worst of all the abuses the Soviet Union perpetrated on its Jews was not the closure of Jewish schools and theaters, but the spiritual impoverishment that its policies brought about. No one in the USSR believed in anything wholeheartedly. Cynicism was all-consuming; nothing was sacrosanct. As a result, people's inner strength was sapped, and they were more likely to break under interrogation and denounce friends.

· · · · ·

It's no mere coincidence that I'm reminded today in Jerusalem of Lyosha as a symbol of Russian dissidence. This is the story of Lyosha and his friend: One day, two young soldiers from the Soviet garrison force in East Germany robbed a kiosk there. This was their strange way of manifesting their decision to flee to the West. So crazed were they by the need to flee that they went wild in this kiosk, training their guns on the poor woman who ran it, and scaring her half to death. They would pay a high cost. When the kiosk was surrounded by security forces who arrived on scene, these two, having by this point had not a little to drink, responded by squeezing off rounds from their Kalashnikovs. Lyosha's partner was killed in the crossfire. Lyosha himself eventually threw down his rifle and surrendered. And this is how, twenty-five years after what the Soviets called the Great Patriotic War against Nazi Germany, the Germans took captive the son of a Russian major. Only his father's rank saved Lyosha from execution. He was a good-hearted guy, but some value-less vacuum in his soul had allowed his deviant tendencies to run riot. I regarded him as a cautionary tale about what could happen to me if I lost my grip on faith.

Is it an advantage or a disadvantage to know the language of the enemy? I overheard two guards outside my door. "What's up, Vanya? Problems again?"

"I was at the municipal worker's committee yesterday. Maybe they'll finally give me an apartment."

"Where are you living now?"

"In the dorms, in a single room with my wife and two kids. I've been there for five years now, ever since I left the kolkhoz (collective farm)."

Most of the prison guards were rural villagers lured away from their farms by the good salaries, inexpensive food, uniforms, and apartments that a job in the security apparatus promised. Others were the sons of senior bureaucrats who studied law at night and came to the prison for their professional "apprenticeship." Those in the latter group were aiming for a college degree and a KGB career. You could recognize them by their expensive suits, their eyes reddened from the previous night's drinking binge, their disparaging way of talking, and the annoying thoroughness with which they carried out searches.

Stalin had used the KGB to suck the blood of Soviet citizens during the 1930s, '40s, and early '50s. In fact, it was used to eliminate the political opposition starting back in the 1920s, and from then on its primary function had been to implant terror of the regime into people's hearts. This was euphemistically called "crime prevention." The security services would establish underground movements to draw in unsuspecting citizens, and then "expose" them. This was how new "enemies of the state" were "discovered," men who issued public confessions before denouncing their "partners in crime."

The exhaustive famine in the Ukraine in the thirties, in which millions perished (including hundreds of thousands of Jews), was brought about by draconian taxes imposed on farmers who refused to join a kolkhoz. This was how the authorities tried to hasten the development of Communist econo-mies. But if anything, the truth is even more horrible. Special delegations, sent to confiscate food goods, would visit the same farmer repeatedly, each time demanding taxes. Receipts showing that taxes had already been paid were of no use. The point was to teach a lesson: the state acts arbitrarily, and demands only one thing: unquestioning obedience. When children began dying of hunger, when people started trading in human flesh (I met other inmates who had engaged in cannibalism during that time), the peasants were ready to do anything – to join kolkhozes, to build Communism, to do anything so long as it would let them live. But no. Even this wasn't enough to guarantee their submission to state terror. Die! Eat your own children! Flee the countryside to the cities? The army blocked all possible routes. This is how the power of the state and its security apparatus grew to such immense proportions that in the end there was no one left to kill. But those inside the apparatus were not eager to give up their privileged positions, and so the massive albeit barbaric system remained in place.

· · · · ·

Some Soviet prison guards are taciturn, with dour, depressing expressions; others are chatty, even affable. The latter are the most dangerous, lest you let slip something extraneous, or give in to the temptation to ask to send a letter to the "outside."

It seems that for the time being I am safe, not only due to my abundant caution but because it is becoming increasingly clear that every last one of my colleagues has already been arrested. Last night, in the interrogator's office, I noticed several partially open suitcases (were they left here intentionally?). I thought I saw my cases, with what looked to be the book *The Swift Sword*, translated from the English, and the issue of our magazine on the Six-Day War, an issue we didn't even finish printing before our arrest. It was to be our last. And was that perhaps Leon Uris's *Exodus* in the suitcase Dov Sperling had buried near Riga in 1969? I wouldn't be surprised if they have also discovered the secret hiding place of Leningrad's Zionist committee.

In any case, investigators come and go. They come from as far as Siberia, some five thousand kilometers from Leningrad. The KGB's finest are enjoying themselves at our expense. If we had not plotted our operation, the KGB would have had to invent it, just to prove their usefulness and effectiveness. From generals to sergeants, they all seem to be enjoying this immensely.

To prevent the forming of attachments, guards are rotated every week. They are brought from Kiev, Kazan, or Yaroslavl. The Riga prison finally got its budget for renovations. The Leningrad prison received a significant outlay for the purchase of several hundred meters of red carpeting to allow guards to sneak up to cell doors undetected and overhear inmates' conversations.

When all goes smoothly, the guards like to have a little fun with inmates. On my first Sunday morning in prison, a guard ordered me to step out of the cell. My heart was seized with panic, which must have been apparent on my face, for the guard asked, "Why panic? You think we're going to torture you? You've read too much nonsense about prison life. No torture here." He took me to get my mug shot taken – frontal and in profile – and to take my prints, as though I were a common criminal.

Every night I dream of home, and every day I think about home. My nerves are rattled. I pace feverishly back and forth. Now a commotion in the hallway. They open my door.

"Wanna buy something?"

"I have almost no money," I say.

"Use what you've got."

I have a grand total of five rubles and sixty kopecks from the money Sylva loaned me. This is normally enough for a day; I have to stretch it out for a month, until my family is informed as to my whereabouts. I buy five hundred grams of bread, and one hundred grams of yellow cheese.

"Why so little?" the guard laughs.

I eat contentedly, imagining I am at home.

But the day has other surprises in store. The door opens again, and Major Kruglov strides in with his entourage, epaulets on his shoulders and a chest full of medals. The authorities have decided to pay a visit to my humble corner.

"Any questions?"

I will hear this routine phrase for many years to come, but this first time it catches me off guard. Why are the wardens here? Why are they asking me if I have any questions? Has something changed in my case? Have my colleagues remembered their brother Joseph and made attempts to free him? (I later learned that they did not yet know what was happening to me, and were spending their time debating whether to use open pressure or quiet diplomacy.)

"Yes. When can I take a shower?"

"In ten days."

"Can I write letters?"

"No."

"How will my family be informed?"

"They'll be informed."

"Can I get a newspaper?"

"If you behave yourself and testify, the interrogator may allow you one."

"I've got no money for the canteen. Can I work?"

"No."

"Can I get books?"

"Books are given out once every ten days. In general, your status here depends on your cooperation. If you talk, you'll get everything you need."

The entourage leaves, and I am left alone in the cell, my thoughts whirling. The visit must mean something. Out there, on the outside, something is happening. But what? Can I somehow find out from the interrogator? But then I'd have to talk with him.

As though my thoughts have been read, I'm taken out the next morning for interrogation, once more with Major Popov.

"In fact I don't need your testimony," he begins. "If you prefer not to talk about your little episode, let's just chat about something else. I get a salary, after all, and I have to work, and my work is investigating. But let's just talk about anything. They say you know Jewish history quite well. I recently read a book on the Jewish revolt against ancient Rome. Very interesting. Tell me, how did Rome conquer Judea?"

"Sure, I guess we can talk about that. You see, the Romans first came to adjudicate a dispute between two contenders for the kingship of Judea…"

It seems my interrogator knows something of Jewish affairs; perhaps he himself is half-Jewish, or is married to a Jewish woman. I chuckle aloud at his naïve attempts to make me feel comfortable. He laughs too, and changes the subject. He's no fool. Sometimes I can even sense hints of philosophical depth in him. Not for naught is he a "special investigator." And then:

"Where did you read that? Who gave you the book? Shpilberg?"

"I can't tell you."

"Fine, fine, let's continue."

When we finish, he types up a protocol: harmless, insignificant details culled from our conversation. In this way, he wants to habituate me to signing the protocol after our sessions. But suddenly my eyes fix on two lines he added, something about an underground Zionist organization where I studied Hebrew and Jewish history. I refuse to sign.

"But it's the truth. Why deny it?"

"You said it yourself: I'm to be executed in any event. So what more do you want from me?"

"You must understand my situation too. We've just spent several hours together. My superiors will want to know what we talked about."

"That's not my problem."

But actually this is a powerful tactic. The interrogator doesn't pound on the table or shout threats. It's just a conversation; no need to inform on anyone, only to consider the interrogator's situation: he's a Soviet clerk, just like you yourself may have been not long ago. And why deny the obvious? I just have to affirm what they already know, the testimonies given by my colleagues…and a drop of poison penetrates precisely here: all my friends have already talked.

· · · · ·

I am taken to a cell that reeks of tobacco, where I am greeted by a tall, well built, sturdy fellow, about sixty, with a wolf-like face. Gray hairs top his low forehead. Ivan Vasilevich Morozov.

It's hard not to admire the prison authorities for putting a young, God-fearing Jew in a cell with a former Nazi collaborator charged with murdering hundreds of Jews. His interrogation over, he is awaiting trial. All day, he whines: "Will they really execute me? Really?"

He has already heard of me. In the first days after his arrest, he shared a cell with Alexei Marchenko, who didn't bother hiding the reasons for his arrest from Morozov. Nor do I feel the need to conceal anything from him. We know theoretically that we have to be careful of cellmates, some of whom are informers. But Morozov? Would a Nazi criminal, whose guilt has already been established, cooperate with the KGB?

"You're an idiot, Yosef." That's what I would say today to my younger self. "Why wouldn't he? He's scared to death, and would seek to get a reduced sentence at any cost. And why would he hesitate to inform on a Jew?"

But Morozov proves uninterested in the circumstances of my arrest, sunk as he is in his own memories. He regards me mainly as a listener.

His father was a kulak, exiled with his small children to the far north in the 1930s. As the son of "an enemy of the state," Ivan grew up bearing the mark of Cain. When the war broke out, he was drafted. His unit was surrounded and captured by German forces. They went hungry. There were trees where they were being held, and Ivan tells me that all the leaves within human reach had disappeared. Then an offer from the Germans: a kilo of lard and two kilos of bread to anyone who volunteered for a special unit being assembled to catch thieves and looters. This was nothing less than an offer of life itself: food, clothing, a warm bed. The Red Army was in retreat, leaving captured soldiers behind and branding them "traitors to the motherland." It seemed clear that Hitler was here to stay, and if you wanted to live you had to deal with the new rulers.

Indeed, the war confronted men of weak character with terrible dilemmas. Having been stripped by his Soviet upbringing of any sense of civic responsibility, Ivan's only concern was to stay alive – at any cost. He lacked the strength to stand on principle. And so he switched sides, and joined a German unit that hunted down partisans, whom the Nazis called "bandits."

But there was another turn of the screw. Hitler's forces were weaker than expected, and they began to be pushed back by an advancing Red Army. With Soviet aircraft bombing the Germans, Ivan had to think once more about how to save his skin. The unit mutinied, killing its own officers, and joined the partisans. But this decision proved premature. The German counteroffensive intensified, and Ivan was captured again and sent to the Mauthausen concentration camp.

When the Americans liberated the camp at war's end, they gave Ivan a choice: East or West. He chose to go home, innocently believing that even if he were punished for serving the Germans, his Soviet comrades would understand he had no choice in the matter. The main thing was to get home.

Back in Russia, he was greeted by a trial and a twenty-five-year sentence in Siberia. There his military experience proved useful: he knew how to get along with the authorities, who assigned him to lead a group of inmates, and so he lived in relative comfort. When Stalin died, and a process of rehabilitation got underway, Ivan's sentence was shortened, and he was freed in 1958, apparently cleansed of his former sins. But it was not to be. Ten years later he was thrown into prison once more, "in light of new circumstances." Beginning in 1965, Soviet papers were filled with triumphal reports of the capture of fugitive former Nazis. These were mere parodies of real cases, like that of Eichmann, but the political purpose of such reports was clear: to besmirch the

West Germans, to serve as reminders of Nazi crimes, and to demand similar trials in West Germany, a country in which nearly every public figure, including those in the socialist camp, had been infected to one degree or another with the Nazi virus. It was an opportune time to remind the world of the Soviet role in the war, and thereby to deflect criticism of human rights abuses in the USSR.

"I worked in the postal service," Ivan tells me. "The managers were my friends, and they respected me. Had I reached retirement age, I would have earned a good pension. My wife worked in a shop, and at home we had everything we needed. When I got back from the gulag I decided to give everything to the kids, so that they wouldn't have to suffer in life. My eldest is a Party member, an engineer in Leningrad. My daughter is married to a major, and I recently bought a TV set for my wife. What a pity that everything came apart. Now who will help my wife at home? And what if they really execute me?"

Is there any logic, I wonder, to the fate that has brought Yosef – a descendent of Abraham, Isaac, and Jacob – into a cell not with the chief baker or royal butler but with a despicable murderer? He, too, dreams, but his dreams are so dark that our contemporary Yosef doesn't dare interpret them. Such dreams have Ivan bolting upright and screaming incoherently in his sleep: "Open the door! Now! You – take the ax, there, in the corner. Hit him in the head! Damn, so much blood! Drag him, drag him over here!" Is his conscience afflicting him? Is he the one we should judge, or should we rather reserve our condemnation for those in power and in high office who robbed their own people of spiritual values, mercilessly murdered their own people, and in the crisis of wartime abandoned them to their cruel fates? They're the ones who dragged Ivan through his miserable existence, who wiped out Kazakhs, Ukrainians, and Jews alike, who staged the 1953 "Doctor's Plot" blood libel before the curtain was brought down on Stalin's rule, and who planned to ship Jews off to Siberia. They are the ones who brought us – a Jew and an anti-Jew – to the same cell.

But that is our only point of contact. I regard him as a symbol of evil, whereas I believe that I and my actions – while still in need of purification – are favored by God. I pray in front of Ivan, as other Jews prayed in front of the barrel of his rifle as they kneeled on the edge of graves they dug themselves. (He swears to me that he did not take part in massacring Jews. The amazing thing is that in all my years in the gulag I meet many former Nazi guards, not a single one of whom admits to killing Jews. One wonders where all the murderers went.)

Morozov does not interfere with my prayers. He even reminds me if he thinks I've missed the appropriate prayer times. But in the matter of my trial he is insistent. "They'll execute all of you. The pilot, you, everyone." For good measure, he usually adds a dose of Israel-hatred. "The Arabs will slaughter all of you people." His views are given ample support from the Soviet press, which consistently depicts Israel as an aggressive foreign occupier and the Israeli soldier as a murderous fascist.

I return exhausted from the interrogation. Ivan looks up from his game of dominos. "What, they haven't executed you yet?"

"Not yet."

"They will, they will. All of you. They'll eliminate your Israel, too. The Yids don't know how to fight. Russian soldiers will come in, and that'll be the end of you."

He tries to pick a fight. I retreat to the wall. I don't want to come to blows, but I'm prepared to defend myself if necessary. "The Soviet Union won't beat Israel. If it were within its power, it would have wiped out Israel a long time ago. But it can't, and never will. You'll all fade into oblivion, but our nation will endure forever."

The next day I tell Popov that if that inciter isn't removed from my cell I will refuse even to show up for interrogations. When I return that evening, I have a new cellmate.

· · · · ·

Senya Barbakov was either a gypsy or a Jew; in any case he was a criminal: a corrupter of youth, a thief, a profiteer. I wondered how he ended up in a facility for political prisoners. Soviet law forbade holding "very dangerous political prisoners" (as I was classified) together with common criminals. Apparently he was suspected of transferring large sums of foreign currency from East Germany to the Soviet Union. I suspected him of being planted in my cell as an informer. Be that as it may, it was through him that I got my first acquaintance with the Soviet underworld.

Utterly exhausted by the daily battle of wills with my interrogator, I used to return to the cell to eat some steamed vegetables for dinner and play dominos with Senya. He shared with me stories from his gypsy childhood during the war, about riding horses, galloping wild and free through the plains. Above all, he liked to talk about women and drink, those eternally popular subjects, but I wouldn't allow it. He suffered from the limits I imposed on our conversations, but still treated me well. Once he even said, "Don't chat too much in the other cells; there could be informers around." He himself never aroused my suspicions by expressing any excessive interest.

Truth be told, my interrogator, too, was fond of talking about women. "Mendelevich," he once told me sorrowfully, "we've tried to track down your girlfriends but came up blank."

"You haven't searched diligently enough," I said.

"Give us their addresses. They may wish to testify on your behalf."

I burst out laughing. "I'm touched by your concern, but I must disappoint you. I didn't have the time to meet girls."

This was a common tactic they could exploit to masterful effect: blackmailing a prisoner with secrets from his personal life. Several of my colleagues would come to regret their indiscretions, and were reduced to shamefully begging their interrogators not to reveal them.

Meanwhile, larger problems disquieted me. Who had been arrested? Whom did the investigators know about? How were my colleagues faring? What would become of us? Even the newspapers did not answer my questions, as I was given access only to the official Soviet media – in which the level of detail to be published was strictly regulated.

On June 15, 1970, the Leningrad *Pravda* had published a short report on the arrest of a group of traitors that had attempted to hijack a plane at Smolny airport. The article caused great alarm among Jews in the West, many of whom assumed that it represented a KGB provocation that heralded a new wave of anti-Jewish persecution. Only a small minority, familiar with our appalling conditions in Russia, realized that such an attempt might actually have taken place.

After being questioned in Riga, my family was informed of my whereabouts. But not a word was said about my sister Meri. My father's second wife, Meri's mother, was too afraid to ask whether she had managed to escape. The letter detailing our plan and its participants, which I had left with Ezra Rusinek, was still hidden away. In addition to the packages she brought for me, my stepmother once brought a second package, addressed to Meri, to the Leningrad prison. The clerk checked his lists, and accepted the package. This was how my family knew that Meri was still alive, and was in fact being held not far from me.

The arrival of a package from home was an important event in prison life. By the time its contents reached me, they were often in disarray after being thoroughly searched, but even crumbled treats radiated the warmth of home. The packages never included anything *treif*; for this I was most grateful to my parents. I remembered the care with which my mother had prepared the packages for my father when he had been imprisoned in 1957. I wasn't allowed to receive any letters from home until the interrogation had concluded, but the packages nonetheless conveyed my family's love – and forgiveness.

· · · · ·

But I could not know then how much anxiety we were causing to so many on the outside. Asher Blank had desperately called each member of the Leningrad Zionist committee from Tel Aviv, but no one replied. It became clear that everyone had been arrested. Just when he was on the verge of despair, he got through to Viktor Boguslavsky, editor of *Ha-Iton*. Viktor began to list in alphabetical order the names of those who had been arrested: Dymshits, Fedorov, Kuznetsov, Marchenko. He forgot to mention my name, and when he got to the letter S the line was cut.

Investigations were meanwhile taking place in Leningrad, Moscow, Riga, and Kishinev. Misha Korn, for instance, spent entire days in interrogation rooms. Hillel Shur, a member of the Leningrad Zionist committee, not yet arrested himself, was waiting for Misha at the entrance to KGB headquarters the night of his release. "Misha, I'm coming to you on behalf of the committee to say that despite your desperate straits, informing on others won't save you. Believe me, only silence can bring salvation. Take my hand; let's shake on it."

Without saying a word, Korn got into a taxi and sped away.

The next day, Shur himself was called into the KGB offices. "Citizen Shur. If you do not stop intimidating witnesses, we will haul you in." But Hillel did not lack for courage, and instead of laying low he arranged a meeting between a group of students who had studied Hebrew and individuals who had been taken in for questioning, so that those who had already been interrogated could guide those who already knew to expect their own arrests. Several days later, both he and Viktor Boguslavsky were detained. These men could have easily remained silent and escaped attention, but their sense of loyalty had dictated another path: they had chosen to share our fate.

In Riga, a certain calm set in after the first wave of arrests subsided. A full description of what had happened reached the West, thus assuring that the KGB could not condemn us to permanent oblivion.

Meanwhile, some could not withstand even the first test. First among these was Feibush, a biologist from Riga who had expressed keen interest in matters Jewish and maintained contacts with Zionist circles. Even as we included him in the production of *Ha-Iton*, we had the impression that he was too frail and unstable for underground activism. But after the wave of arrests we simply needed men, and we tasked him with smuggling out of the city a suitcase filled with illegal literature. This was done without a hitch, but several days later Feibush was summoned for a routine questioning by the KGB. It was clear they had no knowledge of the suitcase, but they nonetheless attempted to threaten him in the hopes that in his panic he would reveal something useful. The usual formula – "we know everything about you, we have been following you for some time" – had the intended effect, and Feibush spilled everything he knew: who organized the Rumbuli memorials, who participated in celebrations at the synagogue, and of course everything about that accursed suitcase.

"Who instructed you to move the suitcase?"

"Maftser."

"To whom did you deliver it?"

"I don't know the man, though I remember him well: tall, light-haired."

"What was in the case?"

"I don't know; I didn't open it."

"We know that you're concealing significant details. For your own good, you'd better tell us the truth."

It was clear that the interrogators were bluffing, but fear did its dastardly work, and the next day Feibush confessed to handing the suitcase to Alexander Druk (who was neither tall nor fair-haired). Feibush announced that his wife had asked him "to tell the truth to the authorities, and to renounce his intention to emigrate to Israel." Thus was he saved from arrest, and he made it to Israel a year and a half later.

Druk adamantly refused to testify. He was held by the KGB for a day, and released. Courage turned out to be the best shield. The investigators, having lost the trail, conducted searches at the homes of Maftser, Shpilberg, and Ruth Alexanderovich. They found a mimeograph and illegal literature. All three were taken into custody. The KGB was especially happy to have apprehended Ruth, who had caused them considerable trouble. She had taken part in all the meetings and holidays, smuggled information out of the country, and supplied half of Riga's Jews with Hebrew textbooks.

• • • • •

Of course I knew nothing of all this. At the time, I was still playing "cat and mouse" with my interrogator, trying my best both to remember what had been said yesterday and the day before that, and to deduce from his questions what he had gleaned from my colleagues. In this way, some weeks passed.

"We know that you passed a letter through Sylva to Leningrad. What were its contents?"

Not knowing the source of this information, or what other details about the letter the source might have divulged, I replied: "The letter was intended to inquire about the possibility of getting Hebrew textbooks from Leningrad."

Several days later: "You have not told us the truth. In the letter you asked the Leningrad committee to clarify their opinion of the planned operation."

Now I realized that investigators knew of the letter from someone familiar with its contents – someone in a position to have read it. It was crucial that they not get onto the trail of Boris Maftser, whom I had asked to write the letter. Boris knew a great deal – in fact he was the only one besides me who knew the names of all the movement leaders in Riga. To increase the pressure on him, they could charge him with aiding and abetting our attempted escape. Evidently, they already knew many details concerning our operation, but I hoped it was still possible to conceal some facts and names.

"Your source is mistaken. I did not send a letter regarding an escape plan."

The interrogator was perplexed. "Well, then we'll have to continue to search. Perhaps you'll remember who wrote the letter."

A month later, both the writer of the letter and its addressee had spilled the beans. When I next saw him, Popov boiled with rage. "I'll sew your lies into an overcoat that will suit you well during your long years in Siberia. Our investigation will reveal everything, except perhaps for some insignificant details. For your own good you'd better give us the truth, assuming, of course, you care for your family. I spoke with your father a few days ago. His health is failing. If you behave well, you might even see him."

That Sunday, a guard barked at me through the slot: "Out! With your belongings!"

Senya and I wondered aloud where – and why – I was being transferred. They were banging on cell doors all down the hallway; I wasn't alone. They conducted a body search in an empty cell, and delivered my lunch. I had to throw it away: the soup gave off the aroma of pork lard. I paced back and forth, painting rosy scenarios in my mind: a plane to Vienna, and from thence to Israel! (Ten years later, when I knew with certainty that my release was only hours away, I could not summon even a tenth of the joyful expectancy I felt that day, so depleted was I by long imprisonment.)

My bold hopes grew even stronger when I was taken to the prison's intake room, packed with confiscated belongings. Two men in civilian dress approached. "We are taking you to the airport. Any unusual movement on your part will be interpreted as an attempt to escape and you will be shot on the spot. We suggest you not try any nonsense. On the plane, you will not speak to anyone, shout, or make any hand signals."

This was how I imagined it: we get on the plane, the investigators having been persuaded that no serious crime was committed. No reason even to put them on trial. Maybe they are about to swap us for captured Soviet spies.

Weakened by prison, and by the emotional toll it had already taken on me, I was overcome by nausea, and could not stop vomiting all the way to the airport. When we arrived, the plane was still empty. The security agents allowed a frightened stewardess to bring me water. I was also offered a newspaper, which I snatched up eagerly – and in vain, as it turns out. Not by chance had they given me this particular paper; not a word in it on the Middle East. Gradually, the plane filled. The flight was short, and it soon became apparent that I would not be released. After all the other passengers had disembarked, I was taken from the plane's ramp to a prison van, and I knew I was in Riga, which I had left twenty-three days before.

That is how I got the chance to acquaint myself with the Riga prison, concealed behind the façade of the former Metropol hotel. The inner workings of its bowels resembled those of the Leningrad prison, but not entirely. Here I encountered a chamber pot – a ten-liter bucket that I had to haul to the bathroom, under guard, to empty every morning. During the day, it reeked to high heaven. Even after it got its daily chlorine rinse, it was impossible to breathe in the cell. Sometimes, a female guard supervised our morning visits to the bathroom, where the door had to be left ajar. In the beginning I found this invasion of privacy unbearable; in time, I got used to it, and to the fact that in jail prisoners were regarded as asexual beings. The main staple of our diet, meanwhile, was fish-bone soup, as it was across the Soviet prison system.

For a long time I was spared interrogations. My cellmate, Andreas, was a young Latvian nationalist. He had worked for foreign espionage services and had acquired from his brother maps of a nuclear submarine base in the north. His uncle, who had arrived as a tourist from Sweden, had persuaded him without too much difficulty to cooperate. In Andreas' view, the Russians were contemptible occupiers. On that point, I agreed. We spoke in Latvian, and our relationship was amiable. He had left a wife and child at home, and before his arrest he had been about to begin theological studies. We spoke often of the relation between man and God. In compelling me to draw distinctions between his Christian views and my Jewish ones, he helped me to understand myself. We talked and played chess and the time passed quickly.

Andreas stood watch for me when I prayed. A ruddy guard had once seen me in prayer and threatened that the next time he caught me praying I would be gravely punished.

That guard had been young, and young guards tended to suffer from feelings of inferiority, from a sense that inmates were mocking them. They could easily become angry and embittered as a result. This indeed was one of the axioms of prison life: the younger the guard, the greater the tendency for a certain kind of brutality. It was easier to understand them as belonging to a certain category of person rather than as people consciously serving the Soviet regime. Andreas told me of a case that illustrated the point. His father had served as a young man in the Second World War with the Nazi police hunting partisans. An older officer, noticing the young man's enthusiasm, explained how he should act. "My son, only shoot a partisan when he is about to shoot you, and it's either him or you. If you see him fleeing, don't shoot. Why provoke him? He'll only be frightened, and in his panic will kill you."

I gave Andreas any food I couldn't eat, anything *treif*, and in return he gave me salted fish and bread. He also taught me the invaluable prison skill of talking through the wall by means of pressing an overturned cup against it. I was lucky. The first time I tried, I said, "This is Yosef. Who are you?"

"Tolya here. What's up?" Tolya Altman! In the next cell!

"They asked whether I know Ruth Alexanderovich, and I refused to admit anything. And you?"

"They found evidence that we copied illegal material together," he said.

"Did our families receive the letters we left for them?"

Then a bark from the hallway: "Mendelevich! No talking! You'll be punished!"

But Andreas generally hid me well, and the guards seldom guessed what I was up to. Anyway, during the interrogation period the wardens weren't too keen on keeping a prisoner in solitary confinement. There would be time enough for that after the trial.

Needless to say, I still wasn't allowed to see my father. When interrogations resumed, the investigators were most interested in Riga's Zionist movement: its leadership, its funding, its hierarchy. On the one hand, the movement hadn't been a secret conspiracy, and this amorphousness worked to our advantage. On the other hand, since we had been so open and accessible, the KGB had had little difficulty in planting informers among our ranks.

I shuttled between three interrogators. When my evasions got on the nerves of Major Zaslavski, he began to scream. "Mark the names of the leaders of the organization!"

"There is no organization."

"Your answer makes clear that you have no remorse for your crimes. You and your Aryeh Khnokh, you're fanatics!"

This was the first time – but far from the last – I heard the words "fanatic" or "zealot" spat at me as an accusation. At my trial, the prosecutor Soloviev would characterize me as a "religious zealot." I would hear the same charge incessantly repeated in labor camp. Apparently the formulaic phrase was listed on some official form. Well, if it's a zealot they wanted, a zealot they would get. A fanatic, a zealot, is someone unaware of his impulses and unable to temper his actions to suit the circumstances. Sometimes this works to his advantage. If my faith were true and deeply rooted, there would be no point in revisiting the fundamental questions: Does God exist? Is my faith in Him real? It isn't always easy to realize one's faith, but that is another matter. It's one thing to meditate on your faith in the Creator of heaven and earth and simply leave it at that. It's quite another to decide that your faith commits you to certain actions. For Jews, passive reflection is not enough; deeds – fulfilling the commandments – are essential. No one had taught me this; I had to learn it myself, through great effort.

It was with similar effort that I steadied myself for interrogations: "Remember, you're about to meet the interrogator. He is your adversary. You must despise him and oppose his every move. This is nothing less than a commandment, your duty to God."

On the way to interrogations, I used to pause for a moment in front of a mirror in the hallway. I saw the reflection of a young bearded man, his face yellowed by prison, but his eyes still alight with faith – an innocent tent-dweller who had found himself thrown into a lion's den.

• • • • •

"Mendelevich, we have learned from the other detainees that Ezra Rusinek was in the possession of a large quantity of typewriters, and that he had organized the printing of all illegal material."

My heart clenches. After all his years in Siberia, this is the last thing that Ezra needs. "I've never met Rusinek," I lie, "and do not know him."

"We have evidence that in March 1970 you gave him the second issue of *Ha-Iton* to print, and that you received from him a copy of the book *The Swift*

Sword by Brigadier General S. L. A. Marshall. We will now present you with ten photos. You will identify the one of Rusinek."

As stipulated by law, two "men off the street" (but then what would they be doing in KGB offices?) materialize to witness the identification, along with two interrogators. An official form, complete with signatures and seals, is put before me, and then the ten photos. Ezra gazes out at me from one of them. The other faces don't appear Jewish.

"This identification is not legal," I tell one of the interrogators. "There is only one photo of a Jew here. Since you asked me about a Jew, it would be logical to assume this is the man you want me to finger. In any case, you're attempting to get me to pick out someone I don't know." The identification charade has failed.

The interrogator, desperate to find some angle to get to me, goes so far as to read Dostoyevsky. When he tells me he has started to read *Crime and Punishment*, I cannot help but laugh. What good will the masterpiece about the Russian soul do him in his match against a Jewish soul?

When Popov realizes his threats and pressure-tactics are making no headway, he changes tactics and adopts an excessively friendly manner. "It's difficult to understand you. You say you're a committed Jew. But where did you get that from? You were educated as a Russian, in Russian schools. You know more than I do of Russian culture, of Pushkin, Lermontov, Dostoyevsky. You are, in fact, a Russian. Even your face isn't really a Jewish one. Drop your obstinacy, admit that someone confused your mind with Zionist notions which you now realize are mistaken. Your present course is a march toward the death penalty. Confess that you were mistaken, and you'll live; you'll serve a six- or seven-year sentence and be released while still young. You mustn't always stand on principle. Think about your life."

When they take me back to the cell, I am in the grip of a pall of gloom. At last, someone who is merciful. Yes, it is a trick. But it is pleasant to sink into illusion once in a while…to save my life…

And then, just as quickly, I become enraged. What does he want, to turn me once again into a vulgar Soviet student, a man without identity? I remember with what joy I found myself, discovered my people, and realized that I am not alone but belong to an ancient and unique people. In this I have found meaning. And now they want to strip that away from me too? Yes, I tell myself; Yosef Mendelevich can remain alive, but only at the cost of killing – with his own hands – his own life's purpose. What kind of life would that be? No, no. I will remain a Jew to the end.

Then the first voice returns. Maybe Popov is right after all. Of what does my Jewishness consist? When I lived among my friends, I felt myself in a special environment that connected me to my people. But now, alone in prison, I have become a prisoner like any other.

On the other hand, I must fight to remain Jewish, to ward off Popov's temptations. More to the point, I must fight my own inner weakness, and save me from myself. I sorely regret now the delay in keeping my vow when I was saved from the Red Army's draft – the pledge to live a religious life. I have wasted an entire year. Had I continued to learn with the underground mohel Mordechai Dinur, I would have acquired a body of Jewish knowledge and known how to behave like a real Jew, and then my Jewish identity would have been impregnable to Popov's attempts to assail it.

To be a Jew!

This is the salvation from my weaknesses. To act in such a way that everyone will be made to understand that. Then they won't stand a chance of breaking me. How does one act like a Jew? By keeping the commandments. But I know almost nothing of them.

I do know, however, of the custom of covering one's head. I had a beret at the airport, but it has been long since confiscated. I take a handkerchief from my pocket and tie its corners together.

Just then, I am called into interrogation. I walk in with the handkerchief on my head. Popov raises his eyebrows. "What have you put on your head? What is this rag? Have you gone nuts? Take it off at once. You're a civilized man."

I have anticipated just this reaction. "Among you, it is considered civilized to take off one's hat upon entering, but among us, among Jews, the tradition is different. We cover our heads. And anyway, you yourself said that I'm a man of Jewish culture." I proceed to deliver an entire lecture on everything I know of Jewish history. He faithfully transcribes my words, but I can see he is steaming.

"Sign the protocol!"

For the first time, I gladly affix my signature to what amounts to a summary of an introductory class in Judaism.

"I see you're pleased with your own cleverness," Popov says. "But you're being a fool. You're simply digging your own grave. You'd better think again about your behavior." At this, he rings the bell, and orders that I be taken down to the basement.

His anger, however, only goads me to consider other ways I might outwardly express my Jewishness. What more can I do? Yes, I'll start praying. I remember my first prayer, the pure plea of a Jewish boy before the court that stood in judgment of his father. Then, my prayer had seemed to work. My father had been released within the year. So why shouldn't I pray now? I begin to recall what Mordechai Dinur taught me in the Riga synagogue about the Amidah, the central prayer of the Jewish liturgy. I could try, with my vocabulary of five hundred Hebrew words, to reconstruct it. I know that it began with praise of God: "The great, mighty and revered Lord, the Most High…"

To conclude my improvised prayer, I say: "Master of the universe, save the people Israel from its Russian exile, show mercy to my father and sister, and release me from my difficult imprisonment." Fortunately, in this prison I am permitted paper and pencil. I wrote down my prayer, and kept it in my pocket.

One more obstacle: how could I face Jerusalem in prayer without knowing its direction? I remembered a description in the book of Daniel of the prophet in Babylonian captivity going to an upstairs room where the windows opened toward Jerusalem to pray three times a day. It gladdened me to remember this beautiful and inspiring description. I stood beneath my cell's barred window, lifting my eyes heavenward in a gesture, as the psalmist put it, of "Out of the depths I cry to you, Lord" (130:1). I directed my heart toward Jerusalem, to the Temple Mount, to the Holy of Holies. Each time I returned from an interrogation, I would stand beneath that window and call out, "Please God, deliver me."

After a few days of this, guards burst in. "We've been watching you. What are you always doing under the window, leaning on the wall? Plotting an escape?" They checked to make sure I hadn't been sawing through the bars like some Count of Monte Cristo. Finding nothing, they conducted a body search, and found the paper in my pocket. "What is this? Are you trying to pass a note in a foreign language to your colleagues?"

In a sense, they were right. They had indeed found a letter – to the Holy One. But I wouldn't tell them what it was. "Fine, we have excellent translators. Soon enough we'll discover the secret."

Several days later, I saw my "letter" on Major Popov's desk. He was evidently enraged. "Yosef, what is happening to you? You're becoming religious? Who has been influencing you?"

What could I possibly tell this atheist? That God had been influencing me? "Yes," I replied, "I am a religious man, as I've been trying to tell you!"

He ordered me back to the basement to think things over. Back in the cell, I felt elated, as though my first religious steps were protecting me from the attempts to break my spirit. And then, another epiphany: Shabbat. I'd keep the Sabbath. What could be a more Jewish expression? If I couldn't exactly observe the Shabbat, at least I could prepare for her arrival. I asked the guards for a rag and bucket so that I could clean the cell. They were only too happy to comply, since the cell seemed to have accumulated filth since the days when the building had been occupied by the Gestapo.

As I washed down the walls, I felt something sharp. I discovered a nail that a previous inmate had jammed into the wall. I resolved to use it to scratch out the outlines of two Shabbat candles. The truth was that my mother had not lit Shabbat candles, but I remembered seeing a postcard from Israel that depicted a woman lighting, covering her eyes as she blessed them. At the bottom of the postcard was printed: "Blessed are you, Lord, our God, Sovereign of the universe, Who has sanctified us with His commandments and commanded us to light the candles of Shabbat."

By this time I had already started to save a bit of my daily bread ration for Shabbat. I couldn't tell when the sun set on Friday, but I could hear the changing of the guard at 5:00 p.m., and shortly thereafter I began Kabbalat Shabbat. Facing the candles I had scratched into the wall, I closed my eyes. When I opened them, I saw two flames, and my heart leaped in otherworldly joy. I began to whirl in dance and song: "David the King of Israel lives and endures!" "The people of Israel lives!" It seemed almost as though Abraham, Isaac, and Jacob themselves were visiting me, accompanying me in my cell.

"Enough with the noise in there!" A guard interrupted my reveries.

"It's the Sabbath," I said, "a Jewish holiday."

"Yeah, sure. But no more noise."

I imagined KGB experts watching me in puzzlement: how could this Jew facing a harsh sentence manage to find such joy? Indeed, for a few moments I had detached myself from prison reality – and from all its attendant anxiety.

Needless to say, reality would soon intrude once more.

· · · · ·

As I reviewed the events of the last several months in my mind, I suffered above all from the fear that the entire Zionist movement in Riga had been wiped out in the wake of our arrests. That worry noticeably weakened my resolve. If I had only known how despite the arrests and searches, their activities – and support from the West – were just growing stronger! One way or another, I had to summon the will to plan my line of action. The main weapon in the interrogators' arsenal was the constant reminders of my colleagues' confessions, the implicit suggestion that while I stubbornly refused to cooperate, they already knew everything. "You have faithfully protected your colleagues, but they have not returned the favor." I cannot say this tactic had no effect. I sometimes had a hard time believing that some of the details the interrogators mentioned had not been given by someone close to me. At other times, I would be confronted with confessions in familiar handwriting. So I had to devise a way to shield myself from such tactics. I made a resolution: from this day forward, no matter how persuasive the evidence to the contrary, I simply would not believe – even for a moment – that one of my friends had incriminated me or denounced me.

Strangely enough, it was good to be in solitary confinement. I would pace, sunk in thought, without the need to make conversation. Andreas had left a pack of cigarettes behind, and it occurred to me that here I was, a twenty-three-year-old political prisoner, and I had never smoked. The cigarettes – the strong Russian Belomorkanal brand – and matches were within easy reach, and I lit up, feeling manly. But my smoking career did not last long. After several days, I began to feel ill, and I developed a revulsion to smoking. In any case, it was idiotic to smoke in a cell without ventilation, where bread would grow a greenish film of mold within two days.

I once complained to my interrogator about the conditions. "Not our fault," he said. "During the war this place was given over to the Gestapo, and was nicknamed the Green Monster. Everyone knows how cruelly the Germans treated their prisoners."

The explanation seemed reasonable, and left open only one question: why did the Russians choose to so faithfully carry on the German tradition?

• • • • •

In memorizing the Hebrew calendar prior to my arrest, I had made sure to know the date of 9 Av, the fast day commemorating the destruction of the Temples in Jerusalem. When the day came, I fasted and refused to take part in the scheduled shower. The guards mocked me. "Don't want to wash? Then we'll force you. We'll teach you to be civilized." They locked me and another inmate into the shower room. I stood naked while my partner washed himself. But Heaven looked kindly on me, and at least I wasn't called to interrogation that day.

Soon after, however, interrogations moved into high gear. Every day, including Sunday, I was interrogated for twelve consecutive hours. Moscow must have ordered that the investigation be brought to a close. "Your behavior isn't normal," the interrogators would tell me. "You are not testifying truthfully. We may have to refer you to psychiatric evaluation."

On Sunday, September 5, 1970, lead interrogator Colonel Nyeizvstni informed me that my father had submitted a request for the release of my sister Meri due to her pregnancy. They would do so if I gave them the names of the Zionist organization's leadership in Riga. I desperately wished to avoid another stay in a mental hospital, and I was concerned for my sister and mother.

"There is no such organization," I said.

The colonel pressed the buzzer. "Take the prisoner away."

I was sent for evaluation to the Serebski psychiatric ward in Moscow, a truly awful place run by a Jew named Daniel Romnovich Luntz. He was known to commit perfectly sane political prisoners to rot in various psychiatric institutions, where they really would lose their minds. Serebski was housed in a decrepit old building in the middle of a park adjacent to Moscow. Intake, paperwork, disinfection. I was shoved into a filthy scum-lined bathtub, where a female attendant wielding rusty scissors sheared the hair from all parts of my body. Couldn't this have been done by a man? "An ashamed lunatic!" she exclaimed delightedly. I am given pajamas and taken to the wing for political prisoners, where one more search was conducted. The head nurse, an elderly, full-bodied Polish woman, scrutinized me with a magnifying glass, checking for pubic lice. She took her time, as though she derived pleasure from the exercise.

The cell consisted of three patient rooms guarded by a KGB man wearing a white smock over his uniform. Additional security was supplied by an elderly nursemaid sitting in the corner in her headscarf and slippers, appearing alternately to be knitting or napping. She watched our every move and reported to the administration. To me, she resembled the wicked witch of children's stories; her image mingled in my mind with the ghosts of the princes expelled by the Bolsheviks, lending the whole scene a nightmarish quality. It seemed to be the kind of place in which you expected to hear the creak of a door in an abandoned room, or the hoots of an owl at midnight. There were no owls here, but there was also no shortage of screams.

In my room I found Valid, a partially illiterate Crimean Tatar who had worked in a Soviet-Iranian construction project in Turkmenistan. He had been charged – the very idea was laughable – with spying for the United States.

He spoke Russian only with difficulty, and I couldn't imagine what threat he could possibly pose to the Soviet regime. Over a glass of beer one night, he had mentioned to a friend that on account of the Soviet expulsion of Tatars from the Crimea, he didn't want to live in Russia. This friend denounced him to the authorities, and a high-ranking officer swooped in to arrest poor Valid.

Another interesting character in the ward was a professor from Moscow University who, having come under the influence of Trotsky's ideas, left the academy, and decided to live among common villagers. As a result, the pitiable fellow was declared insane.

My first evaluation took place in a room with six doctors, most of whom had typical Jewish faces. At the head of the table sat Daniel Romnovich Luntz himself, a short grey-haired man who struck me as a kind of Soviet Dr. Mengele. He was sitting on an antique armchair as though it were a royal throne.

"So, young man, you wished to flee to Israel."

"I wanted to leave together with my family, but this was not permitted to us."

"Did you consider becoming the president of Israel?"

I was holding up my buttonless pajama bottoms in an attempt to save them from dropping off, and keenly felt the absurdity of the situation. Luntz sounded as though he himself were interested in the post and saw me as a rival.

"Actually, I just wanted to study."

"And what do you know of Israel?"

"That it is a country where Jews live."

"What have you read about Zionism? Have you read the writings of Herzl? Pinsker? Borochov?"

● ● ● ● ●

My psychiatrist, Margarita Abramova, would summon me from time to time. She would be holding the protocols of my interrogations with Popov. As it turned out, my conversations with her would not differ too much from my discussions with him. She wanted to know about certain episodes about which my interrogators had been unable to obtain precise information. My unwillingness to talk about such things troubled her. "Why do you avoid speaking about your past? Do you experience night terrors? Did you suffer traumas as a child?"

Silence would result in "coercive therapy." Although I steadfastly refused to testify, I tried in other respects to act like a normal Soviet citizen. I was deferential and well behaved, both in my room and in meetings with the doctors. For instance, if a patient napped for more than half an hour in the afternoon, they would mark in his file: "depressed." I swore to myself that I wouldn't fall into that trap. Once, as I nodded off, I heard a thundering voice: "Yosef, awake, your hour has arrived." Startled, I jumped up and looked around, wondering if I had finally gone mad. To this day, I can't explain that voice. My greatest fear was that in this awful ward that dark force that lurks in every man's soul would rear its head and consume me. Among my fellow patients, meanwhile, I could not easily tell who was sane and who was not.

Dr. Ivan Stepanovich Suk seemed more normal than the rest. This young biologist from Donetsk had a hobby: in his free time he would research the October Revolution, using documents that had come to light in the first years after that uprising. In those days, the Soviets had not yet felt ashamed of their viciousness; in our day, they attempted to cleanse the past and paint it in glorious colors. As befitted a serious researcher, Suk shared his findings with his colleagues, several of whom were members of the Ukrainian Central Communist Committee, but in the end it was his wife who had informed on him. She had envied his mistress. Under the pressures of fearful intimidation, his distinguished colleagues affirmed that he had distributed anti-Soviet literature. Now he could expect three years of labor camp or a course of "coercive therapy." He was extremely tense. Once, during a chess match, he threw the board at me. Still, he retained a Soviet worldview. He was one of those frightened intellectuals who made easy prey for criminals in the gulag. Even in our ward, he was the object of mockery. "Look at this intellectual running to the bathroom again. He must have a woman's problem. Hey, you: are you a man or a woman?"

The mocker, in this case, was Kolya Ivanov, a rude, loud-mouthed taxi driver who had been arrested for distributing anti-Soviet pamphlets. (His father, interestingly enough, had been a prison warden under Stalin.) He liked to compose awful anti-Soviet ditties:

> *Communism, my friend,*
>
> *Is coming to an end,*
>
> *Its force spent,*
>
> *Nothing to lament.*

Kolya was hauled into the ward screaming melodramatically. He demanded to be put into another cell on the grounds that here his life would be endangered. He even declared a hunger strike.

"Kolya," the nurses would say, "won't you eat a little?"

His strike lasted a mere four hours before he called over an attendant and asked her what was for lunch.

"Porridge," she said.

"Fine, bring some." And he proceeded to wolf down a double portion.

Here, normal people were considered insane, while the actually insane often lacked treatment and were punished as though they were compos mentis. In the closed ward, a patient named Grinya Sobol would shriek like an animal as though that were the only way he knew of affirming his own existence. Yet he of all people was slated to be released. He had been imprisoned for nine years. A colleague who wanted his post in a government ministry had informed on him. The injustice had driven him up the wall. He began to have delusions that Khrushchev, with whom he had once worked, was personally persecuting him. The KGB, not knowing what to do with him, sent him to a special psychiatric hospital in Kazan, which ultimately stripped him of any last vestiges of sanity. He received so many forcible injections of drugs that his legs became paralyzed. He would lie in bed all day composing primitive poems full of disturbing lines. Having spent hours on his "literary" creation, he would recite it to the attending nurses, who would only nod their heads. "Grinya, you were talented enough to have become a minister, and now you occupy yourself with this drivel?" At which, gravely insulted, he would snatch a towel and try to choke himself. As the nurses gave him another injection, he would let loose maniacal laughter and roll his reddened eyes. His latest work was occasioned by the visit of his daughter, who had begged him to cast aside his paranoid delusions. The poem called her dirty names, accused her of serving the KGB, expressed doubt as to whether she was actually his daughter at all, and cast aspersions on her femininity in the most vulgar terms imaginable.

He once invited me for a "Jew-to-Jew" talk. His mentality proved to be Soviet to a tee. The only evidence of anti-Semitism he acknowledged was the fact that he was prevented from being appointed a minister. I excused myself and turned away from his incoherent ravings as soon as I could. Even the nurses understood that nine years ago this had been a normal man. Now that his millionaire uncle abroad was agitating for his release, the authorities were prepared to release Grinya. But he didn't want to go free.

"Sobol, take a look at the newspaper. Here's an obituary for Khrushchev. There's no one to persecute you anymore."

"You don't know Nikita Khrushchev," Sobol said. "You can't believe a single word of his. I demand an appearance with him before the international court in The Hague. There we'll determine who's right."

· · · · ·

My evaluation included an exam in a spacious neurology laboratory equipped with a French-made machine spitting forth a ribbon of graphs. Two white-coated doctors, undoubtedly Jewish, were debating some scientific point. I was placed in something resembling a dentist's chair as electrodes were placed on my head, hands, and feet. The younger of the doctors interrupted his conversation and said, "Images will appear briefly on the wall. You will report what you see in the images, and we'll determine the maximal speed your brain can process them."

I was left alone, in darkness and in utter silence. I wondered whether it was to my advantage to show rapid or slow reactions. Images began to flicker on the wall, sometimes flashing so quickly that it was impossible to register them at all. This took place that day and the next, for a quarter of an hour each session. I became so tense that I started to tremble, and when I tried to conceal it, the strain only made the trembling worse. Meanwhile, the young Jewish doctor was chatting up some young female technicians. Could he not understand the suffering he was causing to one of his brethren?

As the images continued to flicker, I gnashed my teeth and imagined I was seeing the headlights of cars in the streets of Jerusalem. I think that helped, but by the end I decided that undermining my sanity through these tests was as bad as committing me to a mental institution, and I refused to go on.

A fellow inmate, Yermak Sergeyevich, once asked me whether I'd prefer to undergo "coercive therapy" but be spared a trial, or to be sentenced to labor camp but be spared psychiatric treatment.

"To go to labor camp," I answered, "no matter how many years the sentence."

"Right choice. You have no idea how terribly the psychiatric ward distorts a man." Sergeyevich had spent two years in Kazan, where he underwent "coercive therapy," and had now been brought to Moscow for final evaluation. In 1941, when as a colonel he had served in the Red Army during battles near the Don River, he deserted and crossed into Nazi occupied territory. After the war, he moved to Belgium, worked in a mine, joined the Socialist party, and became a member of the Soviet-Belgian Friendship League. But he still had family in the USSR. In 1968, Sergeyevich came to the USSR as a tourist to visit his family, but was caught and taken away. Neither his family in Belgium nor his Russian family knew his whereabouts. Facing the death penalty for treason, he pretended insanity – with remarkable success. But sometimes it seemed that the pretense went too far, and that he edged into real insanity. He would sometimes scream in his sleep: "Don't torture me! Yes, I know, you have a drug that goes straight to the brain. But I'm an honest man. I've told you everything. No! Oh no!"

I talked with him about Belgian Jews, and their relationship to Israel. He would tell me about daily life in the West. "Every government office displays the Declaration of the Rights of Man. If a staffer gets out of line, you can show him that he violated this or that clause. In Russia, no one even knows there are such things as human rights." Then he realized that the old witch-nurse was listening, and quickly revised himself. "But here, workers enjoy many more rights; and, of course, everyone here is equal."

Here Kolya Ivanov interrupted. "Shut your damn mouth! Some political prisoners! One a Communist sermonizer, the second has caught some woman's disease, the third stole a suitcase of gold and tried to flee to Israel. Russia is collapsing, and you're playing chess!"

The eve of Rosh Hashanah found me in an entirely unfestive mood. Then they announced the death of Egyptian President Gamal Abdel Nasser. The news signaled that significant changes were afoot in the Middle East, and I took it as a signal to me, too, hinting that embers of hope still glowed even amidst the darkness in which I was imprisoned. To make matters even better, a nurse brought in plums that had been left over from her jam-making. A real feast.

Several days into the new year of the Jewish calendar, the doctors held a kind of summary meeting on my case. Hours earlier, I had learned that my former cellmate, Ivan Morozov, had been sentenced to death. The news troubled my spirit. The doctors based their evaluations on their conversations with me. One asked me with great interest to elaborate on life in Israel: prices, groceries, the real estate market, etc. Though I was well acquainted with this tactic from my interrogation sessions with Popov, I was glad to speak openly about these things.

Then I was to meet Lunz himself. Ordinarily, he would talk to inmates one-on-one, but this time, to avoid any suspicion that he favored me, he talked to me in the presence of Margarita Abramova.

"Why do you refuse to testify?"

"I am not refusing to testify. I simply know very little."

"Why did you want to live in Israel?"

"I was brought up that way."

"What would you prefer: therapy or trial?"

"Whichever would be better for me."

"Would you like to ask me for anything? Perhaps I could help you." His voice betrayed a hint of warmth. For the first time, it seemed, he was meeting a young Zionist. I knew, of course, of his cruel reputation. Some inmates had nicknamed him the Executioner.

"I ask of you only one thing," I said calmly. "Don't harm me."

He looked perplexed. "I wish you success, young man. And don't worry."

• • • • •

The next day I am transferred to cell number 37 in the infamous Lefortovo prison for political prisoners in Moscow. The cold stone walls have been painted in black and red. Each new cell takes some getting used to. Who knows how long I'll be held in this one? As was the case in the previous prisons, until you've managed to make contact with those in adjacent cells, you have the feeling that you're utterly alone in the world. At the same time, I feel an unusual presence beside me, guiding me. I don't know whether others have the same sense: a feeling of serenity borne of faith in God.

Lights out. Bedtime. Outside the window, it is a dark, chilly night. What will happen to me? Will they coerce me into psychiatric treatment, and thereby make me insane, or will they imprison me for long years? A night of silent crisis. The only illumination is the occasional sweep of a searchlight, which sometimes coats the cell with a gloomy radiance. I pray silently all night.

In the morning, a shout: "Quick! With your belongings!" A KGB captain reads out to me a warrant for further interrogation. I have been saved from the world of madness, but I feel neither joy nor hope.

The eve of Yom Kippur. I am brought to a train station, and put on an ordinary passenger train, where I am surrounded by guards with concealed weapons. The captain of the police escort team offers me an apple and a book about Flavius Josephus. Coincidence? I immerse myself in the story of the Jewish rebellion of 68 CE, and ponder the rise and fall of Josephus, also known as Yosef ben Mattityahu. There are lessons here: about being wise and decisive, about leading men, about the courage required to die with equanimity, with the knowledge that death itself comes from the Creator, about the courage needed to sit in a cave with neither water nor bread and to endure, not for the sake of glory, but because one cannot do otherwise – and because it is clear to you that you are not just Yosef, but a leader of a people, and that you must never surrender.

We arrive in Leningrad an hour before Yom Kippur is to begin. By the time I am given dinner, the fast has started. I don't have a prayer book, and I don't know the prayers, but I feel totally immersed in my memories, in renewed reflections about what has happened to me. Our failings, after all, derive not from our life's tactical errors but from our moral flaws. The greatest sin, therefore, is to avoid a clear-eyed look at yourself, a realistic assessment of your powers; to act as though you determined the will of God rather than vice versa. Every man of faith knows in his heart when he crosses that line, just as he knows when he strays from carrying out God's will. Above all, you must be candid with yourself.

I am not called to interrogation for several days. During my stay at the Serebski psychiatric institute, the investigation had advanced, and the investigators now want to conclude the case. The best thing for me is to avoid having to be represented by a public defender. No Soviet lawyer, after all, would declare to a court: "Given that every man has a right to live in his homeland, my client – who was robbed of this right – is innocent." In fact, no lawyer could say such a thing without landing himself in jail.

Popov informs me that since the Latvian bar association wasn't keen on sending one of its members, a lawyer from Leningrad has been appointed to represent me. Even at first glance, it is clear that my lawyer is a KGB man, just like Popov.

In his presence, we observe Article 210 of the Soviet criminal code, which requires the accused to review the evidence amassed against him. I am confronted with twenty files, a virtual library of falsehoods, distortions, and forced confessions. The first page of the first file opens with a June 14, 1970, report from the operational department of the KGB about the treasonous attempt of a gang of criminals to flee the country by hijacking a plane. If only it were possible to reveal the source of the report! Indeed, this isn't the first report, but the last. When, then, had they been tipped off? And why not let these Jews leave, if that's all they wanted? And why had the KGB knowingly let us get to the stage where we could be arrested? In effect, the KGB had permitted us to continue our efforts, and thus the KGB itself should be the primary defendant.

The rest of the documents allow me to trace the methods of information gathering: mainly blackmail, by pressing on the vulnerabilities of interrogatees.

The pages are awash in the tears of those who had been pressured to testify. I read with great interest what my co-workers said about me. The Russians among them were mostly hostile: "A talented young man, but keeps his thoughts to himself, did not join in social activities, preoccupied with getting to Israel." The Latvian manager, however, went as far as he could in praising me. "Diligent, progressing well in his work, does the job of an engineer without getting paid as an engineer, does not pretend to be more than he is." I was grateful to him for that, and for not turning me in. It was with him, after all, that I had discussed the radio news broadcasts during the Six-Day War.

During pre-trial preparation, I meet with Viktor Boguslavsky and Leib Korn, who were discovered to be in the possession of books I had given them on March 7, 1970. They couldn't explain how they had come into possession of the books without mentioning my name, but I have no intention of confessing that I had in fact given them the books in question. The position is awkward, for me and for Leib Korn both. The investigators demand that we agree on a single, true version, but we decline their request. We each stick to our own version, and leave it to the investigators to figure things out.

Viktor acts confidently, going so far as to debate his interrogator on the true essence of Leninism. "Viktor Noyevich [son of Noach], although you are our enemy, I must admit you know more about Communism than I do," the interrogator concedes. "Then again, you've had more time to read up on it."

· · · · ·

The concluding phase of investigations is usually an auspicious time for a prisoner to make requests. I had heard that during the file-review stage, prisoners are sometimes allowed to get food from home, and even to exchange letters with family members. I wanted my kippah back, along with several books that had been taken from my home during the search.

"I refuse to sign the protocol until you return my kippah," I insisted.

"It is forbidden to wear a kippah in prison."

"Then I will not sign."

The kippah was brought to me, and I put it on at once. Until then I had been compelled to wear a handkerchief, which served as source of amusement for them. Now the jokes stopped. They merely looked at me contemptuously, and harassed me at every opportunity.

One day I poked my head into the office of Kuznetsov's interrogator and asked how Eduard was doing.

"Not bad, but of course you know that he will most likely be sentenced to death." They knew the sentence before the trial commenced.

In early November my interrogator, perusing the newspaper, remarked, "Now you're really in for it."

"Why?"

"Yesterday, two Lithuanians, Berazinskas Sr. and Jr., ordered a Soviet pilot to fly to Turkey. When the stewardess, Nadia Korchenko, blocked the cockpit door, the father lethally shot her with a homemade rifle and wounded the two pilots." To deter further hijacking attempts, Moscow had decided to impose severe punishments. We would have to pay a high cost for the crimes of others, so that, in the phrase of Deuteronomy, others "shall hear and fear."

· · · · ·

I relinquished my right to the attorney given to me by the authorities. A rank smell of primitive anti-Semitism had permeated his every utterance. I requested legal books so that I could prepare to defend myself. I received nothing. Two weeks before the trial was set to begin, I was summoned to the visitation room, where a black-haired man of average height looked out at me with a penetrating stare.

"My name is Ariya. Your parents hired me to defend you in court, but since I heard that you prefer to do without representation, I must know if you refuse my services too."

"Let's talk, and then I'll decide. How are my parents?" I hadn't had any word from them in six months.

"They're fine. They asked me to say that there's no cause for worry. They love you and remember you."

"Who asked you to defend me?"

"Your 'brother' Mendel. Before he left the country he met with me in Moscow."

I was nearly struck speechless with joy. "Mendel? Gone abroad?"

"Yes, to Israel. Many people are emigrating now."

Now this was news! Rather than arrest him, they let him leave for Israel. A sign that perhaps not all was lost. On the contrary, this was a victory.

"How do you see the strategies for defense?"

"Well, I generally don't take such cases. In fact, everything is determined in advance. Besides, if the defense attorney isn't careful, he can lose his position. At present, I know your case only superficially. I had heard something of it before. Many Jews are worried that in the wake of the case Jews will no longer be permitted to serve in high positions or engage in scientific research."

"As it is they have no business being here. They should emigrate to Israel."

"Not everyone agrees," he said as he opened my file. "Tell me, it says here that you testified to the effect that you knowingly harmed Soviet sovereignty. Did you really say that?"

"The prosecutor Katukova posed that question to me, and I replied to the effect that if she meant to ask whether I knew that crossing the illegal border amounted to harming Soviet sovereignty then the answer was yes."

"But you must understand that there is no connection between harming state sovereignty and crossing a border. They simply took advantage of your lack of legal expertise in order to get you to testify against yourself. In effect, you have admitted treason."

"I reject that charge."

"You see? Yet the protocol records show that you admitted it, and I'm not certain that document can be contradicted. In any case, will you allow me to represent you?"

I admired his agile, incisive intelligence, and I accepted his offer. Afterwards I would discover that he was one of the most prominent legal scholars in the Soviet Union, the author of a number of books on jurisprudence. He was Jewish by origin. His fees were no less impressive; they were the equivalent of an average worker's annual salary. Without considerable assistance from abroad, my family could never have afforded him.

· · · · ·

The summer faded into fall, and fall into a rainy Leningrad winter, with its long nights, gloomy days, and bone-chilling winds. My morning walks in the courtyard were sunless. Everything seemed depressing, and the days passed with monotonous rhythm. Between mealtime and our daily walks, we slept, read, and talked.

Once more I was given a new cellmate, and as before his arrival was no coincidence. The KGB sent me an intelligent, engaging fellow who could be relied upon to inform them of my views. This he did dutifully, but that did not prevent him from treating me with frank admiration. The story of his life bears telling, since it sheds light on certain dimensions of Soviet life generally.

Dmitri Lesov, as he was called, had been arrested for illegal trafficking of yeast. As was the common practice, the factory where he had worked produced a "surplus" from material that had been "saved" – in other words, stolen. The manager ran a kind of private business within the state-run factory, selling the illegal stock together with the legal, and dividing the profits among the retail stores. Dmitri had a share in these profits, and would, in addition, steal crates of yeast outright and sell them without the factory's knowledge. He would go to a shop and ask the salesgirl, "Want some yeast?"

"How much?"

"Two crates."

"Good. How much will it cost me?"

"Two hundred rubles each, plus a bottle of vodka."

"Deal."

And so forth, from shop to shop. In a city of four million inhabitants, there was always bound to be a need for yeast, and Dmitri had no doubt helped many families. As far as the company was concerned, he was an entirely honest man; theft from the state was not considered a moral crime. Yet when he was caught, the factory manager saw to it that Dmitri was put on trial. He was sentenced to three years.

Though not well educated, Dmitri was far from an ignorant boor. His father was a well-known film director, and he himself had moved in actors' circles, and had sometimes served as an extra. Due to his mischievousness, he had been transferred from a prison camp to a KGB jail. The vice-warden of the camp, who was responsible for "reeducation," had once approached him with an offer.

"Dmitri, you head a prisoner's group, and you know the inmates in your group well. Would any of them be interested in early release?"

"Sure. But they have records of behavior problems, so they wouldn't stand a chance."

"No matter. Just mark the names of some trustworthy men. I'll put a positive recommendation in their files, and take out reports of reprimands. It will cost them five hundred rubles each."

Not a few succumbed to the temptation to cough up the sum in order to earn an early release. When the fraudulent scheme was inevitably discovered, they thronged to Dmitri's room, begging him not to reveal their involvement. To alleviate this pressure on the ringleader, the KGB was compelled to transfer him to their prison. The KGB always overlooked the blunders of their "colleagues."

As I mentioned, this thief and informant harbored some admiration for me. One morning, he recited a poem that he had been inspired to write during the night and had dedicated to me: praising my modesty, good nature, and so on. Needless to say, the KGB had not instructed him to write poetry. But it turned out to be our last day together. That afternoon, he was taken away, together with his belongings. As a collaborator, he must have known this in advance.

• • • • •

Each of my cellmates – a gypsy cash-smuggler, a former Nazi policeman, an enterprising thief – had been far from ethically perfect. From none of them had I been able to receive moral support. With the interrogations behind me, time seemed infinite, monotonous to the point of nausea. My spirits fell.

A week before the trial was set to begin, a letter arrived from my sister Eva. "Why haven't you written? All the others have sent letters to Riga. What's happening with you? Father isn't feeling too bad. Write to us. We love you very much." This was the first letter I'd received in prison, and I would save it throughout all the years in camp. (It would be confiscated just before I was released.) It moved me to tears: tears of love for my family, tears of concern for them, tears of anger that to avenge my refusal to break under interrogation those bastards had neglected to pass along the letter I had written to my family. I wrote to the prosecutor-general, demanding that my letter be immediately delivered to my family. To no avail.

As I awaited trial, I considered how I should conduct myself in court. At the end of the day, I regarded the trial not as a significant event but as an empty formality, a show without substance. Soviet courts, corrupt to the core, were packed with carefully selected spectators, and so appearing in court seemed to me like playing a role in an absurd play. (I couldn't have known that my every word in the courtroom would be broadcast to millions of listeners in the West.) I was not a politician who sought to grandstand or use the trial as a platform. I was just me, and I had no higher ambition than to stay true to myself and to my Creator. I therefore resolved to behave with self-confidence, to avoid pathos, to speak as I would anywhere else. The things I was about to say in court were modest, but I knew that God listens equally to the voices of the powerful and the weak. The real trial wouldn't be taking place here, where everything was predetermined, so I would keep my words short and to the point, like the Shema Yisrael.

Still, I carefully chose what to wear in order to look my best when I saw my family. The vest my mother had knitted me, along with Mendel's sweater, warmed me with the affection of those closest to me.

The morning of the trial, the prison filled with high-spirited tumult, as though we were about to celebrate an important holiday. We were taken to be shaved and were given new underwear. One by one we were then brought to a room to await the escort guard. The colonel appeared wearing a long military coat, as though he were in the entourage of Stalin himself, and a severe expression. "Do you have in your possession any weapons, gold, or anti-Soviet propaganda?"

"I've already sent the gold to Israel," I quipped.

After a search, we were taken downstairs into closed vans, which were designed to carry up to thirty inmates. Each of us got our own. Thus there traveled a convoy of ten vans, surrounded by a phalanx of blue police cars and rows of policeman lining the streets, offering a mysterious, almost celebratory sight. Years later, someone who lived in Leningrad then told me how he watched our convoy from his window in the dawn light, but that the sight had made him so gloomy he'd had to close the curtain.

Our friends were waiting at the entrance to the courthouse. The moment Mark Dymshits stepped out of the first van looking steady and firm, he was surrounded by a joyous throng shouting blessings and words of encouragement. The police quickly shoved everyone aside. Each van stopped only steps from the entrance; we were hustled upstairs and through corridors lined with police. This production must have been an expensive one.

I was taken into a still-empty courtroom. We were seated in a very particular order to prevent us from plotting a political protest, God forbid. Sylva was brought in first, Eduard last. Mark and Eduard sat on the front bench separated by Marchenko (a so-called "neutral"). Fedorov and I occupied the second bench, and so on.

Looking around, I saw that we were in the largest room in the district courthouse, with a capacity of some 150. The defendants' section, behind a screen, could seat thirty. For the first time since our ordeal began, I saw my friends. It was forbidden to exchange words, but we nodded to one another in greeting. Sylva's eyes conveyed an enthusiastic hello. Behind and beside us stood armed guards who watched for the slightest word and stared at us with contempt. And why shouldn't they, really? For we were "enemies of the state." It would be interesting to chart how they slowly softened towards us as the trial progressed.

The spectators were then allowed in. Words cannot express the emotional storm that raged within me when I saw my family. They weren't crying; they were trying to put on brave faces and smiles. My father had brought me some apples in a familiar basket but wasn't permitted to give them to me. Instead, he waved from afar. I did my best to show him that I was calm, collected, and confident.

My memory can only retrieve a few details from the haze of boredom that surrounded the trial: prosecutor-general Soloviev's microphone, which looked to me like a desk lamp; his cup, which resembled a lampshade. These thoughts amused me, as did watching the lawyers oddly sipping his leftover tea.

For the duration of the trial – wonder of wonders – we were permitted paper and pencil, which had been denied us for the last half year. A great deal of time was consumed by procedural matters, as though prolonged legal deliberations would prove the rigor of the proceedings against us. In fact, the whole thing could have been concluded in a matter of hours. The result was a foregone conclusion (to the judge and prosecutor alike), determined in advance by the KGB investigators. It wasn't even a show; they were merely going through the motions. Two members of the jury, uneducated people, could barely even understand what was being said.

Mark Dymshits was the first to speak. He pushed out his lower lip contemptuously, and spoke persuasively, with barely concealed, prideful rage. It occurred to me that even the Communists attending the trial by special invitation could not fail to be moved by the justness of his cause. I imagined the judges expected something quite different from this from a man who faced the death penalty.

"The Soviet Union threatens the Jewish people," Mark said. "You have closed our cultural and religious institutions and have actively sought our assimilation. Your aid to the Arabs in the Six-Day War resulted not from strategic considerations but from simple hatred of Israel."

"That's enough!" one of the attorneys cried. "Sit down!"

Mark's speech seemed not to leave the rest of us very much to say, but then Sylva rose to speak.

"Sylva Zalmanson, you sought to flee from our Soviet motherland?"

"We are pledged from birth to remain loyal to the land of Israel, to declare '*Im Eshkacheich Yerushalayim Tishkach Yemini*: If I forget you, Jerusalem, may my right hand forget its skill.'" This she said in Hebrew.

"What did she say?"

Sylva translated the verse – Psalms 137:5 – into Russian. The prosecuting attorney nearly fainted in anger.

"Sit down."

Suddenly it came my turn.

"Why did you want to flee to Israel?" the judge asked.

Having expected to speak only the next day, I hadn't even prepared notes or talking points, but my position was clear. I told the court what Colonel Kaiya had told me in the interior ministry when I had applied for an exit visa: "Forget about Israel! You will rot here." I dismissed the charge that I had betrayed my homeland, since my homeland was Israel, and concluded with the insistence that the longing to live in Israel was not some private, personal whim but a result of God's charge to Abraham, Isaac, and Jacob.

At this, the prosecutor turned to the judge. "Your question to Mendelevich was wasted. He's known as a religious fanatic. It's incomprehensible how a man raised in our Soviet reality could cut himself off from Russian life and preoccupy himself only with his Torah and his Israel."

At that moment, my lawyer jumped to his feet. "Is it not true that you underwent psychiatric evaluation?" With this question he wanted to suggest to the court: don't pay attention to my client's drivel about God and religion, which may just be symptoms of his mental illness. I regarded this as a low tactic.

Eduard Kuznetsov spoke at length, and his claims – about humanitarian and legal considerations alike – were well grounded, and delivered with both rigor and humor.

In general, my colleagues performed superbly. None tried to shift responsibility onto the others. On the contrary, each stressed his own role in the operation. Not for nothing did Mark go out of his way, in summing up, to praise our "fitting behavior" and our refusal "to squabble like spiders trapped in a jar."

Cross-examination focused on whether we had planned to use violence to hijack the plane. We testified that we had intended to resort to violence only if the pilots resisted. The question was: would the pilots have managed to react at all? One of the pilots was put on the stand. "Imagine," said assistant prosecutor-general Katkova, who had proved capable of shameless exaggeration, "imagine that you are clubbed on the head, gagged, cuffed, and stuffed into a sleeping bag. Would you like that?"

"Would you?" the pilot answered. Laughter in the courtroom. From this we were to deduce that the pilot would have resisted, and that we would then have violently used our weapons.

Dymshits would have none of it. "Tell me," he said to the pilot, "what would you manage to do if two men were clutching your arms?"

"Nothing," the pilot admitted with embarrassment.

Katkova interjected. "But he had a sidearm!"

"Isn't it true," Mark continued, "that your pistol was stored in a bag? Do you think you would have been able to reach it in time?"

"No, I would not."

Katkova again: "The cockpit door must by regulations remain closed. In other words, the pilot would have managed to reach for his gun."

Now Eduard: "When a pilot emerges to welcome passengers, or to bid them farewell when they disembark, does the cockpit door usually stay open?"

"Yes, it does."

"And what do the regulations stipulate?"

"That it remain closed."

Thus did Mark and Eduard contradict the prosecution's claim that we would necessarily have had to resort to violence. A small victory, but a telling one that perhaps illustrates our fighting spirit during the proceedings.

A similar skirmish concerned the cost of the plane we allegedly intended to steal. The prosecution used an inflated figure: 64,000 rubles. Dymshits countered that such an aircraft does not cost more than 30,000. I leaned forward and whispered in Mark's ear: "I remember the plane was an orange one."

"That type of craft costs 30,000," he said.

"Do you think it's worthwhile to mention that?"

"You can try, but in any case the law mandates the death penalty for any theft of state property higher than 10,000 rubles," Mark said.

I raise my hand. "Your honor, I recall that the airplane in question was orange, and bore the call number 245. I request that the official price of the craft be found."

"Mendelevich, you remember too many facts that are in your interest to remember. We know very well the color of the plane. Look, do you perhaps remember these?" Judge Yermakov held up two gags that were three times larger than the ones we had brought. A murmur went through the courtroom.

"There were indeed gags in my pack that day, but not that size."

"Aha, now your memory doesn't serve you so well. Sit down and try to remember better."

The second pilot testified that the plane was worth 35,000 rubles.

· · · · ·

Next to be called to the stand was the artist Gilberg, who had taught painting to Boris Penson. At first glance, it was obvious that he was intimidated to death and prepared to say anything they wanted him to say. On arriving at the witness stand, he bowed thrice – to the prosecutor, the judge, and the court secretary – not daring to make eye contact with us.

"Penson had never been satisfied by conditions in the Soviet Union. He once remarked to me that it was impossible to obtain anything in stores."

Everyone in the courtroom knew that most stores' shelves were chronically empty. Gilberg's testimony sounded odd to say the least.

"In your view, does Penson represent a danger to the public?"

A difficult question to put to someone who had been Penson's teacher, but the judge appeared to enjoy humiliating this Jewish artist.

"Had he posed a public menace, I would have taken appropriate measures."

"And what measures might those be?"

"I would have informed the NKVD," Gilberg said, referring to the no longer existing predecessor of the KGB. The slip of the tongue underscored how deathly frightened the witness (one of the most prominent painters in Latvia) must have felt. And then, with exaggerated deference, he retreated to the exit, pulled on his painter's cap, and congratulated himself for managing to appease the scary goy's anger. Gilberg was then fifty-five. He had received some Jewish education before the war. It seemed to me that despite his fears, in his heart of hearts he still disdained the non-Jews who had compelled him to testify.

· · · · ·

The next two witnesses were of a newer "model," individuals who retained not even a memory of their Jewishness. These two were traitors not reluctantly, but by choice, and that day I vowed to myself that whatever happened, I would one day tell their story publicly.

A year earlier, Aryeh Khnokh had been visited by a relative from Kazakhstan named Anya Aptayker who joined our circle and participated in our meetings during her stay. Our passionate love of Israel and our faith inflamed her, too, and she returned home brimming full of new ideas and longings, which she shared with her brother and his friend. One day, this brother and his friend – two students on vacation – arrived in Riga, where Aryeh took them in.

Aryeh loved stimulating argument and vigorous conversation, and it's doubtful whether the two guests were prepared for the flood of words Aryeh let loose on them about Israel, the Jewish people, the Soviet invasion of Czechoslovakia, the state of the Soviet Union, etc. This wasn't a pedagogically designed approach carefully calibrated to open the eyes of his listeners, but a ruthless barrage, an assault of the enlightened on the unenlightened. Not surprisingly, it was counterproductive. Far from adopting Aryeh's Zionist enthusiasms, the two students went away confused and embittered. Anya was right to reprimand Aryeh by letter: "Rather than telling them how Israel is good, you told them how the Soviet Union is evil."

That letter was discovered in a search of Aryeh's home, and led investigators to Alek Aptayker and his friend Zacharavich, the very witnesses who had now taken the stand, only too happy to expose Aryeh's "anti-Soviet views." The prosecutor Soloviev was practically dancing in his chair with joy. For us, no gloomier sight could be imagined than these two young Jews eagerly condemning another to years of suffering.

Aryeh's lawyer attempted to cast doubt on Aptayker's testimony. "Can you quote for the court any conversation you had with my client?"

"No, I can't."

"How then can you claim that the conversations were of an anti-Soviet nature if you cannot remember them?"

"The same way you can read a poem and remember its subject without necessarily memorizing its lines."

"Smart fellow!" the prosecutor exclaimed, nearly falling out of his seat with excitement.

· · · · ·

Subsequent days were taken up with procedural matters, mostly devoid of substance, though the defense attorneys delivered some superb speeches. If I were the prosecutor, I would most certainly have shed a tear and sent everyone happily home. Still, even as the attorneys' legal fees were wiping out our family savings, their talents would ultimately be of no practical consequence.

Each began with the standard disclaimer. "As an upstanding Soviet citizen, I strongly condemn my client's actions." But skillful defense work – including that of my counsel Ariya – would follow that cold formulation. It focused on certain key points:

The charge of treason should be mitigated to the lesser charge of attempted illegal border crossing.

There had been no intent to commit theft of the aircraft.

Consideration should be made for the fact that no actions were carried out, and that therefore at most only our intentions could be judged.

There had been no intent to overthrow the Soviet state.

I, on the other hand, felt that the defense strategy should have been built on the claim that I had been denied my rights, first among them my right to emigrate to Israel, together with the claim that the literature that I distributed and wrote concerning the state of Soviet Jewry contained nothing but the truth.

In his closing arguments, the prosecutor Soloviev did not trouble himself to engage the points raised by the defense, choosing instead to reiterate his original claims. Though his closing speech may not have been well grounded in fact, it was marked by an impressive and uncompromising rigidity. (In the 1960s, he had sent many Jews accused of theft to their deaths.) In it, he again characterized me as a fanatic, and saddled Fedorov and Marchenko with Article 64 of the criminal code, for "betrayal of the fatherland." To do so, he had had to establish the anti-Soviet nature of their views. During the trial, he had asked Marchenko, "Did you become an upstanding Soviet citizen after your first imprisonment?" He knew full well that there could be no greater insult for Marchenko than to be called "an upstanding Soviet citizen," and that the defendant would reject the term. Now, in his closing, he relied on Marchenko's denial to paint him as a self-confessed anti-Soviet activist.

With Fedorov matters were even easier. During his first imprisonment, in 1960, Fedorov had written to his mother that if released, he would continue his struggle against Soviet oppression. The letter not surprisingly fell into the hands of the KGB and Fedorov was imprisoned. That time, he had been lucky enough to receive a pardon and early release. Now, waving the same letter, Soloviev declared, "You see, even back then the defendant was hatching his sinister plots!"

Then it was the turn of the "people's representative" Mednonogov, his voice muffled under the many medals and military decorations he wore on his chest. "These base traitors sold out their Soviet motherland for Coca Cola and chewing gum," he said. "Surely it's no coincidence that they planned to carry out their sordid crime on the year we celebrated Lenin's hundredth birthday. They wanted to spoil our international celebration of our Great Leader." He concluded by requesting that all of us be sentenced to death by firing squad.

On the evening of December 24, 1970, we were brought for the final time to the courthouse to hear the verdicts. According to Aryeh Khnokh, Chanukah had begun the day before. I had memorized the dates of the Hebrew holidays only through Yom Kippur; I hadn't imagined I would be in prison after that. Since I had no candles, I wondered how to mark the holiday, so I brought apples and cakes that I had received from home and shared them with the others. Eight Jews stood before the corrupt court like the eight candles of Chanukah as testament to the fact that although the Jewish tradition had been suppressed in the Soviet Union for sixty years, there remained enough oil to light the fires of struggle and purification in the hearts of young Jews.

The judges conferred behind closed doors. We had been kept waiting for two hours. When Boris Penson got up to stretch his legs, the old colonel rushed over: "Order in the court! Stop this at once!" Whereupon Boris' nose began to bleed, and he was taken to a clinic.

We knew these were our last hours together, and we wanted to exchange a few words of farewell. Yisrael Zalmanson began to say something when he was interrupted by shouts. "No talking! We'll punish you!"

"With what punishment exactly?" we asked.

"No more packages from home."

We burst out laughing. We were fighting for our very lives, and the guard was threatening not to allow us care packages?

"We'll manage somehow," Anatoly Altman joked, "the main thing is that the Basques survive." As though prophesying, he was comparing our trial to the trial of Basque terrorists in Franco's Spain.

"Have you heard what's happening in Poland?" Marchenko asked. "Port workers in Gdansk have started a strike." Hearing such optimistic news made imprisonment slightly more bearable.

The verdicts were read. We rose, hanging on to Judge Yermakov's every word as he listed our sentences. Standing there, I felt like a soldier in battle. I was sentenced to fifteen years imprisonment for "harming Soviet state security," fifteen years for attempted hijacking, and seven years for illegal Jewish activity. Since under Soviet law one can serve a maximum of fifteen years, I essentially received a fifteen-year sentence. As death sentences were handed down to Mark and Eduard, applause erupted. Applauding a death sentence! This, I reflected, was a characteristic Soviet response, rooted in a society that had been corrupted by the show trials of the 1930s. Our families shouted: "Disgrace!" Not a muscle moved in Mark's impassive face. Sylva broke down crying. "How much blood have the Bolsheviks sucked," Eduard exclaimed, "and still their thirst has not been slaked. One day, they will choke on the blood they have spilled."

The other sentences were received calmly. Spectators brought bouquets of flowers up to the judge to congratulate him for condemning us. Then our families stood on their chairs and called to us. "Don't worry, you won't have to serve out your sentences! In the West they know of your plight!" I noticed my father arguing with one of the "people's representatives." This isn't the time or the place for such debates, I thought. Having had several heart attacks, my father didn't need the excitement.

I can't say the verdicts came as a shock to us. We had been prepared for any cruelty. I felt the need to demonstrate dissent, to sing "Hatikvah," maybe, or the Palmach anthem. But somehow the tone wasn't right, and none of us felt like doing something dramatic or ostentatious.

As they took Eduard out of the courtroom, Sylva leaped toward him. Several guards restrained her. I pushed one of them aside, and the others helped Sylva, her face streaked with tears, reach her husband. Then reinforcements arrived – a group of soldiers headed by a major – and tore Sylva away.

My lawyer tried to say something soothing, but I instructed him to attend to my father. "You'd best escort him out; otherwise he might be arrested himself." I already noticed the familiar faces of several KGB agents surrounding him.

I embraced Mark and Eduard, ardently kissing them in the hopes of seeing them again. Not for a moment did I believe that their death sentences would be carried out.

For the next several days, Sylva's sobs would disturb the sleep of everyone in the prison...

· · · · ·

After the trial, we were finally permitted to see our families. Inmates and families alike felt a sense of awakening joy in the knowledge that another stage of our struggle to return to our homeland was complete. We did not regard the trial as a terminus, or as a failure. My reunion with my parents was charged with emotion. My father – his lips trembling, his cheeks streaming with tears – could hardly speak. I had always been proud of him, and I wanted to see him strong. It was hard to bear the thought that I had caused him such sorrow, or that my actions had undermined his health. My stepmother Ella didn't cry. So that the guard wouldn't understand, she used Yiddish phrases to help update me on what was going on outside the prison walls.

There seemed to be no doubt that the means of our escape had been very unpopular, mainly because of the lethal hijacking of a Soviet plane not long before. That hijacking enabled the leadership of the Central Communist Party to decree harsh sentences for us; however, it was clear that they had overstepped their bounds in handing down a death sentence for a crime that had not actually been carried out. In retrospect, it's hard to understand how the

KGB apparatus, which meticulously planned the investigation and prosecution of our case, hadn't taken this into account.

The way in which Mark and Eduard were spared the death penalty may not have been miraculous in the usual sense of the term – it may not have resulted from supernatural forces that could not be explained rationally – but in my mind it did belong to the category of miracles we sometimes encounter in the Torah. Here, too, we were witness to the astonishing fact that from time immemorial, when the Jewish people struggles for its survival, for a return to its homeland and its faith, it enjoys divine providence. Today we tend to regard miracles with skepticism: was there an Exodus from Egypt, or not? Did the walls of Jericho come tumbling down, or not? Did the Chanukah miracles really occur? Yet in our case, you could read about the remarkable events in the newspaper, or see them on television. To be fully understood, I believe, our episode must not be considered in isolation, but as part and parcel of the progress of Jewish history over the last several generations.

It turned out that wondrous things were happening beyond the walls of our prison. Activists had been giving daily reports of our trial to foreign correspondents; each day, in exchange for handsome compensation, a special courier brought to Moscow unofficial transcripts of the trial that our families had secretly noted down. In Moscow, the transcripts were translated into English and worked into press releases for Western consumption. Well-known dissidents like Vladimir Bukovsky, Vladimir Telnikov, and Galina Ladyzhenskaya took part in this.

Naturally, the authorities would have liked to suppress this material, but they were unable to prevent its publication. In this way, the Soviet Jewry movement cracked the walls of silence erected by the totalitarian regime, and by drawing attention to the problem of human rights showed the Soviets and the West alike that suppression could not continue forever.

On December 23, 1970, six Basque terrorists were sentenced to death, and three days later General Franco commuted their sentences. By handing down death sentences in our case, the Soviet authorities were depicted as more brutal even than the fascist Franco. Twenty-four countries made formal appeals to the Soviet Union concerning our case. The Communist parties of France and Italy anxiously (and rightly) feared that public attention on the lack of human rights in the Soviet Union would harm their own image. The Socialist International sent a protest cable. Even the Pope registered his disapproval, as did a petition signed by a number of Nobel laureates. The Soviet Jewry movement in the United States, headed by Glenn Richter and Yaakov Birnbaum, organized mass rallies. In Long Island, Lynn Singer and the Union of Councils for Soviet Jews led a demonstration of fifty thousand. In the Soviet Union itself, Andrei Sakharov sent protest telegrams to both Brezhnev and Nixon.

· · · · ·

Yet the view from prison looked quite different.

The day after our sentences, a guard stuck his head into my cell. "Mendelevich, have you written your appeal yet?"

Normally, appeals were submitted two weeks after sentences, if the prisoner chose to file one. "No, I have to think it over."

"There's nothing to think about. Write it. I'll be back for it in half an hour."

Taken aback by the pressing hastiness of the request, I sat down to write: "All of my actions derived from my national and religious views, and my desire to live in Israel. In my opinion, the court's sentence is cruel, and ought to be reconsidered."

The guard rushed in. "Ready?"

"Ready."

He came back not ten minutes later. "Here's a nicer piece of paper. Write your appeal again." I did so, only to see him come back once more.

"Why have you written so little? You should add something."

Here was a novelty: a guard instructing a prisoner on how to write an appeal. All this panicked urgency seemed ridiculous, but the matter could not have been more serious. For the first time in the last sixty years of Soviet trials, the authorities flinched. Instructions had arrived from Moscow to reexamine the case, and our appeals were passed along to the capital that day, despite the legal stipulation that at least a week must pass for appeals to be filed.

On December 29, 1970, at 10:00 a.m., the Soviet Supreme Court began deliberations on our appeals. The next morning, at 11:00 a.m., the court rendered its decision. This took five hours, though it's not clear, given that the instructions came from Brezhnev himself, why it should have taken so long. In the end, Mark and Eduard's death sentences were commuted to prison terms. As for the rest of us, our prison terms were shortened.

Mark and Eduard had spent the days following the trial on death row, where everything was done to prevent suicide attempts. The tables and chair had rounded edges and were bolted to the floor; hands were cuffed at all times; reading and taking air in the courtyard were forbidden. Mark would later tell me how easily the thought of impending death could drive a man crazy.

Through sheer willpower, he had convinced himself from the outset that a quick death was preferable to years in the gulag.

On New Year's Eve, Mark was summoned to the warden, Kroglov. For a moment he wondered whether the day of his execution could have arrived so soon. Kruglov handed him a telegram. "Here's a cable from your lawyer. Your death sentence has been commuted. Congratulations. Although I've received no official instructions in the matter, I've decided to remove you from death row and into a shared cell." Behold, a progressive warden.

I myself learned the news only on January 2, when a copy of *Pravda* was brought to my cell: "Certain elements hostile to the Soviet Union have been agitating in the West on behalf of a gang of criminals who plotted to kill Soviet pilots...." The usual drivel. But what's this? "The Supreme Court has humanely found fit to commute the death sentences...." Not a word about the rest of us.

I knock twice on the wall, and hold a cup against it. "Aryeh, does it say anything in the *Leningradskaya Pravda* about the rest of us?"

"Yes. They've shaved three years off your sentence, and two years from mine and Tolya's."

"Congratulations!"

A guard interrupts. "No talking! You'll be punished!"

Luckily, my cellmate had been blocking the door slot with his body, so the guard couldn't prove a thing.

At the time, I didn't appreciate the magnitude of the Chanukah miracle that had befallen us. Years later, after my release from prison and the fall of the Soviet regime, I learned that at some point during the planning of our escape, word of our intentions had reached the KGB. In discussing possible responses, one of the heads of the KGB had suggested "helping" us reach the plane so that we could be caught red-handed. Such a spectacular arrest, they thought, would allow authorities to arrest all Soviet Jewish activists – from Hebrew teachers and their students in the illegal ulpans to actors in the Yiddish theater. In the days of Stalin, no pretext would have been needed to wipe these people out. But times had changed, and Russia now sought better relations with the West. Authorities therefore needed a pretext, and our attempted hijacking would give them just that. In fact, after we were apprehended at the airport, the authorities arrested many other Jews who had no connection whatsoever to our operation: Hebrew teachers and Jewish educators were picked up and charged with abetting our plan.

The authorities planned on breaking us under interrogation so that during the trial we would express remorse and denounce Zionism. Thus part of our

Chanukah miracle was that they failed to put together such a trial, for the simple reason that none of us were intimidated, nor our loyalty to our people shaken, by the threat of a sentence of death or life imprisonment.

Our sentences caused great shock among Jews in the West, many of whom had believed the Soviet line that Soviet Jews were happily assimilating into Russian society. Suddenly, it became clear that Soviet Jews desperately wished to remain Jews. In this way, our trial, rather than serving as a triumph for the authorities, became instead a Jewish victory. We had exposed Soviet tyranny, and indirectly given birth to a worldwide human rights movement that ultimately helped bring down the Iron Curtain.

I also later learned that in her attempt to prevent the death sentences from being carried out, Israeli Prime Minister Golda Meir had sent a special envoy to Marshall Franco in Spain, which had just sentenced several Basque separatists to death. Golda's message was succinct: "We know that you are a descendant of Marranos [Jews who had been forced to convert to Catholicism in the Middle Ages]. We ask that you pardon the accused in order that innocent blood not be shed." The message was simple: Franco's pardon of the Basque separatists would make it politically harder for the Soviets to execute us. And this is exactly what happened. After Franco pardoned the Basques, the Soviets had no choice but to appeal our harsh sentences to the Supreme Court, which commuted them to lesser sentences.

Thus did the authorities' expected triumph end in their humiliation and in a wave of protest in the West calling for the right of Jews to emigrate. David had once more defeated Goliath. Truly a Chanukah miracle.

· · · · ·

My new cellmate was a Frenchman named Marius, who deserves a few words of introduction. He had worked as a driver in Magadan, in Kamchatka, located on the Pacific shore on the far east of the Soviet empire, the legendary capital of Stalin's gulag system. He, too, had been imprisoned for trying to escape the Soviet Union. His Communist parents had brought him to Russia from France after the Second World War, but Marius never quite fit into Soviet life, never even learning how to write Russian. He found work in the far northeast of the country near the Bering Strait, where only fifty kilometers separate Kamchatka from Alaska. He had already served a three-year term for trying to cross the border.

While planning his second escape attempt, he had visited a number of port cities, including Odessa, Riga, and Klaipeda (formerly known as Memel), in the hopes of bribing a guard and boarding a foreign vessel. In Vyborg, he met Tolya Mokrousov, a senior member of the local Komsomol and owner of a motorboat. Mokrousov volunteered as a guide on KGB-supervised boat tours near the Finnish border. For three days, Marius supplied Mokrousov with rivers of vodka and cognac, somehow managing himself to stay sober, and then offered the boatman two thousand rubles, an enormous sum, for Mokrousov to take him across the international sea border. But it seems that he had given the boatman rather too much to drink, for instead of Finland they found themselves at a Coast Guard station. This, at least, is how Marius reported the story in the *Vyborbskaya Pravda*. I later met Makrousov in prison, and asked him about Marius. "Despicable man. He plied me with vodka, and I ended up in jail. So be it. I'll get out and return to building Communism. The pity of it is that I'll never again be permitted to own a boat." This patriot had stashed away the sum he had received for his services, and couldn't wait to get out of jail to spend it. In fact, although he had sold himself out, he was indeed pardoned and released and went about "rebuilding Communism." As for us, our attempts to leave meant we would stay imprisoned.

In prison, Mokrousov got basketfuls of excellent apples, which he would share with me. Before the war, his family home in Vyborg, along with its apple orchard, had belonged to Finns. His parents were allotted their pastoral residence after the Soviet invasion of Finland.

"You condemn Israel for belligerence," I told him, "and you yourself live in a house stolen from its rightful owners."

"They attacked us first, and only then did we take their lands."

"The Russians invaded Finland without cause, as everyone knows. And in any case it seems clear that the lands belong to the Finns. Israel, meanwhile, has retaken territory that from time immemorial belonged to Jews."

"Israel must return all the territories to the Arabs."

Facts are useless in such arguments. When Israel is discussed, reason very often goes out the window, and the "logic" of anti-Semitism more than suffices. In their years in camp, Mokrousov and Marius served together with many of my friends. In all those years, the former remained impervious to any idea except those implanted into his mind by Soviet propaganda. Marius, on the other hand, was quick to grasp Zionist ideology, asking many questions about Israel, and even making a stab at learning Hebrew.

· · · · ·

In the meantime, the other trials continued. Zev Zalmanson, who had been drafted into the army after finishing his studies in computer science, was for that reason to be tried in a military court. One day, I was brought to the courthouse to testify. I was made to wait for quite some time in a closed police van. At some stage, I realized that there was someone else in the van on the other side of the screen. It was Eduard Kuznetsov.

"Eduard, it's a shame we didn't have the chance to coordinate our positions before our trial. And our behavior under interrogation wasn't exactly stellar either."

"Only matches are made in heaven," he replied. "We are but flesh and blood."

"What will we do if we're not released for a very long time? How will we continue our struggle?"

"We can initiate hunger strikes, but only if we act in coordination and prepare ourselves for the long haul."

At this, the guards who had been listening to us hastened to remove us from the van and put us in separate courthouse cells.

At the trial, I was asked to explain what had motivated Zev Zalmanson's attempt to flee. "His motivation," I said, "was simply his desire to live in Israel, the only country in which Jews can live full lives."

"Mendelevich, this isn't a Zionist rally. There's no need to indulge in propaganda."

As I was taken back to the van, a large crowd had gathered near the courthouse entrance. An elderly woman hurled abuse at me: "You degenerate! Sold out your motherland for gold. Give him to me. I'll rip him to pieces!"

The escort guards burst into laughter. "Relax, grandma. What are you going on about?"

I remembered how my lawyer Ariya had told me that many Jews were angry with us for imperiling their position in Soviet society.

· · · · ·

After the trial, I spent another half year in prison. Once in a while, they would drag me to testify in trials in Riga and, later on, in Leningrad. The local authorities were not eager to hold additional trials in Leningrad; the first had caused them headache enough. Moscow, however, was not pleased by the Zionist committee of Leningrad and wished to see the group on trial. On August 5, 1970, Brezhnev arrived in Leningrad, demanded a full report, and reprimanded first secretary Tolstikov for his "obduracy." The court date was put off so as not to interfere with the twenty-fourth Party Congress.

Finally, the trial of the Leningrad Zionists began on May 11, 1971. Once again, I found myself in the role of a witness in the same courtroom in which I had not long before sat as a defendant. Sitting on the defendants' benches now were the nine members of the Leningrad committee; their pale, fearful faces were not familiar to me. I prepared my statement in advance. "I refuse to give testimony on the grounds that in this trial I am not a witness. The distinction between these trials is arbitrary and artificial. The trials in Riga, Kishinev, and now Leningrad are in fact a single trial, in which the national Jewish movement is being judged. Thus in the present trial I appear not as a witness but as a defendant."

The judges, seeing that I would be no use to them, let me go. On the way out, I turned to the defendants and said, "Shalom." In their frightened state, they did not reply.

At that moment, a man rose from the press box. It was Yevgeny Yevseyev, correspondent of *Izvestia* and author of an anti-Semitic tract called *Fascism Under the Blue Star*, an official publication of Komsomol, the Communist Youth Organization. "You clown!" he shouts.

Surprised that a correspondent could behave this way, and never very fast on my feet, all I could say was, "You're a clown!"

Guards shoved me forward. "Let's go. No stopping."

This time, as I exited the courthouse, I was greeted by the friendly faces of the families of the defendants. Some among them waved to me, and passed on greetings from my father. My last week in Leningrad was drawing to a close. Because of my apparent uselessness as a witness, it was decided that I be sent at the earliest opportunity to a labor camp.

My family had hoped to see me one more time at the Riga trial, but when my name was called the court secretary announced: "Ill. He cannot be present." My family felt acutely disappointed – and worried. In reality, I was perfectly healthy.

Now I know that the struggle continued even after our arrests. In government offices in Riga and Moscow, Jews staged sit-in strikes to demand exit visas (among them were my sister and brother-in-law, Rivka and Chaim Drori). Dozens of open letters, appeals, and telegrams sent by Soviet Jews to the authorities were publicized in the Western press. The movement, driven forward by many other brave souls, had not lost its momentum.

• • • • •

May 29, 1971. Amidst the barking guards, I collect my belongings. I have neither suitcase nor basket; everything is in packages. Yet I have only two hands. To make matters worse, I'm given bread and salted fish for the trip. I can't carry everything, and no one offers to help. Just as I'm stepping into the police vehicle, the warden says, "You have mail. We didn't have a chance to give it to you." I read a telegram: "On May 29, we are leaving for our homeland. Farewell. Chaim, Rivka, and Eva."

Certain moments bear too much symbolic meaning to be dismissed. The very day that I was being shipped off for a decade of labor camps, my family left behind everything it had known to go Home. We would meet there many years hence. The road of faith, long and circuitous though it may be, leads in the end toward Jerusalem.

That day was the holiday of Shavuot.

Chapter Three

Gulag

They say that when a man uproots himself from one place to another, the changed circumstances bring to light new dimensions of his character. My journeys represented movement not merely through time and space, but also motions through my own soul. Thus this story documents not just my ordeals, but also a man in search of the truth and of himself – in other words, a man in search of God. I should say that I always sensed His presence in mundane life, precisely in those seemingly insignificant coincidences. A man of faith finds himself in a state of continual seeking in which despair, hope, and discovery intermingle. "One thing I ask from the Lord, this only do I seek: that I may dwell in the house of the Lord all the days of my life, to gaze on the beauty of the Lord and to seek Him in His temple" (Psalms 27:4). This is our daily seeking after simple human joy, and the ensuing transformations would indeed shed new light on hitherto unseen facets of my character.

• • • • •

Overburdened with my unwieldy packages, beset by a headache, my strength sapped, I feel suffocated in the sealed police van as it winds its way through the streets of Leningrad. I vomit up the stale sour cabbage they've given us in prison for lunch. In this hapless state I arrive at the train station where I am transferred to a train car reserved for prisoners. On the side of the car opposite the windows are narrow, barred cells meant to hold eight inmates; the guards push some twenty into each cell. A terrible stench arises, along with cigarette smoke that gathers above us like a dense fog. Luckily, as a "dangerous security prisoner" (my classification), I am put into a solitary cell. I sink onto the bench, happy to be relieved of my burdensome bags.

I begin to unpack the suitcase my father gave me before I'd boarded. I had put together the list of contents myself, based on advice offered to me by a veteran convict, and my father had followed my instructions meticulously.

The case contains real treasures: one two-and-a-half liter pot, ten packages of tea, two chocolate bars, a packet of ground coffee, a white enameled mug, a stainless steel spoon, two shirts and sweaters, and leather boots. These are essential camp items, and thus critical to have there. In a large canvas sack, I find eight books (regrettably, a Torah is not among them) along with two kilos of stone-hard sugar. I feel like a Rothschild. But what's this? Feeling along the bottom of the sack, my fingers touch a packet of letters. The prison authorities had never delivered them. Fortunately, rather than being destroyed, they had been kept and placed in my bag.

Among them I discover a letter in Hebrew from Mendel, and a photo of him at Masada. He is living in Jerusalem, he reports, and studying in an ulpan. He has not forgotten me. Other letters are from the Kamyeski and Gelfond families: "We realize that we have been able to come to Israel only because you are imprisoned there. We shall never forget you." I feel overjoyed – people on the outside remember me with affection and are going to Israel. I am infused with a renewed sense of purpose.

Then I begin to sew a rucksack out of my coat, suturing shut the front and the collar, and turning the belt into shoulder straps. Now I can carry the bag on my back and the suitcase in my arms. I am ready to go. I hide my needle in a tea packet.

I quickly learn to act like a veteran prisoner. On finishing the "housekeeping," I look up and cock an ear to the adjacent cell of the train carriage.

"Hey, neighbor. Who are you?"

This could be dangerous. Criminals are a troublesome bunch, and if I open my mouth I'll end up having to tell my entire story.

They try to be encouraging. "You got twelve years? Bastards."

But soon their attention turns to another matter. "What kind of things you got there?"

"I don't have anything."

"Nonsense. Shoes, a suit?"

"No."

"You got money, maybe? We can get you anything…"

"I've got no money."

"So what's with the big suitcases?"

"Books."

"So give me something to read. Something with spies and girls."

"I've only got textbooks."

"You want to study in camp? It's not school, you know. Listen, you got a notebook? I write poetry."

"A notebook I do have. I'll give it to you at the transfer station."

As we had been talking, the train had started to move. Prisoners gazed out at pastoral scenes they had forgotten existed. "Look! A dog running behind a peasant!"

The tension abated, at least among the older prisoners. The younger ones tried to get acquainted with the female inmates in an adjacent cell. "Hey, is there someone there named Nadka?"

"Yes, there is? And what's your name?"

He answers with a vulgarity, and women react with wild enthusiasm. "Hey, guys, how's your health? We've already dried up over here."

"Any young ladies in there?"

"We're all young."

"Under fifty?" The men chuckle.

Introductions are made, mash notes are passed, and I start wishing that I wasn't in the cell located directly between the men and the women. I'm forced to become a messenger, even though I could be in danger were I caught with one of their notes. But if I refuse, twenty fists begin pounding on the wall. "You bastard!"

The distribution of water provides further entertainment. "Guard, there's no water."

"We forgot to fill the tanks. Wait till the next station."

"But we're dying of thirst. You feed us salty fish only to deny us water? Fascists! You're torturing us." In the commotion, a tank of filthy water is found somewhere. Each prisoner gets 250 grams. They drink up, and demand more.

Then the next pressing issue: going to the bathroom. "When can we go? When?" The criminals had wolfed down the bread and salted fish – meant to last for the two-day journey – in one go, and now demanded to go the bathroom or else they would urinate in their pants. The guards remain unconvinced, and the prisoners start kicking the door. The chief guard, dressed in a T-shirt and half asleep, appears. He emanates the smell of warm food. "What's up, boys?" He is tranquil, having spent vastly more hours on this train than any prisoner, and he calms them down. He instructs the guards to lead prisoners to the toilet one by one.

My turn arrives. "Did you read about Operation Wedding?" a sergeant asks one of the soldiers standing outside the bathroom door. "The whole world is talking about him, and I'm taking him to the toilet." His appetite for power has apparently been satisfied. I return to the cell accompanied by taunts. "Hey, professor, I'm gonna smash your glasses." Or, "Hey, guard, bring him into our cell so we can have a little fun with him."

I press up against the bars of my cell, praying, only to be interrupted by a spot-check – intended, I understand, to reveal the private life of a "world-renowned figure," as the guards sarcastically call me. "What's this? Books? Forbidden!"

"The prosecutor permitted me to bring them."

"I'm the prosecutor here." In the end, having had their cat-and-mouse fun and having asserted their control, they confiscate nothing.

"Why do you look so despondent? Don't worry, everything will turn out fine. You'll serve out your term, get married, have children…" Could this be the same soldier who moments ago had been trampling on my letters?

"I'm not despondent. And I know everything will turn out fine."

"But don't even dream of reaching Israel. You'll die here!" His friendliness couldn't last, and he returns to his barking. "Tell me how you tried to hijack that airplane. No? Never mind, after eleven years of imprisonment you'll be more talkative. I once escorted a prisoner after he'd served twenty-five years, and he was desperate to talk with me the whole way home. You'll be like that too. You'll be like them." And with that he goes to curse out the criminal prisoners.

I'll be like them? Never. I withdraw once more into myself, into my letters and into the photo of Mendel at Masada.

．．．．．

For two days, I cross a large swath of the empire imprisoned in my iron cage.

At last the train pulls to a halt. We hurriedly gather our belongings and jump from the boxcar, and are instructed to sit on the ground facing a thicket of gun barrels. Then we are ordered to run to the closed vans that will whisk us away.

The Ruzayevo transit station is a greyish three-story building erected in the previous century in a particularly desolate area. A fat captain with a Jewish appearance says cheerfully, "When I read roll call, you will pass before me, say 'I,' and doff your hats."

"And if I don't take off my hat?" I ask.

"You must."

"Just imagine that I had."

"Just imagine getting socked in the face," he says.

After a search, our belongings are taken to storage. I hold on tightly to my only Yiddish book, a volume of Sholem Aleichem.

"What were you arrested for?" asks the surprised captain.

"I'm a Zionist."

"Ah, so you're the 'bridegroom.'" It seems he too has read about Operation Wedding.

Unfortunately, as the only political prisoner in the convoy, I am put into solitary confinement, even though I've done nothing wrong. No matter. In the future, solitary confinement will oppress me, but I'm as yet young and healthy and have bread.

For half an hour, I hear the nagging of another prisoner. "Sergeant, I have no bread. I'm hungry."

"You've already eaten your ration. Now be silent!"

"Sergeant, I'm dying of hunger. Give me bread."

"This is no grocery store."

I call the soldier over. "Give him my ration."

"Impossible. If they see me do that, I'll be fired."

But after more whining, and my repeated requests, he relents. "Fine, hand me a little of your bread." I look into the slanted eyes of his narrow face. He looks like a Tatar. I give him my morning portion and a moment later hear thanks from the adjacent cell. I'm happy to have had the chance to feed a hungry man, and relieved by our jailer's humane gesture. It turns out that my neighbor is a Jewish student from Moscow, sentenced to ten years for purchasing dollars on the black market. What a pity, I think, that our energies are being wasted here on foreign soil. It would have been better had he been imprisoned for trying to blaze a trail to our homeland.

A couple days later, I hear: "Mendelevich! Want to take a walk?"

"Sure," I say. I put on warmer clothes and am taken out of my dark cell into the courtyard, where it turns out to be a balmy day. Flies buzz, and clouds of brown dust whirl through the air beyond the fence. A farmer and his horse are plowing the black, brilliant earth. Having been cut off from the world for so long, I now long to rejoin it. Just then, a clap of thunder and a burst of rain send me scrambling for cover under a small shed. The wonders of creation.

The time comes for us to be sent to our respective camps. Another search is conducted, this time in the prison's communal bathroom, which fifty inmates can use at once. A barrel of foul-smelling fish is brought in, and everyone takes as much as he wants.

At midday, we are taken back to the station and loaded onto the train in full view. It seems that people in this town are used to such sights, and before guards shoo them away, they even try to offer us cigarettes or slices of bread.

I leave my civilian clothes on the overhead rack. Better that than to let the guards confiscate them. We arrive at the last station, Potma, whence we are dispersed to the various camps in the Dubrovlag system. Although we number 360 prisoners (among them mothers of infants), only four trucks – each of which has thirty seats – are there to greet us. "Women with children will walk," a fleshy major announces. "It's not far."

As a "dangerous political criminal," I get my own compartment, but someone else is already occupying it. I have to sit atop him. He doesn't complain – merely requests that I don't rest my shoes on his head. We get acquainted. I learn that he has been imprisoned for seventeen years now, and that he's being taken to a new camp because he had participated in a strike. He listens to my story with interest.

When we arrive, the doors open, and we tumble out like ripe plums from a basket: dark, bruised, and damp. All of us are crammed into a cell meant to hold a hundred people. Some sit, some have to stand. One man is sitting on a urine-splashed pail that serves as a makeshift toilet. Beneath the window, however, conditions are more spacious. Only five or six men are there, sitting on a blanket, sucking candies and eating preserved fish. There are the heads of the "mafia," the leaders of the underworld, for whom separate laws apply. No one picks a fight, steals, or murders without their knowledge. Since they enjoy unrestricted rule over their colleagues, the camp authorities do not threaten them.

As my eyes grow accustomed to the surroundings, I notice a group of thieves crowded into the cell that look different from the usual rabble. They sit quietly mending their clothes. One, a man with an Armenian accent, invites me over, and asks me about the hijacking. Those around us listen intently and without mockery. Gradually, the entire cell quiets down to listen to me. When I conclude, my audience barrages me with questions about Israel and Judaism: is it true that Israeli scientists have discovered a cure for cancer? Does Israel really have the atom bomb? Why do Jews bake matzah with blood? The Armenian takes out a Soviet almanac on Israel, and shows off his knowledge of Israeli crop yields, exports, and armaments.

As a gesture of hospitality, they begin the sacred ritual of preparing tea. This is forbidden in prison, but then again, so is stealing, and everyone steals. They wrap a rag around a spoon, which is inserted through the handle of a mug heated by burning newspaper. In five minutes or so, the water boils. Only the thieves sip the tea. I'm invited to join the elite sitting on the blanket, but I choose to stay next to the Armenian.

At night we sleep pressed up against one another like sardines. In the morning, I discover that some of my belongings have been stolen, but there's little to be done; the earlier shipment of prisoners has left, and a new shipment has arrived.

That evening, everyone but me is evacuated from the cell, and I sleep soundly in the suddenly empty space. I throw the keys of our Riga home out the window; I will never return there. Despite the superstition that dictates that we will return to a place where we tossed a key, I resolve that my next home will be nowhere else than Jerusalem. But before I throw them away, I use the keys to scratch a picture of an airplane into the wall above the Hebrew words: "To Israel!" Many of my friends will later tell me that they had seen my graffiti.

My address in the labor camp is 389/17, Ozyorny district. Before we enter, we are searched yet again. The camp orderly has alert eyes set in sharp, intelligent features. He too has read about me in the paper, and treats me respectfully, even permitting me to bring in my shoes and the beret I received from Israel. The boots and sweater, however, I have to leave behind. When he later discovers the needles I have hidden in my tea packets, he bursts out laughing. "Why did you conceal these? You knew they're forbidden."

Then I'm allowed into the camp, which consists of a broad courtyard surrounded by five wooden barracks, grass, foliage, even flower bushes. It is a tranquil sight, and I can hardly believe that I am standing on real earth, basking beneath the sun. Incredibly, I can walk right or left, as I choose. I try the handle of one of the barracks, and the door swings open. After my time in prison behind locked doors, this in itself seems miraculous. I can walk about, open and close doors freely!

The chilly barracks is lined with beds covered in white sheets and azure and pink blankets. The windows are covered in nets to keep out flies. Some old men are sitting on stools, and politely return my greetings. On second glance, I see that the walls are peeling, the floorboards rotting, and the ceiling barely holding up. Still, in contrast to the stone walls of a solitary cell, this is quite livable. The adjacent barracks not so long ago served as a pig sty, but these seem to be peripheral details.

The camp was built in 1944 by German POWs; their bones are rotting in a swamp not far from here. In fact, the camp is surrounded by swampland, making any tunneling impossible. The swamps also fill the camp with mosquitoes and a humid, heavy air. Beyond them stretches a green forest canopy.

Being new to camp customs, I begin putting my foodstuffs into a cabinet, earning a stern look from the elderly inmates that says, "What does that Jew have there?" I hadn't realized that they would expect me to offer them some of my provisions.

The orderly enters. "We've made a mistake. In accordance with camp regulations you must be quarantined before entering the camp proper." The quarantine isolation area is some three hundred meters outside the camp, and to reach it I am marched through the adjacent town under guard. These towns are amazing phenomena in themselves: they house only workers connected to the camp. Since the early 1930s, the Republic of Mordovia has been carpeted by such towns. The republic is home to some 1.5 million inhabitants, but an escaped convict stands no chance; anyone trying to hide in the local population will be immediately turned in. In fact, anyone who turns in an escaped prisoner will be rewarded with half a bag of flour.

Ostensibly, quarantine is designed to prevent the spread of infectious diseases; in reality, it is used to break the prisoner upon arrival, to show him "who's the boss." To wit: "How long do you intend to hold me quarantined?" I ask. "I was sentenced to camp, not to solitary confinement. I demand to speak with the commanding officer."

"You're demanding your rights? It is precisely the function of quarantine to teach you that you have no rights here. The quarantine will last as long as necessary, and the commander will come whenever he finds it appropriate to do so."

"How dare you talk to me like that? Answer me straightforwardly."

The door clicks shut, and I am left to contend with my anger, an anger that will do no good here. In camp, time has no meaning; the more you want something, the longer you'll be made to wait for it.

This is how the attempt to transform you begins. You can either submit to their concept of time, or you can withdraw into your interior world, there to navigate your own spiritual waters. My world is Israel and the Jewish people; my time beats to the tempo of Jerusalem. I am both here and not here. I am out of my jailers' reach.

Next to my cell sits another man building his interior world, which is both similar and dissimilar to mine. I had heard long before about Edik Chimilainin, a Finn from Leningrad. At a street fair in honor of Lenin's centennial, he had set fire to a stand, and passersby set upon him, beat him, and brought him to the police. In consideration of his youth, investigators intended to charge him with disorderly conduct, which carried only a three-year sentence. Edik wouldn't hear of it. "I did what I did for ideological reasons, because I believe that the Bolsheviks have destroyed democracy," he insisted. So the arsonist was charged instead with Article 70, subversion of Soviet authority, and got slapped with five years. He was satisfied. Through a window, he tells me: "I realized my place is not in Russia. I don't want to change their regime. Each nation gets the regime it deserves. I just want to return to my homeland, to Finland."

Then he recites a poem that glorifies his country, its lush valleys and azure bays, and its industrious citizens. It seems clear to me that his longing for his country (a country unfamiliar to me) has been inspired by the passion of the Zionists. Herein is the answer to those of our critics who called on us to break out from the "Zionist ghetto" and join the larger prodemocracy movement. Why did we not understand that a man must become what he is by nature – be it Jewish, Finnish, or Tatar – and that rather than cultivate a hatred for Russia, he must harbor in his heart a love for his country – be it Israel, Finland, or Tatary? Why not replace hatred with love?

· · · · ·

As soon as I no longer asked how long the quarantine would last, it passed quickly. After five days, having understood that it would not succeed in break-ing me, the guards let me into the camp. Each barracks held seventy men. I had, first of all, to find a bunk. One of the old men, a former Nazi Polizei, pointed to an open spot. "Grilius requested that if a Jew comes he be brought to a bunk near him." Grilius, I thought; sounds like a Lithuanian. Why must I make my home near him? "Mendelevich, hurry. Grilius is calling you. He's waiting for you by the factory fence." What did this Grilius want from me?

As I approached the fence, a man with a wild red beard called to me in Hebrew, "Shalom! How are you?" Although it soon became apparent that his knowledge of Hebrew didn't extend much beyond those two sentences, I was still flabbergasted. A Jew! Here! I am not alone! We couldn't speak for long. Shimon Grilius was at work, and missing work could land you a harsh punish-ment, so we decided we would talk that evening.

After work, I waited by the entrance to the camp's residential area. When he appeared, Shimon and I embraced. "Do you believe in God?" he asked. "Do you know Torah? Hebrew? Jewish history?"

When I answered in the affirmative, Shimon's excitement grew palpable. "Incredible. My prayers have been answered. For a long time, I've yearned to keep the Torah, but I never knew how. A year ago, I heard about the arrest of Jews wishing to escape to Israel. I prayed that a religious Jew would be among them, and that he would be sent here, to me. What a miracle. You can start teaching me right away."

"Listen, it's late. Let's start in the morning."

"How can you say such a thing? I have waited for two years to begin living a Jewish life. Each moment until then is a wasted one. And you want me to wait another full night?"

"Fine, I'll tell you everything." I could offer him the totality of my limited Jewish knowledge in a matter of minutes. "We must cover our heads, which means sewing kippot. And we must do our utmost not to eat non-kosher food, or work on Shabbat."

"Making a kippah should be no problem," Shimon said. "We can use material from our prison uniforms, and I have a needle and thread. I'm just not sure they'll let us wear them. It's strictly forbidden, and may land us in solitary confinement." As he said this, he was already taking out his needle and thread – treasures under camp conditions – and I stitched together two kippot. Putting them on, we felt transformed.

As for the other issues, Shimon did not have ready answers. "I don't see how it's possible to keep kosher here. Our meals are prepared in a single giant pot, and who knows what goes into it. Also, there's no way we'll be permitted to rest on Shabbat. Failure to work is considered a grave violation around here, and they can really make us suffer."

"I don't care," I said.

But several days later, Shimon, a veteran prisoner, had found a solution. "I spoke with a Ukrainian inmate who works in the kitchen, and he agreed to siphon off some cooked vegetables – carrots, potatoes – before the lard is dumped in. And even when he can't manage that – he's under constant supervision – he'll at least warn us when the stew is *treif*."

And that's exactly how it transpired. Imagine prisoners lining up at the kitchen with their aluminum bowls. When my turn comes, I thrust my bowl over the transom, only to get a signal from the prisoner inside that today the stew was *treif*. Our very own camp kashrut supervisor. Even when we sometimes went without a meal in this way, we didn't starve. It was usually possible to get a few pieces of bread. As time wore on, we learned to supplement our diet with herbs and certain edible leaves that sprouted around the camp, and that were supposedly rich in vitamins.

We also managed in time to find a solution for Shabbat. "I talked to the prisoner who records the daily work quotas," Shimon told me one day. "If we fulfill our quotas by producing more on the other six days of the week, he said he'd be willing to list us as though we had fulfilled our quota on Saturday too."

On the bunk of his neighbor, a Latvian nationalist named Gunnar Astra, Shimon prepared a welcoming dinner for me: white bread and honey from Gunnar, and sugar, coffee, dark bread, and sausage that I had brought from Leningrad. Shimon and Gunnar both complimented the Leningrad bread, which was far more flavorful than the camp fare. Camp bread looked like mortar and tasted like mud. (I wouldn't have imagined that two years hence Shimon and Gunnar would no longer be on speaking terms.)

I accepted Shimon as I accepted myself, almost as though he were a second "me." Gunnar, however, was something else. He stood more than six and a half feet tall, and had been on both the Latvian national basketball team and the Soviet rowing crew. By profession he was a radio engineer, and had worked, like me, in Riga's main radio factory. Oddly, we had no friends in common. I disappointed him, too, in my ignorance of the streets of the city I had inhabited for twenty-two years, which just goes to show how disconnected and alienated I had felt there. My streets awaited me in Jerusalem.

Gunnar also turned out to be a dedicated anti-Semite. "Just look at the photos of those who so eagerly greeted the invading Russian troops in 1940. They're all Jews. What did they lack in democratic Latvia? Were they not satisfied with their Jewish schools and theaters? No wonder the Latvians slaughtered Jews during the war, though of course I'm not justifying it." It is absurd to condemn an entire people to annihilation on the basis of a few photographs, of course, or to deny that there were far more Latvians in the Latvian Communist Party than Jews. But no reasoning could shake Gunnar's convictions.

After several months together in camp, he told me, "I never thought there could be Jews like you: Jews who aren't cunning, who aren't greedy hucksters. I've even developed something of a fondness for Israel."

Most of the time, however, Shimon and I avoided engaging Gunnar's views, most of which were based on the teachings of Nietzsche. Instead we concentrated on imposing a new reality on our little corner of Mordovia: the sounds of Hebrew, prayers, blessings, Kabbalat Shabbat, and Israeli songs. I

felt content. I talked with Shimon with great openness, I read the poems of
Bialik, I sang.

Shimon would listen silently, immersed in his own Jewish longings. He
had been arrested in 1969 together with Aryeh (Yuri) and Zev (Vlodya) Vudka
and Asher (Alexander) Frolov for distributing an anti-Communist tract by
Aryeh in the cities of Ryazan and Klaipeda (Memel). Aryeh had contended
that Communist theories, more precisely, Marx's teachings in *Das Kapital*,
were anachronistic, and no longer applied to modern realities. In the last
year, they had become involved with Zionist circles in Moscow, and had even
weighed emigrating to Israel. During their trial, the prosecution had labeled
them "Zionists."

Shimon had been the group's administrator. His friends, without hope of
getting accepted into a technical college in a bigger city, had come to Ryazan to
study. One day, a young poet declaimed his poems at the entrance to the student dorms. An informer in the audience reported him to the official in charge
of the dormitory, who in turn asked the poet to leave. The poet refused, and in
the end was forcibly removed. This enraged a group of students, who hurled a
stone through the official's window. Police arrived, and arrested the most vocal
of the group. Other students began to demonstrate, joined by young workers
who had problems of their own: their salaries hadn't been paid for months,
and the police had been making their lives miserable. All told, some five hundred gathered in protest. Taken by surprise, the police sent representatives to
negotiate.

By this time, 1:00 a.m., Shimon was returning home from a date when
he stumbled onto the scene, and was struck with an idea. "Let's march to the
police station and free our colleagues." This kind of student-worker demonstration was unheard of in Ryazan – or in the whole of Russia, for that matter.
Police reinforcements arrived to block the roads. The police commissioner
himself was alerted and rushed to the scene. "Who's in charge here?" he asked.
Many in the crowd pointed to Shimon and several others. They were taken
to the commissioner's office, and when the negotiations were completed, the
police agreed to release the prisoners, fire the official in charge of the dorms,
and pay the workers' salaries. "We promise no one will be punished if you disperse at once," the commissioner announced. Then, turning to Shimon: "You
could have been a fine officer."

The next day, the "student rebellion" was the talk of the town. The BBC
reported it. Shimon became "the big man on campus," and thus came to the
attention of Aryeh Vudka, who needed someone to help distribute his essay.

Shimon agreed to help. But every underground group in the Soviet Union is sooner or later discovered, and they, too, were arrested.

"We now must above all commit ourselves to aliyah, to knowing our own tradition, and to fulfilling the word of God," Aryeh declared. Immediately upon arriving in his labor camp, he circumcised himself with a razor. His brother Zev reached Israel after three years in the gulag and today is an observant Jew who spends his nights studying Talmud and the writings of Maimonides. So close was Shimon's story to my heart that I found myself immediately identifying with him.

Before I was shipped off, my lawyer Ariya had said: "Don't despair. Paradoxical though it may sound, there is life in the camps too." Reality exceeded my expectations. Life here proved to be diverse, crosshatched by tensions and passions, boiling with intensity.

On my first night, Shimon introduced me to his friends: Mr. Goren, a Ukrainian nationalist; Mr. Soroka, a thirty-year veteran of the camps, who as a leader of Ukrainian guerillas had fought the Soviet army in the Ukraine; Mr. Pirus; Mr. Pidgorodchki; and Yonis Kagionis, a Lithuanian guerilla who was serving a twenty-year sentence for shooting a local police officer who had collaborated with the Soviet occupiers. Amid the introductions and handshakes, I felt that this band of prisoners, these fighters for justice, regarded me as one of them, while also accepting me as a Jew who was struggling for his faith and his people. This was new to them, since they had met only "victim Jews," who in the best case were intimidated creatures and in the worst case were spineless grovelers before the authorities.

That night, a commotion seized the barracks, though I remained sound asleep. In the morning, I found out that Mr. Soroka, the oldest inmate, had died. Before he was arrested by the Soviets, he had been imprisoned by the Poles for his participation in the struggle for Ukrainian independence. His fellow Ukrainian prisoners, accompanying him to the last, held a one-day work strike in his honor. Later, the Ukrainians would say that I had inherited Soroka's legacy.

It was my first day in the camp factory, where prisoners slaved over sewing machines for eight hours a day making gloves out of coarse white canvas. Would I manage? I took my place and pressed the pedal; the machine screeched and the needle promptly snapped. This wasn't working. I tried lowering the handle, which moved the cloth, only to see the thread hopelessly tangle in the needle. On either side, prisoners were pressing pedals like madmen, hastening to fill the daily quota. Next to me, Shimon pasted some English words on his sewing machine so that he could memorize them as he worked. We whispered to each other, like two schoolboys, casting glances at the door to watch for guards. Next to us, Gunnar towered over his machine, and nearby sat an old prisoner with a white beard named Rodenkov, who crossed himself before setting to work with a concentration approaching prayer.

Our salary amounted to eighty rubles a month. Half of that was withheld by the interior ministry; in effect, we were paying our own jailers. From the remaining forty rubles, half was deducted for food, lodging, and electricity, as though this were a hotel. We were permitted to send the remainder to our families. Rodenkov worked to be able to help support his "old lady" back home.

"Shimon, did you lose your kippah? We'll make you another one."

I cut four triangles from Shimon's old uniform, and stitched them together. I can't say the result was very impressive, but it was nonetheless his own kippah, and he was moved to have this symbol of Jewishness restored to him. In a place that was designed to strip us of our identities, this was a significant gesture. A Turk named Issa, for instance, would wear his scarlet tarboosh when the guards weren't looking, and the Ukrainians embroidered their shirts in the traditional fashion. Each of us tried to hang onto some semblance of national and ethnic individuality.

In general, group belonging took on special importance in the life of the camp and in the social dynamic that gave camp life its shape. There were Ukrainian nationalists, led by Gorin and Kandiba; Lithuanians; and a large contingent of Byelorussians, Ukrainians, and Russians who had collaborated with the Nazis during the war.

One prisoner in particular stuck in my memory: a former Polish officer who had been brought with other captured officers to be executed by the Russians in the Katyn forest near Lvov in 1939. By sheer luck, he had survived. Even now, he kept his noble appearance, carrying himself tall and erect, his magnificent mustache curling up at the ends. Yet he was totally mad – unaware of his surroundings, and unwilling to use his spoon at mealtimes. His madness stood out in high relief against his otherwise noble manner.

One day, while talking a stroll with Shimon, we noticed a group of twenty men behind the barracks, surrounded by lookouts to warn of an approaching guard. "Those are the Jehovah's Witnesses," Shimon explained, "part of an international cult." Most came from Bessarabia. They openly believed that the Soviet regime was the work of the devil and called on followers not to obey the authorities. Not surprisingly, the Soviets had banned the group and declared its followers to be outlaws. They were based in the United States, where they published a magazine called the *Watchtower*, which was distributed illegally in the Soviet Union. Most had been sent to camp as a punishment for having distributed the magazine, but once here they didn't cease evangelizing. They came to the aid of many a depressed and vulnerable prisoner, who in sheer gratitude would later join their ranks. This is how they recruited many of the former Polizei who felt a need for repentance. They lived modestly, refrained from informing on others, and read Bibles that had been copied by hand and passed around. Many knew the New Testament by heart.

The next day, I was sitting next to the barracks watching a bee buzzing from flower to flower, when a thin, silver-bearded, righteous-looking old man sat beside me. "The bee collects honey from the flower, and the flower grows from the earth," he said. "The earth sustains all. But who sustains the earth? 'In the beginning God created the heavens and the earth.' And He chose one people above all others, yet the Jews betrayed Him and were expelled from their land. If the Jews repent with all their hearts, and return to the true faith, they will save the world."

In a soft, delicate voice, he laid out the principles of his faith for an hour, and concluded with the exhortation that I join his cult in order to save my people. I listened distractedly. His words hardly interested me. "Well," he said finally, "what do you say?"

I got up and left. I am a Jew, and cannot be otherwise.

Soon thereafter I met a recruiter of a different type. Major Grusha, a KGB man from Moscow, arrived in the camp, and summoned a large number of prisoners for interviews. (KGB recruiters usually met with many people, so that the prisoners would not be able to guess who among them was collaborating.)

His room held two chairs, one backed to the wall and the other next to the major's desk. A prisoner who chose to sit near the desk signaled his readiness for an intimate conversation. Nothing here was left to chance. I chose to sit against the wall.

"Come closer," Grusha said.

"No need."

"Well, how are you getting on? Any questions?" The characteristic KGB way of opening a conversation put me into a cold sweat. What does he want from me? "Yosef Mosesovich [son of Moses, my father's name], you're in for a long time. We in the security apparatus are very determined. No one in the West will save you. You can look forward to a very difficult term. You've committed a serious crime against the state and its people, and still you refuse to express remorse. No one but yourself will look after you. But you can still help us. You have some influence over your colleagues, and it's up to you whether that influence will be favorable or unfavorable. Sometimes people do things that only harm themselves. If you were to warn us about such things, you'd be doing your colleagues a favor." Such is the subtlety with which they would try to recruit you to inform on your friends.

"You're fortunate that I'm a peaceful man," I replied, "and that I won't respond the way I ought to."

"Why is that, Yosef Mosesovich?"

"Because you imagined I could possibly entertain your offer."

"But why so rude? We're talking about helping your colleagues, after all."

I got up and left the room, and from that day forward the KGB concluded that there was no more use trying to speak with a fanatic like me. As a result of my unyielding stand, they left me alone for several years. Those who hesitated, who said neither "yes" nor "no," only opened themselves to the KGB's pressure tactics: solitary confinement, denial of food and family visitation rights. Although my strategy of steadfast firmness was difficult at first, it ultimately succeeded.

One of my friends took a different approach. "Fine," he told the KGB agent, "I'll try, as you say, to 'influence my colleagues favorably,' but first I must know that my family has received visas to emigrate to Israel." The family received its visas. Then he demanded to see a cable from Vienna confirming that they'd left the USSR. The cable was delivered.

"Well?" said Major Grusha.

"I'm a different man now. Before I feared for my family. Now I am at peace."

"And what about your promised cooperation?"

"Have you gone crazy? Forget about it."

"Do you think it's so easy to trick the KGB?" And with that he was sent to solitary confinement at every opportunity.

I was reluctant to play such risky games.

· · · · ·

Gulag life is regulated by a thick volume of Interior Ministry–approved "internal rules for reeducation facilities," and a book specifying how these rules are to be applied. These are surrounded by many volumes of commentary written by leading Soviet jurists interpreting each clause – a vast library of rules and regulations. Neither guard nor prisoner could know even a fraction of these, but this didn't stop them from being invoked:

"Prisoner, why did you violate article such-and-such?"

"I didn't even know there was such an article."

"Ignorance of the law is no excuse. You must be punished."

You thus find yourself in an absurd world in which you can be sure that at any given moment you're violating some obscure rule or another.

Being on the wrong side of an unjust punishment naturally arouses in the prisoner the thought of lodging a complaint to one of six authorities: the interior ministry (local, district, state, or central); general prosecutor's office; central camp administration; the administrative department of the Central Committee of the Communist Party; the KGB; or the department of justice. My notebook with the relevant addresses of the offices within this hierarchy would be confiscated every time a search was conducted. A prisoner would petition each authority simultaneously, and receive a negative reply from each. The reasons for denial, however, differed. Another mark of absurdity in the Kafkaesque universe of Soviet life.

The most important man in the camp is the official responsible for enforcing discipline. With the simple words "permitted" and "forbidden," he determines your fate. The most obedient prisoner can't help violate some rule or another at some time. But however unrealistic those rules may be, you must be aware of them. You want to be able to know your rights, to say, "it says in article such-and-such that a prisoner may…" But your rights are illusory; they do not exist. You'll waste your time – and your energies – fighting for your rights to send letters, to receive letters, parcels, and books, and to see your family. The remote chance of succeeding – maybe one in ten – only fuels your addiction to a costly form of gambling with the authorities, a game whose end is a foregone conclusion. Before entering the gulag, I had often declared that there is no justice or legal recourse in the Soviet Union. But these were mere words. In my heart I believed that it must be possible that truth would prevail. Now, however, I learned the bitter lesson not through the newspapers but on my own flesh: there is no justice, no truth. This is the fundamental principle of Soviet "reeducation," upon which was based the gulag's attempt to force into the prisoner's subconscious the denial of the very idea of justice. Only thus would the prisoner become a Soviet citizen, willing to submit wholly to any dictate of the state, no matter how absurd.

A man naturally seeks to infer from his surroundings some semblance of logical coherence. If you persuade him that logic does not pertain, that there is no coherence, he loses his ability to navigate, and it becomes possible to direct him, to tell him what to do. Whoever invented the gulag, that vast machine for "reeducation," surely merits some kind of prize. Here, torture did not mean broken bones or needles under the fingernails, but the plunging of prisoners into a deep state of despair in which they no longer comprehend the world around them – the daily nightmare of denizens of these "reeducation camps."

What can be done? Many who feel the gulag's jaws close upon them and its teeth sink into their flesh succumb to despair, and decide from the outset that all is lost. They submit, and are indeed reeducated. Other, braver souls, insist: "If this is how it is, I adamantly refuse to obey any of these rules." In effect, the individual declares war on the infinitely vast system. But this proves impossible, since rather than struggle against the system itself, he invariably ends up in a battle – as ceaseless as it is futile – against the small cogs who implement it: the petty, coarse, ignorant officials and guards who are its only human face. This, too, works to the system's advantage, since the prisoner exhausts his mental and physical health in a vain and ineffectual exercise. Sometimes the prisoner deludes himself that he has succeeded in winning a small concession (usually a concession that he would have received anyway), but far from granting him a victory, the authorities have merely encouraged him to sink deeper into the quicksand of his futile struggle. The system never regards a prisoner as a lost cause; he is always able to be further broken and "reeducated."

A third type of prisoner seeks to outwit the rules by outwardly pretending to obey them while in fact evading them. This requires a thorough familiarity with camp regulations – written and unwritten – together with the shades of their possible interpretations, which in turn necessitates studying the characters of each of the camp officials and how they understand the rules. For this to work, the prisoner must persuade the authorities that if need be he would not hesitate to join the ranks of the second type of prisoner (that is, one who does not fear punishment), and that he enjoys the respect of his colleagues such that he would get their full support when needed. The camp administration usually prefers to bother with such prisoners only occasionally, to test their mettle, but no more.

· · · · ·

The above is no mere abstract classification; I drank from this poisoned chalice every day for eleven years. This was the cost of my lifelong dream of Jerusalem, the Zion from which Torah springs forth. How distant and unattainable it then seemed. How, then, was it possible, under such circumstances, to hold fast to faith in God – and in myself? How was it possible, here of all places, to think about Israel? "*Shema Yisrael* – Hear O Israel, the Lord is our God, the Lord is One." I felt the embracing presence of the One who transcends time and space, and thus was out of reach of this monstrous system, and my sense of being a part of that omnipresent Oneness is what saved me. "God watches over me," I would tell myself. "He is here, even when I am in solitary confinement, He who stands guard over the people Israel, and over a son of that people, Yosef the son of Moshe."

I resolved that I would not play around with the rules, but that I would isolate myself from Soviet reality as a whole; this would be the key to my survival. To be a Jew, I thought, meant to find a way of serving out my sentence while remaining until the end a man of sound mind.

Not that I learned the secrets of the gulag system immediately; it took years. The system, after all, existed long before I was thrown into its maw. Yet from it, and within it, I learned a great deal about human life. Though it was an inhumane creation, it was nonetheless a human creation, the product of the human mind. As such, its meaning and relevance extends far beyond Russia. In some way, it exists anywhere a nation or society loses sight of its own animating essence: "And now, Israel, what does God want of you? Only that you remain in awe of God your Lord, so that you will follow all His paths and love Him, serving God your Lord with all your heart and with all your soul" (Deuteronomy 10:12).

The harshest of the gulag's many deprivations was being denied visitations, which amounted to a denial of communication with the outside world. Not for nothing did they take from us the possibility of having a pen or paper; in fact, they took away even candy wrappers, lest we compose essays on them for Western consumption. Not for nothing did they search family members before visits, even though the law required a warrant for each and every search of citizens charged with no crime. But here, as I said, the law did not apply; rules were arbitrary.

Most of the legal arguments I had with Captain Zhuravlyov ended the same way: "Mendelevich, you've already shown you can talk, now we want to see you can obey. We will interpret our own rules, thank you. This is not your Talmud."

Here's how a typical conversation went between us:

"Mendelevich, since you were late to work, your next family visit will be canceled."

"But in the first clause of the Interior Ministry code it is stated: 'The prisoner has a right to visitations.' By definition, a right is something that cannot be negated or suspended. I have a right to my next visit."

"It's a right, but not an unrestricted one. As it is stated in the second clause: 'A prisoner who has violated camp discipline may have his visitations canceled.' You have violated camp discipline, and therefore your right has been abrogated."

"My tardiness does not constitute an infraction of discipline. The regulations stipulate that a prisoner must work with devotion. I fulfill my quota 101 percent, so clearly I am working devotedly."

"The workday includes a break between 12:30 and 12:45 in the afternoon. You returned late from that break. By infringing on the work day, you infringed camp discipline. The punishment is thus legally sound, and we're denying you your next long visit."

"The regulations provide the prisoner the choice of which visit will be canceled, and I choose the short visit."

"Last year, three of your visits were canceled for disciplinary reasons: one long and two short. The next cancellation must therefore be of a long visit."

"I could count the other way: short, long, and two shorts. Also, I was denied visits for three years, so I've accrued three visits."

"Visits do not 'accrue' or roll over from one year to the next. The count begins anew each year. You lost those visits through your own doing. The last visit permitted to you was a long one, so our calculation is correct. The code starts to calculate the next visit from the day of the cancellation of the last visit, so you cannot get a long visit before the anniversary of the cancellation of the last long visit."

I made no headway trying to convince the captain of something he knew as well as I did: I had been singled out for punishment for keeping the Torah, not for tardiness. I had been away during a power outage, when no one had been working. I had never violated the work schedule, since that very day a new schedule was taking effect, and since none of us had watches, none of us could know when the break had ended. In such cases, a signal was customarily given to get back to work. No such signal had been given, and therefore the fault was the authorities.

Camp rules permitted each prisoner three visits annually. A short visit meant four hours separated by a glass partition, and a long visit lasted from one to three days, according to the whim of camp management. During a short visit, nothing could be given or passed to the prisoner; during a long visit, the prisoner could receive food packages, but no currency, documents, paper, pens, or clothes. Family members were subject to strip searches before the meeting. If a camp official approved only a single day rather than three, there was nothing you could do about it. Only immediate family – mother, father, brother, sister, and wife – were allowed long visits. Short visits could include relatives and friends, provided that the camp authorities were of the opinion that they might exert a "favorable influence" on the prisoner.

Needless to say, the authorities preferred to cancel long visits. My father was then quite ill, and there was no reason he should travel two days in order to talk with me for several hours (with wardens present). But this time I wouldn't be able to inform him of the cancellation, and his journey would be totally futile. The introduction to the criminal code made clear that the purpose of punishment was not to inflict physical or psychic harm but to correct and "reeducate" the prisoner. In this case, the cancellation would inflict great harm not just on me, but on my innocent family.

"Listen," an officer told me, "we don't wish to cause you any suffering. All this is the consequence of your infractions. Your father bears partial responsibility for those infractions in raising a son to be an enemy of the state. Therefore it seems reasonable that he should bear part of the punishment."

The end result was the cancellation of the scheduled visit – my parents were callously turned away upon their arrival – and it was unclear when the next one could take place. For months, my parents entreated the camp authorities, when at last came a response: "Ask your son." I managed to send them a message through covert channels. "Come on such-and-such a date without giving prior notice." In this way, I thought, we would circumvent the system, as the authorities hopefully would not deny me a visit if my family arrived unexpectedly on the specified day. But it took a month for such messages to arrive, and the thought that I was causing my father to suffer – or that I was shortening his days – oppressed me each and every day.

· · · · ·

As a beginning apprentice, I didn't suffer too badly from the workload. Whenever possible, I would lie down under a tree behind the factory, drinking in the azure of the sky, the white of the clouds, the emerald tints of the grass…until Shimon would shout, "the pigs are coming," to warn me of the guards, and I would rush back to my work station.

The guards Oreshkin and Kosoy ("one-eyed" in Russian) didn't pay us too much attention, preferring to pass the time playing cards with prisoners too weak to work. Almost as soon as he came on duty, Oreshkin would summon a thin, anemic prisoner named Vasilyev by his nickname: "Buchenwald! Bring the cards!"

"Leave me alone," Vasilyev would grumble. "I've had enough."

"C'mon, bring them, or else I'll have to punish you."

This kind of affection was reserved for the ex-Polizei who had collaborated with the Nazis, and who now, almost to a man, displayed fervent Soviet patriotism. Such prisoners would go to lectures on Communist doctrine, vocally praise the Soviet regime, and submit reports on "unreliable" prisoners to the KGB. Gunnar Astra used to call them either "two-legged trash" or "sharp ears" for their knack of showing up in the vicinity to listen the moment you started a conversation with someone. "It must be awhile since you've cleaned your ears," Shimon would say in a loud voice, and they would retreat shamefacedly. The greater their sin against the Soviet regime during the war, the more did they grovel before it today, and the more eagerly did they cooperate with camp authorities. All of the ex-Polizei, without exception, hated Jews, and persecuted them to the best of their abilities.

On my very first day in the camp, I came across the silver-haired Ivan Arzubov, "chief prisoner and superintendent" – in short, an important personality. All the prisoners despised him; for many years his chief occupation had been to inform on others. Due to his "exemplary behavior," the camp authorities recommended his early release from the camp just after my arrival there. At the hearing, the prosecutor asked him, "What did you do before the war?"

"I served as head of the village council."

"And during the war you collaborated with the Nazis?"

"Yes, I served as a regional police commander."

"You must have tortured a large number of people to death."

Silence.

"And where did you work after the war, before your arrest?"

"I was chairman of a kolkhoz."

"And it appears that in the camp, too, you served an important role. How is it, Arzubov, that you always seem to rise to the top?"

"That is my fate, citizen prosecutor." And in a fit of self-pity, he wiped a tear from his cheek.

He was released a year later. Indeed, he had not brought much harm to Soviet rule. All in all, he had perhaps killed several thousand Jews. The night before his release, he sat on his bunk crossing himself and kissing his cross.

The camp elite included two other prisoners: a former KGB lieutenant colonel who had murdered so many men in Stalin's day that during Khrushchev's "Great Thaw" he was sentenced to twenty-five years; and a former commander of a Nazi field police unit. Both worked at the library, "the ideological frontline," disseminating propaganda and interpreting items from the Soviet press. They posted articles about Israel and Zionism on a board, underlining essential passages and phrases: "Zionists and members of religious Jewish circles cooperated with Hitler....";"Jewish capital allowed Hitler to gain power....";"Zionist elements in Israel collaborate with radical totalitarian regimes the world over...."

The former Polizei would taunt Shimon and me: "Jews are at the root of all wars; it's all because of the Jews." The Jews were responsible for all woes. "They robbed us of our gold, and now they flee to Israel." I listened in bewilderment as they claimed that Brezhnev, Gromyko, and the Politburo were Jewish; that the Jews had started the October Revolution in 1917 in order to usurp the reins of power. Others conceded that while Brezhnev himself was no Jew, Jews in scientific centers everywhere were plotting advanced ways of oppressing the Russians and achieving world domination.

Even as the Jews' alleged ambition to dominate the world aroused revulsion, these same prisoners felt proud of Russian expansionism: Soviet military and political power, the conquest of new territories, triumphs in international sport competitions – all these were met with wild enthusiasm. In this respect, they shared the same views as the camp authorities. Soviet propaganda had implanted in jailers and jailed alike the very same opinions. Gunnar Astra liked to count the number of times the word "Russian" was broadcast over the loudspeakers that boomed at full volume all day, chasing away conversations and private thoughts: "The Russian skies," "the Russian nation," "Russian wafers," "Russian tea," "Russian passion," etc., as though no other nation existed on earth.

The educated prisoners, too, thought along similar lines. The camp housed a group of Leningrad academics, supporters of the All-Russian Social-Christian Union for the Liberation of the People, who had been arrested in the mid-1960s. They took up the cause of forcibly replacing the Soviet regime with a Russian state founded on the principles of Christian Socialism, democracy, and tolerance. Yet they proved just as capable of expressing both the most loathsome anti-Semitism and admiration of Nazism. "You brought Communism to the Russian people and now you want to flee? No, you must stay here with us and atone for your sins."

The sum of their subversive, "dangerous" activity had never amounted to much more than a political game: distributing portfolios for the future government they would install, discussing abstract ideas, and composing a manifesto and political platform (years of studying the Communist Party had left their mark). The head of the group, one Igor Ogurtsov, was sentenced to fifteen years; Mikhail Sado, who had also founded the Assyrian national movement, received thirteen years; the others received shorter terms. In camp, members of the Union talked a great deal about Russian history and literature, and the greatness of the Russian people. Like the camp administrators, they hailed the Russian invasion of Czechoslovakia, the threats directed at Poland, and the invasion of Afghanistan.

How is it possible not to remember in this context that from 1917 to 1921 the czarist officer class went over to the side of the Bolsheviks in their struggle against the Social Democrats (the Mensheviks) and the Constitutional Democrats (the so-called Kadets), guided by the belief that only the Bolsheviks were capable of preserving the Russian imperial order. They were proven all too right.

In our camp the only active member of the All-Russian Social-Christian Union was Ivan Ivanov, a scholar of Semitic languages. His friendship was sought by Yuri Galanskov, active in efforts to democratize Soviet law within the extant Communist framework, and a Communist named Yuri Fedorov. A young Estonian fascist named Rayo modified his prison uniform to give it a Nazi look, and joyfully proclaimed his readiness to obey the every command of his personal Fuhrer, Ivanov. (Of Ivanov's effeminate style it must be said that it lent him the appearance not of a fascist leader as much as a priest.) Each day, these three – the ideologue Ivanov, the guard Oreshkin, and the former Polizei Arzubov – would gather by the loudspeaker at the center of the camp and chat about Russia's fate. It was clearer than day that the guards treated the Russian nationalist Ivanov very differently than they treated Grilius and Mendelevich, "enemies of the Russian Empire." In fact, we did not count ourselves among Russia's enemies; we simply longed to be Jews, knowing full well that with our scant knowledge of Hebrew and religion, we had some way to go.

For instance: Shimon asked me to teach him some Hebrew. We had no textbook, only a dictionary. I made some index cards with words and phrases. But I was ignorant of the niceties of Hebrew grammar, and generally felt insecure about the language. So the project faded. We had not yet learned to commit to it fully.

I did have an English textbook and a bulky English-Russian dictionary, and I started to teach myself English at night. Even the guards encouraged me. Surely, a prisoner preoccupied with studying English would not have the time to plot subversive activity. As far as they were concerned, we could have turned the camp into a college for the study of botany or astronomy.

Actually, botany already occupied a place of honor; each prisoner tried to grow some edible vegetable or another. The rules forbade us from growing vegetables or having pets; they likewise forbade us from receiving honey, chocolate, or vitamins. You might say we were forbidden anything that carried a whiff of health or pleasure. But the Soviet guards were as lazy as the Soviet laws were arbitrary, and the prisoner who could maneuver between the laziness of the one and the stringency of the other might be able to steal for himself a bite of forbidden pleasure. A resourceful prisoner could grow an onion, a radish, and some dill in a patch of earth no larger than the palm of his hand. Some even managed to grow a carrot – a pathetic, wan thing, but a carrot nonetheless. The biggest growers were the old nationalists among the Ukrainians, Lithuanians, and Armenians. Generally, the nationalists showed a higher appreciation of life and a more developed ethical sensibility than the criminals who had been arrested for their activities during the war. This, I think, resulted from their confidence in the justice of their cause.

I arrived at the camp just when the stifling air was retreating in the face of the annual resurgence of life-giving foliage. In the center of the camp, a riot of colors had broken out in the flowerbed of Papa Antos, as we called him, a native of Bessarabia who had refused to join the kolkhoz. I'm quite sure that the town adjacent to the camp did not raise finer yields of tomato, radish, lettuce, and onion than ours. How we hurried to gather garbage, our only fertilizer!

Encouraged by the camp administration, the grounds were ornamented by many flowers, which served to distract high-ranking visitors from the general state of filth and neglect of the grounds. For the prisoners, the flowerbeds served to hide the illicit dill, onion, and lettuce. At the beginning of the school year, we would watch the commandant's wife, Anna Mikhilovna, instruct a guard which flowers to pick for her, after which the other staff wives did the same. On September 1, after all, the beginning of the school year, students had to present wreaths to their teachers. "How ironic," Shimon remarked, "that gulag flowers are decorating the schoolhouses."

Shimon and I inherited a small vegetable patch, with sorrel, onion, and an unidentifiable herb, from a Ukrainian prisoner who had been unexpectedly transferred. We had to water and prune our tiny piece of farmland, situated behind the outhouse, and as I tended our patch I felt as lucky as the owner of a sprawling villa.

I was once so absorbed in gardening that I failed to notice the arrival of two ranking officials visiting from Moscow. Lieutenant Colonel Zhervichov, a departmental head within the central camps authority, must have wondered at the sight of a prisoner stripped down to his waist probing around in the earth.

"Prisoner, come here!"

Even from five paces away, I could notice the high-ranking epaulettes glinting in the sun.

"What is that on your head?"

"A yarmulke."

"What? Remove it at once."

"No, I won't remove it."

"I command you to take it off!"

I remained stubbornly silent as he glared at me. Though taken aback by my chutzpah, he didn't want to be drawn into an open confrontation in front of the prisoners who had started to gather around us. "Go put on the jacket of your uniform and appear at headquarters at once," he ordered.

I appeared at headquarters wearing my jacket and a visored hat, to find all the ranking officials there.

"Remove your cap."

I did so. Under the hat I had on my kippah.

"Take that thing off!"

I refused.

"Explain this impertinent disobedience!"

"The Jewish faith forbids me from going bareheaded."

At this, the lieutenant colonel signaled two thuggish guards to forcibly remove it. They were of course far stronger than I was. Though my whole being burned with humiliation, I neither shouted nor cursed. Instead, I put my hat back on, and noted that the Germans had tortured Jews for refusing to take off their hats.

"You're not being punished because you're a Jew, but because of disorderly conduct. Now go. You will be punished for insubordination."

I was distressed only by the thought that now they might cancel my next family visit. Back at the barracks, I was greeted with a barrage of questions and expressions of concern. Vladilen (named after Vladimir Lenin) Pavlen-kov approached: "In several hours I have a meeting with the famous Jewish orchestra conductor Schwarz, who will be traveling soon to America. (He had been granted an exit visa thanks to our struggle.) I'll tell him how they forcibly removed your yarmulke."

As I walked to work the next morning, Schwarz called to me from the barracks roof. "I'll give a report to Moscow. And greetings from your father."

I stitched myself a new kippah. Amazingly enough, the promised punishment didn't materialize. Apparently our case was still too fresh, and the authorities weren't eager to provoke a new wave of condemnation in the Western press. The authorities weren't alone in their respect for the influence of Western opinion. Not infrequently an older prisoner would say, "They haven't released you yet?" or "Look, he's still here." They imagined that once the West had taken up your cause, the authorities in Moscow would capitulate at once. "You'll see, you'll be in Israel in a month." I heard that sentence at least once during each of my 3,863 days in prison. Fortunately, I didn't believe it, for if I had, I'd have certainly gone raving mad. It seems likely that had the outcry continued after the death sentences in our case were commuted, we'd have been released. But the uproar had died down after the sentences were changed. If the authorities had indeed issued special instructions for our treatment, we certainly never felt it.

· · · · ·

I waited with great impatience for my parents' first visit. I had to persuade the guard, or the supervisor of the visitors' booth, to let me take some of the food that would be brought for me back to the barracks – a significant addition to our very modest kosher diet. This was strictly forbidden. The supervisor was a former Polizei nicknamed the Son of Belial (Hebrew for "scoundrel"), who was capable of selling out his own father. Shimon bribed him with the offer of ten rubles and a small portion of the food.

In the end, they exacted their revenge for the kippah incident by allowing a visit of only a single day. The head of the camp, Captain Garkushov, had explained the matter in the plainest terms: "In cases of outstanding accomplishment (i.e., collaboration with the KGB), you get a three-day visit; if you stay on good terms with the administration (i.e., collaboration with the interior ministry), a two-day visit will be approved; and if all you can say for yourself is that you haven't violated regulations, you get a day." I was lucky to get even a day. "Not including work hours," he added.

Since the camp day included ten hours of work and six of sleep, that left only eight hours of twenty-four for a visit after a year of separation, and only

God knew when we would have the chance to meet again. "I demand to have the meeting on a day when I'm not working," I said.

"But your parents have already agreed; they're here waiting. If you start making demands, you won't get a visit at all."

"You've tricked my parents. They didn't know that they could have requested to see me on a day off."

"You have to decide: either you see them like this, or you don't see them at all."

I stormed out of the office. What could I do? At the entrance to the visitors' booth I found the short sergeant who had searched me the day of my arrival. He treated me more agreeably than other guards did. "Listen, let me in to say two words to my father." After some hesitation, he agreed, and we entered together. My father ran towards me, but I stayed unmoving. That had been the sergeant's condition for letting me in.

"Why did you agree to a visit on a workday?" I asked him.

"They told us there was no alternative," my father replied.

"Request a meeting on a day I don't work. I'll wait."

The door clicked shut behind me, and I returned to camp heavy hearted, wondering whether I should have accepted the abbreviated visit offered to me. I sat down to write complaints to the usual authorities, but even before I could finish, I got word that the matter had been decided: I would be permitted a full-day's visit without having to go to work.

The visit was heartbreaking: embraces, kisses, tears, as though I had returned from the afterlife. And who knew if we would see each other again? (In all my years in the gulag, I would see my father only once more.) My stepmother plied me with the kosher food they'd brought, my father showered me with news from the outside: who had received exit visas, what they were reporting from Israel. On a piece of thin paper, I recorded conditions in the camp and described the kippah episode. I handed it to my mother, and she concealed it. Suspecting that we were being listened to, we turned up the radio and passed notes to one another.

I learned to my amazement that my father, despite his three heart attacks, had taken my place in the Zionist movement. He told me that just as that year's commemoration at Rumbuli was set to begin, a column of tanks emerged from the adjacent army base for maneuvers, stirring up an awful din. The cemetery was spread out over an enormous area, and my father led the group to the Children's Grave at the back. The memorial began again, only to be interrupted once more by the arrival of security agents.

My father was standing next to Jean Lipka, a Latvian who had saved forty Jews during the war. "I know these types," Jean remarked. "They're the same types who used to come around hunting Jews in the days of Hitler." (The following year, my father was placed under house arrest before the Rumbuli anniversary to prevent his attendance.)

Our meeting, though brief, buttressed us with hope, and reminded us that we could rely on one another absolutely.

· · · · ·

After the meeting, camp life resumed, and letters became the only connection to home, to friends, to the Jewish people, and to the outside world.

One month after my parents' visit, I received my first letter. It arrived from Israel, and heralded great news: Jews continued to receive exit visas, and Eva, Rivka, and Rivka's husband Chaim Drori were studying at an ulpan in Dimona. The letter was accompanied by a postcard in vibrant colors depicting a celebration of Israel's Independence Day outside a synagogue in Tiberias.

I shared the postcard with Grilius, who had never seen one from Israel, and we in turn secretly showed it to some Ukrainian and Latvian nationalists, who started to see Israel as a symbol of national self-determination. In admiring tones, they told us that all the doctors in the ranks of the Ukrainian Insurgent Army had been Jews. "If the tiny Jewish people can establish and defend its own country, we can surely found an independent Ukraine." Because these nationalists occupied an important place in the camp hierarchy, their newfound respect for us acted as a counterweight to the Jew-hatred that characterized the group of former Polizei. The cook Vasil Pidgorodetski, a nationalist whose twenty-five-year stay in the gulag had not dulled his sharp Ukrainian humor, was the one who had agreed to help Grilius and me keep kosher.

Things greatly improved with the arrival of Hillel Shur and Eliezer Trachtenburg (today a mathematics professor in the US). Although their case was intimately bound up with ours, the authorities had artificially separated them, and they had been tried in Kishinev, rather than in Leningrad as we had. Those tried in Kishinev were natives of Bessarabia who had studied in Leningrad and had affiliated with the Leningrad Zionists. On completing their studies, they had returned to Kishinev and founded a network of ulpans.

The interrogations and awful conditions at the Kishinev prison had left Hillel and Eliezer utterly depleted. Many of their colleagues, shocked to discover that studying Hebrew had landed them in prison, had not comported themselves well during the interrogation and trial. After the trial, therefore, a kind of trial by peers was held by Kishinev Zionists under the direction of Aharon Shpilberg. Its operating principle was: you must be morally worthy of living in Israel. Those defendants who had failed the test, it was decided, would have to tell the truth and express remorse upon arriving in Israel. Everyone accepted the verdict. But when Hillel and Eliezer arrived in camp, they still carried the mindset of this trial by peers, and eyed new acquaintances with some degree of suspicion, as if to say: "And how did you act under interrogation?"

Shimon initially treated them like heroes, and accepted them as brothers. They'd heard good things about me from Shpilberg, and our relationship soon blossomed. Shimon, however, liked to pick fights, the stormier the better, and in the camp any fight threatened to escalate into something more. I would often find myself in the thankless role of mediator and peacemaker.

The main argument centered on the question of the role of ethics in camp, where human relations are like nowhere else, and where social significance attaches to the smallest gesture. Let's say, for instance, that you drink tea with someone. Elsewhere, this fact might be insignificant and forgotten the next day. Here, however, it announced your political worldview. Hundreds of pairs of eyes followed your every move: what you eat, how you sleep, when you go to the toilet, what you read, and how diligently you follow the orders of camp officials. Everyone knows whether you're a coward or a decent man, a straight shooter or a sly trickster – "rotten," to use camp parlance.

The "rotten" prisoner accepts tea from security officials and agrees to work overtime for Lenin's birthday, while scorning the Soviet state in private. Then there are those who buy extra food from the guards; these are called "fish." The important thing is to take a consistent stand in relation to the internal rules, and to declare one's stand clearly and openly. There are those who refuse to obey the rules; a Jew, of course, must obey the halachah. But how could Shimon and I know the halachah? There was no one to ask.

Over time, a prisoner develops a way of accommodating to camp life in accordance with his ethical principles. He must stick firmly to those principles while at the same time not harming himself. (Such constant weighing of priorities and values proved exceedingly difficult for me.) On one side, a line separates principled courage from stubborn foolishness, and on the other, another line marks off justified caution and self-preservation from cowardice. In not straying over these lines, I tried to retain my dignity – and that of my people.

Take an example: greeting the commandant. Is this a gesture of shameful groveling, or one of justified self-preservation? Answering such a question requires knowing something about what awaits the prisoner who refuses to comply with "internal regulations." One clause of those regulations stipulates that a disobedient prisoner may earn himself the right to solitary confinement in a cell of two meters square for the entire duration of his term (up to fifteen years). The prisoner thus confined is to be denied letters, newspapers, radio, walks, visitations, and conversations with other inmates. He may sleep and use the toilet only during designated hours. His food rations are 1,600 calories a day. On "bad" days, he receives bread, salt, and water. On "good" days: bread, water, forty grams of fish, thirty grams of grits, and two hundred grams of potatoes. Cell temperature remains at about eight degrees Celsius. The prisoner is not permitted a mattress, pillow, blanket, coat, or hat.

Now, in light of all this, and in light of the probability that you will be punished if you refuse, should you greet the commandant? You must calculate that probability and measure it against the international significance of the Soviet Jewry movement, the level of support you can expect from your fellow prisoners, as well as your own determination and stamina. You feel yourself to be on a knife's edge as you gauge all this, for you also see yourself not as a submissive slave but as a descendent of the Maccabees, as heir to the fighters of Beitar. So, do you greet the commandant, or not?

A further question: should you attend the camp's politics classes? The views of two men whose courage was unquestioned – Shimon and Hillel – differed on the matter. On the one hand, such classes are a formal requirement, devoid of all substance, a duty of all Soviet citizens, from the minister down to the lowliest prisoner. The camp's political education courses included lectures on Communism. Is it wise to take one's stand over such nonsense that no one takes seriously? On the other hand, as a Jew who recognizes no other faith than his faith in the Almighty, can I subject myself to Communist sermonizing and indoctrination? On this question, Shimon and I decided not to attend such classes; Eliezer and Hillel did participate. "And why not?" they said. "You can attend without listening."

"Cowards! You're harming the dignity of the Jewish people."

"How so?"

"We must prove that we are not slaves." Such exchanges were fraught with pain and fury.

· · · · ·

"I have a visit coming up," Hillel said to me one day. "If you'd like to pass something to the outside, put it down on a piece of paper."

Indeed, I did have something to say. My sister Meri had been released from camp just before her son Yigal was born in January 1971. Aryeh Khnokh, her husband, was still imprisoned. I thought she should leave the country at once, before the authorities changed their minds, but she had been denied an exit visa. So I wrote a letter to Brezhnev's wife: "Do you want to compel me to once again take desperate measures?" I wanted to smuggle my letter out.

Hillel himself had prepared far more serious material. He had memorized his interrogators' openly anti-Semitic outbursts and various violations of the law, and had subsequently written them down in list form. Despite the many searches, he had managed to smuggle this list with him into the camp, and Eliezer, who could compress sentences into the tiniest handwriting, had copied it onto cigarette paper. As he was copying, I had stood watch, on the lookout for guards. The cigarette paper was tightly rolled and inserted into a quarter loaf of bread. We had received word that Rosa Lipin, Hillel's mother, was due to visit. Rosa had assisted her father in underground Zionist activities in the 1930s, and we had no doubt she would agree to pass along our material.

Hillel was taken to the meeting straight from work to prevent him from taking anything along, but he had the paper roll with him at all times precisely for such eventualities.

"May I use the toilet before the meeting?"

"Fine, but hurry."

Hillel inserted the paper into his anus. At the visitor's booth, the usual strip search was conducted, and he was made to bend over. Luckily, the list was not discovered, and it would later be published in the West. When Rosa left the visitor's booth, Shimon and I presented her a bouquet of camp flowers. (I would get them back from her, in dried form, on the day of my release years later.) In return, she gave us a basket of apples, but a guard snatched them from her hands, and cast the fruit to the ground.

• • • • •

This is perhaps the appropriate place to tell the story of how Hillel rescued a Hebrew textbook called *My Teacher* from the clutches of the KGB. The book had been confiscated during a search conducted in the home of a student of one of the underground ulpans, and was then sent to the central state library. Hillel filed a petition with the prosecutor: "If the book in question has been deposited at the library, then it must be permissible to use it. If, however, it is permissible to use it, on what grounds was the book confiscated in the first place?" The astonished prosecutor instructed that the book be returned – not to its original owner but to Hillel. And that was how we came to have with us in camp a Hebrew textbook with the imprimatur of a state institution, thereby ensuring that it could not be confiscated.

Eliezer had started to teach Hillel some Hebrew on the train journey, and continued after they had arrived at the camp. For both, the process of study itself held greater significance than the end result. Upon returning from work, Hillel would scan the paper and then settle down to study. Shimon pored over Hebrew words and sentences, and even did homework I had assigned him. Eliezer studied mathematics, and I learned Hebrew and English. Our choices of how to spend our free time differed in this respect from other prisoners, who napped, tapped out domino games over long tables, played cards, and sipped tea.

· · · · ·

Tea in the gulag is a subject entire unto itself. Camp tea is prepared in an especially strong way – fifty grams to a cup – which, at that concentration, has the addictive effects of a mild drug. Thus tea becomes a currency of commerce and bribes.

Until 1978, tea was sold without restriction at the camp canteen. The average tea drinker required some thirty grams a day. But if a prisoner spent his monthly food allowance on tea, he had nothing left over for bread or margarine.

In fact it was easy to identify the tea addict: wiry build, fatigued appearance, tattered uniform, smoking homemade cigarettes of cheap tobacco rolled in newspaper, and always trying to mooch something to eat. His day begins with tea anxiety, which grows sharper toward the end of the month as his allowance peters out. Just after waking up, he hurries, glass in hand, to a friend. "Senya, have you got a little tea?"

"I gave it to Petya earlier in the month."

The two of them shuffle over to Petya, and ask for some tea. "I've got enough for one cup. For the other, we'll 'recycle.'" Recycled tea is tea that is boiled for a second time after it has already been used. Our two prisoners are satisfied.

Drinking brings pleasure in the first stages of addiction, after which ever larger doses and ever higher concentrations are needed to satisfy the craving. Hence, the addict forced to go without tea for a full day is beset by headaches.

Though the preparation of tea is technically forbidden, the authorities look the other way. Their attitude bears some similarity to the attitude toward vodka outside camp: better that people drink themselves into a stupor than engage in politics. Tea is stewed in a wood-heated iron oven; while flames dance above the twigs, sticks, and newspaper, prisoners wait patiently in a long line. Three tins are placed inside the oven, and when the water boils, a measure of tea (the equivalent of a matchbox) is poured into each. After a few minutes, the tins are taken out with the aid of thick, singed gloves, and after the tea leaves have settled they are taken ceremoniously to the barracks. Here, each prisoner gets a candy (rather than a lump of sugar), the mug is passed around, and tea is sipped over conversation about the price of meat or the national struggle.

An outsider can't possibly fathom the complexities of this ritual. Where do you drink? Will there be enough for another round? One serving of tea will get your boots repaired. Two can be exchanged for a tomato from Papa Antos's garden. But how does one get the tea? Steal it? Indeed, whoever can, steals. Once they discovered a tunnel leading to the canteen; all that engineering know-how directed at stealing tea. It is possible, too, to earn tea, which is a common currency in which KGB informers are paid. I remember a KGB man arriving once with a bag bursting with packages of tea. "So you've brought salaries," I quipped. He didn't find it amusing.

Informers would return to the barracks satisfied with their earnings of fifty or a hundred grams of tea. I once argued about this with a dissident who told me, "I went in to the KGB officer, told him to give me some tea, and he did."

"You shouldn't have taken it," I said.

"Why not?"

I felt we should resist getting used to accepting their gifts. With a wolf's cunning, they sensed that a man – no matter how independent – who accepts such a gift already shows signs of rottenness. "I won't accept their tea, period. And I also won't drink with you."

"As you wish. But you really ought to get off your high horse."

It seemed so clear-cut to me, but trying to explain my position to others was something else. Then again, does one always need to explain oneself? And what if the person to whom you're trying to explain oneself is an informer?

We Jews would prepare tea only for Shabbat. Eliezer and Hillel had by this time received packages. In general, only a prisoner who had served more than half of his sentence could get packages, and they had been sentenced to two

With my father Moshe, my mother Chaya, and my two sisters, Eva and Rebecca, in a park in Riga in 1957. Six months later my father was arrested and a year and a half later my mother passed away.

In Riga with members of the Jewish underground, 1968

Headstone in memory of mass extermination in Rumbula, Riga, 1965. Rumbula was also the site of the Riga Jewish movement's revival.

With friends at the wedding of my sister. Among those later arrested: my sister Meri, her husband Aryeh, and to my left, Yisrael Zalmanson.

Perm 36 Labor Camp (photographed in 1972). In the center, the hut in which I was imprisoned. Photo taken from the guard post.

The prisoner's gaze a few hours after his release from prison, March 1981

Beit Hatfutsot, Tel Aviv, at an exhibition commemorating forty years of the struggle for aliyah. I am looking at a drawing of an exercise yard in Chistopol prison. It was there that I gave the text of Kaddish to Natan Sharansky.

The code name for the hijacking had been Operation Wedding – and here I am like a bridegroom being carried on the shoulders of the people welcoming me at Israel's Ben-Gurion Airport.

My first request – to pray at the Kotel. I am pouring out all my hardships to G-d.

Menachem Begin also served time in a KGB prison. He received me as a friend.

With President Reagan, Vice President Bush, and Avital Sharansky at the White House, 1981
Courtesy of the Ronald Reagan Library

Reception in New York, 1981. One hundred thousand Jews came to rejoice in my release. To my left, the US advisor on national security, Richard Allen.

Receiving an honorary doctorate at Yeshiva University

This really is a wedding: my bride, Katy Seroussy, an activist in Shomer Achi Anochi for the release of Prisoners of Zion

Immediately after the wedding, back to the struggle: my new bride and me at a demonstration in support of Natan Sharansky's release; with Rabbi Avi Weiss and Glen Richter.

The president of the national association of olim from the Soviet Union during the great wave of aliyah, together with Ephraim Kholmyansky and Knesset member Victor Brailovsky, both former Prisoners of Zion

Receiving rabbinical ordination, 1986. Left to right: Rabbi Shimon Grilius, Rabbi Aaron Rakeffet-Rothkoff, Rabbi Haskel Lookstein and myself.

With Chief Rabbi Mordechai Eliyahu (of blessed memory) during the wedding of one of my children

With my students, Russian immigrants I teach in Jerusalem's Machon Meir Yeshiva, at Me'arat Hamachpelah (Cave of the Patriarchs)

Speaking during a Jewish Agency Board of Governors Assembly at a ceremony in honor of those involved in Operation Wedding. Seated at the table: Natan Sharansky, Yuli Edelstein, and the chairman of the Board of Governors.

Courtesy of Mark Kruglyak

At an exhibition of a small tallit and kippah that I made in prison.
Courtesy of the Wolfson Museum of Jewish Art

years. (I would receive my first package in 1976, six years after my arrest.) For Shabbat, Shimon, our resident chef, would prepare omelets from powdered eggs (made in Israel) and onions fried in soy sauce (also from Israel). To this he would add soup, prepared from soup cubes, and salted fish. In short, a royal feast.

On Fridays, we had to prepare our work quotas for Shabbat. I could usually fulfill the quota of an eight-hour shift in seven hours, since I didn't bother too much about the quality of the gloves that flew off my sewing machine. We would hide the Shabbat quota, telling the supervisor where to find it the next day. Finishing work, we would gather wood to heat the oven, taking care to hide the stash so it wouldn't be confiscated in the event of a search. Fortunately, Friday was shower day; I soon got used to communal showering in the steam-filled washroom.

Then we would rush to the oven to prepare our food. At last, the sun set, and four Jews, decked out in our Shabbat finest (which wasn't saying much) sat around a table, surrounded by some fifty prisoners chatting, cursing, throwing glances our way. And yet, from the moment we recited the prayers, a Shabbat serenity descended upon us and made us feel as though we were elsewhere, greeting the holy day of rest together with our brethren. We would bless the bread and raisins (our substitute for wine), and if one of us had received a letter from Israel or from home, it, too, would sanctify the day. We had no sacred texts, and couldn't learn Torah together, but one way or another our conversation would circle back to the same question: What is the meaning of being a Jew?

Most weeks, however, just when the atmosphere of Shabbat began to draw us in, two guards would burst through the barracks door. "What kind of gathering is this? Disperse!" Prisoners were allowed to eat in the barracks, but not to gather in groups of more than three. Someone had taken the trouble of tattling on us. The former Polizei taunted us. "Not letting you celebrate again, huh?" Their eyes betrayed not just wrath, but also envy of the very existence of Jews faithful to themselves and their tradition. Our home was bright and our faith solid; their corner was dark, devoid of both hope and faith. For all their plentiful food and lard and butter and vodka, they sensed that our modest Shabbat table was infinitely richer. They wondered at these strange people so faithful to their traditions. "Do you avoid pork because it is unhealthy? Do you avoid work on Shabbat in order to rest? Do you pray out of fear? Do you want to go to Israel in order to exploit Arabs? Explain yourselves. Why is all this necessary?"

"God has commanded it."

"That's it? You must be hiding something. There must be some rational explanation. How do you explain it to yourself?"

"I don't explain. I believe. Every man has the capacity for belief. Every man is aware of his Creator, though he may sometimes conceal that awareness even from himself."

• • • • •

The next morning, we had to go to work. Shimon and I had mulled over whether we should go to the factory on Saturdays. I decided it was best not to provoke the authorities needlessly, that Shabbat was between us and God, and that there was no need to involve the entire administration in our day of rest. So, like the conversos of old, we would go to the factory and only pretend to work. There we sat amidst the buzz of activity, a rest that was no rest. During the morning inspection, the guards would come to my workstation and stare at me as I pretended to be occupied. Sometimes they would move on, and sometimes they would say, "Mendelevich, why aren't you working?"

"But I am working."

"You're not. We see everything. You'll be punished. And take that thing off your head."

I am silent. My name seems foreign on their lips. I must do what I must do, and you can do as you please, I think to myself. It's a war of wills. I will not react or take their bait. I will not give them that pleasure. But neither will I work. I cannot desecrate the Shabbat. I cannot be otherwise than who I am.

The war of wills ended in my victory. For seven years, week after week, they gave in. Shimon, on the other hand, often lost patience. "This Shabbat I refuse to go to the factory."

"But in refusing you're starting a quarrel in my name, too," I said. "You have only three years left to serve; I've got ten."

"I still don't think this is the right approach. I'm not afraid of them and their threats."

"Neither am I afraid. But we must not provoke them needlessly."

But Shimon persisted, and so they dragged him into solitary confinement until Hillel and I persuaded him to resume the old approach.

In midwinter, the pilot Mark Dymshits arrived at our camp. Along with Hillel Butman and Misha Korn, he had been held in Leningrad, and then in the KGB prison in Mordovia for half a year longer than the others. The entire time, the KGB had tried to "reeducate" them, hoping to extract an expression of remorse.

Misha was scared to death. One day, after hours of interrogations, he sat on his bed in utter silence.

"What's the matter? Do you still fear execution? They've sentenced you to seven years."

"My friends, I've agreed to cooperate with the KGB."

"In other words, you're making your own life easier at our expense."

"No, no, I won't inform on you." But how was it possible to tell who he would denounce, and who not? And Misha had seemed so brave, his eyes had burned with such Zionist idealism…

Mark, on the other hand, had changed not at all. Still sturdy, still steady. "Do you not regret joining me?" he asked.

"What? I thank God I met you," I replied.

Camp life is especially hard on a pilot. He was assigned tree-cutting labor in the minus thirty degree Celsius conditions. In the evening, as we were being taken back from the factory, he was still outside sawing trees. When he finally returned to the barracks, he would collapse onto his bed exhausted. As a former soldier, he wasn't used to Shabbat meals, but over time he too joined our Shabbat rhythms.

· · · · ·

The month of Kislev arrived. At Hillel's urging, we wrote to the commandant to request permission to celebrate Chanukah. Captain Garkushev, his face blotched by chronic drunkenness, summoned us to his office.

"What kind of a holiday is this Cha-NU-kah?" He stressed the middle syllable.

"It marks the victory of the Jews over the Greeks in the second century BCE."

"If it's not a Soviet holiday, I cannot allow it."

Our appeals to the prosecutor, the central camps authority, and elsewhere were denied.

"How did you plan to celebrate?" asked Captain Byelov, who played the "good cop" to Garkushev's "bad cop." "We're not opposed to Jewish holidays, you see. But what would things look like if we allowed every ethnic group to celebrate its own holidays?"

"But every other group does celebrate its holidays. Only Jewish holidays are excluded."

Byelov proceeded to lecture us on camp ethics. "Don't you know the unwritten rule: Never whine about what someone else gets."

"Well, we didn't intend anything out of the ordinary. But this is our national holiday. Imagine the response when Jews abroad learn that we weren't permitted to celebrate it."

"Don't threaten us with your Jews. The Soviet Union does not fear Jews – even Jews."

And yet we remained determined to celebrate. I procured some candles, and Shimon had a Lithuanian prisoner named Kadzhionis carve a tiny *chanukiyah* (or candelabrum) and dreidel out of wood. The *chanukiyah* was only ten centimeters long, which would allow us to smuggle it out of the factory. On the first night of the holiday, we were prepared for anything, but no guard intruded into the barracks, so we lit the first candle and enjoyed a meal. It was only a pity that we had no potatoes with which to make latkes. We even dared to go to the empty dining hall to play dreidel, using matches for our Chanukah gelt. We returned to the courtyard in high spirits. "One day, we'll celebrate in Jerusalem!" At that, we broke into song, belting out every Hebrew song we knew.

• • • • •

Several days later I am called to a family visit. What has happened that my parents would travel several hundred kilometers to see me for a few hours in the presence of a guard? It must be something important.

Embraces and handshakes are not allowed, so we smile at one another. "Your grandfather Aharon was a pious man," my father begins, "but he never fasted more than three days." It seems he wanted to tell me about a hunger strike. Aharon could only be Shpilberg. He must be starting a hunger strike.

The guard would not allow us to use Yiddish. We'd have to say what needed to be said in plain Russian. Referring to Aharon's daughter, I said, "And how is Yocheved? Is she pleased with her father?" A twinkle in my father's eye signaled that I had guessed right.

"She's pleased, but he spares no pity on himself. It's not good." Ah, so my father opposes the hunger strike. But I wonder about the purpose of the strike.

"Perhaps there's a reason he's being so merciless with himself," I say. "Maybe he's not happy at work and wants to leave it?" (I meant to ask whether he'd requested transfer to another camp.)

"No, his work is fine. He's planning to mark his wedding anniversary."

This raises the guard's suspicions. He calls in the sergeant from the next room, and they both listen in. But the news is clear: Aharon is calling for a hunger strike to begin on December 24, 1971, the anniversary of our trial. My father wishes both to inform me of it, and to register his opposition to my participation. "Everyone is writing now to Leonid," he adds, "to inform him that they can no longer continue their friendship with him, since it's impossible to befriend both Leonid and Iziya." I understand this to mean that those who are joining the collective strike are writing to Brezhnev to renounce their Soviet citizenship and to say that they recognize only Israeli citizenship.

Now I permit myself to ask about the family. "Does Meri still live in Tivon? And how is Yigal?"

"Stop speaking in code," the guard barks.

"What code?"

"Tivon, Yigal – what is that?"

"The names of a town and a boy."

"Another foreign word and I'm terminating this meeting."

It was to be one of the last times I saw my father.

· · · · ·

Aharon was being held at Camp 17, only a hundred meters or so from ours. From the small hill near the watch tower, you could make out prisoners on the second floor of their barracks. We tried to signal them in Morse code using our arms: one wave – dot; two waves – dash. On our side no one other than Shimon knew Morse code, and we weren't sure whether anyone in the adjacent camp would see our frantic arm waving. It turns out that Yuri Fedorov, a former police captain, did see our signals; but so did the Camp 17 watch tower, which contacted the guards in our camp, and I just had time to warn Shimon as they came running and ended our experiment.

In the end, without being able to consult the others, we decided to begin a hunger strike. We prepared detailed statements that described the trial and requested immediate permission to emigrate to Israel. "As I regard Israel as my homeland," I wrote, "I no longer wish to remain a citizen of a Soviet state that condemns its Jewish community to discrimination, anti-Semitism, and forced assimilation. I hereby renounce my Soviet citizenship, and declare myself a citizen of Israel."

The authorities did not react in the slightest. In subsequent years, every "Prisoner of Zion Day," I would send out a similar statement, but with each passing year they got shorter. Eventually, my annual statement consisted of two sentences: one renouncing my Soviet citizenship, and another insisting on our right to leave the country. I had become fed up with wasting my breath, with the futility of sending these texts into oblivion. Only it turns out that the KGB had all along been acutely sensitive to our statements, and starting in 1980 such anti-Soviet expressions would be harshly punished.

After we had completed our hunger strike, we wished to publicize it. One of the only ways of communicating with the outside was through the hospital, located close to Women's Camp 3, where Ruth Alexanderovich and Sylva Zalmanson were held, and Camp 5 for foreigners. This single hospital served the four Mordovian camps, and was the only place where prisoners from different camps could meet and exchange information.

Hillel Shur suffered from chronic stomach ulcers, and was listed for medical care, which he got several months later. He took with him to the hospital the announcements of our hunger strike and of our appeal to the Knesset to recognize us as Israeli citizens. (The law affirming this was passed by the Knesset on June 13, 1972, a year after our imprisonment.) He didn't really hope to receive medical treatment, nor did he. Gulag medicine couldn't be simpler: either you die, or recover on your own. But Hillel did receive abundant news about our colleagues in other camps. Once he climbed onto the hospital roof to talk with Sylva, who reported that hunger strikes had taken place in each of the camps, leaving the KGB to wonder how we had coordinated. He also managed to see Eduard Kuznetsov and Yakov Suslensky, who mentioned that prisoners in Camp 3 had started receiving letters from Israel.

Soon enough, we too began to get batches of letters from Israel, which the guards would have been happy to burn were it not for special instructions from Moscow. And so every Friday we would hear: "Shur, Trachtenburg, Mendelevich, Grilius: come to the censor." The censor, Buyanov, treated us not only to letters, but to notices of confiscated post.

Receiving or sending mail proved no less convoluted than arranging visitations. Legally, a prisoner held under "special conditions" was permitted to send two letters a month, and to receive as many as arrived. Corresponding with another prisoner was forbidden unless the correspondents were related. Camp administrators were obligated to post a letter within three days of receiving it from the prisoner. These matters were spelled out in Article 30 of the "Penal and Reeducation Code of the USSR."

Now try to imagine a dialogue between me and operational division head Lieutenant Rozhkov.

"Why are you violating Article 30 by refusing to give me my letters?"

"The clause is to be interpreted as granting the camp administration the power to permit the prisoner to receive letters. If we have the power to permit it, then we also have the power not to permit it."

"The law does not grant you the power to permit it or not; it grants the prisoner the right to receive letters. It does not say that prisoners may receive letters only at the administrator's discretion."

"You know too much, Mendelevich. As long as I have power, I decide whether to pass along letters."

Powerful reasoning, indeed.

A prisoner in solitary confinement cannot send letters, although in a camp where "special conditions" apply, he may send one letter every two months. If he does not send it at the right time, his right to send it does not roll over to the next month.

Internal regulations require all correspondence to pass the censor. Any letter containing the following is confiscated: information that cannot be made public; details about the camp itself, including its staff, location, and number of prisoners; news of uprisings, natural disasters, or epidemics; encoded information; anything deemed to distort Soviet reality; pornographic material; impermissible attachments like currency or products. In short, the prisoner may describe neither the conditions of his life nor his thoughts. The fate of his letter depends solely on the censor, who operates not according to the law but according to the latest covert instructions from Moscow. If he wishes to confiscate a letter, he will have no trouble finding a legal provision to do so. But of course any letter must pass through not one but multiple layers of censorship: in Moscow, at the district level, at the central camp administration, and finally at the camp itself. In most cases, the prisoner will not even receive the mandatory notice that a letter has been confiscated. In the best of cases, he will receive one such notice for every ten letters confiscated.

The notion that a stranger's eyes will be scanning the intimate lines you have filled with affection and homesickness disgusts you and drains your will to write letters in the first place. An officer even has the right to summon a prisoner to discuss a letter. Imagine receiving a letter, only to have to discuss with a member of authority the intricacies of your relationship with your wife.

The law grants you the right to receive letters, and the law takes it away, in which case your only alternatives are to write complaints, argue with officers, or announce a hunger strike – in other words, an exhausting daily struggle. For how can you give up on getting a letter from your father, or a letter on matters of faith, or a postcard from Israel? How can you reconcile yourself to the knowledge that of the hundred letters sent to you by Jewish schoolchildren in England you've received not a single one?

"Why do you tell us that no one sends us letters?" Boris Penson once asked a senior interior ministry official. "Better simply to admit that you steal them."

"And what of it? You can report it to the West, if you'd like, but either way we won't pass along your letters." They did not expect Boris to pass to the West a detailed account of being denied letters, including that very conversation. He did so through his mother, whom he managed to meet before she left for Israel.

It would have been better had they forbade all correspondence, or allowed just one letter a year. But each letter sent and never received caused profound suffering.

At a meeting with American Jews I was invited to address after my release in 1981, I was once asked whether the gulag was as bad as all that. "After all, they didn't murder their prisoners." Why should they have murdered us, I replied. Only to cause another international outcry? It was more effective to wear us down with petty battles over another ten grams of bread, another line of a letter, another minute of being with your family.

One way to cope is to cease caring: if a letter arrives, fine; if not, never mind. But you cannot instruct your soul to stop loving, hoping, expecting. Thus for me, the only way to cope was by means of the faith that far from standing alone, subject to the authorities' every whim, I belonged to a great and noble people. This hard-won awareness came to me not by means of theoretical reflection, but through solitary suffering. Like every Jew in the Soviet Union, I had felt alone and disconnected, but through my pain I prayed for the chance to join myself to the corpus of the Jewish people.

But this is getting ahead of myself, for we were still in our first year of imprisonment, and had not yet learned how to comport ourselves or to control our spirits.

Eliezer Trachtenburg was summoned to the censor's office one day. He was married not long before his arrest, and letters were a sore point for him. Only after a year did he begin to receive letters from his young wife, and even then for every letter he received another was confiscated.

"Sign here! A letter from your wife was confiscated on the grounds that it contained unpublishable material."

"But what could she possibly disclose? Did she try to pass me a military secret? To inform me of a planned assault on the camp by Israeli paratroops?"

"You may file a complaint with the prosecutor, if you wish."

"At least write to my wife explaining the reasons for confiscation. Otherwise she'll continue to write whatever she's writing without knowing that her letters aren't getting through."

"We don't owe anyone an explanation. It is her responsibility to know the rules."

"But she's not in prison. How can you expect her to observe camp regulations?"

"If she continues to write what she's writing, she'll end up in prison too."

For days afterwards, Eliezer paced through the barracks, from wall to wall, chain-smoking, dusting his clothing white from repeated brushes with the wall plaster. Finally he got word from his father that his wife Tanya was planning to visit. On the appointed day, Eliezer gave the camp officers no rest. "Has my wife arrived yet?"

"She's here," Captain Garkushev said, "but we can't allow a meeting. The time hasn't yet come."

"Not true. It's been four months since our last meeting."

"And there should be six months between visits."

"Allow the meeting, or compensate her for the three hundred rubles she spent on the journey to Mordovia from Kishinev."

"It is we who decide if you deserve a visit or not. Your wife can come another time." Then he turned his back and sat on an empty beer crate to watch a half-drunk tractor driver who was trying to repair his tractor. Garkushev, who had himself worked as a mechanic, appeared far more interested in the repairs than in continuing the conversation with Eliezer.

Eliezer returned to the barracks furious, vowing to begin a hunger strike. We tried to dissuade him. He had only a year left to serve. We tried to cajole Captain Byelov into permitting a meeting between Eliezer and his wife. We hinted at passing word of it to the West. Nothing helped.

I gloomily thought about my own twelve-year sentence, and about how a hunger strike could be very risky for me. Who knew how long it might last? And yet I also felt that this was not Eliezer's problem to bear alone, and so I announced that I would join his proposed strike and sat down to write a declaration.

Shimon decided to join, too, but wanted to know how long we thought it would last.

"Until the authorities give in, or the strike poses a danger to our lives."

We began the strike, and stopped going to the dining hall. A guard would visit the barracks ten times a day: "Why aren't you in the dining hall?"

"We're on hunger strike."

"Why?"

"It's all explained in the declaration."

"I haven't heard about any declaration. If you don't want to eat, don't eat. You can rot to hell for all I care."

Despite the strike, we had to go to work as always, otherwise we'd be put into solitary confinement, where we would suffer both hunger and bitter cold. On the fourth day of fasting, you begin to experience severe dizziness, feebleness, and alternating waves of warmth and chills. We couldn't go to work in that state.

Captain Tokhtachev summoned us to his office for what turned out to be a long but useless conversation. "It's a waste of your health," he said in conclusion. "We won't allow Eliezer's visit in any case."

"Then we'll continue our strike."

That evening, a guard arrived on a horse harnessed to a sled, and ordered us to gather our belongings. Each of us put our mattress, pillow, and books into the sled, which took us to isolation chambers that were just inside Camp 17. According to procedure, a prisoner who persists in a hunger strike for four days is locked in an isolation cell.

At the gate, we were made to carry our belongings on our backs along side paths, so that we wouldn't encounter other prisoners. Fortunately, we chanced across Arkady Voloshin, a former ulpan teacher in Kishinev, who greeted us in Hebrew. He could be counted on to tell the others. The very decision to isolate us was another stroke of luck; at least the authorities weren't ignoring our strike entirely.

We found ourselves in the very same quarantine cell where I had spent my first days after arrival. After collapsing onto the bunk boards and resting a bit, we began to study: I read Sholem Aleichem in Yiddish, while Shimon exercised his Hebrew and Eliezer his English.

When dinner was brought, we refused it. The guards insisted on leaving the dishes in the cell. "We're under orders to leave you some food. If you want, eat. If not, not. Either way, we'll come in the morning to collect everything."

"But this is abuse! You're trying to tempt us with the sight of food. And tomorrow you'll no doubt claim that we ate part of it."

"Those are the rules."

The moment they placed the plates on the table, Shimon jumped up and took them into the hall.

An officer arrived on the scene. "Why did you spill out the food?"

"We didn't spill anything. We just put it out in the hallway."

"Look, some of it spilled. You have no respect for food. First earn it, and then throw it away."

"You're the ones who don't work, you who live at the expense of prisoners."

The officer angrily clanged the door shut behind him.

The days passed, and our stomachs contracted like deflated rubber balls, our lips became parched, our mouths filled with a vile taste, our heads felt heavy. Still, we studied Hebrew and sang Israeli songs – our small triumphs.

Once in a while we were taken to a doctor who measured our blood pressures, inspected our tongues, and sniffed the odor emanating from our mouths. The rules allowed for force-feeding when a prisoner's mouth emitted a sulfurous, rotten-egg stench.

"Why are you insistent on ruining your health? It's a pity," she said.

"If it's such a pity, allow the family visit, and we'll end the hunger strike."

"I'm a doctor. I don't have a say about visits. But you should know that once you ruin your liver, it cannot be healed, and that prolonged hunger can cause permanent loss of vision."

Were it not for the sadistic expression on her face, we might have believed the sincerity of her concern. Not for nothing had she been nicknamed Ilse Koch, after the notorious wife of the commandant of Buchenwald. She was a dental technician by training. What real doctor would agree to work in a hole like this? So she fixed teeth, and meanwhile tried to treat everything else, too, rarely referring a prisoner to the hospital.

"Acute stomach pain? Show me your tongue."

"But doctor, I have an ulcer."

"The tongue is the key to the digestive system… I don't see anything. You're healthy. You can go back to work."

"But I suffer from chronic stomach ulcers. Medical experts confirmed this ten years ago."

"In that case, you've recovered. Fine, take this," she said, offering a white pill.

The patient could not be confident she knew which pill she had prescribed. "Do you have something else?"

"Why are you always asking for something else? You want to feel different? Take my advice: don't try to be different. Act like everyone else, and everything will turn out fine." This was the farce of camp medicine.

· · · · ·

Every day of the strike we force ourselves to take a half-hour walk. "You must be deceiving us about your strike," a guard tells us on the eighth day. "Most prisoners can't walk after a week without food."

"But we're Jews!" He looks at us in astonishment.

But in fact our energies have ebbed. "That's it, my friends, I can't go on," Eliezer says. "I need to end this."

"We haven't come this far to stop now. We agreed to carry this through to the end."

"I've changed my mind. We've shown them what we're capable of, and now it's enough."

We try to persuade him that stopping our hunger strike now will represent not just our defeat, but the defeat of our colleagues. On the ninth day, however, wonder of wonders: I'm given a letter from Israel, a report of my sister Eva's wedding, with the first photos I've seen from Israel. How much my family has changed! How Israeli they look! One photo shows my sister with a robust-looking, mustached soldier. The very sight of him encourages us to endure.

Out of the blue, both Eliezer and Shimon also receive letters from home. The superintendent of the quarantine cells, a veteran Lithuanian nationalist named Antanas, whispers to us that our strike has been causing a stir, and that letters are being sent protesting the canceled family visit. We hatch a plan. Since I speak Latvian and Shimon knows Lithuanian, we would pretend to hold a conversation while in fact passing on information through Antanas.

Lunchtime arrives. The guards outside our door taunt us. "Well, looks like fried potatoes with chicken and white bread."

"Enough of your lies," we say. "You yourselves don't even remember what chicken looks like. Open the door and bring in our mash." As Antanas brings in the plates, Shimon and I start our Latvian-Lithuanian conversation. "Tell the others that we'll be taken to the showers tomorrow at 6:00 p.m."

The next day, the twelfth of our hunger strike, we stagger to the showers to find the others waiting. Leib Korn peeks in to say Shalom. I spot Aryeh Khnokh, looking thin in his cotton wool pants. As we enter the wash room, nearly fainting from the humidity and steam, Arkady Voloshin, who has somehow evaded the guards, pops up at the window. "If you continue your strike," he says, "we'll all join you. Still, we must advise you to try to find a compromise."

"If we had been looking for compromises, we wouldn't have started the hunger strike."

"As you wish, friends. One more thing: we received a letter reporting that in the last year alone more than ten thousand Jews were allowed to leave the country."

At this moment he is whisked away, but we have heard enough to allow us to take great joy in the news that our colleagues are supporting us and that so many have been allowed to emigrate. An extraordinary rush of jubilation seizes us, emboldens us. We begin talking excitedly about Jewish cooking: I remember Lithuanian dishes, Eliezer argues for the unparalleled wonders of the Bessarabian Jewish cuisine. "Have you lost your minds?" Shimon protests. "Enough of this verbal feast." But these are not hallucinations, just reminiscences of Jewish home cooking.

· · · · ·

That day, the authorities decided to start force-feeding us, informing us that it was useless to resist; one way or another they would get something down our throats. We knew of cases in which a prisoner's teeth were broken by a device designed to force open a clenched jaw.

"Who's first?"

I went in to find a full committee: doctor, medic, senior warden, and an officer.

"Will you agree voluntarily to eat?"

"I refuse."

"Then we will feed you involuntarily. If you resist, we'll use force. Sit." I'm held down on both sides and pressed into the back of a chair. A thick rubber tube is thrust into my throat until I gag, tears streaming down my face. A liter and a half of white liquid is funneled into the tube. My stomach, not used to food, can't handle the sudden intrusion, and sends up shivers of pain. As soon as the tube is removed, the liquid comes back up, spraying white drops over the floor and the guards' boots. Not wishing to frighten my friends outside, I stifle my cries. Returning to the cell, I give them a word of advice: "Breathe through your nose."

We all get through it – exhausted, but pleased with ourselves. The next morning finds us deep in conversation about fate. Could any of us have imagined a year ago that we'd be here, starving, fighting for our basic human rights? The discussion is cut short when a guard brusquely summons Eliezer.

We wait nervously for him to come back. When he finally does, he sits down and lights an American cigarette. "I'll tell you everything in order. I was summoned to Garkushev's office. The deputy interior minister for Mordovia has come to resolve our problem, along with a representative of Jewish prisoners, Lassal Kaminski. The deputy minister listened to both sides, but his decision was made in advance: 'The commanding officer acted within the law in not permitting the visit. However, your wife can visit next month. In order to avoid future difficulties, I'm instructing Captain Garkushev to publish the list of prisoners who have visitation rights. As for you, Trachtenburg, I suggest you call off this hunger strike.'"

We took this compromise as a victory. "So, should we stop? It's doubtful whether we can get a better offer."

"Yes, we can stop. But there's no need to rush. We don't want to give the impression that we're eager to accept their every offer. We've become used to the hunger; let's wait until morning. In the meantime, they might as well remain anxious, and they might even give us some letters." Sure enough, they distributed several more letters from home that evening. It seemed that when it was in their interest to appease us, their postal service markedly improved.

As we lay on our bunks that night, we wondered aloud: "Does this not remind you of the biblical Joseph, who in a single moment was raised from abject prison to greatness? Here we were, hopeless and starving, and suddenly the door opened, Eliezer was called, and the unexpected – even the miraculous – started to happen. We must not despair. We must have faith."

The next morning we halted the hunger strike, on condition that over the next several days we would not have to work and we would receive extra nutrition. As we were taken out into the courtyard, its snow gleaming white in the sun, it seemed as though our souls, too, were awash with radiance.

All our friends – Aharon Shpilberg, Lassal, Khnokh, Leib Korn, Misha Korn, and others – were there to applaud our victory and to wish us well. Here in Camp 17 the Jewish community was stronger, had rules of its own, and had been able to forge ties with other groups of prisoners. Even so, it permitted each member to choose his own stance. Aharon and Lassal, for instance, chose to abide by camp rules, and even to attend the politics lectures. I myself couldn't understand this. I preferred to wear my opinions openly, without pretending any interest in obeying Soviet law.

The Jewish prisoners of Camp 17 also celebrated the Jewish holidays in the presence of the other inmates, while Voloshin and my old cellmate Lyosha Safronov would strum a guitar. Lyosha had become quite close to the Jewish prisoners, learning Hebrew and Israeli songs, and taking part in discussions of Jewish matters. Dmitry Chakhovsky, a friend of Voloshin's, was another Russian who felt connected to the Jews. He had been arrested in the Crimea for his part in founding a workers' rights organization. In camp, he tried to get along with everyone. It was he who convinced the group not to accept one of the camp's most controversial figures, Jan Makarenko (born Yaakov Hershkovich), as a Jew (though both of his parents were Jewish). Due to the "ambiguous" nature of his relationship to the authorities, no group would take Jan in, and yet he succeeded in maintaining contacts with each group.

Another unusual character there was an Israeli citizen named Yehuda Halevi. He had defected from the Red Army in Berlin at the end of the war and traveled to Palestine with a group of concentration camp survivors. There he had served in the Haganah, fought in the War of Independence and the Sinai campaign, and established a family and a shop in Tel Aviv. It seems that he forgot from whence he had fled, and in 1962 returned to visit his brother in Kherson, a city in the southern Ukraine. One day he went out for a pack of cigarettes, and ended up in prison, sentenced to ten years for defection. Even the intervention of Golda Meir could not save him. Placed at first in a camp for foreigners, where the conditions were relatively easy, he was already living in Camp 17 by the time the Leningrad defendants arrived. Their relations with him were chilly. They found it strange that a former Haganah soldier should be acting like an exile Jew, currying favor and avoiding confrontation with those more powerful than he.

"Yehuda, why do you drink tea in the company of Karp, that repellent overseer?"

"As the Eastern saying has it, 'Throw a dog a bone, and it won't bite you.'"

Yehuda was proud of his country – he would describe it fondly, and read aloud letters from Tel Aviv – but this pride did not prevent him from abasing himself. The contradiction bothered some young Jewish prisoners, who preferred for that reason to study Hebrew with Leib Korn instead. It seemed that combat and imprisonment require two very different kinds of courage.

Aryeh Khnokh encountered another kind of difficulty entirely. His classic Jewish features and his behavior irked Captain Garkushev from the beginning. Aryeh had once secretly received a hundred rubles – a princely sum in camp terms – from a visiting relative. He hid in a ditch in order to conceal the bill inside a tube of toothpaste, but Garkushev spotted him and ordered him to stop. Aryeh fled, with the chubby captain huffing in hot pursuit, and managed to toss the money behind a stack of bricks before guards apprehended him and tossed him in solitary confinement for ten days. Ever since, Garkushev had found ways to punish him. Because Aryeh was conscientious enough at work to produce flawless gloves, he had trouble filling his weekly quotas. (I myself found it easy to prioritize quantity over quality.) This was deemed a serious breach of discipline, and he was punished time after time until the Jewish group intervened and begged Garkushev to cut Aryeh a little slack. Aryeh's determination, pleasant demeanor, and familiarity with Middle Eastern affairs endeared him to everyone.

These, then, were some of the friends from our sister camp who had gathered to say farewell; quite diverse men, united in the common aim of living in their homeland.

After the hunger strike, we returned to our camp in triumph, though not everyone viewed things that way. The famous Russian dissident Yura Galanskov, for instance, saw our victory as a hollow one; his group of dissidents generally couldn't come to terms with us as an independent nationalist group. They had become used to Jews of another sort: democracy activists who were totally invested in Russian culture. "Those Zionists are narrow-minded," they said of us. Generally the pro-democracy dissidents ignored Soviet propaganda, but they swallowed whole the parts of the propaganda message directed at Jews and Israel: the charges that Israel exploited Arabs, for example. Ivan Ivanov and his ilk believed all the anti-Semitic canards about "international Jewry." In their view, Jewish activists in the human rights movement had to atone for the harm Jews had allegedly inflicted on other nations. "So you want to flee to Israel? Who then will bear responsibility for the fact that Jews brought about the Communist revolution?" Against this anti-Semitic libel it should be superfluous to point out that both before and after the revolution, Russia had always been a cruel tyranny that denied its citizens their human rights and freedoms. The revolution merely exchanged one tyranny for another. For what, then, do the Jews have to atone for exactly?

It's a truism that assimilating Jews seek to ingratiate themselves with whoever happens to be the majority in their host society. For this reason, we weren't much liked by the "true Russian democrats" in camp. They cooperated with us only when they needed our help. For my part, I avoided their company. Naturally, the ranks of the "democrats" included some Jews who also sympathized with the Zionist cause, but in my view one's soul could not simultaneously be partly Russian and partly Jewish. Jewish belonging demanded total commitment. Thus they seemed as strange to me as I to them.

Take, for example, the birthday celebration of a prisoner named Witold Abankin. The moment we gathered to drink tea, guards dispersed us and called Garkushev. Things got heated. "I'll find a way to get even with you," Abankin told the commandant.

"You're threatening me?" Garkushev exclaimed, and promptly ordered the prisoner to solitary confinement.

Calls went out to begin a hunger strike in response, and the prisoners asked whether the Jews would join. Not a single one of them had lifted a finger during our strike. "We'll see how things turn out," we said. Insulted, they initiated a hunger strike without us. As expected, on the fourth day they were taken into quarantine in Camp 17. Soon their resolve eroded, and they wondered whether it was really worthwhile to strike over such a petty issue. In order to boost their morale, Fedorov, the self-styled "fighter for the purity of Communism," lied and told them that many other prisoners would soon join the strike. Upon learning that the message was false, the hunger strikers pounded on the door and demanded to be fed.

The authorities were pleased; such abortive strikes only sapped the will to protest. They called a prisoners' assembly. "We announce that for the crime of organizing a hunger strike, Ivanov, Fedorov, and Galanskov will be transferred to the internal prison for six months."

Fedorov submitted a desperate and incoherent appeal: "I request that Galanskov be spared punishment on the grounds that he is ill and in accordance with the Geneva Conventions should be accorded medical care. In addition, I demand that all political prisoners, together with prisoners whose health is too delicate to withstand camp conditions, be freed." The appeal had no support, and no one took it seriously. And these are the people who had wanted us to join their strike for the sake of "common objectives."

Our sole objective was returning to Zion, and the path to realizing that goal was exceedingly long. In the meantime, we would have to traverse many byways.

• • • • •

One Saturday night in June 1972, prisoners were assembled as a list was read out. Everyone on the list was ominously requested to come back with his belongings. Shimon and I were on the list; Hillel and Eliezer, who had less than a year remaining to serve, were not. Rumors had long been rife of an imminent transfer of large numbers of prisoners. The camps in our area, it seems, had become too well known in the West, and had leaked too many reports to the outside. It was decided to transfer most of the prisoners – some six hundred of us – to more remote camps in the interior of the country. But where exactly would we be sent? One of the Ukrainian prisoners, who was from the same hometown as Captain Byelov's wife, had heard from her that our destination was somewhere in the Urals.

We began to pack. Our belongings were pathetically meager, but it still pained us to have to leave some behind. Then there was the question of what to do about the small stashes of money that our families had smuggled in for us but which we hadn't been able to use. (It turns out the guards did not do business with Jews). We wrapped some of the money in plastic and concealed it in a jar of honey Hillel had received from home; the rest we hid between pages of books.

But on the way out, our Hebrew textbook was confiscated. We insisted that we would not leave until it was returned.

"It's in a foreign language. We have to send it to be checked."

"That's anti-Semitic discrimination. You can see for yourself that it's just a textbook!"

The head of the transfer department promised that it would be returned just as soon as it could be inspected. But could we trust him? We decided that if it weren't returned within two months, we would take steps to get it back. Amazingly enough, some time later a new Hebrew textbook, published in Israel, was sent to us – an event utterly unique in all my years of imprisonment.

At last, the preparations for our departure were complete. Hillel and Eliezer had given us their most valuable possessions. We sat together for a few moments in silence. Who knew when we would meet again?

We were loaded onto flatbed trucks lined with armed soldiers, which took us to a train standing in an open field surrounded by yet more troops. They ordered us to jump from the trucks and to run in a line to the train. At the door to the rail car, we were handed two kilograms of bread and two cans of food for the journey. These signaled a long trip. But the journey ahead couldn't be longer than life itself, I thought, so what's to fear? Everything will unfold in due course according to God's will.

Though our physical loads as we embarked may have been slight, our spiritual burdens weighed upon us heavily.

Chapter Four

"And Joseph Was Brought Down to Egypt"

Since political prisoners must by law be held separately from criminal prisoners, on most transports we were each placed in our own cell. But this time, the train of cattle cars carried only political prisoners, so we were packed eighteen to a compartment meant for nine. The train had not yet begun to move, and already conditions were insufferable. The windows were sealed shut, and thick cigarette smoke stifled the air. Some prisoners had already devoured the rations that had been intended to last several days, and were on their knees begging to be let out to the toilet. But this was forbidden so long as the train was not yet in motion.

Shimon and I sit ourselves down near the cell door, where there is slightly more air, and immediately this stirs envy from others. "Hey, get away from there! Let us breathe." Everyone has stripped down to their filthy undershirts, and the stagnant air reeks with the odors of sweat and tobacco. Our books have been confiscated on the suspicion that we might use the paper to write anti-Soviet messages. All we can do is sit and stare at one another.

Shimon leaps up. "Open the windows! We're suffocating!" The entire compartment begins to shout. Finally, the guards jam sticks into the windows to prop them open a little, which improves things a bit.

The train jolts into motion, and guards begin to escort prisoners to the toilet. But the guards leave the toilet door ajar, and watch prisoners as they take care of their needs. Shimon once again flies into a rage, and demands to see the commanding officer. He doesn't show up, and as our turn for the toilet draws closer, Shimon decides to raise hell. At last the officer arrives to see what all the tumult is about.

"What kind of abuse is this?" Shimon says. "Do you think we are creatures without shame?"

It appears the very concept of shame is new to the officer. "What have you been imprisoned for?"

"I'm a Jew," Shimon declares.

This elicits a cluck of recognition from the officer, who instructs the guards to close the toilet door especially for us. "And when we get to camp, I'll see to it that you're punished," he adds, as though unable to sustain a humane attitude for very long.

As the train pulls into a small station, I glance out the window. I see young men and women vociferously playing cards and drinking vodka. A girl leaves a shop carrying a large loaf of bread. A woman drags her drunken husband from the station as he curses at her wildly. It is Sunday, a grey, dusty day.

As I gaze out, I think to myself: is this all you can offer me as an alternative to the precious sanctity of Shabbat? Are not these drunks in more dire need of "reeducation" than I am? And what if I'm confronted with a similarly bleak scene when I get to Israel – young people "killing time" like this in some shabby backwater town? Will I disavow them just like I disavow these scenes today? No – because it is not the shabbiness of what I see that repels me: even without knowing Israel, I never for a moment imagined that the outward appearance of its cities and towns would be much different than anywhere else in the world, that its grime would be somehow purer than grime anywhere else. But I also know that Israel, whatever I might find there, is my country. I discovered this simple truth not through books or lectures, but from within my own being, and I know, too, that it must have been implanted there by divine hand.

I notice orange containers on the adjacent tracks; they are labeled in black: "Made in the U.S.A." and the name of a Jewish company. I feel no anger that Jews may be involved in supplying these containers to the Soviet Union at the very moment that I am being hauled off to a camp in the Urals. No, I am simply amazed at the paradox of it all. Someone overseas is at this moment worrying about the delivery of his merchandise. That man is no doubt a decent, well-respected individual, and a good father, and his decency is harmed not one iota by the fact that he is offering no help to the obscure Yosef Mendelevich. I myself cannot possibly offer aid and succor to all the world's sufferers. Would such thoughts forever trouble me?

As the train at last reaches its destination, I find myself looking out over a small industrial town filled with metalwork factories: piles of slag metal, thickets of chimneys billowing dark smoke, low-slung apartment buildings

– all surrounded by forested mountains. It seems the rumors had been right: we are in the Urals.

Many people imagine that Siberia is the worst place to be imprisoned. But Siberia, which occupies an area roughly as large as the US, is very diverse; it includes frozen territories as well as milder ones. In fact, before we knew with certainty where we were heading, the veteran prisoners expressed the hope that we would be taken to Siberia. Besides, the climate is not the only factor that shaped camp experience; people and personnel were far more important, and Siberians had the reputation of being more humane than residents of central Russia.

The Urals, on the western edge of Siberia, were dotted with labor camps. Measured by either the harshness of the climate or the number of prisoners who found their deaths there, the northern Urals actually did not lag far behind Siberia. During the Second World War, Stalin had moved much of the Soviet military production to the Urals, and many areas there became restricted military zones, impossible to access without special permits. Afterwards, many nuclear arms facilities were based there, together with large concentrations of forces. Many prisoners were put to work in the military industry, and thus the camps were wrapped in a double isolation: as labor camps, under the authority of the interior ministry, and as military sites, under the auspices of the office of military production. In case of an attack on the Soviet Union, we were ideally located to be among the first victims.

· · · · ·

"Collect your belongings! Hurry!"

We had been cooped up in box cars for four days. At the guards' orders, we sprinted toward our belongings like athletes bolting from the starting line, falling over one another in a mad scramble to find our suitcases, parcels, and mugs.

Then to flatbed trucks, where we again sat on the floor surrounded by soldiers and dogs. The early morning air, though ice cold, buzzed with oversize mosquitoes. We greedily drank in the sight of open spaces and forest. Strange that in our state we could still take pleasure in natural beauty. We were being taken to God knows where, shut up like dogs in kennels, and still we could not help marveling: "Look, a jet-black raven!" "See those fir trees? Those dramatic mountains?" We had been released from the past; the future could only be worse. Yet we felt liberated in spirit – at least those of us capable of feeling inner freedom. It seems that even at a time of crisis, a man needs natural beauty no less than bread: "It is not by bread alone that man lives" (Deuter-onomy 8:3). The most beautiful paintings or sculptures would not have drawn our eyes away from the natural beauty we glimpsed that day: a reminder of the Creator and of the continuity of life.

As usual, the secret service did its best to give our convoy the air of a state funeral: two red and white police cars in the lead, motorcycle escorts on both sides. In this way we passed through muddy villages with crumbling churches, places that looked as though time had stopped in the 1950s, not long after the war.

After an hour's ride deeper into the forest, we came upon a long, grey fence and behind it a bloc of grey-white structures: the camp itself. Adjacent to the camp was a miserable village of decrepit wooden huts that looked like they hadn't been inhabited in twenty years. Perm 36 Labor Camp was built near a settlement called Kutchino, forty kilometers from Chusovoy. The nearby Chusovaya River had created marshes that made tunneling impossible. Prior to our imprisonment there, the camp had held some five hundred police and correctional officers being penalized for "turning bad" – who were consistently subjected to more comfortable treatment by their fellow officers in authority.

Upon our arrival, 280 of us were brought into this camp; the others were sent to Camp 35, some hundred meters away. The date was July 17, 1972. With the exception of three years in jail, I would go on to spend the rest of my imprisonment here. On February 18, 1981, I would be taken from this camp's factory to the guard booth – and thence to freedom.

Was it really necessary to serve the entire length of my term in order to develop mature self-awareness? If that were true, I could console myself with the thought that my time had not been wasted, that my character was built here, and that had I reached Israel without overcoming the difficulties of imprisonment, I would have arrived as an entirely different man. But I don't think that's true. It is not for me to understand the intentions of the Almighty, who tested me with eleven years of servitude. Rather than spend those years learning the bitter lessons of imprisonment, I would have preferred to come to Israel as a young man to study in a yeshiva. That lesson was bitter not due to the hardships I endured, but because of the ways all the pettiness of prison life limited me, robbed me of my Torah, my people, my homeland, and above all of my family's love. I could not subsist all those years on prayers and dreams alone; my soul was restricted within the narrow confines I came up against every time I wanted to become myself – i.e., a Jew. Needing to clip the wings of my lofty ambitions to conform to camp life depleted my energies.

What lessons, then, did years of imprisonment teach me? Other than gaining certain experiences and encountering certain people – myself included – what did those years really consist of? It would be premature to try to express a single, conclusive answer, since my life is not yet at its end, but I can say that my imprisonment gave me something that is difficult to express and that eludes easy definition. Sanctifying God's name, perhaps? Returning to the fold and acquiring God's law? It is not for me to judge. Only God is omniscient. It is not possible to discern the meaning of life in every event, in every fleeting episode. A man who tries to do so will at best discover a fragmentary truth. But perhaps the best way to put it is that my years of prison taught me how very far the world is from perfection and wholeness – myself very much included. This awareness stirred within me the desire to become whole, to live a more just life, even as I realized that the matter did not depend on me alone. I came to understand how wholeness is to be found only in clinging to God. I learned, in other words, the meaning of the endless quest for the ideal, the dissatisfactions of reality, and the measure of the distance between the ideal and reality. Camp life is compressed; in an almost miraculous, revelatory way, its inexplicable and incandescent intensities stamp themselves on your mind, your heart, indeed on every cell in your body.

As usual, pettiness intrudes on my lofty thoughts. A corporal is opening the jar in which we had hid our cash, and sniffs at it with his bulbous red nose. "What is this?"

"Honey."

He gives the jar back, and shakes one of my books. Nothing flutters down from its pages. With the search over, I notice a pile of belongings that had been taken from me in Mordovia: boots, sweater, and my kippah. I tiptoe over to my backpack behind a red-faced guard, and silently draw out my Israeli kippah. Mission accomplished.

As I enter the living quarters, it seems a celebratory mood has seized the officers gladdened by their new shipment of prisoners. The colonels and majors stand there puffed up with self-importance, surveying the new arrivals like lords at a slave market. Then they notice that some of us are bearded and wear a cross or Star of David.

"What's this? You're religious?"

"Yes."

"Apparently they've spoiled you over there in Mordovia. No matter; we'll educate you." Such threats have ceased to bother me; I've learned that "reeducation" efforts are forgotten after a while and soon fade.

Still, Captain Zhuravkov appears joyful. He gives us orders us as though we were soldiers. "Get into formation. To the washroom, march!"

Despite the captain's idiotic gaiety, and despite the repulsion I feel toward marching in lockstep, when we get to the showers the warm water feels good on the skin. But the real delight is the reunion with some Jewish friends: I greet Uri, Michael, and Shabtai (fictitious names). Zhuravkov, the only one who isn't stark naked, cuts our reunion short and tells me I must shave my beard. I don't reply.

"How long have you got to serve?"

"Ten years."

"So you see, it's not worth the risk of punishment. Give up on this and go shave. Make things easier on yourself."

I'm not even paying attention. I've heard too many of these orders couched as though they were they were in my best interests to obey. As we leave the showers, my friends and I arrange a time to meet.

Asher Frolov is preparing tea. The transition from student to prisoner has done him good. He looks well in his reddish beard and grey uniform; glasses perched on his nose. He's kindling a fire from some twigs and readying a two-liter pot of water. Other prisoners, too, after a protracted lack of any pleasure, poke through the garbage to find kindling material. Shabtai, Michael, Mark Dymshits, Shimon, Asher Frolov, Uri, Yaakov and I gather on the grass between the barracks and the dining room. At Shabtai's suggestion, we've each brought our Israeli postcards. There seems no better way to get acquainted with one another. Shabtai has the most postcards, and is as familiar with Israeli history and geography as someone who has already visited the country.

We learned a great deal about Israel from these postcards, from our books, and from our own hearts, so that when we ultimately did reach our homeland it was to feel like a return after a long absence. The twelfth-century sage Maimonides recommended study of the commandments that could only be performed in Israel on the grounds that although they were presently irrelevant, they should not be entirely unfamiliar to us when Jewish sovereignty returned. It was similarly important to us that our attachment to the country be not merely abstract, but concrete, and it was precisely this weave of the symbolic and the palpable that gave us the strength to carry on until our ultimate arrival in the Promised Land.

• • • • •

From then on, the eight of us Jews acted as a group among other groups, existing within a series of concentric circles that determined our lives over the ensuing years. This is how I saw those circles:

The Creator of the world ultimately guided and set in motion everything in it, including everything that happened to the Jewish people.

Camp policies were designed to quell disobedience. Their modus operandi was to induce or intimidate the weak, and to annihilate the rebellious. The way the camp's policies were applied depended to a large extent on the degree of connectedness its inhabitants managed to forge with the outside world.

The authorities first attempted to force us into submission, and then to bring to bear the full weight of suppression – now tightening sanctions, now loosening the leash. Jewish prisoners suffered especially harsh conditions. If we were prudent enough to avoid getting too caught up in camp life, our conditions improved. The guards' extreme severity, however, sometimes resulted from sheer sadism.

Each prisoner sought to avoid unduly hard labor, to hang on to whatever minimal comforts he chanced to enjoy, to receive and transmit as much information as possible, to receive packages, and to hold some sway over the camp staff.

Most prisoners exhibited hostility toward Jews. All of them, to one degree or another, suffered from some psychological complex: a superiority complex, a persecution complex, depression, etc. Many would stop at nothing to ensure their own survival, not hesitating to bare their naked greed, envy, or selfishness. This behavior could usually be explained by personal traits (sometimes dressed up in political clothing), and by the cruel, clawing struggle to survive.

On matters of principle, we were united with the rest of the camp's political prisoners. This entailed a blanket refusal to enter into any explicit agreements with the authorities.

In order to preserve our Jewish identity, we avoided forming close connections with other groups, cooperating with them only on matters pertaining to camp discipline. In exchange for our restraint, we hoped to be able to observe Jewish law and study Hebrew.

We consistently studied Hebrew and Jewish history, celebrated the holidays, and dreamed of emigrating to Israel.

★ ★ ★ ★ ★

To return to our arrival, I must admit that beneath the joy we felt in meeting one another, we also felt deep anxiety. I felt especially tense. Would I manage here, as before, to keep some semblance of the Shabbat? What kind of labor – and of how arduous a nature – would I be assigned to do?

Each prisoner was called in for a conversation with the camp commandant Kotov, his deputy for camp discipline Fyodorov, and the officer in charge of "reeducation," Zhuravkov. As in Mordovia, the roles were well practiced: Zhuravkov as good cop, Fyodorov as bad cop, and Kotov transcending it all.

Kotov was a new type in the camp system: neither a bloodthirsty murderer, like the typical gulag officer from Stalin's day, nor merely a bureaucrat going about his dull, monochromatically cruel work. Kotov was young and well educated, and wished to prove his superior intelligence to everyone, prisoners included. He attempted to base his control over prisoners not on hierarchical power alone but on his personal superiority. This is not to say that he wasn't a product of the Communist system. It's just that it was in his nature to broaden the reach of his rule by means of a wicked kind of game of commanded and commander, of masking and unmasking.

"Why are your uniform and shoes in such tatters? You must fix them."

The speaker who expressed his concern to me with these words was neither Zhuravkov nor Kotov but Fyodorov, of all people, the bad cop. Whence his excessive concern? Fyodorov wasn't your typical depraved camp official. He had a round face, reddish hair, small reddened eyes that would scan you closely, and a blunt, revolting nose through which he was constantly inhaling and sniffling. We nicknamed him Guinea Pig, though there was nothing cute about him. Indeed, the political prisoners in Camp 35 discovered that their predecessors had defaced the walls with the phrase "Death to Fyodorov." Apparently he had embittered their lives before coming to us. Unlike most guards, he knew how to exploit a prisoner's vulnerability, to touch on the prisoner's most sensitive and secret inner wound. Despite his outward cleanliness, he aroused in us deep disgust. Even his kind gestures felt like the condescending pat on the head given to a naïve child or to a slave. This kind of humiliation was more corrosive than the more obvious varieties.

This might be the right place to parenthetically address a common question: "Well, life in the gulag may not have been pleasant, but was it really so terrible?" Although it is true that life in a "corrective labor camp" did not pose a daily danger to the lives of prisoners, its relentless repression did grind away at our sense of self as it aimed to efface our personalities. For the sake of comparison, imagine that you are trapped in a kindergarten where the teachers refuse to treat you as an adult. You want to read a newspaper, and the teacher says, "Don't touch. That's not for you. Why aren't you playing with the others?

Why are you so antisocial? Why are you so angry? If you keep this up, I won't take you outside with the others. Oh, why are you crying? Here, have a candy." Obviously you're not crying because you don't have a candy, but because you want to be regarded as an adult, not as a child who needs his diapers changed. And you can't deny me privileges because I'm upset, since it's your fault that I'm upset in the first place. You're torturing me!

We're torturing you, Mendelevich? To say so is to spread anti-Soviet propaganda. You have everything: three meals a day, a library, and still you're not satisfied. Get back to work, you lazy loafer!

I'm no loafer. I labored in a factory from age sixteen. I know how to work. My refusal to work is intended to protest your cruel treatment.

You'll be punished for that piece of impertinence, Mendelevich.

Labor edifies man – this is the fundamental Soviet principle, and it divides mankind into two. Good men are those who labor and who are materially productive. They are deemed honest and righteous. Whatever they regard as right is right, and whatever they determine to be wrong is wrong. Bad men are those who, not wanting to work themselves, exploit workers. This category includes doctors, engineers, clerks, and businessmen. Criminal prisoners are those who didn't want to earn their keep. They must be "reeducated" before they can be reintegrated into productive Soviet society. Hence in the Soviet Union there are no forced labor camps, only "reeducation facilities." Whoever claims otherwise libels the state. These facilities teach men to work, to maintain order, to become obedient. Whoever points out that high levels of crime are a testament to a sick society libels the regime. Whoever notes that the huge number of prisoners in the gulag is itself a mark of oppression, or that the punishments there are excessive, is an enemy of the state. There are no prisoners, only men who have been judged by "the people" as enemies of the state. In this Orwellian universe, there is no punishment, only "reeducation"; no guards, only "educators." There are no political prisoners; such prisoners exist only in states in which the proletariat is at war with the class of its exploiters. In the Soviet Union, those who do not accept the Communist ideology are not political prisoners but simply criminals.

This strange, not to say absurd, doublespeak results in a paradox: there is officially no difference between a thief and a writer of anti-Soviet essays. The same vice, sloth, may turn a man into either a thief or an intellectual or nationalist. We'll reeducate each of these men, dear comrades, through labor, for the betterment of our socialist society. If we were to recognize the need to treat political prisoners differently, it would imply that they are not after all criminals. But as we've said, there are no political prisoners in the Soviet Union, because all of its citizens are pleased with the regime. Those who express displeasure with the regime are agents of foreign intelligence services who have sold out for money. All Zionists are agents of the CIA. They are all lazy parasites.

"Mendelevich," Fyodorov says, "why did you fail to appear at the labor department? Are you trying to shirk your work? Everyone must work. If no one worked, you'd die of starvation."

Does he understand what he's saying? Does he realize what lies behind his preaching? Does he really imagine that I'm lazy and that he must teach me the value of work? Or does he wish merely to humiliate me, and to enjoy the humiliation? That might explain the cynical twinkle in his eye. This son of peasants enjoys his power over an educated Jew with a university diploma whose name has been broadcast over all the Western airwaves. "The whole world is talking about him, and here I am taking him to the toilet!"

Fyodorov had joined the army at age seventeen. During the war, kids his age had been used as cannon fodder. Luckily, however, he had been sent to the interior ministry's military college, which put him on track to serve in the part of the army that ran the gulag. Even during the war, the authorities had to attend to the gulag, which killed as many victims as Mauthausen and Dachau. What could a young man from a remote village in the Urals be expected to know, except that the Russians dominated the world, possessed absolute truth, and therefore had the right to do as they pleased? The wildness of a villager had intermingled with the dogmatism of Communist ideology to fruitful effect: At twenty, Fyodorov had tortured to death a prisoner who had attempted to escape, and then jammed his bayonet into the victim's eye socket. Today, at age forty-five, the wild murderer had become a refined sadist, a master of humiliation. The instructions he received from Moscow were intended to drive home a single message: whatever is in the press is for mass consumption; you yourselves must believe in force alone.

I don't know whether someone consciously designed this satanic system of "reeducation" and "psychotherapy" facilities, or whether they evolved on their own, unplanned. But there can be no doubt about the satanic character of the gulag, and Fyodorov was its ultimate product and personification.

So what could I possibly reply to him, except: "I'm not refusing to work. In the previous camp I fulfilled my work quotas, and I will do the same here."

My panel of officials is not satisfied by the answer. They see quite clearly that I am not submitting, and so they must find something else to fasten on. "Why don't you shave off your beard?" Kotov asks.

"I had a beard in Mordovia too."

"Here it's forbidden. Shave it off. If you refuse, we'll have to punish you."

"My religion does not permit me to do so. Jews do not shave their beards."

"On the outside, or in Israel, you can do as you please. Here you will obey our rules."

Here Kotov senses he can discover a way to reeducate me. "Do you believe in God?" he asks.

"Yes."

"I'll allow you in this exceptional case to keep the beard, but if you violate any other rule, we'll shave it off." His plan is clear: in getting me to obey him in order to keep the beard, I'll gradually become enslaved, after which they'll find a pretext to shave the beard anyway. Otherwise, they'd have a bunch of bearded Jews on their hands, and other prisoners would ask why the Jews are allowed to go unshaven and they're not.

Many prisoners are persuaded that Kotov is Jewish. For them, nothing is easier than projecting Jewishness on someone they hate, as though his Jewishness could explain everything hateful about him. Thus I confront him alone. No one can be expected to help if things with him got bad. To whom could I turn? To the authorities?

Don't think that standing there before Kotov I ran all the possible variations through my mind. In retrospect I may be wiser, but at that moment I knew only one thing: I will not enslave myself to the authorities. I will follow the dictates of my faith and conscience, no matter how difficult. I arrived in the Urals with a clear decision to keep the Shabbat, but the uncertainty of how I will be able to do so is weighing on me, and even more so now that Kotov is telling me that if I remain religious, then…

"I want to add that I do not work on the Sabbath," I said. "In Mordovia I fulfilled my Saturday quotas on the other six days of the week."

Fyodorov's jaw drops, and then he lifts a receiver to his ear. Will he order an assault on me? No, he merely smiles the gaping smile of a crocodile just before it eats you alive. "Well, if you work diligently…"

I left the office and rejoined the others who had been waiting for me outside, and together we went with heavy hearts to the immense camp dining hall. Each long table could seat forty. In the center of the room stood a tank of pea stew, and next to it portions of fish. This is how we were to become an army of worker-slaves, filing off to the factory every morning, dreaming of a thin stew for lunch.

On our way back, Yaakov appeared, looking pleased with himself. "I told them that I too am religious so that I won't have to shave my beard."

"But that's a lie. You're not religious."

"So what? Must I tell them the truth?"

"No, but if they discover that you lied, you'll be in trouble."

"Don't worry. Nothing will come of it."

But something did come of it. The very next day, guards ordered Shimon and I to shave our beards.

"But the camp commandant expressly permitted us to keep them."

"Because of your lies, he has rescinded the permission."

"We did not lie."

"Does it matter which of you lied? The commandant is not about to start making fine distinctions."

Herein, then, a lesson about the importance of truth telling, consideration of the other, and responsibility toward fellow Jews. Not that Jews alone were affected. Another twenty prisoners refused to remove their beards and proposed we join a hunger strike. We had to decide quickly.

The camp administrators were meanwhile assigning work for the new prisoners. Because our transfer had been made suddenly, they hadn't yet managed to find workplaces for all of us. For our part, we were simultaneously trying to organize ourselves, on the principle that although each of us individually was holding onto lofty goals, we could achieve them only if we united. Jewish strength has from time immemorial depended on acting not as isolated individuals but as a unified and cohesive community. Shabtai in particular began emphasizing this value of organizing ourselves, but each of us was already well aware of the need to work together and to join in common cause. This simple notion was so deeply rooted that it required no external validation or proof; we had inherited it, as it were.

It was in that spirit that we gathered that evening, eight young Jewish men, in the not-yet-completed headquarters building. The camp's fence was illuminated by bright lights spaced every five meters, as though the camp were a theater stage without actors. Though no one uttered the thought aloud, we had convened to discuss whether to found a Jewish underground in the camp.

The first item on the agenda was the question of joining a hunger strike to protest the order to remove our beards, and on this matter we decided that we could not put our full trust in the strike's organizers. In my last camp, we had already witnessed the failure of the strike Yuri Fyodorov had organized. Tempting though they were to believe, we could not trust the reports that the strike had attracted broad support. We decided instead to take a "wait and see" approach.

Being old hands, Kotov and Fyodorov simply refused to acknowledge the strike. On its sixth day, the strikers – by then flat on their backs – could not summon the strength to go to work. Guards arrived to drag prisoners out of their bunks. "Let's go, you loafers. Go and earn your bread. Here even the dead must work, let alone hunger strikers. You're striking because you're simply too lazy to work."

"No, we're striking to demand to be able to keep our beards."

"Then it's fifteen days in solitary confinement for you."

Once in solitary, the prisoners suffered a failure of nerve, and the strike fizzled out. Who knows how the administration would have reacted had they continued to strike and work at the same time, but the prisoners gave in. In this case it was possible to discern the precise moment when resolve either was to be broken or redoubled. It is that moment when if you resolve to carry on, despite the pressures, a glimmer of hope begins to dispel the darkness; if you give in, all is lost. But the line between those outcomes is exceedingly thin, often a matter of just a few moments. Many of the disasters we inflicted upon ourselves could have been averted had we simply had the faith to wait another moment.

One of the young dissidents was the first to break. He emerged in shame, sheepishly trying to hide his clean-shaven chin. It wasn't long before everyone had shaved, and the strike was over. At first glance, you might imagine that we would be relieved not to have joined prisoners who didn't have what it took to see the strike all the way through. This was in fact a common pattern in camp life: someone tosses out an idea, and suddenly everyone joins a protest, but they do so halfheartedly, exhibiting typical Russian recklessness, with neither much forethought nor an unshakable confidence in their cause, merely a hope that the next guy will be strong enough to carry on. The protest begins with flourishes of big words: truth, justice, dignity. But after the protest reaches its first stage, you look around and realize that nearly everyone joined in by chance, and you, as a Jew, are expected to save them from disgrace. And that's how you lose. Then, the next time you hear those lofty speeches about truth, justice, and dignity, you say: "Gentlemen, one second. Have you considered the circumstances? Are you really prepared for a protracted struggle?" To which the reply is usually: "Stop calculating like a Jew. We'll storm the barricades and die heroes." So you lower your eyes and say, "No, I haven't got time for this. I must go study Hebrew," and retreat to the sound of their cat-calls: "Coward, traitor! We'll manage without you." They manage without you by bursting into fiery battle, but the moment they're singed they beat a hasty retreat, no longer remembering their platitudes about justice and dignity.

And yet, their defeat is to some degree our defeat too. From now on, declaring a general strike will be extraordinarily difficult, and even if a strike is launched it will take considerably more effort to convince the authorities that they will not get away with an easy victory, like last time. We all pay the price of surrender.

Now we are being called into the guard booth one at a time. "Mendelev-ich, your turn to get shaved." When I refuse, guards tackle me, cuff my hands, force me into a chair, hold my head, and shave off my beard – and some skin too. They do the same to Shimon. Coercion? Yes, but only in the interests of good hygiene. I stumble out, on the verge of tears. Some prisoners come up to me, their eyes full of compassion, but none finds words of consolation.

The next days are spent in mourning; I feel no desire to do anything. We are being humiliated, and are powerless to resist. How is it possible not to wist-fully think at such a time about a free country in which they do not forcibly shave beards and remove kippot?

"Since they're shaving non-Jews too," I say to Shimon, "this isn't an instance of anti-Jewish persecution. I have ten more years to serve, and I can't devote all of them to a struggle over a beard. There are many other religious duties, and fulfilling them will require a great deal of our energy and health."

"But I can hang on," he says. "I've got eighteen months left, and I can hang on."

They start harassing him, inspecting his face every month as though he were a lamb to be sheared, admonishing him for growing out his stubble. "Shimon," I say, "this is just making the humiliation more acute."

"No, I can hang on. I'll complain." He writes complaint after complaint. He fights the camp administration tooth and nail. He memorizes all the rules pertaining to beards. He learns that all of the rules about shaving are deduced from a single line in the interior ministry regulations: "Upon arrival at a re-education facility, prisoners will be disinfected, including trimming of the hair on all parts of the body."

"'Upon arrival' implies only once," he said.

"No, in the next clause it states: 'Disinfection is to take place once a week.'"

"But that clause says nothing about hair removal."

"We interpret it to include shaving. We don't require your interpretations of our regulations."

It becomes a battle of wills. Shimon tries to hide his chin, and the authorities pursue him. Every day he kindles the same hope. "You see, it's been a month since they've made me shave. Maybe they've given up." And the next day, they apprehend him, force him to the ground, and shave him against his will. Then they send him to solitary confinement.

• • • • •

Meanwhile, we had been planning our "academic year," using the experience we had gained in Mordovia in order to continue our Hebrew studies. Even before their arrests, the Leningrad Zionists had studied in underground ulpans (in fact it was these ulpans that had given birth to the Zionist movement there), and after their imprisonment they had continued to devote great effort to their studies. Michael, for example, had arrived in the Mordovian camp with a vocabulary of some one hundred Hebrew words; after a year he knew three thousand words, and could speak the language. He was appointed our first teacher, and I served as the second instructor. Shabtai would give a seminar on Jewish history. We were confident we could succeed, in no small part because of the books we had collected between us: parts 1–4 of a Hebrew workbook called *1000 Words (Elef Milim)*, *Book of Legends (Sefer Ha-Aggadah)* by H. N. Bialik and Y. H. Rawnitzky, and others.

How did these precious books come into our hands? Therein lies a tale.

Shlomo Dreizner from Leningrad, whom we had met in Mordovia, excelled in being able to talk to anyone, including thieves and former Nazi Polizei. "To get along with such people is an art," he used to say. "Let's say I want to buy a loaf of bread from the camp baker. I could simply say, 'Give me some bread, and I'll pay you.' But he has money without my contribution, and so is unlikely to take a risk for my sake. Instead, you might offer him a cigarette or share some tea with him, and strike up a friendly conversation. Then he may himself offer you some bread. You say, 'It's really not necessary, I'll get by...' Don't say, 'Yes, bring me some and I'll pay you.' When he brings you a loaf, by all means do not ask how much it costs; he's given it to you as a gesture of friendship, and friendship is not purchased. Instead, give him some money casually, a gesture of generosity 'from the heart,' as the Russians say. Better yet, offer him not cash but a gift – a 3D postcard or a pen from Israel. It is similarly wise not to give him something right away, but a short time later. He may be a thief, but he has pride. If that same baker would himself be starving, he wouldn't hesitate to rip your throat out and crush your bones. But in the meantime, he's a human being, and you should treat him as such. Just now he's getting a shirt made to order from the 'camp tailor.' It will be made not from the rags that we prisoners wear but from regular work clothes; it will have two breast pockets and even a collar. His undershirt, meanwhile, gleams white, and he shines his shoes every day. His most precious treasure is his pair of boots, polished like a mirror. Of course on the 'outside' he would look ridiculous, but here his appearance distinguishes him from the political prisoners, who have no time to think about fashion. Our pants are filthy with mud, our shirts are missing buttons, our socks are pocked with holes…" Thus does Shlomo sum up his accumulated life wisdom.

At that moment, by way of demonstration, he turns toward one of his "friends." "Shura, a relative of mine is coming for a visit. I'll need to get some packages into the living quarters. Do you think you could help?"

"Why not, Shlomele?" Shura pats Shlomo on the back and sips some of his tea. The two are sitting next to a rough-hewn plank table in the smoke-filled barracks surrounded by the usual clamor: dozens of prisoners milling about and getting ready for bed. Who would have thought that they were hatching a special Zionist operation to smuggle in banned books?

That night, Shura's friend, Lieutenant Chakmaryov, is on duty. During the night, Shura gets up as though to use the toilet, and sneaks through the court-yard in his underwear to the guard booth. He checks to see that Chakmaryov is alone, and taps on the window.

"So, what have you got for me?" the lieutenant says. Shura hands over the payment for a shipment of two kilos of sugar that had been smuggled in the day before. The sugar was for Jews, and the money came from the Jews, but Chakmaryov isn't troubled by that fact in the slightest. Money has no smell, as the saying goes, and cannot be tainted. The only drawback is that there's no comfortable way of carrying the sugar in his trench coat; it fits only with great difficulty into his pockets, and anyway the pay is low. In the old days things were better. Prisoners wanted vodka, and he could make a good profit. For some reason, Shura has lately been asking for worthless things, though today Shura requests a kilo of coffee and a kilo of cocoa, which is good because he'll have to go to town to get it, and can raise the price. But Shura is not yet finished; he has something more to request. Chakmaryov scans the area; his fellow guards are due back at any moment. "Well, what is it? Spit it out."

We don't know whether Chakmaryov works for the KGB. He may just be involved for personal profit. A more complex possibility is that he has received instructions to trade with prisoners. The KGB knows that prisoners are always in need of some good or another, and that guards always need money. Rather than permit black market trade to go on unsupervised below their radar, then, the KGB allows guards to trade with prisoners so long as they report the trades to the authorities. The guards get to supplement their incomes, and the KGB gets information. Trading without the KGB's knowledge would be impossible. When Shura gets up "to use the toilet," his fellow prisoner Mitya, on the next bunk, wakes up and watches from the window. He's quite familiar with these nightly visits to the toilet. Tomorrow morning, everything will be reported to the KGB, and they'll determine just how "legal" the previous night's illicit trade was. In the same way, Oreshkin, Chakmaryov's partner, and the duty officer Tuchtashev know exactly what is going on, and are playing their own roles. The same law that governs Soviet life in general governs life here too: everyone informs on everyone.

Here, then, you have fact number one: In contravention of interior ministry instructions, the KGB turns a blind eye toward this kind of illicit trading. And what if it is discovered? Precautions have been taken to ensure that this does happen: The upper echelon of camp staff is composed of interior ministry men who have been recruited into the KGB. But everything lies under a cloak of secrecy. The commandant does not know which of his officers works for the KGB. Everyone, therefore, fears everyone else. It's even possible that the interior ministry fields its own espionage network. The KGB, after all, operates beyond the law. Not that it matters much. Everyone meets in the Kremlin and papers over what needs to be papered over. The law is for the common people. Still, there is sometimes friction and competitive jealousy between the interior ministry and the KGB, and woe to the prisoner caught between them as between the hammer and the anvil.

Many thousands of rubles are illicitly smuggled into camp, much of it going to bribe guards. An equal volume of prisoner's letters flows directly to the KGB. But in order for the game to go on, some material must be allowed to reach its destination. The majority, however, is used as evidence for indictments of other political prisoners.

This brings us to fact number two: The KGB itself allowed and even encouraged us to send and receive illegal material, on the basis of which they would send others to prison.

So the way we had chosen to obtain the books in question was anything but straightforward. Assuming everything was inspected, why did the authorities allow us to receive the books? Did the KGB intend to soften us up, to allow us to occupy ourselves with Hebrew so that we would be less inclined to join protests within the camp? Or perhaps they permitted us to get something we'd be afraid to lose so that we'd be more hesitant about confronting camp staff? All of these factors almost certainly played a part. Clearly, whatever it was, this was not an expression of goodwill born of a desire to help us learn Hebrew before our emigration to Israel. The main reason to let us smuggle in the books was this: the Soviet regime was bowing to the pressure of the burgeoning Soviet Jewry movement abroad. God comes to the aid of those who cling to Him, and strengthens those who are strengthened through His commandments. We remained steadfast in our commitments, and our enemies sensed our firmness. But permitting us our books in fact did nothing to improve the Soviet image abroad; the transfer being illegal, they couldn't very well take credit for it or publicize it in the press. But the illegal transfer – like our illegal possession – gave the authorities the power to take away, at any moment, what they had given. The books were granted us without promises, and thus could be confiscated without breaking any promises.

I've already remarked on the uncertainty that resulted from the amorphousness and arbitrariness of camp rules. Those rules stated, for example, that a prisoner may submit complaints. Was this an irrevocable right or a revocable privilege? The word "may" was chosen precisely to engender such ambiguity.

I've also mentioned another kind of uncertainty, which derived from the set of rules that are both unknown and unknowable. You might characterize the relationship between prisoner and camp administration in terms of an implicit agreement or unspoken contract. For example, although prisoners were forbidden to visit other barracks, I was not punished for my regular visits to Shimon's. The first few times the guards on duty discovered me in Shimon's barracks, I was filled with dread. How was it that I had missed being warned of their arrival? I had carefully chosen a time when they were supposed to be elsewhere. I had sat facing a window so that I could see them coming, and still I had missed seeing them. But then something very odd usually happened. They either pretended not to notice me, or told me to go back to my own barracks, and then walked out without making sure that I obeyed. It seems they were under instructions not to harass me under certain circumstances, and all I could do was guess why. But in this way an informal understanding was reached, though neither the guards nor I had made any promises. So I had to guess which rules I was expected to follow, and where the lines of submission would have to be drawn. Would I be asked to give up on my kippah, on celebrating Passover, on studying the Torah, on keeping the Shabbat? How must I act in order to play the game by their rules? Even when it gave me temporary respite, this uncertainty played to the authorities' advantage.

One day, everything changed. The guards began to treat me harshly and to punish me for visiting other barracks, and when I tried to explain that it had until then been permitted, they insisted that of course it had always been forbidden; indeed, it became a punishable behavior from then onward. In some cases, they said, "Yes, the guard erred in permitting it. Good that you reminded us. We'll discipline him." Prisoners, as a rule, did not inform on guards or try to get them into trouble. We did not want to imply that we recognized the legitimacy of their rule, and besides, they could easily exact revenge on us.

This experience reflected a typical example of the fluctuating uncertainty of camp life: Just when the prisoner begins to relax, to accustom himself to the comfortable circumstances, the rules of the game change, and he finds himself bargaining with an officer: "I'll do such and such for you if you do such and such for me." But the officer never accepts this formulation. "Mendelevich, you're in no position to dictate terms. You're a prisoner like any other prisoner, and must submit to the rules. As for your requests, we have no intention of altering policy. Our function is to carry out the interior ministry's directives."

A few days later, for no apparent reason, the old understanding comes back into effect as suddenly as it was suspended. The officer smiles at you when you next encounter him: you have become a partner in his game of ambiguity, in which words and rules constantly shift meanings.

In the midst of this world of chimeras, a group of young Jews dreams of Israel, each of us wounded, bloodied, entrapped in the devilish thickets of "reeducation." How is it possible to bear this long enough to reach Israel?

There is only way: to be loyal to yourself and your people, to know why you're here, and where you're headed – not in an abstract way, but as a lived reality, manifest in your every act and decision. Only then do you stand a chance in their game. They think that if they've given me something, I will have to offer them something in return. Although I pretend this is the case, in reality I don't trouble myself trying to understand what they want from me. I refrain from work on Shabbat, I greet the Shabbat in my friends' barracks, I study Hebrew, I maintain contacts with the Ukrainian, Armenian, and Latvian nationalists. We smuggle out information and organize hunger strikes. And yet the authorities do not revoke our informal, unstated understanding; they're more invested in it now than I am. They think they have me hooked. We want books; fine, they'll let us have them, but the dark cloud of worry – knowing that this nebulous permission could be revoked at any time – hangs over us throughout.

We had successfully acquired books back in the Mordovian camp as well, albeit in a slightly different manner. Michael, who had trained as a specialized engineer, had been working then in the factory's office. The other office staffers were loyal administration people, one of whom, Oneshichenko, agreed to accept a package for Michael. When the package was delivered, however, the foodstuffs were missing.

"There was no sausage, honey or butter," Oneshichenko said. "I gave you everything that came in the package." When Michael opened the package, he was stunned to find all the books intact. The truth of the matter was that Michael didn't care about the food. The books were the main thing. And since his colleague had pilfered the food, it was unlikely he had reported the package to the KGB, and the authorities were unaware that they might have had new leverage over us.

Transferring these books from Mordovia to the Urals had proved no easier. Thorough searches were conducted before each journey (this was how my Hebrew primer *My Teacher* had been confiscated), so we paid Shura (as a "loyalist" his bags were not searched) to take them. The money for this came from our relatives. My father, for instance, had brought me two hundred rubles during one visit, and had mailed me another seven hundred rubles in Dutch guilders.

Michael took it upon himself to give some of the Hebrew lessons; Asher, Shimon, and Shabtai studied with me. Although I could read reasonably well, I wasn't sure my own error-ridden Hebrew was good enough to allow me to teach others.

My new surroundings, which encompassed so many more fellow Jewish camp mates than previously, compelled me to reassess my place in the social structure: would I consistently maintain an independent stand or begin to follow the majority? Here too I came up against a widespread human failing: the inability to muster all of one's energies to achieve a goal. All of us have experienced the failure to fulfill good intentions – or even to try to succeed. I now understood just how dangerous this insecurity could be. To overcome that fear of failure and follow through on an endeavor, I realized, one must believe in the truth of that endeavor not only intellectually, but emotionally as well.

And so I girded my belt, so to speak, and we began to study. My "advanced" group focused on Part Two of *1000 Words*; my students would discuss passages, and I would broaden the subjects of discussion and try to link them to our life in the camp. The moment I returned from work, I would rush to my bunk, pull out a textbook and dictionary, sit in a most uncomfortable position between bunks, and get down to business: translating texts, grappling with grammar. The light was dim, and my friends castigated me for damaging my eyesight, but I was utterly immersed. Meanwhile, each of us was copying the textbook by hand in case the originals were confiscated. Thus was born what we playfully called *The Yosef Notebooks*: a complete translation of the textbook together with commentaries, appendices, and glossary. Later, I know, Dymshits, Shimon, Shabtai, and Yaakov would use "my" book when there was no possibility of studying with a teacher. In fact I translated two textbooks, one geared for a vocabulary of 1,500 words, and the other 3,000 words, and began work on another that assumed a vocabulary of 5,000 words.

To study and to teach – these were my true pleasures. This was no mere exercise in linguistics for people with nothing better to do, but a practical preparation for our future lives in Israel and a way of forging our identities as Jews. It created a kind of cycle: our "Jewish souls" awakened us to study, and our study in turn enriched the soil of our Jewishness. A prisoner who refused to become enslaved or abased would find a way to resist the authorities. Such a person would be able to transcend a way of life forged by constant conversations with likeminded colleagues (usually over tea); by an extended dialogue with officials, KGB agents, prosecutors, and others; and by an endless series of punishments, including cancellation of family visits, revocation of canteen privileges, and solitary confinement. Yet from the moment we decided to make our studies and preparations for a life in Israel our highest commitments, we had a standard against which to measure the prudence of joining this or that protest or hunger strike. Given our commitment to our studies, we couldn't take part in every campaign. Getting punished, after all, involved a great deal of wasted time. It took a long time to recover from a stay in solitary confinement. On the other hand, we recognized that we had to take a firm stand on certain issues: for example, when the authorities, acting on instructions from Moscow, canceled family visits for the entire camp without cause or explanation. Because the connection to the outside was essential, here we had to join hands with other prisoners.

Do not imagine that it was a simple matter to keep aloof from certain adventures and stick to our Jewish activities alone. Although each of us had belonged to the Jewish movement, we had been educated in Soviet schools. Each step toward Judaism, therefore, represented a negation of our pasts, of our very essences. It is likewise a mistake to accuse prisoners of foolishness in opposing the authorities' arbitrariness. Even if a certain act of resistance seemed to have failed, in the longer view it sometimes took on another aspect; sometimes the first signs of success appeared only much later. Every operation had its positive side. We had been sent to camp precisely because we had engaged in a certain struggle, so naturally we had a fighting spirit, and all else being equal we tended to fight rather than sit on our hands. At the beginning, our default was to ask ourselves: why not join an action or a strike? After a while, we learned to begin with a different question: why join?

Those who belonged to the Jewish group enjoyed a certain status in the eyes of other political prisoners. Had we wanted, we easily could have acted as leaders. Each of us had to suppress in himself the temptation to lead, and to persuade himself that he was among equals.

It's not easy to articulate the significance of the isolation in which we layered ourselves. It's not that we feared punishments or the cold or hunger. We were past that. Rather we perceived events in the camp as ephemeral; only our studies held lasting value. Thus our way of organizing ourselves vis-à-vis our surroundings served as a means both of self-preservation and collective development. This was no accident, for as I've mentioned the remarkable strength of our people has always rested not on individualism but on unity. The Ukrainian, Lithuanian, and Russian prisoners, by contrast, fragmented into small groups that were forced to expend a great deal of energy in internal fractiousness.

At a later stage, when I remained alone in camp, I more keenly felt the significance of our group. For now, I didn't have to feel ashamed for not taking part in a hunger strike. I would merely say that our group had elected not to join in. Other prisoners respected our unity and the serious consideration we gave to our decisions. The authorities, too, were aware that any move against one of us would bring about a response from the entire group, and that this response would come not from intimidated individuals, but from a strong, collective commitment.

Shabtai acted as our historian. Drawing on a deep reservoir of knowledge, he charted for us the entire course of Jewish history, from the Creation to the present day, complete with names, dates, and analyses of larger patterns. We had to be careful in our note taking not to mention Israel, the Jewish people, or God. We were under constant watch. When they noticed us sitting in a corner, listening to Shabtai and taking notes, they accosted us and demanded to know what we were up to.

"We're studying history."

"Which history?" And they would grab our notes and peruse them: events, dates, 163 BCE, 2 CE, Rome, ancient Greece… A record of the Jewish encounter with civilizations long past. "Fine, you may continue."

Over time, we amassed what amounted to a proper history textbook, which we would go on to use after Shabtai's release. It would have been effortlessly easy to fill our time with tea and vapid talk; Shabtai, Asher, and Michael could chatter away endlessly about the most trivial matters. But the moment we had to prepare for a class, or wished to discuss what had been learned, we moved quickly on to subjects of greater significance.

The closer we became, the greater were the possibilities of rejection. We had too many points of contact, too much in common. Shimon, in particular, had a hard time getting along with the others. He was just then "embracing the Torah." You couldn't say he was "returning" to religion, exactly, since he had never left it. As the son of staunch Communists, he was more akin to what the Talmud calls a "captured infant" – someone who through no fault of his own is raised in total ignorance of Judaism – and his move toward faith involved a painful severing of ties with his family. He grew to hate his past, unable to acknowledge the ways it had auspiciously shaped the present. He would pronounce definitive judgments: "that's a Jewish quality," or "that's an un-Jewish quality," without pausing to realize that such a rigid black-or-white approach might itself be a rather un-Jewish attitude. He couldn't see that even if he thought himself a more "authentic" Jew than someone, this was no cause to act with condescension or disparagement. You cannot say to a Soviet-educated man of fifty: "Why don't you pray? You betray our faith. You're no Jew at all." That man, after all, had not interpreted his Jewishness in terms of observing Jewish law.

"Do you too think I'm not a Jew?" he asked me.

I had no trouble answering the question, though I did not think we had the duty to pronounce on the question of who is a Jew, or the authority to banish the "not sufficiently Jewish" from our ranks. Instead, fearing that our already tiny group would fracture, I did everything in my power to avoid exacerbating the situation. Better a less-than-full Jewish life in camp than no Jewish life at all.

"Do they not distinguish between 'authentic Jews' and 'inauthentic Jews' in Israel?" Shabtai asked.

I didn't know what to say, but I tried to express my feelings on the matter. "Naturally, I don't take any pleasure in the fact that you don't observe Jewish law. I believe that the duty to fulfill God's commandments rests as squarely as you as it does on me. The fact that you don't believe doesn't render you exempt. But I'm not interested in tagging people. My own faith is flawed, and I'm in no position to determine who is a Jew."

My reply more or less gave Shabtai rest, but Shimon could not accept it. He was under the impression that unbelief calls one's ethical integrity into question. Every day, he said something like, "Shabtai is so selfish; everything he does in the group he does for himself." In our history classes, he constantly challenged Shabtai: "Why do you characterize the Torah as our cultural heritage? It's our spiritual heritage. Why do you portray the Maccabee revolt as a war for national and religious independence? You should have said that the essence of Chanukah is in the miracle of the vessel of oil." And so on, ad infinitum.

Is it not a terrible feeling to begin to grow apart from your closest friends? To lose sleep and to suffer from high blood pressure over the dissolution of the bonds of friendship? Is that not some kind of divine retribution? In a free society, I would be free to choose my friendships; here I was compelled to live in maximal and continual contact with people who had been chosen for me. If someone's spirit breaks after years in camp, it is not the guards' abuses alone that have reduced him to that state. Who can say, in the end, who inflicts the sharper pain: your enemies, or your friends?

It annoyed me that my friends were so intelligent, and so brave, and yet I had become unable to enjoy their company. It fell to me, moreover, to iron out the difficulties between them, so that Shimon would reconcile with Shabtai, and Michael would no longer clash with his students. One day we received letters from Israel, and I would have liked to see us reading them together rather than each man in his corner. To experience a sense of unity between us here and them over there – that is precisely what lends meaning to our time in prison.

· · · · ·

The unity of our group was threatened not just by our internal social dynamics but by external forces too. Some among us had one foot inside the group and one foot sunk in the camp's political morass. Take Yaakov, for instance, a forty-five-year-old former English and gym teacher. Although we had included him in our celebrations of the Jewish holidays, his heart wasn't in it. He had grown up in the lap of Soviet culture but then came to understand that it was a culture founded on lies. And yet, he had continued to educate Soviet children into the Communist faith. When Nikita Khrushchev opened the door a crack and allowed criticism of Stalin's crimes, some took it as an invitation to level charges against the regime as such. In their excitement, they failed to notice when Brezhnev took power and took a new approach. Brezhnev frowned and said, "Nikita Sergeyevich weakened the people's discipline. We must tighten the screws."

To be more precise, it was Mikhail Suslov who had uttered those words, and Brezhnev who implemented the "tightening." Yaakov, meanwhile, together with some other Jews, began to dig deeper into Soviet reality only to discover that the rottenness at the surface was but the outer layer concealing the true decadence and decay within. Some tried digging for the truth and arrived at the KGB. Yaakov continued burrowing, and sent earnest suggestions to Brezhnev about how to improve the regime. He also told jokes about Dzerzhinsky, founder of the Bolshevik secret police, the Cheka.

The KGB in Moldovia started to look into Yaakov out of sheer boredom and idleness. The political opposition had long since been wiped out, and here were a few buzzing flies to swat. Thus they knocked one day at the apartment of the author of those proposals for building a more perfect and more "Soviet" education system. There they found a copy of *Doctor Zhivago* by Pasternak and a photo of Brezhnev taped to a toilet seat. They rubbed their hands gleefully: they had stumbled upon an instance of the anti-Communist plague. Although Yaakov was taken in for questioning, they didn't have enough evidence to charge him. Just then, however, competition was heating up among the various KGB field offices. In Leningrad, they had netted a big catch: thirty-five arrests, fifteen-year sentences – with the resulting promotions, medals, and awards. Envious of the success of their Leningrad colleagues, the Kishinev agents "discovered" that Yaakov and his friends were Jews – in other words, Zionists. (Every Soviet citizen knew that all Jews were Zionists bent on world domination.) Since Zionists were well-known enemies of Socialism and progress, Yaakov got not the usual two-year sentence but the maximum sentence of seven years, and that is how he arrived in our camp together with real Zionists.

"Yosef," the others said, "you must persuade Yaakov to decide once and for all which group he belongs to: us or the pro-democracy prisoners." Naturally I didn't wish simply to give up on him. Over the course of several weeks, we had soul-baring talks in which I told him that the struggle against the Soviet regime wasn't a Jewish struggle, that there was no Jewish future in the USSR, and that it was better to join us and eventually emigrate to Israel than to waste away here.

Not long before, Yaakov had suggested to the KGB in Moldavia a solution to the "Jewish problem." "You know why the Zionist movement arose? Because of the lack of Jewish theaters and cafes. I'll develop a plan for the rehabilitation of Jewish culture, and you'll be rid of the Zionists." The KGB officers, putting on serious faces, said that they'd consider the idea. Obviously they had not the slightest interest in Jewish culture, but if this little Jew is trying so hard, why not amuse him a little? He may agree to collaborate, and then he could be planted inside the aliyah movement, which had until then remained impenetrable to moles. So they let Yaakov work on a plan under the title "Saving the Jews from the Zionists," and to write an article on the subject for the camp paper. Since only KGB collaborators published there, the moment his piece came out Yaakov was shunned.

"Yaakov, do you really believe this is the best way to prevent Jews from leaving the Soviet Union? Do you really believe the KGB takes a genuine interest in your proposals?"

According to him, he himself didn't believe in his proposals; they were meant to lay bare the anti-Semitic character of the regime. But in practice, he hoped they would have another effect. "This way they'll grant me an early release," he confided to a close friend, "and I can return to work in Moldavia." Of course that didn't happen, and Yaakov, now embittered, was full of imprecations for the state. "Yaakov," we would say, "calm yourself. Better that you study Hebrew and history than spend your energies on this futile fury." But in Yaakov's mind, to study Hebrew when the fate of the USSR hung in the balance was impossible. Only after a month-long campaign of persuasion did he relent, promising to coordinate his future steps with the larger group.

It later turned out that he had made this promise only because he pitied us, and had relented only under pressure. In fact, his political views remained unchanged, though he had given the false impression that he was working on behalf of the group of Jewish prisoners. In the tense atmosphere that followed, we invited him to clarify. "Why did you renege on our agreement? You promised to let go of your quixotic quest to reform the Soviet system." Yaakov expressed remorse for his actions and promised to rectify things. But having lost our trust, we decided to request that he submit for Michael's approval any future statements and complaints he would write. In other words, matters had deteriorated to the point that we would have to resort to internal censorship.

· · · · ·

Yaakov turned for support to a well-known prisoner – almost a camp institution in himself – named Janovitc (the son of Jankel). He could be counted on for supplying addresses for complaints; indeed his motto was: "Let us bring down the regime with our complaints!" It's doubtful whether he believed in this motto, but his restless nature compelled him to do something, to take action. So why not issue complaints? Well practiced in complaint writing, Janovitc had turned it into an art form. So great was his charisma, that for years one of the more accepted ways of resisting the authorities in camp was the issuing of complaints and petitions. Things got to the point where in 1977 the twenty-sixth Communist Party Congress had to take up the issue of the proliferation of prisoner complaints.

This story actually began in 1939, when a Jewish boy named Misha Hershkowitz (later Michael Janovitc), living in the Romanian town Galati (Galatz in Yiddish), read in the paper about the Communist youth movement, the Young Pioneers. (This was for children aged ten to fifteen; after that, they joined the Komsomol.) The descriptions of the Pioneers' adventures so enthralled Misha's imagination that the eight-year-old decided to run away from home and cross the Dniester River into Soviet Bessarabia. But instead of enrolling in the Pioneers, the boy was sent to a camp for juvenile delinquents. His father searched for him in various Red Cross institutions, but to no avail. He could not get his son back. Misha, meanwhile, was receiving an accelerated education in the ways of the underworld. After "graduating," he fled the juvenile delinquents' center and wandered the country, supporting himself with petty thefts and shoplifting. The German invasion of Russia in 1941 found him in the Caucasus, where he witnessed the chaotic retreat of the Red Army. The woman he'd been boarding with sent him one day to loot a state-owned warehouse of furs. Being quite a thin young man, he managed to slither in through an air duct, but once inside the townspeople wouldn't let him out again until he had passed out every last fur. Having done so, they ran off, leaving him to his own devices.

Somehow, Misha managed to escape, finding his way ultimately to a sanitarium housing dozens of the children of Moscow scientists suffering from tuberculosis. Thirty years later, he still vividly recalled a girl with an angelic face, her beauty unmarred even by a curved spine. With perfect pitch, she would burst out in song every morning. After the Soviet army fled, but before the Germans arrived, the locals decided to "settle the score" with their Russian occupiers. One night, Misha awoke to the noise of locals, in fur hats and long coats, storming the patient rooms, bending over each bed in turn.

A mustachioed Circassian man stooped over Misha, lifted the blanket, and moved on. When dawn broke, Misha found himself in an eerily quiet room. The girl with the beautiful voice sang no longer. The limp bodies of the Russian children who had been murdered during the night were taken away. Although he was a Jew, he could pass for a Circassian, and because of his appearance, Misha had been spared.

As his wanderings continued, Misha was adopted by a unit of combat troops who took a liking to this bright boy; possibly he reminded them of the children they had left behind at home. It's only a pity he's a Jew, they said, but even this was rectified when one soldier baptized the boy in a lake.

After the war, Misha turned to a legal aid office in Moscow to help locate his family. Having discovered they were abroad, a startled lawyer shooed him out of the building. "Get out of here, boy. I didn't see or hear a thing. Forget that your relatives exist." But Misha could not forget, and several years later appealed to the International Red Cross. Unbeknownst to him, his father had meanwhile been making repeated inquiries with Soviet authorities. (Because they had been searching for him under a different spelling of the family name, Misha's sisters would locate him only in 1977, by which time his entire family had moved to Israel.)

In the meantime, Misha had matured into manhood, and although he had barely completed primary school, he had been well schooled by life. By chance, he began to collect artworks, soon discovering both an aptitude for distinguishing fakes from originals and a deep grasp of painting. Before long, he had become a prominent collector of Russian painting (purchasing, among others, some of the first works of Chagall and El Lissitzky). Art collecting was then one of the few fields in Russia still open to entrepreneurship and enterprise. The street smarts Misha had picked up between his wanderings and his stay at the juvenile delinquents' camp, together with his natural talents, allowed him to operate freely. He tracked down pieces of antique art that had not yet been confiscated by the authorities, gauged their values, and persuaded their owners to sell them. All of this demanded ingenuity and guts. Misha Janovitc became rich, and built himself a two-story villa in Leningrad. He married the daughter of a Russian priest who had been executed, and adopted her family name: Makarenko. Just to be on the safe side, he had himself baptized a second time. He didn't put too much stock in his wealth; the main thing was the wheeling and dealing itself. One of his favorite pastimes was to dress up and test his chameleon-like abilities. "When I'm with Russians," he said, "I'm the perfect Slav; when in the company of Ukrainians, I become the most ardent supporter of Ukrainian independence; and among Jews I'm a fervent Zionist." I used to ask myself who Makarenko was really: an altruist who never thought of his own interests; a cunning politician; or a mere rogue? He was so good at identifying forgeries that had he known how to paint he could have been a brilliant forger. But instead of creating artistic compositions, he put together masterful real-life compositions of human destinies and events. Is that not the greatest form of art?

His last "creation" was the founding of a party that he intended as nothing less than a rival to the Communist Party. He gave himself the modest position of member of the criminal investigation committee of Novosibirsk (he was then managing a gallery on the campus of the university there). This "party" had its own ideological line – it criticized the Communist policies that oppressed workers – but its only member was Makarenko's adopted son Sasha. Yet he managed to make it seem as though his party was a well-organized mass movement. Even Communist parties abroad were convinced of its influence. János Kádár, the longtime leader of Communist Hungary, requested the presence of representatives of Makarenko's party at the Conference of European Communist Parties, and had to postpone the conference when none could be found. The party also sent a cartload of documents to the Kremlin, leaving no doubt about its existence. With the KGB exhausting itself trying to pick up the trail of this great party, Makarenko was arranging for Marc Chagall's visit to Novosibirsk. Chagall had long dreamed of returning to visit Russia from his Parisian exile, but had always refused an official reception in Moscow. Here, too, Makarenko displayed his persuasive powers, promising the famous painter that he could come straight to Novosibirsk without having to stop in Moscow. The main attraction of the trip would be bear hunting. Makarenko bought a bear from a circus, and arranged for the hunting party to be accompanied by a professional sharpshooter, who would shoot the bear at the same time Chagall took his shot to ensure a hit.

All this would have continued smoothly had Makarenko not stumbled by chance one day into the apartment of a diamond dealer (among his clients were Soviet Premier Alexei Kosygin's daughters) who also happened to be active in an underground group. By a stroke of bad luck, a search was scheduled for that apartment that day, and Misha Makarenko was arrested. At first he aroused no suspicions, but when investigators began to connect the dots, and when the KGB discovered a cache of his party's documents, their interest was aroused. Still, they couldn't solve the riddle of this Jew who had been twice baptized and had thrice changed his name. On the orders of the very highest Soviet authorities, the investigation was extended three times. The KGB tried in vain to find his hidden millions. Makarenko's adopted son twice gave them false leads, and finally agents demolished his house in the hopes of discovering bars of gold stashed away in the structure. When this failed to turn up anything, they sent him to labor camp for eight years.

There Misha was something of a mysterious figure. To the camp administration he presented himself as a Communist; to the dissidents, he portrayed himself a pro-democracy activist. In short, he was an actor by nature, and played his roles to the hilt. Other prisoners called him a "fish," but meant it as a term of respect. (In camp parlance, a "fish" is a prisoner who could "go with the flow" and comfortably swim in any waters.) Camp staff feared and despised him; fellow prisoners admired him. Even within the gloomy routines of the camp, he knew how to enjoy life. He was generous of heart – never refusing to help someone in need. A witness to his boisterous, frenzied activity might imagine him to be driven by a single-minded sense of purpose. In reality, he had absolutely no comprehensive view of the world, merely an unwillingness to accept the Soviet regime and an aspiration to realize the highest ideals – an aspiration to believe in something for its own sake. He did not have a broad education: primary school, as he himself recognized, can only take you so far. Among Jewish prisoners he was quite open; he felt that we could understand him. We were the first aliyah activists he had met; until then he had known only Jewish businessmen, not Jewish idealists. "But I'll never be a Zionist," he insisted. "I ask only one thing of you: when you get to Israel, look for my family. I'm convinced that they are there."

Only those who knew him well were aware that this man who so generously dispensed bread and smiles to his fellow inmates was at heart a Jewish boy who longed for the familial warmth he never had. We accepted him even as we remained wary of him. Some believed he would one day gallop into Red Square on a white steed (never imagining that this sturdy, bearded Russian was Jewish). Others suspected he was a KGB mole (the KGB encouraged such rumors).

When he came from Mordovia to the Urals, he brought with him several new ideas. The first was the suggestion that we put together a campaign of writing complaints and petitions. Second, he claimed that we would all be pardoned in 1977 in honor of the fiftieth anniversary of the Soviet Union. Third, he thought it likely that all war criminals would be released. And finally, he proposed organizing a "political prisoners' day."

For certain people, it often happens that however incoherent their plan of action, their behavior appears to the outside observer to follow a consistent course. This is how it was with Makarenko – not merely in the eyes of prisoners who were used to labeling every Jewish activity as belonging to some alleged worldwide plan, but also in the eyes of the KGB's experts in identifying "enemy intentions."

Another of Makarenko's ideas was that an enemy is best struck at his most vulnerable point, at his Achilles heel, and for the USSR this was the fear of negative publicity and bad international press. This fear granted prisoners a weapon: their right to send complaints and petitions to party institutions, professional unions, public figures, and journalists. Until then, the authorities had used the complicated phrasing of the internal regulations to deny us that right, but we learned we could use the same complexity to our advantage. The camp staff simply did not know the subject as intimately as Makarenko, which meant that we could use the internal contradictions of the regulations to challenge the authorities. They tended to focus on small infractions: an open button, a cap that wasn't doffed, a one-minute tardiness to work. But their infractions were greater than ours, and our complaints could bring about requests for clarifications and investigations, and draw attention to the camp administration's missteps. In such a way, we might burden them so much with the work of having to answer our charges that they would have less time to persecute us. At the same time, we would increase the export of information to a population that might begin to understand the essence of the regime. For who staffs state institutions if not Soviet citizens? Our stream of complaints, then, could only help raise awareness about the camps. In short, Makarenko counseled, we must strike at them with their own laws.

Many political prisoners were well practiced at writing complaints, but Makarenko perfected the art. It was he who coined the phrase "complaint campaign." Even before his arrest, he was a master of this art, as he was in the art of submitting legal claims and lawsuits. It came naturally to him. It proved even more natural for prisoners like Yaakov, who poured all their bitterness into their complaints, and who enjoyed giving the dignified veneer of "political struggle" to their exercises in therapeutic catharsis.

The first such campaign quickly took on immense proportions. Every self-respecting prisoner was expected to produce at least five complaints a day. Makarenko produced even more, and in addition checked the drafts of other prisoners. Many prisoners, however, opposed the campaign, arguing that there was little hope of its improving matters and that our appeals for help were humiliating. "Whom are we complaining to? To the same bastards who threw us into prison? This is who you expect justice from?"

After much discussion, the Jewish group took a stance slightly different from Makarenko's. We preferred to use complaints not as carpet bombs but as precision weapons aimed at specific instances of suppression of our rights.

Makarenko's second campaign was also geared to stirring the prisoners to complaint writing. He spread the rumor that the law stipulated that a prisoner who had served three-quarters of his sentence could request to live outside the camp in a kind of house arrest. The veteran inmates, at first not believing it, hesitated to lodge complaints on the matter, lest they be punished. But Makarenko was also a master at starting rumors, tossing out a well-placed word or two at the right moment. "I received a reply from the prosecutor's office confirming my understanding of the relevant clause." Or, "They say that Camp 35 has already released a few prisoners to house arrest. You'd better hurry to act before the window of opportunity closes." The rumor had its desired effect. Every morning, a line of illiterate old prisoners would form, and Makarenko would compose complaints on their behalf. Some said he received gifts from them, but whatever compensation he may or may not have received it is certain that he exerted himself tirelessly for them for days on end. The authorities, of course, threatened him: "You'll be punished for slander and for intentional disruption of the work schedule." But they lacked sufficient proof to do anything about it.

Yet they could – and did – prosecute his supporters. Polouchov, for instance, was sentenced to a half year in the camp's internal prison for "failing to keep his sleeping area clean," as though anyone could be meticulous about cleanliness in our conditions.

Makarenko would sign his complaints, "the Communist Makarenko."

"Makarenko, you're not a Communist. You don't have a Party membership card."

"I'm a Communist in my soul." He would go into raptures of delight when he remembered this retort of his. "You're not satisfied with my signature?" And from then on he signed his petitions: "dangerous political criminal Makarenko."

It's not easy to describe the style of his complaints, which were laced with a breadth of legal erudition and with a mocking humor. For instance, we were treated to a weekly movie screening, invariably depicting the October Revolution and the founding era of Communism. Although all of us grew to hate this ritual, we felt powerless to do anything about it until Makarenko came up with a solution. "Lately," he wrote in a complaint, "the camp staff has seen fit to screen films about Lenin. When enemies of the Soviet state here in the camp see the great leader of our revolution on screen, they mock him and mutter obscenities. As a Communist, I cannot bear to hear how they scorn our great leader, and so respectfully request that such movies no longer be shown." Ultimately, the goal was achieved: for a long time, there were no screenings at all.

Generally, though, Misha's complaints were well reasoned. He had managed to bring with him into camp the full set of the multivolume penal code, which content he would then invoke to harass Soviet jurists, not hesitating to exploit legal ambiguities by distorting the meaning of some clause. Take, for example, his complaint that "in solitary confinement prisoners receive bread and water every other day." This implied that every other day, prisoners in solitary got nothing at all. In fact, however, one day prisoners would receive 450 grams of bread, 50 grams fish, 30 grams porridge, and soup consisting of 60 grams of vegetables and 300 grams of water. On the next day, prisoners would get only water and bread, as Makarenko wrote. On the "good" day, each prisoner would get about 1,700 calories, when the average grown man requires 2,200 to 2,400 a day. In other words, the average caloric intake amounted to a diet of gradual starvation. But Makarenko's phrasing made matters sound even worse than they were.

"But Misha," we'd say, "it's a lie."

"And what of it? Don't they lie to us?"

"But why must you take your example from those bastards?"

Another of his complaints, however, was entirely accurate. It had to do with the guards' practice of confiscating our warm clothes in the dead of winter, when temperatures could fall to minus fifty degrees Celsius. In submitting his complaint, Makarenko volunteered his own clothes. "I request that my clothing be given to the children of Vietnam." (During the Vietnam War, Soviet propaganda harped relentlessly on the suffering that American troops were causing to Vietnamese children, without of course mentioning that the Soviets had inflicted similar suffering in every country they conquered.) This gesture earned the support of a great many prisoners, and the winter confiscations ended. This highlighted another factor that could increase a complaint's effectiveness: if many prisoners complained, it sent a signal to the authorities that there was a danger of a larger outbreak unless they agreed to make changes.

As for the rumors of imminent pardons for political prisoners, Makarenko reported that he had overheard two officers speaking of it. But it wasn't clear to me why so many inmates believed him. It is true that the possibility was hinted at in other ways. December 30, 1972, marked the fiftieth anniversary of the formation of the USSR. For three months before, some prisoners felt optimistic, and more readily joined Makarenko's letter-writing campaigns. Even the guards took seriously the possibility that the Kremlin might announce a general amnesty and they acted with relative restraint as a result.

Prisoners eager to grasp the slimmest thread of hope saw signs of optimism everywhere. "Did you see how good the fish portions were today? Pardons must be in the offing." Or, "Did you see that? The guard didn't blink an eye when he saw I wasn't working. It's clear I'm to be pardoned soon." Or, "They haven't made me shave my beard in almost a month. It could be a sign that they'll let me go."

We also interpreted the usual hints in our letters from Israel in this hopeful light: "We visited Uncle Sam, who says the kids will recover soon" (i.e., American sources were predicting our release). Or my father would write, "Aunt Golda [i.e., Golda Meir] has found some good medicine." And so on. Then someone would say to me, "This can't be coincidental, Yosef. Your father is a serious man, and wouldn't mention Golda frivolously. Something must be afoot."

From all of the above I concluded one thing: I should redouble my Hebrew studies. I studied for hours upon hours, and the time flashed by at lightning speed. Bent over my bunk, I filled whole notebooks with translations and exercises. Michael showed me how to use cards small enough to store in matchboxes with Hebrew words on one side and Russian translations on the back. Unlike vocabulary lists in notebooks, this allowed me to put hard words aside so that I could practice memorizing them more frequently. By the end of my imprisonment, I had some ten thousand cards categorized by level of difficulty. I would take a matchbox to work in my palm and review five hundred to eight hundred words a day, including sixty new words.

Guards would occasionally rifle through the cards and scatter them. Once I was so absorbed in copying a passage from *1000 Words* that I failed to notice a figure standing behind me until I heard a familiar snorting sound. Lifting my eyes, I saw Fyodorov himself, the nastiest of them all, and my blood froze. I steeled myself to fight tooth and nail for my textbook.

"What are you doing, Mendelevich?"

Sensing that he would confiscate the book whatever I said, I saw nothing to lose. "I'm studying Hebrew," I replied with pride.

He fixed an expressionless gaze on me. "Well, then, study!" And with that he headed for the door. It seems he had merely been strolling around, as was his wont. He regarded the camp as his home. We had learned how to read Fyodorov's moods by certain signs: facial expressions, the twitching of his nose and volume of his snorts, his uniform (he would dress up when he was primed for special abuse). We had the impression that the many crimes he had committed had thrown off his mental balance. Very often he would behave like a man possessed, which is why his response to catching me studying Hebrew had been so unexpected. Was he under special instructions not to interfere with our Hebrew study? Or perhaps he was simply too drunk to register my answer.

Strangely, I sometimes thought that Fyodorov was capable of empathizing with another's pain. I never once shared this observation with my friends; they would have eaten me alive. "Fyodorov? A human being with sympathies? Have you lost it?" Perhaps he treated me differently. In any case, even when he punished me I never sensed a sadistic pleasure. He seemed at such times to be an exhausted clerk, a man worn down by his duties. Was this because I never hurled abuse at the camp's officers or guards? (Other prisoners would hatefully call them "Gestapo.") I seldom argued with them. When I resisted their attempts to prevent me from observing Jewish law, I did what I did without fuss.

It's also possible that Fyodorov's Jewish wife – an accountant named Esther Rabinovich – influenced his attitude. They had met during the war, when a great many Jews fled from the Germans toward the Urals. Oddly enough, their children would have qualified for Israeli citizenship. Their slothful son worked as a camp guard before going off to university, and their fine-featured daughter (quite Jewish in appearance), who worked as a camp censor, attracted the gaze of many a prisoner.

· · · · ·

As soon as I arrived in camp, I was made to do construction work: mixing and hauling cement, digging trenches, loading bricks onto trucks. Though it was strenuous, I didn't fear the work; I preferred working in the open air to suffocating in the constricted and polluted factory.

Ivan Bogdanov, our half-mad foreman, had been imprisoned for stealing radioactive material. He had planned to sell it to the Americans in return for vodka. He was sentenced to ten years, and was considered loyal to the camp administration. But the real brains of our construction team was none other than Misha Janovitc Makarenko, who had been promoted from simple laborer to "personal secretary," which meant that he was our acting foreman, leaving Bogdanov with not much more to do than preparing our tea. Makarenko's "rule," if you could call it that, was a bright time. He somehow gave the authorities the impression that we were exceeding our work quota by thirty percent when in fact we had fulfilled barely half of it. This meant food bonuses: an extra bowl of porridge and another hundred grams of bread.

Makarenko also enabled me to keep Shabbat by reporting some of my work during the week as though I had done it on Saturday. We would be studying Hebrew after work, and he would come over to say that if I agreed to unload a recently arrived cement truck, he would list the work as having been completed on Saturday. We would interrupt our lesson and spend an hour unloading the truck while conversing in Hebrew.

But Fyodorov, with his uncanny sense of smell, soon sniffed something suspicious in these "Jewish dealings," as he put it, and together with the other dissidents we were replaced on the construction job by the former Nazi Polizei and sent to work at a factory producing electric heaters. This was exceedingly exhausting work – and harmful to one's health – and on the day I was supposed to start it I presented myself at the office of the camp physician, Dr. Petrov. I informed him that my glasses had broken, and that there would be little point sending me to perform work that required great dexterity. Several times, I was called into the administrative offices, and each time I presented my shattered lenses. In the end, they gave in and let me be for several happy months. I used the time to learn the Jewish blessings, to study the Torah and the Passover Haggadah (a copy of which had been brought from Mordovia), and to talk with Shimon about matters of faith.

· · · · ·

On December 30, 1972, the camp went silent with anticipation of the promised pardons. That day and the next, when Russians celebrate the New Year holiday, we couldn't pick up the usual radio broadcasts from Moscow. On January 1, we went to work. The winter sun had not penetrated the dawn mists of the Urals. Snow had blanketed the earth in white. All the camp officers stood by the gates, hands thrust deep into their long overcoats. The column of prisoners stood across from them in suspense. One gate led toward the factory, the other toward freedom. Which would open now?

Kotov raised his arm and the gate to the factory swung open. "To work – march!" The guards, like dogs smelling blood, seemed eager to leap at the passing prisoners. They read our names from their list, calling us to the room where searches were conducted.

"Ivanov."

"Here."

Onanesku, Kudirka, Lukyanenko, Nikolyenko. "Nikolyenko! Why do you have your hands in your pockets?"

"It's cold; my hands are freezing."

"Arguing with an officer? Fifteen days in solitary."

And so on. "Uzlov, why is your cap not in order?"

"It was torn, sir."

"Damaging camp property. Ten days in solitary."

And so forth, meting out punishment after punishment as if to say: "You thought today you'd win your freedom, that our rule would be over? Well, you're still under our thumbs and we'll do with you as we please." In this way they revenged our three months of anticipation and quickly made up for the lost time by returning the shocked prisoners to a state of submission.

There was indeed an amnesty officially announced on that December 30, but it specifically excluded "political criminals." As a matter of fact, not a single prisoner was released. The announcement was a sham, meant to advertise Soviet "humanitarianism," while the amnesty law was composed primarily of clauses specifying who was excluded. We used to joke that to qualify for amnesty you had to have been a pregnant Communist Party member who had joined the ranks in 1902. (This of course was an impossibility.)

They managed to find a factory job even for a half-blind prisoner like me, putting me and Makarenko (who seemed to suffer every known ailment) to work on making joints for heat regulators. Every day, we were expected to put together 3,100 joints, which meant laboring at a backbreaking pace. By the end of the workday, our eyes burned, and we couldn't so much as hold a spoon in our fingers. But that was just at the beginning. Before long, our fingers were so dexterous that the finished product flew out of our hands as fast as words could come out of our mouths. We talked nonstop, pausing only when we were visited by fellow prisoners (in my case, fellow Jewish prisoners) who came to take a break in our dark corner. The much-beloved and much-consulted Makarenko was visited by everyone, so much so that our corner sometimes resembled a legal aid office, giving me a front-row seat to observe the secret of Misha's success. He would talk to a peasant as though he were a simple villager, to a dissident as though he were an intellectual, and to young people as though he himself were young – all the while remaining true to himself. But the main thing was that he made his listener or conversation partner feel as though he were the most important person of all. I often saw people who had been prejudiced against him develop a fondness for him after a few visits. Nor was he stingy with compliments, discerning the best features of every person who came to ask his advice. "Yosef," he often said, "your dignity amazes me. You follow your principles without ostentation but with admirable decisiveness." He had hit the bull's eye; even when I failed, I did aspire to act that way, and his words flattered me. "Better go easy on the praise," I replied. "When I hear praise being laid on too thick I start to suspect that something's up, especially when it comes from you. Don't forget that I watch how you flatter others." Still, despite these skepticisms, one couldn't help wonder, "Well, what if he's right about me?"

After the failures of his campaigns, Makarenko came up with a new idea: marking a Memorial Day for Victims of Soviet Prison Camps. He chose September 5, the day the Cheka issued its "Red Terror" decree in 1918, which called upon the Bolsheviks to annihilate their enemies. This unprecedented decree, which in effect legalized mass murder, ushered in a bloodbath in which tens of millions perished. Since hundreds of thousands of Jews were among the victims, our group decided to participate in the hunger strike called for that day. The strike announcement made explicit reference to "the memory of the victims of the Red Terror."

That night, we snuck into an empty warehouse to meet with representatives of the Armenians, Lithuanians, Ukrainians, and Russians. I represented the Jews. Makarenko delivered a rousing speech that would not have seemed out of place in any Soviet newspaper had the phrase "red murderers" been replaced with "fascist murderers." At its conclusion, a sack of dirt was ceremoniously dumped on the ground in a symbolic gesture of burial. Each community lit a candle, and I recited the Kel Malei Rachamim funeral prayer. Even without understanding the Hebrew words, many prisoners were moved to tears.

"You're becoming a real rabbi," Makarenko remarked the next day.

"Woe is us if all our rabbis are as ignorant as I am," I replied. But he wouldn't hear of it, and from that day forward many of the non-Jewish prisoners were convinced that I was an ordained rabbi.

• • • • •

I knew a great deal about Makarenko, but he by no means confided all his secrets in me. That ceremonial sack of earth in the warehouse, for instance, turned out to be from an escape tunnel being dug by a group of young prisoners led by Abankin. They had spotted a white tree fifteen meters outside the fence, and reasoned that it must be rooted in dry soil rather than in the swampland that otherwise surrounded the camp. It was toward this tree that they aimed their tunneling. Lyosha Safronov, my old friend, was one of the operation's architects, and Makarenko was invited to supervise the digging. There were considerable obstacles to overcome in concealing the digging and the removal of dirt, and in planning the escape itself. The daring plan involved coming up some twenty meters outside the fence, sprinting to the train station with Makarenko (who could no longer run) on their shoulders, then stowing away on a train that would take them to the northern forests, where they hoped to lie low in an abandoned house. After a month or so in hiding, they would travel to Mordovia to free Sylva Zalmanson and Zina Vassilyeva. (In 1969, Zina, together with her husband and brother, attempted to hijack a plane to West Germany. Her husband was killed in the attempt, and her brother, a prisoner in our camp, was part of the escape plan.) If all went well, they would then hijack a plane at the Perm airport and head for Iran (then under the Shah). The far-fetched nature of the plan well suited the personalities of its principal organizers, Lyosha and Wytold, two brave Russian "heroes" whose heads were in the clouds. When they invited Dymshits to fly the plane, he looked at the two boys and turned away without a word. He'd had enough of this kind of derring-do.

The tunneling was carried out in three shifts. An opening was hidden beneath floorboards, and the excavated dirt was hauled out each night by means of stolen sheets into a nearby ditch. When they decided that they could no longer dig by candlelight, they turned to Viktor Tchamovski to help install electric lights. We had gotten to know Viktor back in Camp 17 in Mordovia. Though not Jewish, he used to join the Zionists for tea. When he felt we hadn't accepted his "Zionism," he reverted back to his old form as a warrior for the ideological purity of Leninism. After Viktor was let in on the secret plan, he revealed it in turn over a cup of tea to two other loyal Leninists: Alexander Tchachovsky, a former Komsomol activist from the eastern Ukrainian city Voroshilovgrad (also known as Luhansk), and Yuri Fedorov, an ex–police captain and son of a colonel in the KGB (whom we have already met above as the organizer of failed hunger strikes). "The escape plan will surely fail in any case," Yuri said upon hearing of it. "Too many prisoners already know of it, and one of them is likely to inform the authorities. Why then should we not be the first to inform? We can get out early, and resume our struggle for true

Communism!" Before long, Tchachovsky was in negotiations with the KGB about the terms of turning informant: early release, admission to university, etc. On successful completion of the negotiations, the "merchandise" was sold, and the escape plan was betrayed.

But these two were hardly the only sellers of this particular merchandise; everyone was prepared to inform in the interest of early release. A foreman named Gorgiashvili, a collaborator with the Germans who had been sentenced for his role in suppressing the Warsaw uprising in 1944, discovered the tunnel in the course of renovating the warehouse, and hastened to report it to the KGB. Unbeknownst to him, a young Latvian named Shovarmanis who had been invited to join the escape had also informed his countryman, the KGB major Malenzov.

The KGB sprang into action with a general search and an investigation into which prisoners had known about the plot and *hadn't* inform the authorities. Those found to be involved were taken for interrogation in Perm, where each was told: "You took part in an escape attempt, which carries a sentence of an additional three years of imprisonment. If you help us, you won't be brought to trial." Some agreed to cooperate; others refused. Tchamovski and Tchachovsky returned to camp as KGB informants; Makarenko and Fedorov came back as declared enemies of the KGB, waiting to settle their scores with the agency when the time was ripe. Yet neither pair talked about it.

Makarenko, apparently in need of support, revealed to me what had happened only in utmost secrecy. Personally, I had no objection to his growing closer to our group of Jewish prisoners. Clearly it would be imprudent to share our most sensitive information with him, but I saw no reason not to include him in our celebrations of the Jewish holidays, for example. Shimon, on the other hand, registered his opposition even to that level of interaction. "He's not Jewish," he said.

"His parents were Jews, even though fate distanced him from them – and from the Jewish people," I said.

"You pity him, of all people? Misha's more clever and cunning than all of us put together. He's interested in drawing closer to us – for reasons of his own."

Shabtai, who considered Makarenko a friend, became furious. "And who gave you the right to classify who is a Jew and who isn't? What about you? What kind of a Jew are you? After all, you were sentenced not for Jewish activities, like the rest of us, but for anti-Soviet activities." Thus did the threatening

Shabtai-Makarenko-Shimon triangle come into play. I stood apart, and had to listen to the complaints of each.

Things in our group only got worse after Uri was released from the camp's internal prison. When I noticed that he had started to go bareheaded and to work on Shabbat I took him aside and told him that fulfilling divine law was the very foundation of the Jewish faith, and that a believing Jew could not live by philosophical reflections alone. Even in our daily lives, I said, we had to try to conform, with our every step, with the most mundane of our actions, to the precepts of the Torah. This was the month of Adar 5733 (March 1973). He and I were walking between the linden trees of the camp's main path, shielding ourselves from the sharp winter chill. (Winter in the Urals usually lasts until May.) "We can't simply philosophize endlessly about Judaism," I continued. "We'll reach Israel in order to learn, not in order to teach. In the meantime, we have to acknowledge that in this swamp of ours we have nothing other than the divine spark within. It is only this spark that gives us the strength to one day escape this place. That's the real miracle. And if we do succeed someday in reaching Israel, our very first task will be to restore for ourselves what the Soviet regime robbed from us – a real Jewish life – and then to raise children who will be better-informed Jews than we have been. In fact, the one thing that worries me is that I've lived in exile for so long that I won't be able to educate my children properly." I was trying by means of this monologue to explain that we must acknowledge our own imperfections, and the need to perfect ourselves by means of a deepening attachment to the Torah rather than by means of sterile philosophizing. But Uri was entranced by the idea of struggle, attracted by writing complaints and declarations (at which he excelled in volumes even greater than Makarenko's). Under this spell, Uri soon grew close to Makarenko, much to Shimon's chagrin.

When Purim arrived, we decided to celebrate it together, even though we all lived in separate barracks and were forbidden from entering one another's quarters. This meant celebrating outside, sitting on the ground; gathering in the half-built guardhouse where searches would be conducted; or meeting in the dining hall. In the end, our hopes disintegrated. It was too cold to sit on the ground, which had not yet unfrozen; the guard house had in fact been completed and moved to the factory area; and the dining hall was now locked between mealtimes. We had no alternative but to request a permit from the camp administration.

Camp regulations stipulated that a commandant may allow one prisoner to visit the barracks of another – *may*, not *must*. Disastrously, however, a prisoner named Layzer Bergman had warned a duty officer that the Jews would soon celebrate a "militarist" holiday to celebrate the vengeful massacre of their non-Jewish enemies. On this day, he added, Jews were permitted to attack non-Jews. I've no idea what possessed Bergman to offer Captain Rak such a skewed version of Purim – maybe it was a compulsive need for idle chatter or for groveling before the authorities.

Both Bergman and Rak merit fuller description here. Bergman was born in Kishinev in 1922 to an actress at the city's Jewish theater. He studied at a cheder and later at a cantorial school. With the Red Army's arrival in Bessarabia, however, life was disrupted, and in 1948, Bergman was imprisoned on criminal charges. He had been in prison camps ever since (his sentence had been extended in both 1956 and 1960 for "anti-Soviet activities"). From what I had gathered, Bergman once lost his gang's purse at a card game and by the laws of the underworld was sentenced to death. To escape this fate, he tied crude anti-Soviet declarations to balloons, and sent them up into the sky, knowing this would get him sent to a camp for political prisoners far from the reach of his murderous colleagues. This wasn't an unusual practice for criminals who had run afoul of underworld elements. Layzer was reputed to be one of the kingpins of that world in his previous camp, and seeing his aggressive and intimidating demeanor now this wasn't hard to believe. He preferred the company of the former Nazi Polizei, who formed the elite of our camp, to that of the political prisoners. "Well, Petya," he would flippantly say to one of them, "how many Yids did you kill? Don't lie. A hundred? Two hundred? No matter, I forgive you. Let's play cards."

For these kinds of remarks alone we should have shunned Bergman, but for some reason we didn't. Sometimes we hear but do not listen. Moreover, we befriended him, we shared tea with him. He showed us photos of his relatives in Israel, and we considered him one of us, with the same Jewish heart pumping in his chest as in ours.

"Today is my mother's yahrzeit," he said one day as we were standing in the snowy factory courtyard. He lifted his head and recited the Kel Malei Rachamim, his superb voice breaking with emotion. The Ural Mountains had never heard such a moving prayer. He prayed for our lost lives, for the mother who was ashamed of her criminal son. As he finished, his eyes wet with tears, he hid his face and walked away.

And yet none of his deep emotions, none of his feelings for Israel, prevented him from sending Yaakov and Shabtai to the camp's internal prison (about which more later). He sold us out, not by denouncing us as much as by his careless banter with Captain Rak as they chatted about their beloved Dniester football club. That's how Layzer came to induct the captain into the "secrets of the elders of Zion."

Rak, a man of below-average height, wore shoes with heel lifts. He had raven hair, round black eyes, a miniature black mustache, and a foreign accent. At first the prisoners suspected he was a Jew; later, most had decided he was a gypsy or Romanian. He himself hinted that he was of Ukrainian origin. One thing was sure: except for Fyodorov, no member of the camp staff was more of a scoundrel. But being younger than Fyodorov, he harassed prisoners – political prisoners in particular – more relentlessly, and meddled more aggressively into every part of our lives.

Imagine the following scene: a Ukrainian political prisoner named Dmitruk gets his shirt caught in a lathe, and is pulled into its churning teeth. At the last moment, he manages in a desperate effort to free himself, and collapses bleeding on the floor. Captain Rak arrives on the scene, but rather than pay the slightest attention to Dmitruk he rummages in the heap of bloodied clothing until, with a triumphant smile, he pulls out a note containing various lists, and walks away happy with his loot. That is Rak, a man who had to quell his inferiority complex by repeatedly flexing his power.

The captain persecuted other groups, of course, but reserved his keenest spite for the Jews. When addressing one of us, he could not wipe a crooked grin off his face, and his hands agitatedly moved to his belt buckle, as though he were considering when and how to pounce. The best way to neutralize him, we discovered, was simply not to talk to him at all. His method, after all, was to provoke a prisoner and coax forth criticisms of the state or the camp administration. Then he would say: "We'll have to indict you. You've just given us pretext," evidently proud that he knew a fancy word like "pretext."

Lyosha Safronov once scrawled a message in honey on the barracks wall: "Rak, you'll never make it to captain." But if nothing else, the Soviet regime knew how to reward loyalty, and in fact promoted Rak from lieutenant to captain.

"What have you got there on your head?" he said once when he spotted my kippah.

Before, I would have given him a lengthy explanation of the custom and its religious significance, but now that I knew how to deal with him, I replied, "Can't you see what it is?"

"Remove it at once!"

As I stepped out into the courtyard, I dutifully took off my kippah only to replace it with a cap. Rak was disappointed that his provocation had failed to provoke me.

This, then, was the Captain Rak whom Layzer had seen fit to inform of our holiday celebration. It thus came as no surprise on Adar 14 to see guards swarming over the camp waiting to catch us in the act of gathering together. But we weren't yet ready to give up on celebrating Purim together. We pooled together what we had received from our respective families: Mark had two oranges and a packet of chocolate, and I had received a package (I was allowed a package of one kilo every half year) with dry soy beans, which we cooked together with preserved fish that we had saved up over the previous several days and some "white" bread. All of us – including Shimon and Makarenko but excluding Layzer – got together and agreed that I would go to camp head-quarters and ask for permission to celebrate the holiday. Unlike the others, I saw nothing humiliating in a request designed to allow us to celebrate Purim.

I went to camp headquarters prepared to negotiate as though with a representative of an enemy army. Though it was a day off, all the sons of Belial, so to speak, were there: Fyodorov, Kotov, and Zhuravkov were sitting around a table. When I walked in, they gave me a look that said, "What is this Jew doing here?" The scene resembled Esther's audience with King Achashverosh to beg him to spare her people. "I would like to ask your permission to celebrate the Purim holiday," I announced.

"What kind of holiday is that?"

"A national celebration of events that took place some 2,500 years ago."

"Describe it in detail."

I tell the Purim story, imagining as I do so that this must be the first time Mordechai and Esther have become objects of close scrutiny by Soviet authorities. I imagine, too, that had these two biblical heroes lived in our day, they themselves would have very soon been imprisoned for espousing nationalist views.

"Is this not a militarist holiday, then?" (This was Layzer's information at work.)

"The holiday has nothing whatsoever to do with wars," I replied.

"Fine. We'll consider the request, and Captain Rak will give you our decision."

At this point, Fyodorov leans toward Kotov and whispers in his ear. "Remove your coat," Kotov orders. I take it off and hand it to him.

"And what's this?" He points to the interior pockets I had sown in.

"Pockets so that my hands don't freeze."

"You've violated the rules. A prisoner may not sew pockets into his coat. Go now. You will not receive any permission until you cut out the pockets."

So I cut out the pockets. I'll gladly suffer from the cold for the sake of Purim. At one o'clock in the afternoon I'm summoned to Captain Rak for his verdict. "Regulations prohibit religious gatherings. Purim is a Zionist, militarist holiday meant to stoke hatred for other nations."

What could I possibly say to that? We decided we'd celebrate each to our own barracks. The moment we sat down between bunks, Rak arrived, hawkishly scanning the scene. But we had given him no excuse; we were just drinking tea, trying to enjoy something of the spirit of the holiday. Despite the relentless attempts to blacken our joy, we managed to join in the happiness of wise Mordechai and brave Esther. Later, in the courtyard, I told the story of Purim, and we sang songs. I even put on a "Purimspiel" based on the play I had written for the synagogue in Riga:

What can you be thinking, our queen?
We will not again on bended supplicating knees be seen,
Nor project on you our hope,
If you from your own people elope.
As one who has preceded us into the next world,
Pray there that our salvation be unfurled.
But if you your own tribe spurn,
Blacker than black will your soul turn.

In our present kingdom, Achashverosh had been long since toppled by the sons of Haman, who were now ruling the roost.

• • • • •

These same sons of Haman had thrown Uri into the camp prison, after he had gotten carried away with writing complaints.

"Why aren't you shaving?" the guards said.

Uri pretended to be an uncomprehending peasant. "Huh?"

"Watch how you speak to us!"

"What's up?" Uri replied idiotically.

"You do know that you have to shave for reasons of camp hygiene."

"What?"

"You've just earned yourself additional punishment."

"What's the matter, comrade?"

Uri was promptly put into solitary confinement for a month, allegedly for refusing Kotov's order to remove his kippah. After his release, he wrote yet another complaint about the incident. Just at that time, solitary confinement itself was changing in the wake of numerous complaints. The first to experience the "new and improved" solitary was, naturally, Uri. The new conditions involved a crypt-like concrete cell with a twelve-liter toilet pail. No table or chair. Sleep was permitted only in designated hours. Being caught sleeping on the floor during the day meant a lengthier stay. Uri, severely weakened by hunger, was punished not for sleeping, but for failing to be able to haul out the pail. His confinement was extended a second time after Captain Rak found parts of a pen in his cell. In light of these "transgressions," Rak summoned "judges" and held a trial right there in Uri's cell. The indictment read: "The prisoner has intentionally violated camp discipline, has failed to fulfill his work quotas, refuses to reform, regards himself as a prisoner of war, and acts as a negative influence on those around him." The sentence: three years in prison. Between the lines, however, the real charges were: wears a kippah, has become too weak to take out his cell's pail or to make the replacement parts in the camp factory, refuses to abandon his views or his associations with Zionists, declines to see himself as a citizen of the Soviet Union, and longs to emigrate to Israel. Uri's very character and worldview, in other words, were his real crimes.

* * * * *

After Purim came Passover, and the question of matzah began again to become pressing. I had a single kilo, which wouldn't suffice for eight prisoners over the eight days of the holiday. One day, much to our surprise, we were called to camp headquarters and informed that a British Member of Parliament had sent each of us half a kilo of matzah, but that we were not entitled to receive the packages because it had not yet been a half year since we received our last ones. The matzah was tucked away in a warehouse for confiscated prisoner property that some months later went up in flames. At the time, thinking that Soviet property was being consumed, we were overjoyed to see the impressive red-hued flames rising skyward. The fire burnt so gloriously, as it turned out, only because the authorities had no intention of lifting a finger to put it out. Among the thousands of rubles worth of lost property was our matzah.

So my matzah would last only the first day of Passover. But there was another problem: each of us worked different shifts, and I was the only one among us who knew how to lead a seder. Our only chance was to squeeze a seder into the thirty-five-minute break between shifts. Shimon and I decided to do the first abbreviated seder for everyone, and then to make a second, full seder by ourselves on the second night using the Haggadah.

As planned, the moment the first shift ended on the first night of Passover, we began our condensed seder between two barracks. I had prepared everything, including an abridged version of the Haggadah. I feared that we would not get through it, or that guards would disperse us, and so I hurriedly explained the rituals. I needn't have worried, since we managed to complete the seder, right up to singing a shortened version of "Chad Gadya." Later that evening, those of us who were free from work continued the celebrations.

I remembered that according to my father, my grandfather had a peculiar Passover custom: to symbolize the crossing of the Red Sea, he would spill some water onto the floor, dress up as though for a journey, and hop over the water with a staff in his hand. So we decided to run over to the camp's ditch, sticks in hand, and leap over it. Mark was especially delighted: at last some action, not mere words.

In fact, we had little need of symbols. We felt ourselves to be living the Exodus story ourselves, and believed that we would reach the promised land, even if it took many years of wandering in the wilderness to get there. The words "next year in Jerusalem" echoed with special resonance in our ears. We were doing everything in our power to reach Jerusalem, and we knew that more and more Jews were being allowed to emigrate not by our struggle alone, but because Jews the world over were raising the banner of our cause.

At the same time, I felt that human efforts were as nothing compared to divine will, and that the events of the last generations bore the unmistakable signs of providence. One would have to be deaf and blind to miss the signs of God's outstretched arm – even in our day.

The second evening, Shimon and I did the full, unabridged Haggadah, which we joyfully ended with the traditional declaration: "The Passover seder is concluded, according to all its laws."

As far as I was concerned, the real difficulty lay not in fulfilling the commandments, but in *not* fulfilling them. How miserable I would feel when the guards prevented me from praying, or when I had to welcome Shabbat alone in a dark corner, with neither candles nor song. I tried to encourage my fellow Jewish prisoners to welcome the Shabbat together, not from a sense of duty (such things cannot be founded on duty alone), but simply because they were my brothers; I loved them and wanted to be with them. And so each of us, each in his own darkened corner, would welcome the Shabbat with great apprehension, one ear cocked to listen for approaching guards. And yet in that very tension there resided perhaps a certain beauty…

Since nightfall arrived so late, we had to welcome the Shabbat before the stars were out. Asher discovered a way of making candles out of sunflower oil, which we put in small bottles with wicks that would burn out before guards could arrive.

With the help of Shura, a soldier sentenced to ten years for attempting to desert the Red Army in Germany, we each got a can or two of preserved fish every Shabbat. Shura had earned the confidence of the manager of the camp canteen. Regulations allowed us to buy five rubles worth at the canteen every month. You could purchase a kilo of margarine, for instance, for 2.10 rubles, candies for tea (instead of sugar) for 1.80 a kilo, fifty grams of tea for half a ruble, a kilo of jam for 1.60, a box of preserved fish for .78, a kilo of onions for 1.80, and rusk biscuits at 1.80 rubles a kilo. This meant a prisoner might enjoy twenty-five grams of margarine, five cigarettes, and a teaspoon of jam every day. These were considered luxurious conditions. At the Potma camp, for example, prisoners could buy only half of what we could, and their canteen privileges were more frequently suspended.

Our own canteen privileges were revoked once after we had refused to attend the political reeducation classes. This compelled us to find other "sources of income." At first, I would ferret out a plastic-wrapped packet of bills from a crack in the bathhouse wall. My parents had slipped me these hundred rubles during a visit. I would hide some bills between pages of a book, and pass the book to Michael, who would in turn hand the money to Shura together with a list of what we needed. Shura would pay a visit to the canteen, as though he were helping to load boxes. He would pass on our money, and bring us the foodstuffs the next day.

The camp administration tried to contain this illegal trade, of course, forbidding us from getting postcards that we could sell, among other restrictions. When all other avenues were closed to us, we turned to Mikhail Sado, mentioned above. Almost alone among the political prisoners, he was well liked by the administration. We assumed he was a KGB informant. For a certain fee he would act as a middleman and buy food for us from certain guards. During family visits, for example, Sado would arrange for the officer on duty to smuggle in the products at night. He did so not in order to help us, but in order to earn our trust, and perhaps out of the sheer pleasure he took in the thrill of smuggling. After a while, however, he began to find excuses: "they're following me" or "the guards aren't prepared." We had no choice but to wait, and in the meantime to stay on good terms with him. Eventually, we asked ourselves whether it wouldn't be better to end the game he had been playing with us once and for all.

Even when you managed to get your goodies, it was still too early to celebrate. A hundred pairs of eyes followed you, and sooner or later everything was reported to the administration. Because of your illegal margarine, for example, the authorities might reduce your regular margarine allowance, or revoke your canteen privileges for months, or send you to freeze in solitary confinement. And so you had to ask yourself which was better: to get food, or to suffer from its absence? Here, as elsewhere, the middle way was best: to try to get food, but not too hard, and to acknowledge that all lies in the hands of God.

In the meantime, Layzer Bergman would offer to sell us surplus food that he had gotten from guards.

One day, Shabtai said to me, "Bergman says that there's a chance to pass information out of the camp. Do you think we can trust him?"

"How will the information get out?"

"A woman who works in the accounting office has bypassed the censor and gotten some of his letters out. We should chronicle what's happened to us here in the form of a letter, and she'll send it on the mail train that passes through Chusovoy."

"It's been a long time since we've succeeded in getting something like that out," I said, "but I think it's worth a try."

So try we did. Shabtai wrote up a detailed report. Yaakov added a few statements, and then put everything in an envelope that he passed to Bergman, who reported that the letter had been sent. We had arranged that the addressee would send us a coded acknowledgment of receipt, and we were worried when nothing came back. Sure enough, several months later, Yaakov, Shabtai, and Layzer were summoned to the KGB, where they were confronted by the letter, and asked how it had been sent. They replied that it had been sent, as usual, through the censor. (Yaakov had taken the precaution of casting the report as a letter to his wife.)

"No, the censor does not recall seeing this. We have evidence that you attempted to send it through illegal channels. You will be punished for this."

The dread of punishment is often worse than the punishment itself. Yaakov was relatively lucky: he was sent to the internal jail for four months. There he declared a hunger strike. In just a few days his condition had deteriorated so badly that Dr. Petrov himself came to examine him.

That night, several Jewish prisoners gathered by the fence separating the internal prison from the camp proper. When Captain Rak came out of the prison and saw them, he was startled, and turned back into the prison building to request backup. The backup having arrived in the form of a couple of burly guards, he walked out again. "What about Yaakov?" Michael asked him.

"His condition is fine. Dr. Petrov has pronounced the prisoner's heart to be well. If he begins to eat, he'll feel fine. Now away with you! It's forbidden to gather in groups of more than three."

The next day, each of them was summoned to headquarters. "We received a report from Captain Rak that last night you attempted to storm the prison in order to free a sick prisoner. This could constitute an act of uprising, for which you'll have to be put on trial. Sign here to acknowledge that you are aware of the pertinent law." (The law stipulated that a prisoner guilty of participating in an uprising could be subject to execution.)

Each refused to sign. "This is a provocation," they protested. "Captain Rak has a pathological imagination. How could he know our intentions? Can he read minds?"

It's unclear how this would have ended had Rak not made the mistake of listing Mark Dymshits as one of the prisoners who had gathered at the prison gate. "It's a pity I wasn't there," Mark said. "They indeed should have stormed the prison. But at that time I was at work." Mark's alibi was unimpeachable, and Rak's report was made null and void.

As all this was going on, Yaakov had been curled up in agony on the filthy floor of his cell, breathing only with difficulty. "Go ahead," the guards shouted, "the sooner you rot to death the better for us." But the authorities could not allow a political prisoner known in the West to die on their watch, and so they finally transferred Yaakov to the camp's so-called clinic. Two guards dragged him along the ground behind Petrov, while other guards dealt with the agitated prisoners who gathered around the scene. In the midst of all this, Yaakov was kicking and cursing. "You bastards! I believed you! For forty years I built Communism. A prominent educator. I taught your sons!"

As he recovered, it came to light that despite his agreement with us Yaakov had secretly been cooperating with dissidents and Ukrainian nationalists, thereby endangering us. We had no choice but to expel him from our group, while still allowing him to come to Hebrew classes and celebrate Jewish holidays with us. Even after coming to this reluctant decision, however, many of us – myself included – remained on friendly terms with him.

Just after he was released from the clinic, Yaakov went straight to Layzer.

"What are you doing, Yaakov? He's a traitor!"

"It can't be. He's good-hearted. He even brought me milk."

"But he ratted you and Shabtai out to the authorities." Even Makarenko reproached Yaakov for his spinelessness.

"It can't be, it can't be," Yaakov insisted.

One day during a break at work, Shabtai was ordered not to return to the factory. This could mean either a family visit or a transfer to another camp. Both explanations proved wrong. He too was being sent to the internal prison for the letter he and Yaakov had dispatched through Layzer Bergman. The timing was anything but coincidental. Kotov sent Shabtai to jail the very day his seventy-eight-year-old father, a major in the medical corps, had come for a visit. He had not seen his son in three years. Rather than postponing Shabtai's punishment or telling the old man not to come, Kotov decided that the "enemy" ought to be treated ruthlessly. Otherwise, he would not fear you. This was classic Soviet reasoning. In response to this abuse, Shabtai declared a hunger strike, and fasted for six days. By this point, however, hunger strikes had become so common that many began to question their effectiveness.

And still Yaakov believed in Layzer. How can you believe that a fellow Jew has denounced you and cooperated with the authorities? Either way, it was clear that these were Yaakov's last days in camp. His continuing campaign of complaint writing would surely land him in prison.

* * * * *

One day after work, all the Jews were summoned to headquarters, together with Braun and Sado. Our local anti-Semites did not trouble themselves with fine distinctions; if your nose isn't straight, you must be a Jew. And so we found ourselves in a room with Braun, a German, and Sado, an Assyrian.

Zhuravkov opened the meeting. "Zionists like to sing Israel's praises, but many Jews, lured by the promise of a better life in that country, discover after they get there that there's not a single good thing about Israel, and they ask to come back to the Soviet Union. I'd like to introduce comrade Zeltzer, who recently returned from Israel."

A man with pleasant features began to speak. "It's true that no one dies of starvation in Israel. I myself earned a good salary. But Israel was foreign and alienating to me. You are judged there by how much money you have." He continued in this vein, trying to give his words the ring of objectivity. He also showed photos of Israeli kiosks selling pornographic magazines. "Look at the moral decadence…"

If he thought his stories would impress us, he was gravely mistaken. We knew very well that Israel was beset with many problems. Instead we cross-examined him to determine to what extent he was beholden to the KGB. If he wanted to earn our trust, he would have to answer our questions.

"Do you have family in the Soviet Union?"

"Yes, I left my son here with my family." (In other words, the authorities had the power to take hostages.)

"Why did you ultimately decide to come back here?"

"My wife couldn't bear being apart from our son. He called often and asked us to come back." (In other words, the authorities exerted pressure on his son.)

"Did you decide to return just after arriving in Israel?"

"Yes, almost immediately I felt a wall of suspicion go up around me. The director of our absorption center warned the other immigrants not to talk with me because I was a KGB informant."

The KGB officer who had brought Zeltzer began to seem agitated. "Ask him about life in Israel, not about his family."

"What more is there to ask?" Makarenko said, rising from his chair. "It's obvious you intimidated him, and that he's willing to say whatever you tell him to say. I will not hear any more slanders of my homeland." And with that, he walked out.

So ended the attempt to reeducate us. It was odd that Makarenko, of all people, behaved as though he were the leader of the Zionist group. Neither before nor after that day had he ever presented himself as a Zionist. He did once get a letter from his sister in Israel, with photos and hopes for a reunion. His family had made aliyah after Israel's War of Independence; his father died there in 1971. (Years later, after having been released and making it to Israel, Leib Korn tracked down Makarenko's relatives.)

Several years after this meeting with Zeltzer, a Jewish mathematician from Riga, Leib Lander (not his real last name), arrived to serve out his imprisonment at our camp. When I told him about Zeltzer, he was reminded of a similar case. Leib's friend had been called into the local Party offices and asked whether he wanted to travel abroad. "We could send you to Israel. You'll live there for a time and then come back and tell people how bad you had it there." The friend declined, perhaps remembering how in Stalin's day a Communist who returned from abroad was often accused of acting as a "Western agent" and shot.

• • • • •

For the crime of persistent refusal to shave his beard, Shimon was sent to the internal prison, but because his release date was fast approaching the decision was made not to starve him too much. Nonetheless, he soon grew ill, and so was transferred to the clinic. Despite the very real danger of getting caught, I went to visit him there. The responsibilities of friendship overcame my fears, especially since he felt so alone. He had no one with whom to share his thoughts, to exchange a word of Hebrew or a bit of Torah or even an affectionate smile. God has planted in the human heart the need to love and be loved. If in our normal lives we are surrounded by friends and family, and take their love for granted, we are scarcely aware of this need. But in prison camp, every ounce of love is worth its weight in gold, so to speak. You are separated from your family, and as for your friends, you must make every effort not to see in them the dark sides that regrettably come to the surface at times of great tribulation, but to discern in them the godly and the pure. Otherwise, to live without affection can be the worst of all tortures. Imagine feeling yourself surrounded by enemies, suspicious of everyone. The prisoner without loyal friends lives like that for years on end.

· · · · ·

Yom Kippur of 1973 fell on a Shabbat. Having heard that Jews do not fast on Shabbat but not knowing the law in such cases, I improvised and decided we would mark the day on Friday. I had fulfilled my work quota – at the time I was unloading coal – and met Shimon on the steps of the clinic, where we took a few moments to appreciate the beautiful sight of azure skies crosshatched by the thin foliage of a nearby tree. One's sense of wonder at natural beauty becomes significantly more acute in camp. Just then, a rainbow cut magnificently across half the sky, a sign of divine promise.

Later that evening I discovered the meaning of that sign. Radio Moscow broadcast reports of Egyptian troops crossing the Suez Canal and breaking through the Bar Lev line of Israeli fortifications on its eastern shore. Dymshits and Shabtai, our military experts, optimistically hoped the reports were Soviet propaganda. Our discussions became the focus of interest of the entire camp.

The next afternoon, the broadcasts were cut off just as reports from the Middle East started. I asked the duty officer Proskurov why the transmission had been interrupted. Given that the Moscow broadcasts were a main source of Soviet propaganda, and their interruption could harm our "reeducation," I was well within my rights to make my inquiry. The officer, having no good answer, asked me to come to his office in half an hour. When I arrived, his tone had changed. "Why did you ask about the broadcasts in front of other prisoners? It was an act of incitement against the camp administration."

I couldn't care less about his threats at a time when Israel's very existence was at stake. Knowing very well how to aggravate us, the authorities cut off transmissions for the next two days, and in order to dampen our morale spread the word that they had watched scenes on television of Israeli tanks going up in flames.

That week, my parents came on a scheduled visit. My father, looking unwell, had to lie down for most of our time together. It was to be the last time I saw him. In my mind, the bitterness of the visit was mixed with the bitterness of the war. My father relayed what he had heard from the front: retreats, heavy casualties, Golda Meir's desperate speech. In this case, the Soviet broadcasts had not deceived. Together with Yaakov I had written a detailed account of the conditions of our imprisonment, which I had hoped to covertly pass to my father. But before I could ask him, he told me about the wife of one of the prisoners suspected of passing on information from camp; she had been searched, threatened, and beaten by agents of the KGB. I realized that even though I was permitted only one visit a year and that another chance would not soon present itself, I could not ask my father to take this risk. Fortunately, I had not yet told him about the material I had prepared; had he known of it, he would have insisted on trying to smuggle it out. That night, I went to the toilet and burned the papers, and felt a heavy burden lift from my heart. I needed my father to be healthy enough to make it home, to Israel.

Soon thereafter, one of the men with whom my parents shared an apartment attacked my father, hitting him in the head with an iron. At the hospital they diagnosed him with a cerebral concussion. But neither this nor the increasing pressures and intimidations applied by the authorities gave him pause; he continued his Jewish activism with renewed, even youthful vigor. His apartment filled with advice seekers. One of the Riga newspapers wrote about him: "though he incites others to emigrate to Israel, he for some reason hasn't gone there himself."

One day in 1973 my parents were summoned to the interior ministry's visa department to meet with the same Colonel Kaiya who had predicted that I would rot away in the Soviet Union. "In 1970," he told them with a smile, "you submitted a request for an exit visa for Israel. You may now go."

"But I submitted the request together with my son. Release him, and we'll leave."

"Your son must serve out his term."

"We'll wait for him."

"Show me your identity cards." My father handed them over. "I am confiscating your papers. Your Soviet citizenship has been revoked. You must leave the country at once. If you do not comply, we will arrest you and expel you by force."

Returning home, my father drew up a statement, declaring that he and my mother would leave the country only when their son was released. Seeing that he wasn't giving in, the authorities began to persecute my father, putting him under house arrest, threatening him with imprisonment.

The soul can withstand any hardship, but the heart of flesh and blood cannot. My father suffered a heart attack. The ambulance arrived in time, and he was resuscitated. As soon as he recovered, he resumed his activism, this time with American help. Henry Kissinger, then President Nixon's aide, explicitly asked the Kremlin to return my parents' identity papers. A demonstration was planned, and Congress scheduled a briefing on the matter.

My father was summoned to the police station and told he could have the papers back on condition that he signed a document to confirm he had received them. He hesitated. My stepmother whispered to him to say that he felt ill and needed to get some air. Outside, she persuaded him not to sign. "The only reason we're getting our papers back is because of the planned demonstration. What will people in Washington think when they see our signatures? They might suspect we were deceiving them in telling them about the ways we've been persecuted."

My brave parents went back inside. "When you confiscated our papers, you required no signatures. Therefore you will return them without requiring our signatures."

"Then you refuse to sign?"

"Yes."

"Then take your damn papers." The officer threw the documents at their feet. A kind clerk picked them off the floor and handed them to my father.

This sort of mistreatment persisted, year after year. I thought my father should have left. His presence in the country, as I told him, would not hasten my release. But my father simply couldn't abandon me, and in fact I felt his presence even when I was prevented from seeing him for six years. Somehow I felt him watching over me invisibly. Each of his letters, meanwhile, lavished me with love, with an abundance of international news, advice, Israeli poems and short stories, and even poems from his own hand. I would never again have a friend as close as my father.

As I said, this was to be our last meeting. A year later, I was called to the administration office.

"Mendelevich, your father has arrived for a visit."

"Yes, I know. I've been expecting it."

"You're entitled to a two-day visit. But you will not be granted this privilege if you continue to violate camp regulations. We've warned you repeatedly that it is forbidden to wear a kippah. Take it off at once."

"I will not."

"Then your visit is canceled. Return to work."

I turned away with tears in my eyes, wondering when – and if – I'd see my father again. He wasn't in good health. I looked at the kippah for which I had now sacrificed a chance to see him. A mere piece of cloth. But also an expression of my deep Jewish loyalties and of my refusal to be broken. Let my jailers understand that a Jew does not give up his principles.

Naturally, those wicked guards did not tell my father that the visit was canceled because of my refusal to remove my kippah. Instead, they said, "Your son, as is well known, is a delinquent. Even here in camp he has continued to flout regulations. Write to him and tell him to behave himself."

My father wrote a note. "My son, have mercy on me. Behave better. I want to see you so much." I broke down sobbing. How could I communicate to him the real reason for our canceled visit? Only much later, when Shimon was released and went to see my father, was he informed of what had happened.

This repeated itself for the next five years, until my father's death in 1978. Miraculously, and with the intervention of the US president, my father's body was flown to Israel and was buried near the top of the Mount of Olives in Jerusalem. Today, every time I descend the steps to the Western Wall, I look up to his final resting place and ask for his forgiveness.

But all of these trials still lay ahead. After our meeting that day, I was thoroughly searched. An apple from my father was sliced into four on the suspicion that a message might have been hidden in its core. Nothing was found, but I didn't get the apple back. Then I was stripped naked, and Captain Rak continued his meticulous search. "You've brought soap back from the visit? Forbidden. A toothbrush? Confiscated. Take off your long underwear. Now it's so hot for your people in the Sinai that you won't be needing your warm clothes. Soon you'll be fleeing so fast you won't even have time to put on pants."

"Dream on," I replied. "Our soldiers are not retreating."

"I saw burning Israeli tanks on TV with my own eyes."

A guard entered the conversation. "So you've lost the desire to go to Israel, Mendelevich?"

"Israel is my homeland, and I'll live there, come what may."

"Your Israel ought to be wiped off the map. It's a belligerent country."

"I tend to think belligerence better describes the Soviets who invaded Czechoslovakia and the Arabs who seek the destruction of Israel."

"The Arabs aren't conquerors. They lived there before."

"Israel was – and shall remain – the Jewish homeland. The Arabs have enough countries of their own." At this I ended the conversation. They had by then confiscated everything I had just received from my parents.

My friends were waiting impatiently for news of the war. I told them that this time the Soviet broadcasts had been accurate. We couldn't understand how Israel, with the world's best intelligence services, could have been caught by surprise by what would become known as the Yom Kippur War. Every day at one, seven, and nine o'clock, we would gather anxiously to listen to the news. At first, many other prisoners would gather around us to express interest or encouragement. "Don't worry," a Romanian prisoner named Petrayev would say, "Israel will go on the offensive soon enough. I read in the Bible that the land belongs to the Jews." But as the days wore on, and Israel seemed to be losing, the interest declined, until only our most loyal friends among the Ukrainian and Lithuanian prisoners – Sverstiuk, Lukyanenko, Kudirka, Kadjionis, and Gerchek – came to support us.

Every day, meanwhile, my father sent a postcard with a detailed account of the battles. To give the impression to the censors that he had had taken his information from the Soviet papers, each message started with the words, "I read in the paper that…" The censors, who seldom read the papers, didn't know the difference.

The more the Soviet media exaggerated the casualty counts of Israeli soldiers, the bolder the camp's anti-Semites grew. I remember a Dagestani prisoner named Guchyev shouting and jumping ecstatically. "We'll gouge out Dayan's other eye! We'll shave Golda's head and drown her in the sea!" His friends vainly explained to him that the chief provocateur in the Middle East was the same USSR against which he had fought in Dagestan. But he was too intoxicated by the prospect of Jewish blood to listen. "We'll throw them all into the sea!"

In their joy, the anti-Semites failed to notice the change of tone in the radio broadcasts. Though the talk was still of an Egyptian offensive, it was possible to deduce from the names of places mentioned that their advance had been halted. Mark and Shabtai offered a detailed running commentary. We knew nothing of the ammunition shortage or the airlift through Belgrade, for example, but even in the war's darkest hours, we never doubted that though Israel had suffered serious setbacks, it would prevail in the end. The only thing that remained unclear was when it would launch a counterattack.

One of the factors that had brought me to the decision to take part in the Operation Wedding hijacking in the first place had been the thought of Israelis my age taking up arms to defend their country. I had felt that I had to act while I was still young and battle-worthy. Imprisoned in camp, I took little consolation in the thought that here, too, I was honorably fulfilling my part in the national struggle: after all, unlike my brethren who faced combat, my own life wasn't on the line. I felt uneasy, and on October 16 I felt that I had to do something, to take part in the war in some fashion. After days of eating nothing more than slices of black bread, I began a fast. I composed a prayer for the occasion:

Blessed are You, O God, our Lord, King of the world, Mighty and Awesome, Lord of Hosts. Grant strength and valor to the Israel Defense Forces, bestow upon them a quick victory without excessive losses, save Your people Israel, and gather in Your exiles (including the exiles of Russia). Bring my father and mother to the land of Israel, and grant a recovery to full health to my father, Moshe the son of Aharon. Blessed are You, O God, Who heals the sick.

Hiding behind the barracks on a dark night, with gusts of wind slapping my face, I faced west toward Jerusalem and recited these words with great fervor, with all the faith and passion I could muster.

The next morning Radio Moscow relayed reports from Cairo that several Israeli tanks had crossed the Suez before they were destroyed. On October 18, another version of the same report: six tanks had crossed the canal, but were hit. In camp, even a distortion of the truth can reveal something of the reality. Had the wheel turned? We decided that in all probability the reports meant a counteroffensive had begun.

Several days later, a postcard from my father bore news that no paper had reported: Israeli forces were approaching Cairo and Damascus. Our resulting joy knew no bounds. We immediately sat down for a festive meal as other prisoners looked on in astonishment. Their army is on the verge of defeat, and these Jews are celebrating? The Soviet press implied that Tel Aviv would fall at any moment. (I often wondered how the average Soviet citizen explained to himself the contradictions that so blatantly characterized the Soviet press.

I concluded that most people read the news without analyzing it, and those who did bother to analyze ended up in prison camps.) The subsequent days felt like holidays, full of excited chatter about what we would do after taking Cairo. Would we help the Egyptians set up democratic elections? Force Sadat to accept our terms? These were but details; the main thing was a swift victory without too many casualties.

As reports began to stream in of casualties and the number of tanks lost, our mood became less exalted. I think we were no less aware of what was at stake than the Israelis themselves. Letters from Israel were allowed to come in steadily. The KGB apparently expected the letters to include accounts of defeat that would dampen our spirits. This is how I learned of the Agranat Commission's inquiries into the circumstances leading up to the war, of the negotiations between Sadat and Kissinger, of the conversations between Kissinger and Golda Meir in the prelude to the war, of the number of soldiers at the front lines, etc. Chaim Drori, husband of my sister Rivka, had reached Egypt with his unit, and wrote to me from there. My other brother-in-law, Eliyahu Lisitzin, was also there, and received a promotion for his bravery in driving a tank-refueling truck under fire. In short, I felt almost as though I were there with them, far from the Urals.

The war ended for me on November 24, 1973, the day I received a telegram from my father: "Eliyahu and Chaim have returned home." I joined Shimon for a celebration, so overjoyed that I distractedly burnt our biscuits to a crisp. Still, we knew that soldiers were still being killed on the banks of the canal, and that the politicians were even then conducting talks whose results were still in doubt.

· · · · ·

During Shimon's stay in the clinic, Makarenko joined us on Friday nights. Once we had to hold our Shabbat-eve meeting in the factory area. We had snuck in some of our modest Shabbat treats beforehand, and as dusk fell we gathered in the factory's unfinished warehouse around an improvised table made of some newspaper and boxes. But someone had informed on us, and before long guards burst in with a camera and began to take pictures. At that moment I felt something of what the *anusim* must have felt during the Inquisition as they practiced their faith in dread of being discovered. But we had an alibi: we had been eating during the evening break from work, a break permitted by the supervising officer. Kotov was satisfied with giving us a scare, and did nothing except cancel the evening break to deny us any future excuses for assembling.

It wasn't particularly difficult to smuggle food into the factory. It was far more difficult to get anything out. Searches were conducted four times a day; when guards would take off our shoes and feel our socks. Only rarely were we made to strip entirely. I confronted a special challenge: smuggling in and out six hundred Hebrew vocabulary cards every day, plus sheets of Psalms and prayers on Saturdays. This was exceedingly difficult, until I hit upon the idea of hiding my material in a factory wall.

To smuggle my six hundred vocabulary cards into the factory each day, I would tuck them into my belt. As a kind of competitive sport, the guards would vie with one another to see who would discover my cards first. I had no use for sport, but I could not avoid taking part in their competition. One morning, at the factory entrance, Sergeant Shrinov accidentally poked a finger beneath my belt. His face lit up as though he had discovered the secret of cold fission. "So this is your secret hiding place. You may be clever, but we Communists are cleverer." He was so pleased with himself that he didn't bother writing up a report. For days after, I stuck to the rules and didn't even try to sneak anything in or out. The last thing I needed was for them to confiscate my handmade dictionary. Much to my surprise, however, it seemed that Shrinov hadn't told the administration of his big find. He had done his part, and would leave a little sport for the others. When I realized that the others hadn't been told, I once again dared to resume, but I had to find a more secure method. I began to tie my vocabulary cards and prayer texts between my legs. Over time, I refined the method by reducing the cards to a quarter of their previous size, which allowed me to bring in five hundred at once – some hidden in my mouth, some in my armpit, and some under my cap. I began to feel like a professional smuggler, and even considered smuggling texts in my nostrils. But events would intervene to cool my newfound enthusiasm.

In addition to watching over my vocabulary cards, I especially guarded another treasure: my prayer book, which Wolf's father had once brought to their meeting and then bribed a guard to bring into camp. I had been at work when word came that the long-awaited volume had arrived and been hidden under my mattress. I waited impatiently for my shift to end, and then, rushing back to the barracks, I pulled the book out, taking care that no one would see. It was a beautiful sight: a *Rinat Yisrael* siddur, made in Israel. It set my heart thumping and my hands trembling.

A moment later, however, I felt the eyes of a prisoner on the upper bunk behind me and my heart fell. He had seen what I held in my hand, and this former Polizei – the type who collaborated with the camp authorities just as he had once collaborated with Nazis – would without a doubt inform on me. I took another glance down at the book. It did in fact look suspicious – and too attractive to have been made in Russia. Perhaps those who sent it should have bound it within another, more Soviet-style cover. I almost gave in to anger that they hadn't taken better precautions, but I knew my anger wouldn't help matters.

Then I hit upon an idea. I would copy the prayer book into an inconspicuous notebook. I volunteered that night for the night shift, knowing that when I returned in the morning the barracks would be empty, giving me a few precious hours while everyone else was at work to do the copying. This I did eagerly, knowing that in the case of a search, I wouldn't stand a chance. After several weeks of my new daily ritual, I finished copying out the daytime prayers, and began to pray properly.

Still, I feared that notebooks full of Hebrew letters might draw undue attention, so I copied the prayers once more, this time to small pieces of paper that, like my vocabulary words, I could hide in matchboxes. I copied out two sets of prayers like this, wrapping the matchboxes in plastic and burying them.

And then something surprising happened. I discovered that I knew the prayers by heart – that in all this covert copying the words had become a part of me. The discovery felt like I had acquired another freedom; I could now pray anytime, anywhere, whether it be at work or in solitary confinement. Prayer could never again be taken from me.

The only remaining problem involved prayer times. I had no time in the mornings; we were taken to work immediately after waking up. But for this dilemma, too, I found a solution. The administration had at last built a large bathroom building with several rows each of ten toilets (really just holes in the floor) that altogether could accommodate dozens of prisoners. Before my arrest, I would not have been able to take care of my bodily functions in full view of others. But necessity did its work and I got used to it. Our toilets had no screens; in many cases, you had to defecate in the middle of a cell. It was another form of humiliation, as was the fact that the new toilet building stood 150 meters from the living quarters, which presented a problem during the freezing Ural nights. If you tried to urinate near the barracks, you ran the risk of being ambushed by guards who took a sadistic pleasure in catching prisoners red-handed.

But the toilet's distant location could also serve a purpose. I could get up before the general wake-up call and pretend to head for the bathroom, while in fact I would take a detour from the main path and begin to pray. The moment I heard the sound of an approaching patrol, or the guards' boots crunching snow underfoot, I would return to the path and pretend again to be on my way to the toilets.

Once, Captain Rak spotted me just as I reappeared from behind a snowdrift. He ran over. "What were you doing there?"

"I'm heading for the bathroom."

"No, you've perpetrated something against the Soviet regime." Officers conducted a full body search but found nothing. I had all the prayers in my head. "You won't trick me," Rak said. "I sense foul play. If I catch you again like that you'll be penalized with a harsh punishment."

That day of reckoning came sooner than I thought. I was standing in the factory, behind the changing rooms, reciting the Shabbat prayers from the page of my siddur cupped in my hand. Just then, Captain Rak and Sergeant Privitkov entered from both sides, blocking any possibility of escape. Usually, when I heard approaching footsteps, I had enough time to hide the prayers into my pocket and slip away. This time I had been trapped. If I concealed the papers in someone's coat, an innocent person might be found out and punished. I could put them into my boots, but the two officers were sure to ask me to take them off.

They at once grasped what was going on. "Have you been celebrating the Sabbath, Mendelevich?"

To avoid answering, I said, "What makes you think so?"

I only hoped they wouldn't discover the prayer in my fist, but even if they did, they wouldn't find the whole morning prayer, since I only took out one page at a time from my hiding place in the wall. As the officers closed in on me, the page in my hand seemed to flutter to the same rhythm as my heart. They approached slowly, knowing that I had nowhere to run. Privitkov crouched over me and began to search, frisking my socks, my thighs, checking my pockets. Our uniforms were so flimsy that there was no need asking me to strip. "Show me your hands." I had no choice. If I resisted, they would take the paper by force. They would have been glad to find a secret communication, but instead found themselves looking at an indecipherable text.

"What's this code?"

"It's Hebrew."

Rak stuffed the page into his pocket. "Well, we'll find out. Now back to work!"

When they found out what it was, they sent two burly guards to take me away to the camp's internal prison. Such was daily life in a prison camp – a life of hunter and hunted, of predator and prey.

• • • • •

My father's postcards began to hint at the capture of Soviet prisoners of war during the Yom Kippur War. Our code name for such POWs was "goldfish." The goldfish numbered eighty-six, he wrote. Other letters confirmed this, and we began to hope for a prisoner exchange. Mark was prepared to bet a case of wine that we would be released. So strong is the wish for release that I had to protect myself from possible disappointment by persuading myself that in fact there was no hope of exchange. At the time, I composed a poem in blank verse to tell myself that although I would never reach Israel, I would always hope to meet her, and that death's clasp would seem to me like the embrace of my homeland:

> *If it be true that when my final hour arrives*
>
> *My eyes will dim –*
>
> *O, the night-chill in Beer Sheba!*
>
> *My chest pressed in suffocation –*
>
> *This is the joy of our stirring meeting.*
>
> *My torso trembles in this last embrace*
>
> *Clasping its fate.*
>
> *At last arrived,*
>
> *At last arrived. Forever?*

My relationship to freedom had shifted. In the first days after my arrest, I had hoped and believed that I would be rescued at any cost. In the first years of imprisonment, I waited calmly for my release. When nothing happened, I began to steel myself for a long imprisonment. I don't know whether my colleagues felt the same, but after I realized that I could do very little to hasten my own release, I longed to free myself from dependence on chance events.

I wanted to build my life on immovable foundations, on ground more solid than the contingent combination of circumstances, whether those circumstances be the international struggle for our release or the conditions of life in camp. My search for independence of feeling, as you might surmise, did not last long, for I discovered that everything I needed was already within me. I had but to grasp my faith even more tightly, to recognize that my duty was to fulfill my responsibilities as a Jew and that God would take care of the rest. I had to acknowledge that although my own fate might be very significant to me, I was in fact but a tiny atom in the people Israel, and that even if one or another atom was lost, the whole would endure eternally. This approach allowed me not to worry excessively about my own life, which in turn gave me a more expansive sense of freedom. Feeling freer meant allowing myself to better care for my welfare. Herein lay the paradox: ceasing to care about my particular life freed me to take better care of myself. Clarifying my place in the divinely ordered system of national priorities took the edge off my fear – the fear that shackles us whether we're aware of it or not.

So they might place me into solitary confinement. So what? Or they might revoke my right to receive letters from my family. So what? Or I could remain imprisoned for the rest of my days. So what? The world will go on. The main thing is to know there is nothing in life that a man cannot bear.

Here, of course, another danger presented itself: losing the will to fight. I myself wasn't susceptible to this particular danger, however, because I believed that in the act of creating me, God had commanded me to live, and that therefore I had to do my utmost to live with a sense of purpose and a fear of God – a life lived in service of Him.

So when we celebrated the release of Israeli soldiers from Syrian captivity, I accepted as given the fact that we were not among them, that our names were not listed among those to be set free. Under Russian pressure, the Syrians had demanded all of their POWs, including the Russians among them, be exchanged for the Israeli captives. Some of my friends angrily insisted that it was a mistake to give in to Syrian demands, and contended that Israel should have held out for a one-to-one exchange: one of ours for one of theirs. I had a hard time understanding their outrage. We couldn't know all the considerations involved, after all. Nor did I expect the government, the Jewish Agency, or any other official body to do everything possible – and more – to secure my release. Our contentious debates on the topic sometimes reminded me of our conversations before our arrests about our chances of success. The optimists in the group would say, "How can you imagine that Jews the world over won't campaign for our release?"

Meanwhile, the squabbling within our group grew fiercer, and to my deep regret the mutual recriminations would be a part of its dynamic from now on, even though we still dreamed of Israel, studied Hebrew, and welcomed the Shabbat together. But nerves were taut, and the accumulating tension had to break at some point.

One Saturday afternoon, we heard that Captain Dobchich had beaten a political prisoner named Stepan Sopyelak, a twenty-year-old student from Lvov who had been arrested for organizing an illegal nationalist group in his village in the western Ukraine. This was hardly unusual; unlike in the east, western Ukraine hosted many nationalist groups. Sopyelak had one weakness: he liked to embellish his stories, sometimes straying from the straightforward truth. In addressing the camp officers, he sometimes adopted an aggressive attitude, and was more than once sent to solitary confinement as a result. By the time Shabbat ended, the camp was abuzz, and details of the incident became clearer. Captain Dobchich had apparently noticed Sopyelak in the courtyard wearing an undershirt, and asked him to put on a proper shirt. When the prisoner refused to comply, Dobchich took him to his office and gave him a thrashing, injuring his kidneys in the process. Sopyelak reported the incident to the leaders of the Ukrainian prisoners, who verified his version of the story.

The beating of a prisoner was unacceptable, and many of us felt we had to react at once. Because of the ceaseless infighting and tension in the Jewish group, I was ready to storm the barricades, so to speak. Enough of words; the time had come to act. Word of my eagerness to launch a protest reached the ears of the Ukrainians, in whose hands rested the final decision of how to respond. They invited me to a hearing together with Armenian and Lithuanian representatives. "The question boils down to this," said Prichodko, a veteran prisoner. "Do we believe that we have the power to get Dobchich punished? If so, we must act."

I stepped forward, a gleam in my eyes and a firmness in my voice. "I believe we can emerge victorious. Our dignity demands it. If we don't protest, they may beat any of us at will." (It later turned out that one of those present leaked my position to the commandant. In the authorities' eyes, this made me doubly dangerous: not only was I religious, but I was stirring other inmates into rebellion.)

A decision was made to begin a general strike the next day to demand that Dobchich be fired. No one remained indifferent. Seventy prisoners – about

half of the camp – refused to go to work or obey the guards. It was a real uprising. The guards vanished, and the head of the camp's administration, Colonel
Mikov, arrived to take stock of the crisis. When Sopyelak was called in for
questioning, he insisted that he would go only in the company of witnesses.

Kotov, however, was not shaken, and would not back down. At the next
prisoners' assembly, he made an announcement: "Our investigation has found
that there was no beating. Sopyelak lied. Anyone participating in the strike
will be severely punished." Those threats didn't go over well; in fact they only
strengthened our resolve.

Sado went to Kotov's office to receive instructions. When he came out two
hours later, he said, "This is all a Jewish provocation. The Jews want to exploit
the situation to exacerbate feelings of bitterness."

Prisoners considered more compliant were summoned to headquarters
and offered bribes: packages, more family visits. As with any struggle, the initial enthusiasm cooled quickly, and people began to wonder: what do I need
this for?

The administration announced that anyone who went to work the next day
would be amnestied. Fifty of us were left. A guard came running and ordered
Shabtai to collect his belongings. They also took Lukyanenko, Prichodko, and
Kudirka. As we said our goodbyes, I vainly tried to give Shabtai some food.
"I have just a year left. You have another eight. Better you should keep it." We
embraced tearfully.

Everyone was tried on the same day. Makarenko, Prichodko, and Shimon
(who had only two months left to serve) were sent to the internal prison; Asher
(only two weeks away from his release date) to solitary. In one blow our group
was decimated. Only three of us were left: Mark Dymshits, Michael, and me.

And yet the struggle continued. Thirty of us still refused to work. Fyodorov glared at me at the next morning's assembly. "Why aren't you working?"

"To protest the beating of a prisoner."

"You idiot, we'll punish you. You'll get sick and die and never see your
Israel."

I usually shied away from talking back, but this time I couldn't restrain
myself. "You'll die before I do!"

"How dare you! Fifteen days in solitary!"

• • • • •

I had never felt so free, so unencumbered from daily concerns and fears. What
joy!

But the authorities had no intention of leaving us alone; their approach was "divide and conquer." They attempted to intimidate or bribe each of us individually, and human nature worked to their advantage. For as they well knew, all feelings and beliefs are measured against the simplest and most terrible measure of all: time. Today you love, tomorrow you will hate. Today you believe; tomorrow you will cease to believe. But just a minute, comrades, in my case you have misjudged. You have forgotten that I belong to the eternal people of Israel.

I am sitting calmly on the cold concrete floor of a solitary cell with my old Latvian acquaintance Gunnar Astra. We talk about everything: the Soviet regime, Latvia, Makarenko, God. At night as I climb onto my bunk, I propose binational commerce: "When Latvia gains its independence, we'll buy your timber and fish and supply you with electronics, planes, anything you need." We imagine ourselves importing and exporting, sending shipments and receiving them – two representatives who represent no one, two men sailing on the ship of time toward our destinies.

A rumor (which the administration is only too happy to spread) reaches us that the other prisoners have given up and returned to work. Someone has negotiated with an officer, and received a promise of something. Of what? Something. Those who are released from solitary aren't coming back; they're going to work. It seems we have been defeated.

"It's a pity I didn't have a Torah in here with me," I tell Gunnar, "because then I could have endured solitary until my sentence was up."

He shoots me an incredulous look. "Nothing but a cold floor, bread and water, and a Bible until the end of your sentence? With your kind of faith, you must be a happy man."

As I listen to him, doubt creeps into my heart. Would I really be able to endure ten years here with nothing but a Torah?

Back in camp, the warm weather calls to mind a summer resort. I sit down to write a letter home, where they must be wondering why their eccentric son hasn't written.

I'm prepared to resume the strike. But where are its leaders? Why have they given up? Sopyelak himself has gone back to work. It seems they have all suffered a failure of nerve.

· · · · ·

After the relative "freedom" of solitary, I return to the minefield of camp conventions, where every step might entail a punishment and every expression of will is negated. But I have something powerful enough to allow me to leave everything else behind: the Torah itself. My copy, a small 1910 printing, had been smuggled into camp two months earlier. In return for 150 rubles, Sado had made the arrangements for its delivery. It is a small 1910 edition. Its only flaw is that it was not bound in the cover of a Soviet book and so has the instantly recognizable look of the holy writ. Every time the door opens, therefore, I hide it away. But if I continue to hide it every five minutes I will arouse the suspicion of my bunkmates, so I decide to copy the whole thing out.

Copying a holy text proves no less dangerous than embarking on a strike. Once again, I manage to work the night shifts so that I have the mornings to myself, and soon I become a kind of Torah scribe, taking almost sensual delight in the shape of the holy letters and words. Having studied modern Hebrew, I sometimes get caught on certain biblical phrases. My only aid is a Russian Bible the Adventists use. Because the translation is imprecise, I read the whole thing through in Russian before going back to make my way through the original.

Typically I would work until 2:00 a.m., sleep until 7:00 a.m., and then sit down to begin copying, urging myself on without pause. Another early riser was the Jewish mathematician Leib Lander, who had been sentenced to three years for indulging his hobby of collecting illegal literature. Exclusively interested in Russian history and literature, Leib insisted that Soviet Jewry would eventually assimilate, and he himself tried as hard as he could not to be Jewish. For this very reason, perhaps, the camp's anti-Semites regarded him as the archetypical Jew. Nonetheless, he tried to be liked by everyone, even by his enemies. On his first day in camp, this former university lecturer made a spectacle of himself bowing and scraping before camp officials.

I was quite familiar with this desire to be liked by everyone, evidenced by so many of my fellow prisoners. I, on the other hand, had to force myself every day anew into a posture of obedience and deference. But who said that I must obey? I am a captive, not a slave. Those who sought the middle way discovered soon enough that the KGB compelled them to make a choice: with us or against us. For this reason I broke off contact with Leib. The pretext was a conversation about the eighteenth-century German Jewish Enlightenment philosopher Moses Mendelssohn.

"Why do you insist that a Jew is necessarily someone who observes Jewish law and lives in Israel?" Leib said. He was trying to justify his own desire to assimilate. "Consider the enlightened Jews of Mendelssohn's time who saw no contradiction between a deep knowledge of Hebrew and Jewish history, on the one hand, and an engagement with secular science and life, on the other."

"I have no objection to science," I replied, "but surely there's a difference between a scientist who has received no Jewish education and therefore regards his heritage not as a way of life but as a mere historical phenomenon, and a man who grew up studying the Jewish tradition as a way of life, as a guide to fulfilling the commandments, only to disavow it all. The latter, in knowingly harming the Jewish people, is dangerous. You must understand that the Torah is not the product of mortal minds, but a divine thing. Like a living thing, the Torah cannot be cut or pruned without killing it."

"It's a shame you're so conservative, Yosef. You ought to be more open to new influences."

"That has always been the slogan and the byword of those who betray the Jewish people," I replied. "It's precisely the language of the Hellenizers who spoke so loftily of 'contemporary Greek culture' and brought about the desecration of the Temple. I want nothing to do with such traitors." At this, I turned and left. After that, Leib spoke to his friends of that naïve Mendelevich, too immature to understand the complexities of life and the impossibility of constructing a life on the basis of a single principle. I too believed in the complexity of life, but I also knew that faith, if it is to be anything, must be innocent.

During this time I was searching for a replacement, as it were, for Shimon and Shabtai (both of whom, after being released, respectively, in 1974 and 1975, made aliyah), and our group as a whole. I suggested to Michael that we practice our language skills by speaking only Hebrew to one another every Monday, and only English every Tuesday. We could now hold classes at work. After the strike, enforcement of the rules became somewhat more lax, and while Captain Dobchich wasn't immediately fired, his appearances at the factory did become less frequent, until after a while he disappeared altogether.

Meanwhile, Major Fyodorov stopped persecuting prisoners for possessing "forbidden items." Until now, his main pastime had been to stroll through the barracks attending to every last detail. The moment he appeared, our peace of mind was shattered, and we tensely waited to see who would be on the receiving end of one of his splenetic reprimands.

"Why are you eating?" he would say to Michael, who had returned from work hungry. "This is not dinner time. You will be punished."

Or, "Dymshits, what are you doing lying in bed? You know it's forbidden to recline on your bunk during daylight hours."

"But I've just finished a work shift."

"Sleep at night. Now it's time for you to attend a lecture on Communism."

Or, "Sverstiuk, what is that book on your crate? It's superfluous. Go place it in the storeroom." He would often sweep a book onto the floor and grind it with his heel. Once, much to our delight, he did this without noticing the book was by Lenin.

Or, "Mendelevich, what's that thing on your head?"

"But you know perfectly well what it is."

"I know nothing. Remove it at once!"

I had been about to begin a letter asking my father to come visit me. Now I foresee in my mind's eye what will happen if I refuse Fyodorov's order: they will summon me to the office, threaten me, and when they are convinced that I will not give in, cancel my right to a visit. My father, who has remained in the country just to be by my side, will be denied the chance to see me. In the best case he will be notified in advance of the cancellation. If not, he will journey by train for two days across five thousand kilometers, and spend hundreds of rubles in vain, for he will at last reach the camp only to be told that the visit has been canceled "due to your son's misbehavior." He will return home in disappointment, and will write to me: "Yosef, you know how much I look forward to seeing you. You're a grown man. Why can't you behave yourself?" In my reply, I will not be allowed to explain the true reason I was punished, nor to write how much I love him, nor how difficult it is for me here. And though I can see all this play out, and though I know that my father has already suffered several heart attacks, I refuse to give in.

"I will not remove my kippah," I tell Fyodorov calmly.

"You will be punished."

"It's your right to do so."

On another occasion, during a visit by KGB officers, my wood *chanukiyah* and dreidel from Mordovia were taken. Seeing them casually tossed into the garbage, I lost my temper. "I'll get you for this!"

"Are you threatening us?" To threaten an officer on duty would mean another trial and additional years in prison.

I had to backtrack. "I said that so that you would know that I'm angry. You've sent agents here in order to gauge the mood of the prisoners, and here I've saved you the salary of an agent by directly communicating my feelings about the confiscation of my menorah."

The KGB visitor looked at me in utter amazement.

· · · · ·

Now these petty harassments stopped. One lesson of our strike was that the authorities wished to avoid provoking prisoners into large-scale outbursts of anger, and that therefore when they heard large numbers of us grumbling, they were likely to back down. We had only to know how to direct our complaints. A second lesson was not to expect the authorities' retreat to be immediate or to take the form of directly addressing our demands. We had demanded that the officer who had struck Sopyelak be punished, fired, or reprimanded. At first they categorically refused to do so, but in the end they relaxed their disciplinarian measures, improved our rations, and finally, got rid of the offender.

In the fall of 1974, word reached us that Sylva had been released and at last permitted to go to Israel. She had suffered enough. As harsh as camp life was for men, it was even more arduous for women. Various groups abroad were meanwhile demanding the release of other prisoners, too. "You'll soon be released," my father wrote. "You haven't been forgotten." My hopes were stirred for several months, but it was impossible to live like that for long. I knew prisoners who preferred the intoxications of illusion over the bitterness of reality; I was not one of them. I wrote to my father: "Even if there are reasons to expect my imminent release, I ask you not to write to me of them. If I am freed, I'll be glad to hear about it then." I didn't need such reports; what mattered was the freedom not of an individual but of an entire people.

One fellow prisoner who supported me in this approach was Evgen Sverstiuk, a Ukrainian intellectual who had been arrested for his philosophical research. His pure soul, uncontaminated by materialism, was dearer to me than all his academic credentials. His untainted spirit, keen intelligence, warm heart, and patriotism (he had been active in the Ukrainian underground since age sixteen), not to speak of his fondness for Israel and the Jewish people – all of these made me consider him one of the righteous Gentiles. At the same time, however, he was too dreamy for my taste, too ready to justify those who lived in their imaginations more than in reality. He saw the world as a place of pain and suffering, whereas I regarded it as a place in which living a full life involved both suffering and joy. I found my joy, above all, in the search for God and in the fulfillment of my obligations to Him. It's not that I escaped reality, but as a Jew I made room in my life for both the spiritual – the Torah – and its material manifestation in the nation and the state.

While we carried on in relative peace and quiet, some of our friends who had organized the strike remained in solitary confinement. It's hard to bear the knowledge that your fellow prisoner is suffering and that you are helpless to do anything about it. Even joining him and suffering together would hardly ease his torment. Only once, when they were taken from solitary to the shower building inside the camp, did we have the chance to aid our colleagues. I calculated how long it took the guard to circle the building on his patrol, ran back to my barracks to fetch all the food I had, then hid in the grass some fifteen meters from the entrance to the showers. I crawled closer, and as soon as the guard turned the corner, I got up, my heart thumping, and walked over. Running would have attracted attention. I made it inside (where thankfully no guard was posted), silently shook hands with my friends, and handed over what I had brought them. Making it back to the barracks, I was dizzy with the delight of my mission's success, and began to slip into joyful fantasy. I imagined myself as an Israeli paratrooper liberating Jerusalem, an Uzi in hand. Then I imagined an Israeli helicopter landing in the center of the camp to whisk us away.

· · · · ·

One day a young Lithuanian soldier by the name of Yanovsky arrived in camp. He had been sentenced to two years for distributing nationalist pamphlets. Naturally cautious and reserved, he began with time to trust the Jewish prisoners, and after a while told us his story.

"I did my military service in the northern Murmansk district, where I operated midrange missiles. At assembly one day, my name was called out among others, and we were taken to the city's port, and thence to the belly of a ship where hundreds of other soldiers were already waiting. After we set sail, we were permitted out on deck only at night, and were not informed of our destination. After a week at sea, we were assembled on deck, where the officer announced that the Jews and Arabs were fighting and that we would be giving support to the Arab forces. No further explanation or political briefing was offered. We were given unmarked uniforms, and the next morning, after landing on the Syrian coast, we were taken to a missile base near Damascus with barracks for eighty men. We had heard that soldiers from a similar base had been taken captive by the Israelis. (This validated what I'd heard from my father – that we might be swapped for Soviet prisoners of war. Only later did I learn that the Israelis buckled to Soviet pressure and released their prisoners without receiving any prisoners in exchange.)

"This was toward the end of 1973, but the war was still raging. Some of the younger soldiers, hearing the thunderous thuds of artillery, began to cry: 'Why must we die here?' We had no access to newspapers or radios. Our letters home were specially shipped to be posted from Murmansk so that our families wouldn't know our true whereabouts.

"Every morning we would train Syrians to operate the missiles. They envied our Kalashnikovs, and asked us whether they could at least handle the rifles for a few minutes. Their discipline was extremely lax. When they kneeled during prayer times, their officers would beat them with sticks, but they would refuse to get up.

"I also traveled to Cairo with my commanding officer to retrieve some weaponry. Our convoy was stoned by local residents, and the walls were full of caricatures of Brezhnev embracing Nixon and Golda Meir sucking money from the pockets of an Egyptian.

"Back in Syria, we received orders to transport ammunition to the Golan. We set off in a convoy of three armored vehicles when at a pass between two hills we came under Israeli ambush. The first two armored cars were hit. Our commander jumped out and ran ahead, submachine gun in hand, screaming 'For the motherland! For Lenin!' Just as the other soldiers started to run after him, a burst of machine-gun fire sliced across us. My friend Antanas was struck in the head, and parts of his brain spattered over me. I ordered the others to retreat behind the armored car as I dove into the vehicle for some grenades. Just as I was getting out of the car it was struck, and the explosion hurled me away.

"Medics diagnosed me with shell shock and declared me unfit to serve. I was recommended for discharge. Later, when I was arrested for distributing nationalist pamphlets, the KGB said that because of my service I would get two years rather than five, but that they would remove the certificate of my combat injuries from my file so that I would no longer qualify as a wounded veteran.

"They forbade me from ever talking about this, but I want everyone to know how our Lithuanian boys are being killed defending someone else's interests."

At this he went silent. So profound was the pain evident in this twenty-year-old youth that we couldn't bear looking at his face. His tale left a lasting impression on me.

• • • • •

A year passed. Yaakov returned to the camp, but without our group's oversight he gradually lost control of himself. He fixated on one idea: "I was in prison, where things are preferable to life in camp. There it's possible not to work; you can read. Why endure the abuses and work conditions of a labor camp?"

"But if the authorities get word that you prefer prison to camp, they'll make sure things are doubly harsh for you there," I said. "Would you still refuse to work in that case?"

"I'll mull it over."

"Why didn't you think it over before? Sure, you can demand your rights as a political prisoner, but why go to prison for it?"

"Because it's better for me in prison."

"But you can't base a fight for principles on accidental circumstances."

The Jewish prisoners declined to support him, but Yaakov found many supporters among the Ukrainian "democrats" who had been arrested on baseless charges of possessing illegal books or engaging in "subversive" conversations. These prisoners sought a way to avenge themselves on the authorities and to find a purpose in their imprisonment and thereby a purpose in life. As always, many prisoners who understood nothing of the meaning of the struggle had joined the "democrats" merely for the sake of struggle itself. They wanted to feel that the world was watching them; they wanted to write complaints and to thumb their noses at the authorities. Certain prisoners desperately wanted to believe that their every gesture was reported in the *New York Times* or the *Washington Post* or discussed at United Nations plenary sessions – and they behaved accordingly.

At first glance, this kind of thing might be excused, as long as they were struggling. But I maintained that any struggle based on illusion, or on the desire for attention, could be harmful. I didn't spend my time organizing "operations"; I just tried to live my life. Nor did I feel compelled to search for meaning; I had already found it. I felt no need for publicity. I was quietly content with my bread and books. It's also possible that my fear of losing these brought me to my vehement criticism of the movement for demanding the rights of political prisoners, and that my fear blinkered my vision. Was I perhaps looking for excuses? After all, the authorities did in fact treat us like common criminals, and so it was conceivably my duty to demand our rights as political detainees. I felt ambivalent, in other words. Not for nothing had Shabtai remarked on my fondness for dialectics. It's not easy to consider all sides of an issue simultaneously.

As it happens, events would help me come to a decision. In March 1975, the KGB conducted a general search of the camp aimed at confiscating any material related to the campaign to secure prisoners' rights. That day I was in the barracks reading from my Tanach and studying the book of Job. The moment I looked at the window and saw what was happening, I wrapped my Torah in a towel, picked up some soap, and went to the room where we dried our laundry. I concealed the book in the laundry, and went to take a shower. The moment I entered the shower room, however, I was seized with the panic of a parent who has left his child behind. I ran back to the laundry room, only to find that my precious book was already gone. I approached a prisoner who was tending the oven to ask who had taken it. He told me that Sergeant Shrinov had just left. This left no doubt: the cunning Shrinov had noticed me entering the laundry room and then searched it as soon as I left. Here I learned the lesson that trying too hard can sometimes backfire. I had gone to such lengths to save the book – but in vain. Why had God not come to my aid? This train of thought led me to the conclusion that I had been punished for devoting insufficient time to studying Torah. I could have studied Torah for several hours a day, but instead I also studied English and history. If only I had studied more, I thought, God would not have permitted them to take away my Torah. I wondered whether I should report to the authorities that it had been taken. This would have the disadvantage of admitting that I had smuggled it into camp. On the other hand, if I didn't report it, I'd never stand a chance of getting it back.

I went to camp headquarters to report the loss and to ask for the book back. The officers scoffed at me. "Ah, so this is your book, then. Why did you hide it so clumsily? What kind of a book is it?"

"It's a book about ancient Jewish history, with not a word in it about the Soviet Union."

"Why then did you hide it? We'll have to look into the matter."

"There's nothing to look into. Return it to me now."

"You can't have it now."

Obviously, I couldn't afford to wait for them to discover what the book really was. I had to act before they sent it off for translation. "In that case, I hereby declare a strike."

"I join you," Michael said.

We operated under the assumption that the KGB wouldn't want to complicate relations with the Jewish prisoners when it was preoccupied with handling the crisis over the struggle for prisoners' rights. We made sure news of our strike would reach Moscow. I asked a prisoner about to be released to inform Ida Nudel, with whom I had corresponded.

We refused to go to work. Every morning we were summoned to the administration offices, where we were bombarded with nerve-wracking attempts at brainwashing and intimidation. After two weeks of this, the commandant gave me a choice: "We have checked your book and discovered it was published in Berlin in 1910. Legally, prisoners may only use books published in the Soviet Union, so I cannot let you have this book. But if you return to work tomorrow, you will be spared punishment. You decide." Our discussion of the offer was brief. If they had not given in by now, there was no way to assume they would give in later. We had to cut our losses.

The defeat was hard to take. Resentment and revenge boiled up within. You wanted to prevent me from studying? I'll prove that it would have been better for you to let me study than to free up more of my time. I said as much to Zhuravkov. "Until now I sat and studied. Now I've got time on my hands. You're well aware that the camp hosts various kinds of activities, and you seem to want to push me toward taking part in the campaign for prisoners' rights."

"Don't you try to frighten us. If you want to spend some time in solitary, you can struggle for whatever rights you wish."

The struggle for prisoners' rights had meanwhile gained momentum. Some prisoners had been tried and imprisoned; others waited for their turns in the camp's internal jail. Some spent months there. One morning we saw one young prisoner, Nikolai, who had spent the last several days in solitary, being taken out unconscious on a stretcher. Since we weren't allowed to come close, we could only speculate about what had happened to him. The camp's officers gathered outside the clinic, smoking and chatting, apparently fearing that the incident might spark something. The prisoners were confused and leaderless and didn't know how to react. Since I had been "liberated" from my studies, I decided to step up to the occasion. I approached several of the more trustworthy prisoners and informed them that the prisoner had passed out because of the lack of heating in the solitary confinement cells. I proposed a strike. The next day, seven of us refused to go to work. It was a small group, and the authorities paid us no heed. Still no heating. So I proposed a hunger strike in addition to our work strike. Almost as soon as we launched a hunger strike, guards came running. "Mendelevich! Sverstiuk! Solitary for the both of you!"

I was wearing just a shirt, and the temperature in the cell could not have been much more than five degrees Celsius. I could see my own breath. I started to pace vigorously to keep warm, meanwhile wondering how they knew that I was one of the strike's organizers. Had there been informers among us?

Everything in the cell is exposed, cold concrete, even the table. There would seemingly be nothing wrong with a large table, except that very little eating and no writing takes place here, so the table's only function is to take up space and prevent the prisoner from walking about. Every detail here bears the mark of Fyodorov's meticulous cruelty.

Suddenly I start to breathe easier. Maybe it's the thought that when I get to Israel I'll look back on all this and smile. But then I feel a physical warmth, and following it to its source discover that the hot water pipes are radiating heat. They're heating the solitary cells! This means we've won. The glow of success mingles with the heat radiated by the pipes, and I feel prepared to spend the rest of my term in this solitary cell.

But it wasn't up to me, and I was released from solitary to find the outside colder than the cell. When I got out, I learned that Nikolai had not fainted because of the cold. When the campaign for prisoners' rights began, he had joined it not out of any deep principle but because he would be spared working. Yet getting put into solitary was a different matter, and when the authorities made him work in the internal prison he preferred to drink car oil rather than work, and that was the reason for his collapse.

The struggle for our rights, then, wasn't always smooth sailing. Serious people took part, but so did many others for whom the whole thing was a mere diversion. The most unlikely participants, however, were those who had been "outed" as KGB informants. Perhaps they wished to atone for their shame through suffering with the rest of us. But how could we allow ourselves to struggle alongside them? Who knew when they might go back to their old ways?

And that's how I became involved in the campaign for prisoners' rights. Had our Jewish group existed as before, had there been representatives of other groups with whom I shared a common language, the problem may have been solved otherwise. But at the time I felt alone, caught up in a vortex of emotions.

The Helsinki Accords were signed in September 1975, granting international recognition to the Soviet Union's postwar conquests in exchange for the USSR's vague pledges to respect human rights and fundamental freedoms. I wrote to Deputy Foreign Minister Anatoly Kovalev: "With your signing of the Helsinki Accords, perhaps you may be so kind as to respect the rights of religious citizens. I have been denied the rights to pray, observe the Shabbat, possess sacred books, or consult with rabbis. I ask that my right to fulfill my Jewish duties be recognized. To bolster this request, I hereby announce a hunger strike for the duration of the days set aside to celebrate the signing of the accords."

I starved in peace and quiet as prominent Western diplomats were affixing their signatures next to those responsible for oppressing hundreds of ethnic minorities in the USSR. But I was mistaken if I thought everything would go off without a hitch. One day I was called into the censor's office to pick up a letter that had arrived from Shimon, who had made it to Israel and already married the daughter of a scholar. Enclosed was a photo of the two of them standing in front of their house in Netanya holding a *lulav* and *etrog*. The Sukkot holiday! He appeared wrapped in a tallit.

"A package has also arrived for you," the censor added, "containing the same shawl that Grilius is wearing in the photo, but we cannot allow you to have it. Is that understood?" By a stroke of bad luck, the tallit I had asked for from home coincidentally reached the camp on the same day as Shimon's photo, tipping off the censor as to the meaning of an otherwise innocuous shawl.

The next blow was even harder to bear. "Mendelevich, a second package was delivered from France containing a book of Psalms. This, too, has been confiscated, and here's a receipt for the confiscation, specifying that the book was taken 'since it was found to contain anti-Soviet material.'"

"Do you really think that the book of Psalms contains anti-Soviet ideas? It was composed more than three thousand years ago, long before Russia existed."

"I have no opinion in the matter. The instructions came from above."

I was left speechless.

Several days later, on Shabbat, I was accosted by a guard in the courtyard. "Why aren't you at work?"

"Why do you think I'm not at work?"

"Don't ask us questions. We know what's up. From now on you'll be punished for your refusal to work."

It seems they had decided to settle scores for my strikes and complaints. They put me in solitary on Friday night, a move that had Fyodorov's signature style: if you want to rest on Saturday, you can rest in solitary.

Finally, when I thought the cycle of punishment would never end, it stopped as suddenly as it had arrived, like the sun suddenly reappearing after a spell of rain. To make things even better, Michael had just then managed to bring into the camp, at my request, a siddur and several Hebrew textbooks.

With the arrival of these books, I no longer had time for protests. For days on end I copied out and memorized prayers, studied Psalms, and learned fifty to a hundred Hebrew words a day. My daily schedule was simple: after waking up, I would pray, spend several hours copying the siddur, and study conversational Hebrew with Michael. At 5:00 p.m. I went to work, returning at 2:00 a.m. As the joy of learning surged once more within me, I felt an inexplicable urge to study more. Before going to sleep I would read the *Shema*, always sensing the gaze of Unishchenko, the ex-Polizei in the next bunk. I had no doubt he would inform on me before too long, so I learned the prayer by heart.

At that point my factory work still involved making heat regulators, which meant riveting together, in a certain order, many small parts, some no larger than a match head. Each regulator part was made of ten metal pieces and took fifty separate movements to put together. There were 760 parts in all, which meant I was making 38,000 movements a day. In the West this would have been done by machinery, but in the Soviet Union slave labor was cheaper than any machine. Other prisoners tried to avoid this kind of backbreaking work, but I didn't mind it, since it allowed me to prepare my Saturday quotas in advance, and with my small hands I learned to make smooth, efficient motions, rhythmically using both hands and a foot in unison. The authorities sometimes showed me off to factory visitors. As my hands danced from one part to another, I felt relaxed, sometimes humming Hebrew songs to myself. I was able to get seven days' work done in six, and still have time left over to pray, to study my Hebrew vocabulary cards, and to practice some conversational Hebrew with Michael. At exactly 11:54 p.m., just after the inspection rounds had finished, I would rush to the drying facility where Michael worked, and we would converse in Hebrew as we stood between machines for drying silicone, all the while keeping our eyes on the door. We were so experienced in tracking the movements of the guards that only very rarely did they catch us. I could even sniff them out by their special smell.

Weeks and months passed this way – studying, reading and rereading letters from Israel, and battling the camp administration in all manner of petty ways. On winter nights, for example, outside temperatures fell to minus sixty degrees Celsius, and the temperature inside the barely heated barracks was eight degrees – too cold to sleep. Fyodorov arrived, and pronounced our thermometer broken. He replaced it with another that registered fourteen degrees. I conducted a little experiment. I thrust Fyodorov's thermometer into the frozen snow, and sure enough it showed five degrees, proving that it was a false instrument. We tossed it aside in anger. Fyodorov came running, and demanded to know what we had done with his "excellent" thermometer.

Since my experiment didn't help heat the barracks, I took another tack. Looking through a newspaper, I found the name of a woman who served on the Central Communist Committee, and wrote to tell her we were freezing and to ask for her help. This was of course a joke, since the Soviet practice was to appoint representatives of "the people" to senior positions that had no practical power but that sounded good on paper. In reality, this "senior" member was a dairy farmer. Why not expose two frauds with one gesture, I thought.

For some reason, however, the authorities didn't appreciate the joke. I was summoned to Kotov and asked why I had written the letter.

"Well, because I think she has influence and might be able to help."

"How would she do that?"

"She could call the interior minister and tell him to send us coal."

"Are you serious, Mendelevich?"

Both of us knew perfectly well that the regime's power was very far from being in the hands of "the people," but of course Kotov could not admit that openly. He dismissed me. "You don't have a Soviet mentality, Mendelevich."

"I thank you for the compliment, comrade officer. Indeed I have a Jewish mentality."

· · · · ·

Spring returned to the camp, and so did Uri (after serving three years in the Vladimir prison), who started to issue complaints even before he stepped foot inside. This didn't please the authorities, and he was kept for an extended time in quarantine outside the camp.

"Why are you abusing him?" I said to Zhuravkov.

"He started to write complaints even before the normal quarantine period was up."

"If you continue holding him there, I'll have no choice but to declare a hunger strike."

This was several days before the May 1 celebrations, and the thought that he might have to forgo the celebratory drinking in order to take care of another strike didn't please Zhuravkov. There was also a march planned in New York to demonstrate solidarity with Soviet political prisoners, and I spread a rumor that if Uri were not released from quarantine we would hold a parallel march in the camp. The best way to circulate a rumor was to approach some veteran prisoners and say something like: "Well, if they don't let him go…"

"Then what?"

"I can't say. It's a secret," I'd reply.

"Just tell us already. We're all reliable."

"Well, if they don't let him go then we plan to hold a protest march on May 1."

These people in fact proved reliable, in the sense that within hours a report of the planned march was on the desk of one of the camp administration officials. I began my hunger strike on April 28, 1976. Two days later, Dymshits and Michael were asked to exert "positive influence" on me. "If you don't release Uri," they replied, "we'll join Mendelevich." On April 31, I was called in and informed that if I would end the strike, Uri would be let go on May 2. This is how we won our small battles. The large battles, on the other hand, were in divine hands, not ours.

Uri was released the night of May 2. We had by that point lost hope; with lights-out fast approaching, there had been no sign of him. When he finally emerged, everyone congratulated us on our victory, and Muhamadzhin, Balakhonov, Sverstiuk and Kovalyov welcomed Uri. Except for his prison pallor, he hadn't changed.

With only three months left to serve, Uri began preparing for aliyah by gathering updated information on prisoners and refuseniks to take with him. When I told him he should be spending his time learning Hebrew, he said he would do that in Israel. I frankly couldn't understand his approach. Such matters ought not be treated as military logistics but as spiritual needs. How could one postpone them? Still, it must be said that Uri did document some interesting material.

Take, for instance, the case of a round-faced, middle-aged prisoner named Vladimir Balakhonov whose first question upon arriving in the camp was: are there any Zionists here? (It was common for political prisoners at a new camp to first approach the "Zionist prisoners," as they called us, as a reliable way to get to know the lay of the land.) He was brought to me, and proceeded to pour his heart out. I asked him why he had turned to me. "I heard a lot about your hijacking operation on the radio," he said, "and you're known as reliable. Everyone admits that of all the underground movements in the USSR it is the Jews who have accomplished the most. Hundreds of thousands of people have been allowed out because of your efforts. And it's no longer just Jews who are being released, but many Russian and Lithuanian dissidents too. You stand at the vanguard of the struggle for freedom. That's why I came to you."

"What's on your mind?"

"I have material that needs to get into trustworthy hands."

"Well, I agree that Jews stand at the forefront of the larger struggle for human rights, but you must understand that our fight succeeds precisely because it is focused on the right of Jews to emigrate and to study their own tradition. If we joined too closely with other dissident movements, we would dilute our energies and achieve nothing. But in struggling for our cause, we have, as you say, helped the cause of others. And that has been the Jewish way from the beginning: what appears to be narrow particularism is in fact a means to achieve universal ends. Which is all to say that I don't get involved in smuggling out dissident material."

"But we must all work together."

"There are areas in which we join in common cause, and those in which we choose not to. But I can help you with one thing: I can give you the name of someone you can trust here."

Balakhonov was a graduate of the Institute of Foreign Languages and had served as a translator for visitors from abroad. He was then sent to work at the UN's World Meteorological Organization in Geneva, where his eyes were opened to a Western lifestyle. When it came time to return to the Soviet Union, he sought political asylum in the American embassy. To pressure him, the KGB persuaded his wife and son to go back to the USSR, and after an anguished month, Balakhonov could no longer bear the separation. The authorities promised that he would not be prosecuted if he returned. He believed them, and flew back to Moscow. Several weeks later, he was arrested and sentenced to twelve years for treason. He surmised that the KGB suspected him of having returned to Moscow to spy for the CIA.

By the time I came to know him, he was already repudiating his Russian origins. "I want nothing to do with the Russians," he used to say. "They're a nation of tyrants and oppressors. I'm a democrat by nature, and consider myself a citizen of the world."

Vladimir Muhamadzhin was arrested under entirely different circumstances. Like Balakhonov, his veins pulsed with Tatar blood, but unlike Balakhonov he wanted to be considered a Russian. He had classic Russian features, and when asked about his origins he would say "Muscovite," as though the residents of Moscow were a tribe unto themselves regardless of ethnic origin. (There was some truth to this: urbanized Muscovites are in some respects a different species from rural Russian peasants.) But the truth was that he also felt ashamed of being a Tatar, and desperately wished to become an American. He had devoted years to connecting with Americans working in the USSR, and ultimately had become a regular guest of the American embassy in Moscow. With his impeccable English, he could imitate American speech and behaviors, but it was just this obsession with Americans that landed him in prison. He had been a painter by profession, and one tourist asked him to paint portraits of Soviet leaders overlaid with the concentric circles of a shooting target. The portraits were confiscated at customs, their source located, and their painter sentenced to five years.

Muhamadzhin had a hard time finding his place in camp. His views were those of a dissident, but his cowardice made him afraid of coming out openly as a dissident vis-à-vis the camp authorities. As was their wont, the KGB soon compelled him toward a choice. His well-fed frame, endless supply of tea, and enviable work assignments all made it clear that he had chosen to go down the road of cooperation. Despite his good looks and high society manners, he had become a slave. As we so often witnessed, life in camp ruthlessly unmasks a man and sooner or later shows him for what he really is.

In a prison camp it is not always readily apparent whether a fellow prisoner is trustworthy or not, and in our situation quite a few problems arose from the difficulties inherent in categorizing others. With surprising wisdom, an inmate named Igor, driven insane by camp conditions, used to wag his finger threateningly and say: "Ah, you thought it was simple, did you? Each one to his own category? Now, try living with everyone together."

Professor Sergei Kovalyov, a biologist, was an expert in cell membranes. His scientific colleagues had been astonished to learn that alongside his academic activities he had also been secretly involved in publishing an illegal journal called *Khronika*. In taking on the editorship, Sergei knew that eventually, like each of the previous editors, he would land in prison, but he felt it his duty to supply the truths that had been kept from Soviet readers. He belonged to that part of the Soviet intelligentsia that set itself against the tyranny of the Soviet state, the intelligentsia that was the finest product of the regime, but also its greatest bane. Every regime needs its intellectuals, but their values and views must ultimately clash with the party line. Indeed, this class developed what you might call its own technocratic ideology. Sergei had been a close friend of the dissident nuclear physicist Andrei Sakharov and knew many other prominent scientists. He was of the opinion that the regime's dependence on its scientists would eventually allow the scientific community to push for reforms, and the Politburo would have no choice but to accede to their demands.

In his identity card Kovalyov was registered as a Russian, though his father was Byelorussian and his mother Ukrainian – another example of the vaunted Russian racial "purity." Examination would reveal that a majority of prominent Russian scientists and political leaders were not Russian at all. There used to be a saying that "a Russian is the child of a Kazakh and a gypsy." The circle of intellectuals in Perm 36 was in this respect perfectly representative. Those who gathered around a pot of tea to discuss "the Russian soul" included Sado, the Assyrian, the Russian-German poet Braun (it turned out later that he too was Jewish), and the Jewish mathematician Lander.

On the matter of nationality, Kovalyov regarded himself as free of all prejudices. "To be a nationalist is to limit yourself," he would tell Michael in one of their long discussions on the topic. "Nationalism means regarding your nation as superior to others and thereby fanning the flames of hatred for them."

"As a nationalist," Michael replied, "I can tell you that you're mistaken. I have love for my people, but no hatred for others. I respect all nations."

"Why then pick out one particular nation? Would it not be more proper to love everyone?"

"It isn't explicable in terms of abstract logic," Michael said. "I have a mother, a wife, a homeland, and a nation, and I love each of them because I belong to them and they belong to me."

"Such a view is too narrow," Sergei said. "I can understand Sakharov's recognition of Israel's right to exist. Jews have nowhere else to go. But beyond that I see no need to call for all Jews to immigrate to Israel."

The truth was that the matter was insufficiently clear not just to Sergei but to many Jews. Eventually, Sergei realized that high-minded humanistic theories could only go so far, and that they weren't the main driving force of his struggle. Aided by Sverstiuk, his search for truth led him increasingly toward faith. Why hadn't he felt a need for this before his arrest? Perhaps his love of truth, love of the other, and his philosophical view of the world was no longer enough. It might have seemed that fear compelled him to look toward faith for salvation. But a bravehearted man like Sergei knew no fear. It wasn't fear, then, but something else. The precise cause may not have been discernible, but one thing was clear: once in camp, the moment arrived in which Sergei turned toward God. By stripping away the possibility of self-delusion, life in camp, like the acknowledgment of mortality or of imminent death, had the effect of drawing a man closer to his Creator. These effects could be seen not only in Sergei, but in many prisoners.

So it was this quite humane group – Sverstiuk and Kovalyov on one side, and Lander and Muhamadzhin on the other – that welcomed back Uri after his three years of social isolation, and with whom he became acquainted during the last months before his release in 1977. He drank in their stories thirstily, hoping to commit to memory particulars about these political prisoners to relay to the West. It was amusing to see him attached like a leech to the day's victim; it might be Kampov, who was imprisoned after his election as a Ukrainian representative to the Supreme Soviet (against Soviet wishes), or Odugayev, who in the late 1930s had met the Hungarian Communist leader Béla Kun in the gulag just before he died.

• • • • •

Just at this point, as I prepared to celebrate Shavuot for the first time in six years, I was given permission to receive a package of up to five kilograms. When it arrived, it contained the finest Israeli treats: cocoa, chocolate, honey, butter, and soup cubes. It was meant to last me for a year, but in honor of the holiday we put all our best dairy products on the table. Uri must have thought that we ate like that all the time. I read out some Torah passages about the revelation at Sinai, and then we went for a stroll, wearing handkerchiefs draped under our hats to ward off the mosquitoes.

The authorities were well aware that it was a Jewish holiday. At some stage we had been visited by Lieutenant Rozhkov, the officer responsible for keeping track of such days. I often marveled at the irony that we could – and did – consult him to verify the date of some Jewish holiday or other. (I had been sent a Jewish calendar to help me keep track of them without his aid.) In this case, a young brash officer was dispatched to follow us on our walk, and when he noticed our handkerchiefs he decided that this must be some kind of Jewish custom. He burst out, jangling the keys to solitary confinement, and ordered us to remove our handkerchiefs. When we protested that we were using them to ward off mosquitoes, he insisted that they violated camp dress code, and punished us by restricting our rations.

"Do our mosquito bites also represent a kind of punishment?" Uri grumbled. "Maybe the insects represent the proletariat, and we prisoners, as 'enemies of the people,' must not try to avoid their bites, which after all are only meant to reform us."

Having had our rations restricted, we decided to enrich our daily menu by picking herbs. Uri taught me to identify the edible herbs, like clovers and sorrel. I had already been long accustomed to eating dandelions (soaked for half an hour to dilute the bitterness) and plantains. I would also pick nettles and lop off the tops, and if I happened to have sour milk I could then prepare a proper salad with which to garnish a Shabbat meal. Growing onions was more difficult here than it had been in Mordovia; the guards would douse any vegetable patches with gasoline. Only garden cress could be grown here "legally." But every bit of plant life helped, both to enhance our diet and to lift our spirits. Like a blossom that grows toward the sun, the prisoner is himself drawn to anything green – the color of life. As you walk in the camp, your eye is drawn to green shoots poking up, beckoning to you.

Our ordinary menu did not exactly gladden the heart. In the morning we got a thin soup (this wasn't *treif* since it had no meat, but then again it had nothing else either), two slices of potato, and a handful of grits. For lunch we were served soup with traces of lard, along with porridge (our main staple). Dinner involved some protein: fifty grams of fish. The precise amount was the subject of frequent dispute.

"Look," we would say to the officer on duty, "there's less than thirty grams here."

"It shrinks during cooking," he would reply.

Or, "look, you're feeding us rotten fish."

"Tastes great to me," the medic would reply with a broad smile. "Can I have seconds?"

In order to put an end to this vileness once and for all we began a campaign of complaints. I wrote to the local board of public health, among others. "Please come to inspect our fish. It poses a health hazard. I'm saving a sample in a sealed jar."

Did the camp authorities seize my sample? Not at all. Instead, when I got to the dining room the next morning I was greeted angrily by the cook, Zhuvaga, who had been imprisoned for fighting alongside the Germans during the war. "Why do you have to ruin things for everyone else? If you don't eat pork yourself, why did you request in your complaint that we shouldn't prepare pork for everyone else?"

"Where did you get that idea from?"

"Doctor Petrov told me. What, you didn't write a complaint?"

"I did, but I complained about the rotten fish."

"No, you wrote about the meat, and now, because of you, we have no meat."

The KGB, it seems, had stumbled on an excellent – and well-established – tactic of evasion: better to slander the Yids than to bother improving the food.

Chapter Five

The Lord's Day

As God says in Isaiah: "For My thoughts are not your thoughts" (55:8). The Almighty dictates the course of events without consulting our plans.

Uri's return to camp, and his preparations for aliyah, played a decisive role for me. He was at that time particularly preoccupied with passing on information about prisoners to his father by means of secret messages. He would dampen a piece of paper, cover it with plastic, and then write over the plastic. When the paper dried, it would leave no traces, but his father could read the watermarks by heating the page. Between the lines of his invisible epistle, Uri wrote an innocuous cover letter. We did all this while sitting on the ground in the courtyard; from afar it looked like we were merely reading our mail. Uri was sure that the KGB wasn't on to him. His confidence was based on the fact that his father had so far received each of the letters. As we later learned, however, the KGB had photographed the letters using a special method and had read every one. His father had indeed received them, but had been compelled to read them in the offices of the KGB.

In the wake of all this, Uri ceased to observe Jewish law and began to work on Shabbat. "If I'm punished for refusing to work on Shabbat," he said, "I won't be able to get out the necessary information."

I replied that getting information out, however important, was not more essential than Shabbat. In the end I persuaded him, but the authorities had noticed that he had worked on Saturdays before joining me and refusing to work, so they began to harass him, and then me. When I alone had not worked on Saturdays, I had been more or less left alone. But now that they saw Uri ceasing to work under my influence, they considered it a grave violation of discipline. For the rest of his time in camp, they stopped punishing Uri, who had only a month left to serve. As for me, they did not relent. I knew that keeping Shabbat alone would be far easier than observing it with Uri, which

251

would make it much harder to remain under the guards' radar, so to speak. I might suffer severe consequences throughout the next six years for the sake of Uri's few remaining Shabbats. Should I still seek to share the joy of the Day of Rest with him?

Ultimately, Uri persuaded himself of the importance of Shabbat, and despite my earlier hesitations about him, and although I was aware of the possible consequences, in practice I shared everything I had with him from the day he arrived in camp, including translated biblical texts, Hebrew notebooks, and prayers. (Zev had managed to bring in another siddur.)

I wasn't wrong about the consequences. From the moment Uri left on his way to his release, the guards gave me no rest on Shabbat. Their first step was to steal the parts I had prepared during the week for my Saturday quota. Both Fyodorov and Zhuravkov disingenuously declared they didn't know how such a thing could happen. It seems they assumed that when I didn't find the parts, I would start working out of sheer fear. In general, they were quick to interpret my behavior as a weakness they could exploit by means of intimidation. For many centuries, religious Jews have appeared in the anti-Semite's mind as weaklings and cowards. I felt I must disprove this stereotype.

I decided that since keeping the Shabbat was not a political act, I would not resort to loud demonstrations, but I did change a few things. Rather than hiding in a corner on Shabbat, I sat out in the open, either in the courtyard (in summer) or in the wardrobe room (in winter). This granted me a sense of relief, though the pressure on me remained. They could imprison me at any time, but they preferred to break my spirit, like the attackers during the Kishinev pogrom of 1903 who smeared pig's fat on the lips of Jews. They could compel me to do many things, but they could never make me abandon my fear of God. My power was not the power of the fist, nor my strength the strength of a stone wall. I was rather like sand, which even when stepped on soon resumes its former shape.

And so every Shabbat morning I went to the factory and prayed. The first inspectors came around at 8:15 a.m. The lazier ones went no further than warning me that I'd be punished if I failed to work. Others, however, took special pleasure in abusing prisoners. The worst of these was Sergeant Zainat-ulelin, who was proud of having served as an honor guard at Lenin's tomb, and who in camp pranced around as though he were still in Red Square. Zainat-ulelin was capable of standing next to me for half an hour while pouring forth abuse and venting his hatred for Jews and Israel, trying to goad me. Wrapped in the sanctity of Shabbat, I sat calmly through this storm of abuse.

I knew, however, that these were no mere threats, and it soon became apparent that for every Saturday I did not work I would have to serve a day in solitary, have my food curtailed, or have a family visit canceled.

So I tried another method. Mikhail Sado was then working in the furnace room supervising teams of prisoners unloading coal from supply trucks. We agreed that if I spent evenings unloading coal, it would be considered as if I had worked on Saturday. But the authorities had different ideas. On my first evening, Fyodorov came running. "Mendelevich, finish unloading and return to your quarters!"

"But why? Others are working."

"Others may be working, but you're not allowed."

On Shabbat I went as usual to the factory equipped with the relevant Shabbat prayers, which I had copied from the siddur that Wolf's father had smuggled into camp. Although in the course of my intensive copying I had discovered that I could remember all of the daily services by heart, I still had not yet memorized the Shabbat prayers; so I had to sneak them on small pieces of paper into the camp factory, hiding them under my waistband so they would not be discovered during the searches that accompanied our transfer from the barracks area to the factory.

Upon arriving at the factory, I would immediately take up my strategic position in the dressing room where prisoners kept their work clothes. Here I could hide my prayer notes in the pocket of my work garments, transferring them from one pocket to another in pace with my prayers. At the same time, I could look out the window, keeping an eye out for the guard patrols. The moment they came in, I retreated to the work area, giving the impression that I was simply going to work.

On this particular Shabbat morning, I stood in my usual hiding place, reciting the morning prayer, when suddenly I heard the guards' footsteps approaching from an unexpected direction. I had not seen them coming in through the normal entrance; they had clearly come to catch me red-handed.

"Mendelevich, why are you not at work?"

I spun around. Before me stood none other than the deputy commander of the camp, Major Fyodorov. He eyed me hungrily, like a cat stalking a mouse. They wanted to put on a good show for me, and I would play my role faithfully.

"You know quite well that as a Jew I don't work on Saturdays."

Fyodorov's face twisted with rage. "How dare you! Do you think you're in a sanatorium here? You will work immediately or I will put you under the ground to rot. You'll never see your Israel."

I thought KGB experts might have taught him the Jewish idea that it is permissible to violate Shabbat in life-threatening situations. Knowing this, perhaps he threatened me in this way so that I'd stand down. And in fact, I had been secretly given Chief Rabbi Shlomo Goren's ruling that permitted me to work on Shabbat if refusing to work involved mortal risk. I now had to decide for myself: did I now face such a risk? I made the summary judgment that I did not. What was the worst that could happen? Solitary confinement? That's hardly life-endangering.

"I'm not afraid of your threats. I fear only the Holy One, blessed be He," I answered rashly.

"Take him immediately to be locked up!"

A couple of burly sergeants escorted me through the snow toward the camp prison. Although it may be difficult to understand, I was not in the least scared. On the contrary: I felt joy and even a measure of pride. I told myself, "I'm perhaps the only Jew in the world who does not desecrate the Shabbat even when he is ordered to do so. How many Jews desecrate Shabbat," I thought then to myself, "even though they are under no threat or compulsion to do so?"

Then I imagined those sergeants were two angels – the angels that accompany us on Shabbat – leading me toward the divine throne of glory.

Several days later, Zhuravkov announced his verdict: "Due to continued refusal to work and the negative influence on other prisoners, you are sentenced to a month in the internal prison." This was standard practice, a final warning before putting a prisoner on trial.

The rhythms of the camp prison resembled those of solitary confinement, with which I was all too well acquainted. The only difference was that in prison you were given a mattress and blanket at night, could listen to official broadcasts on Radio Moscow, and could read Soviet papers. For half an hour a day, you could see the light of day from a five-by-two-meter cage surrounded by barbed wire, as though you were an animal. Nights were particularly hard to bear; you felt entombed in the darkness and utter silence.

I felt increasingly remote from my dreams, from Israel, from normalcy, even from my father, all of which seemed unattainable. With neither family nor human warmth, it was an existence lived against the grain of human nature. I began to doubt whether there was still really a world in which people got up, went to synagogue, ate breakfast, and commuted to work. Or was real life nothing but daily abuse? "Mendelevich, do this! Don't do that! Mendelevich! Mendelevich!"

My one ray of light came from my conversations with Sverstiuk, who occupied the cell across from mine. When the guard left the hallway, we could exchange a few sentences through our locked cell doors. Our work involved cutting screws, nuts, and bolts by hand, and we had to fulfill a daily quota of 1,200 grams. If we had worked according to regulation, we'd never be able to make the quota, which would mean an extension of our sentences. But I discovered that rather than clamp one bolt at a time perpendicularly, as we were instructed, I could clamp together thirty horizontally, and then cut them all at once.

Even so, I had to work quickly to fulfill the Saturday quota – a chain of bolts that I hid in notches in the floorboards. On Fridays, my shift started at 4:00 p.m., before Shabbat. The moment the guard left, I took the necklace of bolts from its hiding place. Then I worked at a slow pace until sunset, just to show that I was working. When Shabbat arrived, I stopped, and did nothing for the next several hours of my shift. The feeling as I "celebrated" Shabbat in my silent, cold, bleak cage – detached from time and space – was one of utter loneliness. Having already said all the prayers I remembered, I had nothing more to do.

A slot in the door slid open. "Mendelevich, why aren't you working?"

"I've finished the quota."

The guard is astonished, and smells something fishy, but cannot figure out where I hide the pre-prepared nuts and bolts. Sometimes I am punished, sometimes not, but I've by now become inured to punishments. They deny you a meal? So what? The main thing is not to succumb to fear, not to wait tensely wondering whether they will punish you or not. I do my thing, and the guards do theirs.

We celebrated the first night of Chanukah, the anniversary of our trial, as "Prisoners of Zion Day," and I traditionally marked the occasion by declaring a hunger strike. "You're not eating?" the guards would say. "Fine, your loss and the pigs' gain." (There was a pigsty just outside the camp fence.) I also issued a letter every year on that day that included a formal renunciation of my Soviet citizenship together with my demands for freedom to practice my religion, for immediate release, and for the right to emigrate for all Soviet Jews. This infuriated the folks at the KGB. "We give him punishment after punishment and still this insolent Mendelevich makes demands."

With nightfall, I ended the fast and prepared a Chanukah candle using thread that I had hidden in my rear. Much to my frustration, however, the thread wouldn't light. On the second night of the holiday, I drew two candles on the wall, the same wall in which I had etched my Shabbat candles and my poems about waves lapping at the shore and sunlight shimmering on azure waters.

· · · · ·

Soon enough, I am put back in the old familiar solitary confinement cell, but this time I notice a doormat made of an old blanket. I ask for water so that I can wash it, and when the guards announce lights-out, I begin my elaborate preparations for the night. I put the mat on my back, under my shirt. Then I distribute my socks: one sock for my freezing hands, one foot gets a shoe without sock, and the other gets a sock. I put my mug inside the other shoe, cover it with the removable sole, and put the whole contraption under my head to serve as a makeshift pillow. I cover my body with my coat, using a sleeve to cover my head, and use some old newspaper to cover my thighs. The guard looks on in wonderment, but I take these preparations seriously; my condition the next day depends on them. Sometimes I can't fall asleep, in which case I get up and exercise. The guard taunts me for it, but for me there is nothing amusing in it. If I fall ill while in solitary, no one will come to my aid. Dr. Petrov has already made his position clear: "I'm a KGB man first, and a doctor second." He regards patients as enemies.

One day it is so frigid I have to call the duty officer Leyaponov. Regulations mandate a certain minimum temperature for solitary cells, and it is obvious that the temperature has fallen well below the threshold. Leyaponov happens to be in a good mood, and agrees to loan me a thick winter suit for tonight. The anticipation of a warm night cheers me the entire day.

At night, however, Captain Rak is on duty. When I complain again about the cold, he appears with a thermometer, stands at the cell door, and takes the temperature.

"Captain, you're measuring the hallway temperature. Come into the cell itself."

"You're classified as a dangerous criminal. What if you decided to attack me?"

"Then hand over the thermometer," I say, "and I'll take the temperature myself."

"There's nothing to be done. Look: sixteen degrees Celsius." A balmy 60.8 degrees Fahrenheit.

"How is it possible that it's sixteen degrees if the walls in here have frosted over?"

"Stop arguing," he barks, slamming the door shut.

That night I cannot sleep, but the following day I am warmed by the news of the sudden release of the dissident Vladimir Bukovsky after eleven years in psychiatric hospitals and prison camps. This is December 1976. The news loosens something in me, and that night I dream of flying to Israel, seeing my family, and visiting the Western Wall.

My last Shabbat in solitary nearly ends in disaster. Just as I kneel down to remove my chain of bolts from its hiding place, I hear the approaching steps of a guard, and in my haste the string breaks, and bolts scatter across the floor. But my six years in prison camp have taught me something about planning – and about the law that dictates that while evil can overtake you on its own, good will come to you only if you make a supreme effort to be ready for it. For this reason, I have made sure that my Shabbat store of nuts and bolts is three times larger than necessary, and much to my relief my attempt to get the remaining ones out of their hiding place goes smoothly.

As though a reward for that, I am permitted back into the camp. As I reenter, I realize that my stay in solitary has enriched my awareness of my own inner strength. The authorities have tried their best to intimidate me, but I have learned not to fear their punishments. I realize that everything depends on how you think of those penalties: It is enough for me to tell myself that I can endure them for me to endure them. I have learned that nothing that originates with man, nothing man-made, ought to be truly feared.

· · · · ·

Some interesting reports awaited my return to camp. A young prisoner named Taratuchin, who had developed relationships with Jewish prisoners and with Kovalyov and Sverstiuk, had reported that he had been working for the KGB for two years. He admitted this in a letter he sent to the twenty-fourth Party Congress. Taratuchin had been arrested at age twenty-one after founding a Russian group in the Bashkir Autonomous Soviet Socialist Republic that opposed letting the Bashkirs govern the republic. According to him, he agreed to collaborate with the KGB even before he was sent to camp in exchange for an early release and the promise of admission to university. His first assignment was to incite prisoners against the Jews – for example, by referring to the Jewish plot to dominate the world. His next instructions were to gain the trust of the Jewish prisoners. "The Jews present us with a problem," the KGB had told him. "We don't have an insider source or informants among them."

Then came the instruction to cease his activities entirely, and to prepare for working as a KGB agent "on the outside." His contact was the camp doctor. Taratuchin used to complain of heart pains, and would visit Dr. Petrov's clinic every day to get his instructions – and the packets of chocolate the KGB sent him as a reward. We had often noticed Taratuchin walking alone, apart from us. We imagined he had been contemplating exalted thoughts, whereas in fact he wandered off on his own so that we wouldn't see him eating his chocolate. He had been the one who had informed the authorities about my part in organizing the general strike. The KGB agent Chariak smiled upon hearing the report. "This Jew boy will remember us!" It finally became clear to me why they had started harassing me for not working on the Shabbat.

Before long, another problem arose. Alexander, a dissident with whom I had become friendly, had tried to persuade another young prisoner not to take part in the struggle for prisoners' rights. We had all witnessed this, but failed to understand what was behind it. Despite the attempt, the young man issued an official statement to announce that of his own volition he had decided to change his status to that of "political prisoner." Having decided Alexander was to blame, the authorities sent him to solitary for ten days. But here's where it got interesting: it seems Taratuchin had been there during the attempted persuasion, and therefore the authorities must have known about Alexander's true position. This aroused our suspicion that Alexander's punishment had been staged by the KGB in order to make him look like a victim and to give him credibility. Could it be that Alexander was working for the KGB? If so, the authorities could very well have been collecting accurate information about me and my views for years.

We more or less excommunicated Taratuchin. Once more he walked apart, though this time without chocolate. Kovalyov, however, took him under his wing. "Even a traitor deserves to be treated with Christian love," he said.

But Kovalyov had his own problems. For years he had suffered from hemorrhoids, and lately his condition had worsened so much that the medical staff diagnosed him with cancer of the rectum and recommended surgery in the camp hospital. But to let Dr. Petrov operate on you amounted to suicide, so Kovalyov requested transfer to the central hospital of the penal system (and a post-operation meeting with his wife). To this end, he declared a hunger strike in February, and was promptly put into solitary confinement. When he was let out for his daily walk, however, it was possible to exchange a couple sentences with him in English. At that time, I had gone through the textbook

Essential English, and had practiced with Zev, Balakhonov, and Suslensky, so my English was quite good.

Meanwhile, in early March, *Izvestia* published a piece by Sanya Lipavsky denouncing several prominent refuseniks as CIA collaborators. Among those fingered were Alexander Voronel and Anatoly Sharansky, whose names and faces we knew from photos Ida Nudel had sent us. In the wake of this stunning article, we braced for a new wave of arrests. Once, before Captain Rak could intervene, Kovalyov managed to shout out the English phrase "in prison" while flapping his arms like an eagle. The meaning was clear: Yuri Orlov, whose last name derives from the Russian for "eagle," had been arrested. I assumed a similar fate awaited Alexander Ginzburg and Sharansky. Sure enough, several days later word arrived of Sharansky's March 15, 1977, arrest.

Most prisoners reacted to the news with a studied nonchalance. "Well, soon enough we'll find out how many years they'll get and where they'll be imprisoned." On the surface, such nonchalance might seem heartless, but we saw arrests as simply a natural part of life, and not something to get too worked up about. Like medical students who get used to cadavers, we had become desensitized to the Soviet system of repression. The adaptability of human nature never ceases to amaze.

March 1977 brought several changes. For starters, two of the leaders of Camp 35 – Svetlichni and Gluzman – were transferred into our camp. Right away, Semyon Gluzman sought me out. "I want to talk with you. My friends in Camp 35 want me to go to Israel after my release, but I can't. I've joined the ranks of the 'democratic movement.' I write poems and stories. What would I do in Israel? I have to go to the West and live among like-minded people. It's not that I don't love Israel; in fact I see it as my spiritual homeland."

My weakness is that I cannot say no. If Simcha – as Semyon asked to be called – wished to be considered a Zionist and thought that doing so would enrich his life, who was I to deny him? In fact, if so many people living abroad wish to call themselves Zionists, why spoil their pleasure? Did I see myself as a Zionist? What did the word mean? It had come to designate a party affiliation. But why expect a single word to capture life's subtleties? Was there a reason to be a Zionist after the struggle for statehood was won? I preferred simply to be a Jew, living on Jewish soil, fulfilling the eternal Torah of Israel. Of course I didn't attempt to explain all of this to Gluzman.

He had been arrested for exposing KGB crimes. Many political prisoners were being sent to psychiatric wards, and Simcha, as a psychiatrist himself and son of a prominent Soviet psychiatrist, gathered evidence of this practice and smuggled it out to the West. This was a mission of the utmost importance, which eventually forced the regime to cease its practice of using human beings as test subjects. In Camp 35, Gluzman had continued to act as a leader, and had been more successful than we had been in getting out information about conditions in the camp.

Another Jewish prisoner who arrived at this time was Michael Kazakhov, a physicist from Leningrad. Having decided to leave the Soviet Union, Kazakhov had sent valuable photos, books, and icons ahead through the embassy of Zaire. Having got his valuables out, he began to look for a way to emigrate. As a physicist he stood no chance of getting an exit visa; the authorities regarded such scientists as having been "exposed to sensitive security information." But he put his hopes in the United States, and arranged to meet the American consul in the staircase of the consul's apartment building. Kazakhov brought with him a list of scientists who had been declared security risks in order to ask the consul to help secure their right to emigrate. It's unclear how the KGB found out about the meeting, but later that week they picked up Michael and later sentenced him to fifteen years. It's doubtful whether the nearly worthless list of scientists justified such a harsh sentence, but perhaps, like Mark Dymshits, Kazakhov was judged on his "intent" rather than on any act.

According to Kazakhov, his punishment was a deterrence measure taken to dissuade other scientists in Leningrad from trying to emigrate. He pled guilty and expressed his remorse to the court: "I am selfish by nature, and have never been able to take others into consideration." Though it was rare to hear honest expressions in Soviet courts, this admission was perfectly true. He *was* self-seeking, and even in camp he calculated whether he'd be better off as a Zionist or as a dissident, whether Israel or the US would act more forcefully to secure his release.

But there was a third way: collaboration with the KGB. Kazakhov had learned that members of the Leningrad Party Committee had illegally taken control of a deposit of gemstones and had smuggled gems out to be sold abroad. Realizing that such information might interest the KGB, he proposed exchanging it for his release. But the KGB agent who came from Moscow to meet him took no interest in what Kazakhov had to offer for the simple reason that certain people within the KGB itself had been taking a cut of the profits.

It so happened that Kazakhov was assigned to the bunk bed above mine, and to a great extent his acquaintance with other prisoners was through me. I introduced him to Sverstiuk, Kovalyov, and Gluzman. Kazakhov soon took a far greater interest in Gluzman, a friend of Sakharov and a well-known dissident in his own right, than in me; I was merely a Zionist who prayed and studied Hebrew. "Ethical norms are merely conventions," he would say, "and my norm is to do as I please."

"No," I said, "ethical ideas are God-given, and if people themselves invented the rules to govern their own behavior the world wouldn't last even a day."

"I envy you, Yosef, for your admirable faith. But let's see if you think the same way in, say, three years." (I wonder what he would say about me today?)

Simcha Gluzman was an entirely different personality: a man who searched for meaning, values, and faith. He once recited for me a poem he'd composed about a man waiting for a divine answer to the question of the purpose of life. "I can't accept Christianity," he once said. "The pervasive sense of guilt, the joyless passivity – these are alien to me."

My other friends, however, were not pleased that I had consented to consider him a Jewish nationalist. "You're too pliable," Mark told me. "You would even agree to think of Fyodorov as Theodor Herzl if he asked you nicely enough."

Still, it was Simcha, and not Misha Kazakhov, whom they invited to that year's Passover seder. As before, there was the perennial problem of getting matzah. My father had sent some, but I wouldn't be allowed to receive my next package until after the holiday. I pleaded vainly with the camp administration. Luckily, during that time, Colonel Mikov, director of all the camps for political prisoners, came to tour our camp, and happened to stop in front of my work station at the factory. I leaped to my feet, wrench in hand. "Comrade Mikov, I request that my matzah be delivered before Passover. Afterwards, they're useless. If you do not consent, I'll have to take certain measures."

Mikov stepped back, as though frightened that I might attack him with the wrench. "No need to take measures, no need." Sure enough, after work, the officer in charge of recruiting and bribing informers, Lieutenant Rozhkov, handed me the package of matzah. This was a provocation; as everyone knew, Rozhkov only gave packages to prisoners who collaborated with him. But at that point I cared only about the matzah.

We put together a festive meal of compote and matzah-meal dumplings. Simcha questioned whether it was worth the time and the trouble to prepare such lavishness. "For you," I said, "the main thing is writing yet another complaint. For us, it is celebrating a Jewish holiday – a no less crucial mission."

There was only enough matzah for the seder, so we went hungry for the eight days of Passover: no bread, and no matzah. On April 12, 1977, the moment the holiday was over, Mark brought me some bread. Yet before I could eat it, two guards arrived and ordered me to pack my things. I could feel my heart beating. So, they had decided to put me on trial. I had prepared for this; my bags had been packed and my speech in Hebrew had been ready for a month. Still, my heart pumped wildly.

I was taken on a bus over icy roads through the forest. Mountains appeared in the distance. Finally, we pull up to a building marked "People's Court of Chusovoy." Two soldiers with dogs lead me into the court chambers. It was 6:00 p.m., and all the court staff had left – an ideal time to try a political prisoner. The judge was a one-eyed woman. I'd heard many stories about her from other prisoners she had sentenced. The prosecutor, Dolmatov, was the brother of one of the officers in the camp. In the role of "people's representative" was none other than Lieutenant Rozhkov.

"Since my mother tongue is Hebrew," I announce, "and my remarks have been prepared in Hebrew, I request both a translator and a public defender."

"You are entitled neither to a translator nor to a defender," the judge said.

"But it will be difficult to translate my remarks from the Hebrew."

"That's not our problem."

Better to speak in Russian, I decided, than not to speak at all. "I am charged with refusal to work, but I did not refuse to work. I requested permission to work on Sundays instead of Saturdays."

It seems that the judge had not been fully briefed. She apparently thought I was merely a slacker, and was bewildered to discover that I had acted not out of laziness but on principle. She asked for a calendar and confirmed that each of the days on which it was noted in my file that I did not work were in fact Saturdays.

Rozhkov read out the indictment and said, "It is true that for some time we made the mistake of allowing the prisoner not to work on Saturdays. But he exploited this to incite others to refrain from work. In our opinion, he should be incarcerated in a special prison."

In my statement, I spoke openly. "From the outset, my arrest was illegal. I cannot be held guilty for the Soviet regime's refusal to grant me an exit visa. With its refusal, the state compelled me to attempt to flee. I therefore regard my sentence as illegitimate, and consequently I regard the various demands made of me by the camp authorities as illegitimate. I am not a criminal. In no other country are prisoners forbidden from practicing their faith. In the Soviet Union, even 'free' citizens are forbidden from doing so. I request my immediate release and an exit visa to Israel."

"Mendelevich, you're being insolent and are inflating your own self-importance," the judge said. "Your allegations that the Soviet Union fails to respect human rights are lies." I don't know why the judicial and camp authorities were always calling me insolent. My acquaintances all thought of me quite differently. But for the authorities, loyalty to one's people was itself a mark of insolence. In her ruling, the judge unexpectedly noted that my refusal to work was for religious reasons. No one had compelled her to mention this. Yet ultimately her sentence was perfectly in line with the KGB's wishes: three years imprisonment.

· · · · ·

On the bus ride back to camp, I notice flags marking the anniversary of Yuri Gagarin's maiden space flight and feel that I, too, am about to be cast into the vast emptiness of outer space. After a trial, a prisoner is usually sent back to camp for a couple of months while the paperwork is put in order before he is sent to prison. But rather than being taken back to my camp, I am put into the internal jail of Camp 37, the transfer station in Polovinka. Perhaps they fear my fellow prisoners will revolt after hearing of my trial. My very presence in Polovinka is kept secret. When I am taken to shower, for example, it is only at night, and I have the vast shower room all to myself (except for the two guards keeping watch).

This stay in complete isolation isn't the most comfortable I've had. I become ill, and receive no medical treatment except for once, when I am given unmarked grey pills. Not knowing what they contain, I throw them out.

Some Party apparatchiks from the city Perm visit to have a look at this odd specimen, a Zionist. These young, full-bodied, self-satisfied men come into my cell and start giving commands as though I am subhuman. But they can't harm me, I realize, for I am guarding a secret. According to regulations, a prisoner gets his confiscated belongings back when he is transferred from one labor camp to another, and in this way I now once again have my Torah, the prayers I once copied out, and my tallit. In other words, I have my work cut out for me. I sit in the empty gloom of my cell and study Torah. Every day, I memorize a psalm and practice reciting the Shacharit prayer I already committed to memory in camp. Now that I am free of the incessant daily struggles over Shabbat, my kippah, and everything else, these are some of the calmest and most contented days of my life. Most of all, unlike in camp, where I was constantly surrounded by the oppressive presence of people, here I am alone with myself.

Yet my stay in Polovinka is lasting longer than usual. The duty officer Dzyuba once takes advantage of a moment when the guards aren't looking and whispers, "I think they're planning on releasing you." At that time, a new constitution is about to come into effect, and naturally the prisoners hope that the penal code, too, will be revised and that they'll be freed. In prison, not one day passes without dreams of a pardon; many prisoners subsist on such dreams. But I have long since ceased hoping for a sudden release. At my request, my father no longer writes to me about attempts being made to save me. I think this is better for him, too. Each new miraculous release – like those of Sylva, Kudirka, and Bukovsky – would excite my hopes only to have them disappointed yet again, and nothing is harder to bear than dashed hopes.

On Saturday, June 4, two months after my trial, the new constitution is broadcast on prison speakers that have been cranked up to full volume for the occasion. I follow the broadcasts with great interest, particularly eager to hear the new citizenship law. Until 1977, no such law existed. According to an order Stalin issued in 1938, the chairman of the Supreme Soviet personally decided cases that involved accepting or renouncing citizenship. Now the authorities have pledged to legislate rules on the basis of the Helsinki Accords.

I never manage to hear the new law, because that very day guards burst into the cell and started packing up my belongings for transport. I wonder whether they have intentionally chosen Shabbat as the day to transfer me. The guards spill my postcards from Israel onto the floor and trample them underfoot. "Look what kind of rubbish you've collected."

"What I've collected is none of your business," I say.

"Enough chitchat. Pack your stuff and move."

I am bundled onto a train, and by that evening I am in the Kirov prison, in a cell in the cellar that holds a terrible stench. Traces of urine splatter the floor, and the walls are stained with the blood of swatted mosquitoes. Before going to sleep, I ask the guard for a copy of the paper.

"Why, so you can read about the new constitution?"

"Yes."

"My son, there's nothing of interest in it. As things were before, so they shall ever be." It is said that the truth is the estate of the simple, common man. Whatever his reasons, this old sergeant, in his own way, had shared with me a classic anti-Soviet sentiment. The next morning, as though to confirm that sentiment, I am given a paper. Sure enough, clause after clause, and subclause after subclause, implies that a Soviet citizen may declare his wish to change his citizenship. But afterwards comes a detailed list of conditions under which he may *not* do so. In other words, in characteristic Soviet fashion, this is a law that isn't a law. The preambles of such laws usually begin, "In general…" This allows for exceptions, but the number and extent of the exceptions is set forth only in the secret reports of the interior ministry's visa department.

As I was wading through the legal verbiage I hear voices outside my door. "Well, Gena, have you written?" asks a woman's voice.

"No," a man's voice says. "I'm still reading the court's sentence, not a word of which is true."

"I'm telling you, you must write. Close your eyes and write. Is it not a pity to take leave of the world?"

As far as I am able to understand, a female guard is trying to persuade a criminal prisoner on death row to pen an appeal.

"Hey," Gena shouts in my direction, "new boy, where have you come from?"

"I'm a political prisoner."

"I'm waiting for my execution," he says. "I assassinated a traitor in camp and now I'm going to get a bullet to the head. Listen, have you got something to eat?"

I ask the female guard to pass him fifty grams of sugar from me.

"Thanks, friend," Gena says. "No tea?"

"No, I'm on my way to prison."

"A shame. Some tea could have been my last pleasure. To drink it for the last time, and then to die content."

"Do you believe in God?" I ask.

"I've heard of God, but I don't believe in Him."

I urge him to think things over a bit. "God sees your suffering, and if you pray to Him, He may come to your salvation."

• • • • •

They board me onto another train. We have to walk some three hundred meters from the transport car to the train. I struggle, bent under the weight of my bags. Among my possessions are a suitcase of books and a large file of letters I have accumulated over the years, mainly from my parents but also from Meir Shiloach, a learned man from Kibbutz Yavne who has written to me every week during the entire length of my sentence.

"Hey, what have you got there?"

"Books," I say.

"You should have burned everything a long time ago. Where are you hauling them to? Better to throw them out now."

But how can I contemplate discarding my father's tender letters or Meir's reports from Israel? They have literally sustained me for all these years.

A soldier yells at me to move faster, and as I struggle to keep up with the column of prisoners I think of my relatives in Dvinsk during the war who were forced to march by German troops.

Just then, one fellow prisoner reaches out to help, and another takes my backpack, and we start running. This, too, arouses the guards' ire. "The Jews always know how to manage…"

When a guard at the train asks me who I am, I say I am a dangerous political prisoner. He stuffs me into a cell with hardened thieves and murderers.

"Hey, buddy, what you got?" they ask.

"I don't have anything."

"Come on. Give us an undershirt or some socks." I've no doubt they would strip me bare if it weren't for the authorities intervening in the form of two soldiers coming around selling Shipr cologne for fifty rubles a bottle. Hands thrust money through the bars. The possession of money is forbidden to prisoners, and the soldiers' first duty should have been to confiscate it, but why lose out? The moment they get their hands on a bottle, prisoners chug it down with zest. (The alcohol content is high, after all.) Then, as in any self-respecting shop, they hand back the empty bottles.

The train journey takes only a night, but I need these precious hours to prepare mentally for prison. For example, I have to figure out how to smuggle in my tzitzit. I detach the fringes from the tallit, and tie them to a pair of white wool socks in such a way that they look like part of the socks.

Then there is the matter of my Hebrew Torah. Since the Soviets see this as "subversive literature," I stand no chance of bringing it into prison with me legally. As I thumb through its precious pages, I think about how sorry I will be to have to part with the book. Then I have an epiphany. While in the camp, I once received a book of Brezhnev's speeches in Yiddish – a ridiculous volume, but one that I decided to take with me to prison in order at least to practice my Yiddish. I notice that it is exactly the size of my Torah. I rip out the title page of the Brezhnev book (which lists its publication in the Soviet Union), chew on some bread to extract some starch, and paste the page over the title page of the Torah. And this is how the first "legal" Torah came to be published in the USSR.

Still, my heart is heavy. I look out the train window, watching forests and fields blur by. As though seeing me off on my final journey, a tree waves its branches at me. I feel as though the fear of death and not-being has insinuated itself into my soul, as though I am already disappearing, as though I am almost gone. I fear such thoughts, and know how dangerous they are to a man in my condition. What to do?

Suddenly, it is as though an unknown artist has painted before my mind's eye a tall, sturdy tree, the tree of the people Israel, and upon it a soft leaf – me. An inner voice tells me: you are both the tree and the leaf. Even if the leaf falls away, the tree remains eternally. Therefore I, too, belong to the eternal. My spirit calms. I realize that in negating my own ego, I have acquired something of eternal life, and in reaching this epiphany, I overcome my fear of death.

• • • • •

Eventually the train pulls into Vladimir, a city known for two things: its fifteenth- and sixteenth-century churches, which tourists flock to, and its prison, not as frequently visited. We disembark onto the pleasant station's public platform, a group of outcasts who no longer belong to the world. This place is used to the sight. Already a century ago it was used as a main hub for prisoners on their way to Siberia.

The prisoner transport vans first head for the women's jail to unload some of their cargo, and then to Special Prison ST-2. Soon the most critical part of arrival begins: the search. I must at all cost keep my Torah, my notebooks with the prayers, the shoes into which I have sewn a hundred rubles, and the shower sponge in which I have concealed another fifty.

In the search room I find a long table and two guards. I am ordered to strip naked. My camp clothes are taken – a precaution in case I had sewn something into their seams. In their stead, I get a prisoner's uniform: pants, a shirt, and one pair of long underwear. All the rest is cast aside. When I complain about the chill, I am met with stone-cold silence. I learn the lesson, and say nothing more. They confiscate my belt, mug, spoon, and mirror – anything they can. I can already tell that conditions here will be harsher than in the labor camp. Now they inspect the bag of printed and written matter. Israeli postcards? Forbidden. Letters? None allowed. Empty notebooks? Fine. My trick had worked. I had left the first and last pages of each notebook blank, concealing the prayers inside. My shoes and sponge pass too, as do a scarf, matches, and two pairs of socks. "What if one rips?" I say. But there's no point in arguing. (Once inside I will remove the tzitzit from the socks and sew them to the wool scarf Hillel Shur gave me in 1971, and for the next five years I will never let go of this improvised tallit.) Now for the books. They take my thick Hebrew dictionary to be scanned in some kind of x-ray machine, and in the meantime, like a deft pickpocket, I succeed in slipping my Torah from the table into my bag.

I soon learn that in this prison there is no compulsory labor, and thus I will be able to keep the Shabbat. How ironic, I think, that to punish me for observing Shabbat the Soviet authorities have sent me to a place where for the next three years I can keep the Shabbat, study Torah, and wear tzitzit undisturbed. As the sages say in the Ethics of the Fathers, *mitzvah goreret mitzvah*, one mitzvah begets another.

It is 9:00 a.m., June 10, 1977. I am admitted into the Vladimir prison under armed escort with the bag of belongings I've been permitted to take with me. The prison resembles a city in itself. It was originally built in the nineteenth century, and has been renovated since. The prison church, for instance, had been turned into Ward 4 after the Russian Revolution. (Who needed prayers when there wasn't enough room to accommodate all the inmates?) Ward 3 was built after the war by German POWs. It's a real art to build something new in the style of the old. The Soviet-built wards are identical to the original Czarist ones – the same immense, grey structures with depressingly endless corridors. Each building houses seven hundred inmates, and the prison as a whole is designed to accommodate three thousand. As I walk through its "streets" for the first time, I behold urban bustle: guards and prisoners moving to and fro, rushing to work, going to eat, etc.

A guard leads me to Ward 3 but has forgotten the keys, and as he goes to get them he leaves me alone for a minute. I look over the five-floor building. Its windows are sealed, and those on lower floors are shuttered over with metal plates. Inside the cells, lit by a single bare lightbulb, it seems that eternal darkness reigns. I hear a voice from behind a metal plate on the first floor. "Hey, you, where are you from?" The chilling voice sounds like it came from a man who has been buried alive; the sound of the living dead is even more shocking than the silence of the sealed windows, behind which dozens of eyes are peering at me through the slits, like saplings trying to poke up through asphalt.

"I'm from Perm 36, in the Urals."

"Ah, a 'political.' Do you know Makarenko?"

This is starting to seem more like a national information-gathering center.

"No talking!" The guard has returned with the keys.

• • • • •

The ashen barrenness of the prison is indescribable. It would be hard to find something as cruel and emotionless as the Vladimir prison, and my cell, 91-ZA, is the grayest corner of the place. It's a grave-like corner cell with cracked glass and peeling walls, and I find myself back in the situation I was in seven years earlier after my arrest. But when I collapse onto the bunk, the thoughts astir in me are entirely different from those that preoccupied me then. On the train ride here, I saw a verdant tree, its leaves rustling in the wind, and its image now passes through my mind. It is blossoming, and I feel lifeless. Why has my life been sapped from me? Am I really a criminal, harmful to human society? Israel and my family and everything else seem merely abstract visions, existing in my thoughts alone, whereas in reality I am degraded, without a glimmer of warmth or affection. It is almost as though I am already a corpse. Will I never feel touched by love?

Lunch arrives in the form of a bowl of watery soup. "Is this made with any meat?" I ask.

"Fool! You think anyone would give you meat around here?"

Then it is time for porridge. The door slot opens, and I am instructed to hold out my bowl. I wait like that for five, ten minutes before banging on the door with my spoon. "Bring my porridge."

"No porridge for you. Special political regimen."

I hear other prisoners getting their portions and my heart sinks, not because I am left hungry, but because they have taken everything from me, even my porridge.

The next morning I awake to the sounds of the beating of drums and marching men below. Later I find out that these are cadets in the interior ministry's officers' course. Breakfast consists of water and a bit of bread, which appears to be less than the required 450 grams. Using a rubber band and a mug of water I weigh it to make sure, and surprisingly enough it is 450 grams, but each morning from then on I weigh my bread. If it weighs in at less than the minimum, I take it as a personal insult. But I decide that protesting would only tempt them to give me even less. (One prisoner weighed his bread in full view of the guards, as a result of which his "scale" was taken and his rations reduced even further.)

My silence is rewarded at lunchtime. The prisoner tasked with distributing food opens the slot, glances behind him, and pushes through a bowl of porridge. "I thought I don't get any," I exclaim.

He laughs. "Take it, take it."

I am overjoyed, not because of the bowl of steaming porridge, but because the wall of solitude has been momentarily penetrated. For an instant, prisoner solidarity had overcome dry regulation. Still, I curse myself for having passed on the bread that was offered on the train. "No thanks, I'm not hungry," I said. What an idiotic thing to have done. How I wish I could have that bread now.

As Shabbat approaches, I start thinking about candles, remembering the time I once managed to smuggle some bits of paraffin out of the camp factory. When I left the factory that day, I was not only frisked, but taken to the search room. Clearly, someone had informed on me. As I was being led to the search room, I managed with an almost indiscernible movement to take the paraffin out of my belt, where I had concealed it, and into my gloves. As we were about to enter the room, I stopped and turned to Captain Rak. "Why are you searching me?"

"None of your business. Get in here."

"No, you only search Jews. It's discriminatory."

"Get in here, or I'll make sure you receive punishment."

"Fine!" In a gesture of despair, I threw my gloves in mock anger at a bench by the door and walked in. Rak suspected nothing. As I left after his futile search, I picked up the gloves with the same gesture of exasperation. "You see, there was no need to search me." That evening, I lit the Shabbat candles. After they had gone out, Captain Rak came in and sniffed the air like a dog. "What was burning here?"

"Nothing."

"No, something was burning here. Have you been lighting candles again? If I ever catch you…"

That's how things were in camp. Oddly, I feel less observed here in prison. The guards look in on you several times a day – sometimes without your even noticing – and that's it. There's no constant scrutiny.

As elsewhere, prisoners here are allotted a daily half-hour walk alone in a small asphalt yard with barbed wire stretched above. One day, I hear a tapping from the adjacent yard. "Who are you?"

"Political prisoner Mendelevich."

The next day, the same tapping. "Catch!"

Before I understand what's happening, a small white pellet comes flying over the wall. A guard we nicknamed Ginger sees what's going on and warns me not to pick it up. But I have no choice. If I don't take what appears to be a note, the guards will find it when they open the yard and will punish its author.

Nor can I simply put it in my pocket. So as soon as Ginger turns to supervise other prisoners, I quickly bend down, insert it in my mouth and swallow it.

At the end of my half hour, the guard opens the gate and chuckles. "So, you've fooled me, eh?"

Back in my cell, I drink several cups of water and stick two fingers down my throat, but my empty stomach refuses to vomit anything up. In any case, I have to prepare for Shabbat. I wash the floor three times and clean the toilet until it gleams. With nightfall, I pray, say Kiddush, and enjoy a meal, like in any Jewish home. No matter that I have no wine, and feast only on coarse bread and a meager piece of fish. I can soak the fish in water, or better yet drop it in boiling water to make a kind of soup. Or I can remove the bones and eat it with my bread, and then chew the bones separately. (I did this so regularly that my tooth enamel cracked.)

But neither the illicit porridge nor the fish bones are helping; I feel myself rapidly losing strength, and am reduced to lying helplessly in bed all day, as though I were debilitated by illness. Maybe I am sick with prison despondency. I can move my legs only with difficulty, and my head empties of all thoughts except one: "Why?"

I have to get a grip. I resolve that starting after Shabbat I will start to study, read, and exercise. It's not just a matter of resolving, of course, but of activating that part of the mind that is still capable of thought in order to rip through the veil of indifference that has settled there. Survival is the last imperative. The last thought of a man about to perish of thirst beneath the scorching desert sun, or of a terrified driver behind the wheel speeding toward an unavoidable collision, or of the fighter in the Warsaw ghetto about to leap into the machine-gun fire and certain death, is the desperate will to live, to hang on to life.

That's how I feel in my bare cell in Vladimir prison: the urge to break through the sensory blackout of three comatose days, my mind jumbled by hunger, to get up from my metal bunk, to live, to be a man again, to reach Jerusalem, and to lift up my voice in a prayer to my Creator, who granted me strength even in my weakest hour.

On Sunday, the note I swallowed comes out the other end, and I can still make it out: "I, Ivan Vassilyevich Nachporok, born in 1931, was arrested in 1949 on charges of theft, and sentenced to five years. In 1956, I was sentenced to another three years…" And so on in a long rap sheet of dates of various prison terms. "The authorities persecute me for openly declaring my opposition to the Soviet state. I ask your help. I ask that you inform the world of my bitter fate."

I receive many such requests in the next three years. But go figure what is true and what false. Did Ivan curse the regime because he had been jailed for theft, or had he really been imprisoned for opposing the regime? In order to justify his crime to himself, every criminal prisoner challenges the existing system to one degree or another. If society at large is criminal, then any act against society becomes an ethical act – not a crime so much as a gesture of defiance or a rebellion against injustice. In fact, it gets me wondering about the extent to which an individual can be held responsible for his crime. What kind of society is it that neglected his education and the education of his parents, who lived sunk in corruption and failed to provide their son with a loving home? Many criminals were themselves the sons of absent or drunk or violent fathers, and harbored a profound hatred of the Soviet regime. Yet their hatred did not by any means make them political prisoners. Their bitterness was not a principled protest against violence, but the hatred of a wild animal prevented from devouring its prey. But how thin is the line separating the man imprisoned for his principles from the man arrested for common theft! Both suffer, both despise their jailers, both dream the same dreams of freedom. And this commonality is the foundation of feelings of solidarity between prisoners.

I considered it anathema to associate with evildoers. But if the prisoner on food duty hands me an extra portion of bread, how can I not accept? And once I accept, how can I not thank him, even if he happens to be a thief or murderer?

One day the "librarian" who distributes books pushes some packets of margarine and sugar through the slot. "There's a note inside," he says. "After you read it, write an acknowledgment that you've received it."

The note reads: *"Yosef, we are serving here together, and are trying to join you. In the meantime, we're sending you some margarine and sugar. – Izya and Avraham"* (fictitious names). I could not be more ecstatic. I no longer feel so profoundly alone. I am among friends – old friends from my days as a Jewish activist in Riga. I put in a request to join them and miraculously they transfer all of us into Ward 4. We meet and examine each other. My old friends have hardly changed.

Five of us settle into cell 27: the Armenian nationalists Bagrat and Razmik, Izya, Avraham, and me. There's so much to catch up on, but there's also our daily rhythms. Avraham immerses himself in reading books and newspapers. He doesn't let a single line about Israel get past him as he amasses geographic, economic, and political knowledge about the country. A conversation with him makes you feel almost as though you were there. Heated debates are easily sparked. Avraham, for instance, endorses the existing parliamentary system in Israel; Izya favors instituting an American-style separation of powers.

Not that all our arguments center on matters of principle. We also squabble, for example, about who is using too much of our scarce soap. It can be oppressive even for the closest of friends to be forced to live in a tight proximity in which it's impossible to leave the room even for a moment. Here you cannot hide your flaws or frustrations. Irritations eat away at you corrosively, but the sources of a man's irritation are often mysterious. One of your cellmates insists that he neither expects nor is preoccupied in the slightest with getting an early release, and then one day it turns out that deep down he lives for that hope alone, that he scrutinizes the papers for any hint of a development that might increase his chances. If the day's paper offers nothing on which he can hang a hope, he huffs and puffs and spends the rest of the day sulking.

Another cellmate feels that the others are constantly mocking him, and he seeks both to avenge himself on them and earn their admiration – contradictory impulses that are equally rooted in his insecurity.

A third fears his ethical decline, and so in compensation drives the others up the wall with his excessive "refinement." Each man and his own neuroses.

One day Avraham has something important to tell me, but in the cell everyone hears everything, so he waits until our daily walk in the yard. "I arrived here with a large collection of 3D postcards," he says, "which were of course confiscated. Kolya Obrobov, the KGB officer here, offered to buy them from me. I mulled it over and agreed. He started giving me bread, sausages, and apples. I got two rubles for each card. After several meetings, he said, 'This is becoming uncomfortable. I need an excuse to explain why I'm seen meeting you so often. I'll list you as one of my agents, but only formally.' Several meetings later, he said, 'My superiors are demanding to see results from those listed as my agents. Maybe just write a short report on someone.'" Avraham wrote a report together with the prisoner about whom the report was written. This man was about to be exiled, and had an interest in giving the authorities misleading information about himself. "That's how it started," Avraham continues. "I write a false report, and he brings me food. Do you think I should continue?"

"I think you must stop this game at once," I reply. "It's not worth getting mixed up in for the sake of some food."

Avraham gives me a long, attentive look with his sad eyes, as though he wants to say something else.

The following day, as we navigate the muddy puddles on the roof of Ward 2 during our half hour of fresh air, he says that he hasn't told me everything. "Obrobov is no longer satisfied with informing. Now he wants to send me to Israel to spy there. What do you say?"

I reiterate that to agree to any such thing is to play with fire, and that there is no way to predict how it will end.

But Avraham continues playing Kolya's game, and after each meeting returns to our cell bearing food in such abundance that we give away some to prisoners in other cells. Our own cell becomes a kind of hub for trading food and passing on notes (all of which requires paying off guards). In order to pass notes to Jewish inmates in other cells we even begin negotiating with a female guard named Inesa, who contrary to protocol chats with the prisoners in each cell of the floor under her supervision. It's reasonable to assume she works for the KGB and is expected to keep tabs on our "financial dealings" and contacts with the outside. Sometimes, however, her behavior doesn't at all seem to be serving KGB interests, as when she passes on covert notes hidden inside tobacco.

As the food supplier, Avraham is the cell's acknowledged leader; one of the reasons for his continued contacts with Kolya may indeed be his desire to remain our "patron" and to keep us bound in gratitude. But actually the dynamic is far more complex. Imagine a captain of a sinking, storm-tossed ship who stays in his cabin nonchalantly smoking, contemplating how to prove his superiority in chess over his first mate while his passengers panic. Such is Avraham, who feels he has to prove each day anew, both to us and to himself, that even here in prison he is the only serious, essential man, a man who depends on no one but himself. Without being himself aware of it, he feels continuously compelled to show others that they need him.

"Yosef, take some porridge. I'll get us more."

"No, thank you."

He shoots me a furious look, as though my declining is a personal affront. "You promised you would eat with the others so that they wouldn't feel embarrassed by eating more than you."

"Yes, but I never agreed to please you by eating a lot myself. They eat as much as they like even without me." In other words, I make clear that I don't need his favors. Izya, on the other hand, eats everything, but resists Avraham's dominance and asserts his independence in other ways. In the end, no one remains above the fray, and the only consequence is endless squabbling. Often one of us will refuse to talk to another for a day or two until the anger subsides.

Bagrat, for instance, gives ample demonstration of human frailties; he eats everything, shamelessly keeping the best portions for himself. Once we had an extra loaf and were discussing which of the two loaves to send to another cell. "Let's give them the black bread," Bagrat said. "It gives me stomach aches."

"And keep the good white bread for ourselves?" I said incredulously. "You have a sensitive stomach but they can eat whatever we toss their way?"

Bagrat took this as a grave insult and sulked in silence. Avraham reprimanded me. "As the majority in the cell, we Jews have to take care not to make the non-Jews feel excluded. And then you have to go and insult the man."

"I didn't insult him, I just pointed out that his suggestion is unfair."

"Yosef," Izya added, "you're embarrassing people. They may not be passing your test, but try to let them be."

• • • • •

Sometimes, however, a lighter and more celebratory air pervades the cell. We prepare fish with breadcrumbs and look together at the wonderful map of Israel that Avraham has obtained through Kolya Obrobov. We discuss the Israeli withdrawal from the Sinai, and the oil deposits that may have been forfeited thereby. Izya (who is working through the final part of *1000 Words – Elef Milim*) and I study Hebrew, and talk about our future lives, where we'll live and study, whom we'll marry.

"I'll find a wife quite easily," I say. "I'll go to matchmakers."

"Are you serious?" says Izya in disbelief. "That won't be my approach."

Then we study the weekly Torah portion together, Izya reciting aloud; I correct him here and there.

Our cell is a haven, beyond which brutality is the norm. One day we ask the librarian about Sergei, whom we haven't seen in several days. "They slaughtered him. He lost at cards and couldn't pay up." Every week, announcements come over the speakers of so-and-so who stabbed so-and-so after some dispute, a weekly litany of violence. Amidst of all of this we sit and learn Torah.

Another time, as I recite Kiddush for Shabbat, we hear wild screams and the sound of guards running down the corridor to quell a riot. I've said the Kiddush in a hundred different circumstances, but each time, the words "a covenant between Me and the children of Israel" ring out and summon the Shabbat queen to fill our humble cell with her radiance.

We fail to adequately defend ourselves in only one area of prison life: the matter of "horses." A "horse" in prison jargon is a method of passing a note or package from one cell to another. Say, for example, prisoners in the cell on the floor beneath ours request tobacco. We tie a packet to a string, and push it through a crack in the window grille. Downstairs they're waiting for the packet, but because of the metal shutters can't see it. With the help of a piece of wood they have splintered from a broom, they pull the string and draw the packet in through their window. It's a complex operation, and the risk is high that we'll be caught. Many "horses" are discovered, in which case they're snipped by guards wielding long scissors. As a Russian saying has it, "even with four legs, horses stumble." In our case, he who stumbles ends up in solitary confinement.

In solitary, another supply chain was in effect. Prisoners in the cell above solitary cell 25 drilled a hole in the floor through which they lowered food – including whatever leftovers they could salvage. Another difference: down in solitary they made no distinction between criminal and political prisoners. Everyone was treated equally harshly. How then could we refuse to take part in the risky cat-and-mouse games? Our fellow prisoners in solitary needed food, after all.

Another means of communication was supplied by holes drilled in walls between cells. Such was the superhuman industry and ingenuity of the prisoners that the authorities despaired of fixing the walls. New holes would be drilled the very day the old ones were plastered over. Political prisoners seldom risked solitary for a hole in the wall, but criminal prisoners made no such calculations. These were their lifeblood.

Doinikov, the head of the political prisoners' ward, once visited our cell to tell us he knew we had a hand in passing things from cell to cell. "But you're intelligent men; at least pay a little attention to the kind of contraband you're passing on. You're sending the very blades with which these people are slaughtering one another."

The plumbing afforded another delivery system. A letter would be folded into a matchbox that was wrapped in plastic, attached to a long string, and flushed down the toilet. In another cell on the same floor they would do the same thing at the same time, and the strings would twist in the pipe, allowing the other side to "fish" the message out. The method was tried and true, but required coordination and considerable patience.

Still another method utilized the prisoners who worked in the bathrooms as couriers. Since these men had been handpicked by Obrobov, they didn't have to be too cautious, and were willing to pass messages. Their willingness also had something to do with the fact that they liked to read the messages before delivering them, hoping thereby to pick up a secret or two. The sender of course knew this, and chose his words accordingly. But if the sender was too careful, and his message too bland, the erstwhile courier would make excuses why he couldn't deliver it.

The crucial thing was to know whom the courier really worked for. If he answered to the wardens, the attempt to deliver a message through him always ended in punishment. If, on the other hand, he served the "the men in the blue uniforms," the KGB, then there was no cause for fear. Kolya Obrobov never administered punishments. But of course one couldn't simply ask: whom do you work for?

For this reason, many prisoners preferred to perform the transfer in the yards. The moment the door to the yard clicked shut behind you, you'd hear a tapping from the adjacent yard.

"Which cell?"

"Cell 2-6."

"Catch."

And then as soon as the guard watching the yards from above turned, a package or note would be tossed over the wall. These packages could be up to two kilos: sugar, margarine, tea, underwear, socks, iron rods, metal files, or wrenches. Although the entire operation lasted a matter of seconds, it was hard to fool the guards. Fortunately, they were by their nature lazy.

Small packets could sometimes be launched over several yards with a single toss. None of us liked to take part in these things. Criminal prisoners were punished only very seldom, while if we were caught we were punished severely and immediately. The criminal inmates took advantage of us at every opportunity, and we were in no position to refuse since most of the information about what was happening in the prison came through their channels.

Vladimir prison was one of the few in the Soviet Union to hold both political prisoners and real criminals, including mafia bosses like Brilliant (a Jew with a mother living in Canada) and Ando. The mafia men were held in isolation in the basement, and yet many in the prison worked for them; even some guards received salaries from them. (An Armenian nationalist by the name of Ashot Navusardian told me that he had been in the Tbilisi prison with a group of crime bosses who bribed an officer to bring crates of wine bottles to their cell.)

Another reason not to refuse to deliver packets and messages was simply that as political prisoners we were more likely to be isolated, and thus we depended more on this covert postal system than anyone else. These bold operations – sometimes right under the guard's nose – cultivated a crucial quality: chutzpah. Whoever did not take risks lost out.

These new habits would soon enough prove very useful. One day I was transferred without warning from Ward 4 to the prison clinic, where I was informed that a routine medical check three months earlier had disclosed traces of a virulent disease and that I would have to be admitted for medical treatment.

"Why am I only now being apprised of this?"

"They forgot to tell you."

The whole thing seemed suspicious, but I had no choice. What if I really were ill? In the clinic, I met Bagrat and a criminal prisoner named Vitya Anissimov. Both were quite pleased to be there. In the clinic, they said, you could eat to your heart's content. You were given a cup of milk and thirty grams of butter a day. But I recoiled from the very thought of eating; I continued studying, losing weight, and waiting to be treated. Finally I was made to take certain medicines, and shortly thereafter developed severe diarrhea. Apart from the menu, the clinic was the most awful place in the entire prison. Each cell held three patients and had no running water – only a bucket for taking care of your bodily functions. Visits to the toilet were strictly regimented, and the schedule took no account of the individual patient's needs. I requested and received other pills, but it wasn't clear if the new ones were any different. I started to suffer from chronic stomach pain. Only afterwards did I learn that the "treatment" had been nothing more than a ruse to separate me from Izya and Avraham.

On April 4, 1978, I was discharged from the clinic and transferred to cell 31, which held Prichodko, Gena Shelyudko, Razmik Zagrobian, and Vitya Anissimov. Anissimov had been tried multiple times, but the last time had been sentenced to five years for leaping out of his cell and attacking the prisoner distributing food for giving him less than he felt he deserved. Prichodko, an ex-officer and missile specialist, was serving fifteen years for participating in the struggle for human rights. Zagrobian, an Armenian nationalist, had burned a portrait of Lenin that had hung in Yerevan's central square in protest of a visit of the Soviet prime minister Alexei Kosygin. Shelyudko had been a young financial speculator, imprisoned for the criminal importation of clothing, who had escaped from prison, hijacked a plane with a hundred passengers to Helsinki, and finally gave himself up to Finnish authorities after a three-day siege. He was extradited to the Soviet Union, and in 1977 sentenced to fifteen years. These men were strangers to one another, and they suffered from a whole host of complexes: obsessions with power, paranoia, and just plain frayed nerves. I requested an immediate transfer to my old cell, and when Doinikov refused, I declared a hunger strike. This earned me a promise that I would be transferred in ten days, which meant I would have to celebrate Passover here.

To prepare for the holiday, I set aside one corner of the room as exclusively mine and cleaned it thoroughly. Much to my cellmates' astonishment, I lit a candle and performed the traditional search for chametz, and the next morning burned the crumbs I had found. The problem was that my cellmates continued to eat bread right next to me, and crumbs scattered all over. I couldn't very well ask them to refrain from eating bread for eight days. They already thought of me as an eccentric. Moreover, the iron rule of prison is that cellmates must share everything they have equally, so I had to give out what little matzah I had. Although I tried to explain to my cellmates that I couldn't eat chametz, they didn't take me seriously. My stepmother had sent kosher-for-Passover cookies made of Israeli matzah meal, honey, and eggs, and these were my sole substitute for everything I was giving up: bread, fish, and porridge. But even these precious cookies had to be shared, and no one thought to offer me in exchange something I could eat on Passover.

As in years past, I wrote out the Haggadah, relying on memory, on some letters I had received that described Passover, and even on a postcard from Israel that depicted a seder plate.

Zagrobian helped me with one more mission. During one of our visits to the yard, he climbed onto my shoulders and threw a bag of matzah and raisins to the criminal prisoners in the next yard. These men, in turn, managed to give the bag to Izya and Avraham so that they, too, would be able to celebrate in some fashion.

Just before Passover a letter arrived from home. My father's health had deteriorated badly; he suffered from pulmonary edema and high blood pressure, and was once even declared clinically dead. After his last stay in the hospital, he and my stepmother decided that their health would not hold out long enough to wait for me, and that they had to leave the country and go to Israel while they could. Getting an exit visa in 1978 wasn't terribly difficult. In their letter to me, they even noted the date they had set to leave Riga. Despite the circumstances, I felt uncontainable joy at the prospect that my family would be settling in Israel.

It was accompanied by this joy that I entered into my celebration of the holiday of Exodus. What profound joy to live in a generation of a new exodus! How wonderful that this new liberation was taking place in my lifetime! Where had Soviet Jewry summoned the energy to pick up and leave when by all logic we should have long ago assimilated and disappeared? Many of us had never prayed, never known how to keep Shabbat. Only by virtue of our love of Israel and of our people did we return to our faith. The love of Israel, I reflected that night, can ignite the divine spark in us and light a path from enslavement to freedom.

Since the common table was used to eat bread, I made a table of my own from cardboard and recited the Haggadah, lifting the matzah, covering the afikomen, sandwiching bitter herbs between two pieces of matzah like Hillel the Elder used to do. Before I could finish, my cellmates inconsiderately made me move aside, claiming they needed room to write letters. But I was far away from them, and from the prison; I felt myself part of the great nation fleeing from Egyptian bondage.

For the next week I went hungry. I knew that in cases of mortal danger one is permitted to eat bread on Passover, but I wasn't on the brink of death, and in any case I derived more pleasure from observing Passover properly than I would have in eating bread. Rabbi Chaim Drukman sent me a letter from Israel permitting me to eat whatever rations I was given (asking me to refrain only from bone marrow) and Israeli Chief Rabbi Shlomo Goren had said something similar to my sister Eva. Still, as I said, I derived a certain pleasure from denying myself almost all foods for the duration of the holiday.

A week after Passover had ended I still had not been reunited with my friends. I began another hunger strike. Doinikov assured me that it was just an administrative delay, and that very day – Israel's Independence Day – I was transferred to a cell with Avraham. In fact, I celebrated that day twice: once in my cell on Tuesday, when I had calculated the day to be, and once with Avraham on Wednesday, according to his calculation. Wednesday also marked our joyous reunion after two months apart, and we spent it talking excitedly and reading letters from Israel.

Meanwhile, the trials of Orlov, Ginzburg, and Sharansky were being held. Orlov had served as a member of Helsinki Watch, a group that took it upon itself to publicize Soviet violations of the Helsinki Accords. The authorities regarded the group's activities as a subversive attempt to undermine Soviet power, and so put its members on public trial. Anissimov, called to testify at Orlov's trial, was asked to describe the conditions at Vladimir prison (which had been one of the issues Orlov had raised in bringing human rights abuses to light). As expected, he told the court what it wanted to hear. He described his own conditions in prison, which as an informer and collaborator were exceedingly comfortable. When Anissimov returned from the trial, he justified himself to us: "I told the truth. They didn't ask me about the conditions of other prisoners, only my own." Anyone with half a brain would understand that this "truth" would be taken by the court as a description of the condition of all prisoners. In any case, in exchange for his cooperative testimony Anissimov was promised a shortened sentence.

* * * * *

One morning Inesa woke me up before the usual wake-up call. "They've brought Sharansky."

"Where is he?"

"In a transit cell, looking very weak and pale. They've given him nothing to eat, and are holding him like that every night."

"Can you send him some food from me?"

"No, there are other guards on duty downstairs."

"At least a little tobacco." I wanted to send him a note. Inesa understood.

"I said I can't." And that was that.

I rushed to the toilet bowl, our means of communication, to alert those in the floor below. A Ukrainian nationalist then being held in solitary named Gayduk replied, saying that he could not communicate with the transit cell, which was cut off from the other cells on the floor. I tried contacting the inmates in the cell adjacent to the transit cell, but they had all been taken away to solitary the day before for refusing to get up from their bunks during inspection. The only one left was a prisoner nicknamed Pinocchio (he had wooden prosthetic hands and legs), but he was hard of hearing. Watching my frantic and vain attempts, Inesa burst into peals of laughter. Understandably, since to the spectator the procedure of communicating through the toilets looks ridiculous. You take the water out of the toilet bowl by means of repeatedly dipping a rag into it and then wringing it out (not a particularly pleasant operation), then you stick your head in as far as possible in order to hear, often draping something over your head in order to improve the acoustics. "Enough already," Inesa finally said. "Another guard is coming now to replace me." So despite my best efforts to convey essential information about the prison and about Anissimov to Sharansky, I failed to successfully make contact with him.

• • • • •

One day I received a letter from Sara Zinburg, who according to prior arrangement was to write to me when my parents had safely arrived in Israel. In a coded message, she wrote that they had reached Jerusalem, where they had wanted to take up residence, but underneath she added: "Yosef, I hope you've managed to recover from this terrible loss. Your father was a wonderful man, and everyone loved him." The lines seemed to blur before my eyes. What did she mean? What loss? Why was she writing of my father in the past tense? At first I refused to believe it. Then I realized it was no mistake; my father was gone. All was lost.

I told my cellmates. At first a long silence, then words of consolation.

My father's final days had been unsettled. The authorities demanded he give up the apartment before he could get an exit visa, and he had to move to an unfamiliar temporary apartment. He had not made peace with the idea of leaving me alone in the country, and having decided not to leave, his heart simply stopped. That evening he had been talking with his wife about the nightly news program, and then had gone to sleep. It was the Seventeenth of Tammuz, the day on which Moses came down from Mount Sinai to discover his people dancing orgiastically around the golden calf, the day on which the Romans breached the walls of Jerusalem on their way to sacking the city and destroying the Temple. My stepmother heard my father from the other room saying he didn't feel well, and by the time she reached him he was gone. She sat by him all night, pleading with him: "Moshe, just one more day. Just to reach Israel. After that, do as you please. We talked about everything, about how we would live in Jerusalem, about how we would meet Yosef there. Only one thing we didn't talk about: what I would do without you." As she debated whether to travel or to cancel the trip, she thought she heard my father's voice from within the still, moonlit room. "Go wait for Yosef in Jerusalem."

And so this brave woman rose from beside the cold body, and went out to fulfill his last wish. This proved nearly impossible to do. The law forbade transporting bodies out of the country. No one wanted to help the parents of a "political criminal." A clerk at the morgue insisted she store the body in formaldehyde and sulfuric acid. When she protested that it would damage the body, he took one look at her distressed eyes and relented, agreeing to sign the required forms.

The effort to bring my father's body to Israel took on trans-Atlantic pro-portions. Prime Minister Begin, Minister Haim Landau, and Henry Kissinger made calls, exerted pressure, and finally came through. On the eighth of Av, my stepmother brought my father's body to be buried the following day on the Mount of Olives overlooking the Temple Mount, in the city where his son would one day live. The entire nation mourned on the Seventeenth of Tammuz, when my father died, and on the Ninth of Av, when he was buried. I had fasted on both days, though I had not then known of his death. Know-ing they were culpable in hastening his death, the authorities had neglected to tell me of it – like Cain putting the body of his brother Abel into the earth in order to hide his murder. The authorities feared telling me of the news when it was still "fresh," and hoped that by the time I heard it, the blow wouldn't be as sharp.

Before my stepmother had left for Israel, she had come to the prison to see me, but was turned away on the grounds that she was already a citizen of for-eign country. Her pleadings were to no avail. The authorities had also held up all the letters and telegrams of consolation sent to me, as though they feared my father even in death.

The passing weeks did nothing to dull the sharp pangs of loss. I didn't even try to analyze things; understanding would come later. I just sobbed, shamelessly sobbed all the time. I shed tears for the meaninglessness of things. How overjoyed I had been when I heard of my father's plan to leave for Israel; now death had shattered the dream. Yet beneath the tears, some understand-ing began to take shape. I understood that I was him, that he lived within me, and that I could go on living.

Three days after getting the news, I could start eating again, and talking. I had considerate friends. During the days I couldn't eat, Zagrobian had kept bread and sugar – and even a baked potato – for me. "Eat something, Yosef," he urged. He embraced me, and reminded me of the transience of every mate-rial thing, and of the eternity of the spirit.

Now I was ready to vent my rage on those who were imprisoning me. In order to "compensate" me for cancelling my stepmother's visit and for making my letters disappear, Doinikov agreed to transfer me (along with Zagrobi-an) to Hillel Butman's cell. Hillel and I had a common language, expressed through learning Hebrew and reminiscing about our days as Zionist activists. But there was another advantage: this ward also held Sharansky. As it turns out, Sharansky had indeed been held together with the informer Anissimov, but had taken the measure of his cellmate fairly quickly. Now Sharansky was held in a cell with Gena Shelyudko. Some time before, I had been surprised when Hillel had given a Hebrew-Russian dictionary to Shelyudko. What would this Russian want with such a book? But God works in mysterious ways, and now Shelyudko had passed the dictionary on to Sharansky.

Hillel had persuaded the librarian – an odd chap who in all likelihood was on the KGB payroll – to deliver messages to Sharansky. After a half year in the prison, Hillel had become well versed in its ways. Actually, this was his second stay; he was back after an all-too-short break. His health was giving out, but he was heroically trying to hang on. He had been sentenced to three years for organizing a rally for Yisrael Zalmanson, who himself had been imprisoned after getting into a fight in the labor camp with an ex-Polizei who called him a kike. Zalmanson was sent away; the anti-Semite was not. To protest Zalmanson's imprisonment, Hillel had walked into the camp headquarters, a yellow star on his lapel and a statement in this hand: "In this country, Jew-killers are always right." For this he was promptly shipped off to Vladimir.

We waited impatiently for Sharansky's messages. He would pass on detailed descriptions of the Soviet Jewry movement abroad, and of the Jewish activists within the Soviet Union. The librarian would come around with a book, in which Sharansky had concealed a letter in Hebrew. In this way, he would tell us about the time he had met the interior minister to demand our release, for example, or about meeting Edward Kennedy.

From various rumors, I had heard that during his trial, Sharansky had declared a hunger strike to protest the absurdity of his indictment – he had been charged with the crime of espionage. The KGB had instructed a telepathy researcher to approach Sharansky and ask how his findings might be passed to the West. Sharansky introduced this man to an American journalist. The "research" turned out to be nothing but speculations about the possibility of telepathic communication between people on the moon and people on earth. Because this nonsense was written inside the academy, it was considered "scientific material," and for enabling it to get into the hands of a foreign correspondent Sharansky was sentenced to thirteen years.

In the yard, we sometimes managed to exchange a few words over the wall.

"Anatoly," I'd say, "have you learned how to get extra food?"

"No," he said with a chuckle.

"But weren't you involved in politics? You made connections."

"But I'm no businessman."

His Hebrew – picked up in an illegal ulpan – was excellent. In our half-hour breaks, he and Gena would fill their yard with Hebrew songs, making our yard seem gloomy by comparison. On our side of the wall, I would run back and forth in the tiny space, splashing through puddles, while Hillel would do gymnastics. Both of us remained silent, quietly wishing Sharansky would be transferred to our cell and reinvigorate us.

My father's death nearly broke me. I suddenly felt alone in the world, and realized to my horror that I had been imprisoned for eight years. For some reason, the thought of losing eight years depressed me more profoundly than the thought of the four years I had left to serve. I felt like someone who had already seen too much.

But once again, change was on the horizon. One Saturday night, we were ordered to pack up. Avraham knew the date of this transfer in advance, having heard of it from Kolya Obrobov. In the run-up to the 1980 Moscow Olympics, a decision was made to transfer us from the city of Vladimir, whose famous cathedrals attracted tourists, to Chistopol, a town in the republic of Tatarstan. On October 8, 1978, we were stripped naked and given new clothes to prevent us from smuggling anything out.

The mood on the train was raucous. The "striped" prisoners – political prisoners serving a second term – refused to wear the new clothes until they were given back their belongings. Many of them were ex-criminal convicts, and it showed. They cursed loudly, and aggressively demanded tea. In our own cell in the boxcar, Hillel and I were given two quarter loafs of bread and two salty fish. Everything else was taken from us for the journey. Despite having nothing, however, our spirits were high. We conversed in Hebrew and sang Israeli songs. The guard was convinced we were Israeli spies, and was surprised when I addressed him in Russian.

"Where did you learn Russian?"

"In school," I said.

"They teach Russian in Israeli schools?"

"I've never been to Israel, but I'll live there one day."

We still hadn't had a glimpse of Sharansky. To prevent us from meeting, he was being held on the far end of the car. When he went to the bathroom, guards took him to the officer's bathroom so that he wouldn't walk past our cell. Nonetheless, Hillel craned his neck and caught a quick look. "Short," he said, "maybe 1.60 meters."

• • • • •

When we arrived in Kazan, the capital of Tatarstan, we were loaded into trucks and driven over the Volga River to the Chistopol prison. The town held some fifty thousand residents, mostly Russian, with a Tatar minority. In the nearby city of Naberezhnye Chelny, Western companies were building large automobile factories. It also hosted a Vostok watch manufacturing plant. Prisoners made parts for these factories.

The prison itself was a single, three-story, pre-Soviet building. We arrived there on the eve of Yom Kippur. The next day, the usual searches, the usual haggles over each and every letter and postcard and book. My possessions, taken from me before the journey, were now examined individually to determine which ones would be returned to me – and which ones confiscated. I managed without difficulty to keep my Torah, and when Officer Ogodin's head was turned I tried to sneak my prayer notebook into the bag of "cleared items," but he snatched it from my hand.

"Mendelevich! That isn't fair."

"What do you mean 'not fair'? These are my belongings. You stole them from me, not vice versa."

He appeared shocked by my chutzpah. He confiscated my Israeli postcards ("Zionist propaganda"). There was something especially sullying about this search, on Yom Kippur of all days. As they put their grubby hands on every sock, fingering every hole in every shirt, I could not help despising their vulgarity and pettiness. And yet I had managed to salvage my Torah, most of my prayer notebooks, Bialik's anthology of Aggadah, *The Book of Legends*, and a Hebrew textbook.

Once more I settled into the monotony of prison life: wake-up, prayers, breakfast, walk in the yard, studies, dinner, studies, lights out. Unlike in Vladimir, however, here we had to work (except on Shabbat). In our case this involved weaving baskets meant to carry vegetables. We did this by hand, in our cells. Each basket took an hour and a half, and if we didn't produce eight of them a day our food rations were curtailed.

I had lost weight in the Vladimir prison, so much so that when I was stripped here, the warden, Major Malofeyev, commented on my appearance. "Didn't they feed you in Vladimir? You're nothing but skin and bones. No matter, here you'll work and get fed adequately."

Our food supplies were by this point running low. I carefully apportioned our cell's supply, in such a way that it would last each prisoner till the end of the month: a spoonful of margarine, evened out with a ruler; and a tablespoon of sunflower oil we had brought from Vladimir. Each of us had to exercise self-control. Even the most fair-minded man whose food privileges are revoked will degrade himself to get soup that is just a little bit thicker or porridge that has a few more drops of oil. Gayduk devised a special method of dividing the fish into equal portions. What disgraceful pettiness! Many a man can stand the heat of combat, but cannot bear the daily degradations of a hunger that saps his life force: the dark circles under the eyes, the bloated face and legs, the fingers trembling as they take hold of the plate...

Every day, I struggle to maintain objectivity in distributing food. It always seems to me that I give myself the largest portion. Have I become so weakened that food has taken on so much significance for me? The very thought brings me to resolve from now on to stop taking anything but the bare minimum for myself. I give the extras to my cellmates and pretend I've already finished my own. I immediately feel relieved.

Drawing on food Avraham has brought with him from Vladimir, we manage to put together proper Shabbat meals. It often happens that we can't fill the Saturday work quota during the rest of the week, in which case our Saturday rations are withheld. But with Avraham's food, our Shabbat meals become almost gestures of defiance, as if we're saying to our guards: did you really think you'd break us that easily? We have treats even you don't have at home: sweets, biscuits, sugar. On Friday nights we enjoy a cake that I prepare with crumbled biscuits soaked in sugar water and made into a thick dough, and the whole thing topped with a bit of improvised whipped cream. Hillel pronounces me a real baker. We also reserve our fish preserves for Shabbat. I mix them with bread, put the result on the radiator for a while, and presto: gefilte fish. We feel like princes at a royal feast. After the meal, we read old letters from Israel and study the weekly Torah portion – in short, the good life. Even when our Shabbat conversation prickles with disagreements, we still feel unified.

Meanwhile, we repeatedly request to be joined by Sharansky, but our complaints always meet with dismissal. I propose a hunger strike until our demand is met, but Hillel once kept up a hunger strike for thirty days, and isn't eager to repeat the experience. Kazakhov and Balakhonov, however, who were sent here from the labor camp, declare a hunger strike in support of our demand. Both Shelyudko and Razmik deliberately refuse to share a cell with Sharansky. Since regulations prohibit holding a prisoner in a cell alone for more than a month, we figure that the wardens will have no choice but to transfer him into our cell. They find an alternative, however, and put Sharansky in a cell with a Lithuanian nationalist named Viktor Piatkus. But this too is against regulations, since Piatkus is serving his second term, and Sharansky his first, and therefore they cannot legally be held together. To this Malofeyev has a simple answer: "I was in Moscow and obtained permission," he tells Hillel. It seems Soviet law can be bent at will.

The law also bends when it comes to letters from Israel, all of which are now confiscated. I learned about this back in Vladimir: Obrobov had told Avraham that the KGB had decided to regard all letters from Israel, whatever their content or origin, as Zionist propaganda, and therefore to be confiscated. None of our protests of this policy made the slightest dent.

Unlike Sharansky, however, at least we were still allowed to receive letters from our families. Sharansky wasn't even permitted letters from his young wife Avital. Hillel resolved to pass him our own letters. But how? This wasn't the Vladimir prison, and here we didn't have the requisite connections. The guard who distributed food was not bribable; he wouldn't accept postcards, or even a nice pen we had offered him, and he categorically refused to pass letters to Sharansky. Here the guards did not talk with "dangerous state criminals" like us.

Hillel hit upon a solution: "Let's smear a letter with soap and stick it under the bench in the shower room. Sounds far-fetched? Let's try it." Communicating through the toilet pipes, we told Sharansky of the plan. When he came back from showering, he said, "shalom," the code word for having successfully retrieved the letter. But after that we didn't hear from him for more than a week. Apparently when he left the shower room, he hid the letter in a soap dish, and it was discovered in a search. He was sentenced to ten days in solitary. When he emerged, we asked him, with some trepidation, how it was.

"Better than solitary in Vladimir," he said. "Not too cold, and they don't take away your long underwear. But they also don't let you out to the toilet, and the bucket in the cell is always full."

At least there it wasn't cold. The same could not be said of our cell, where the chill often prevented us from falling asleep at night. On the other hand we weren't starving. With a method Hillel devised, we could even earn some money. If a prisoner fails to fulfill his quota, he is penalized, but even if he works and does manage to earn a little, half of his wages go to the prison, and another fifteen rubles are deducted for his food, shower, and electricity costs, leaving him no money with which to buy food at the prison canteen. In Hillel's plan, we delivered no "product" at all for a month, hiding the baskets we had been weaving, and then we would deliver them all at once in such a quantity that we would earn enough to last me, for example, a couple of years.

One advantage to prison is that no one supervises your work, so long as you deliver the product. So in contravention of Soviet law, we rested on Shabbat and worked on Sunday.

The fruits of our labors helped embellish our Chanukah table. I contact Sharansky through the toilet. "We're lighting candles now. What about you?"

"What are you using for wicks?" he asks.

"Cotton string."

"I think that Chanukah candles should be made of wool or linen, not cotton. I learned this in an underground Judaism class."

"Are you religious?"

"No," he says, "I don't keep all the commandments." Well, by that score, I'm not religious either. But I try…

I remove a string from a linen bag my father sent me back when I was just starting my prison term, dip it in oil, and root it in a piece of bread. Every night we light another candle.

· · · · ·

Thus, locked behind bars, we ride the train of time through the years of our imprisonment. But the train's pace is slowed and delayed by our petty squabbles, by discussions of various vain rumors, and – on a higher order – by studying languages. At a certain point I get tired of learning languages. But what else is there to do? Our train is going nowhere.

Even our "walks" in the yard become a form of punishment. It is cold (minus thirty-five degrees Celsius), sunless, and snow has accumulated. We shovel the snow each morning, but the work hardly warms us. I continue to run, but it is joyless; it is the principle of the thing that keeps me going. I ran in the past, and therefore I continue to run. Stopping would mean surrender. I slip and fall, and Hillel gives me a mocking look. I get up and keep jogging, wiping my perennially runny nose with a glove. Everything follows a rigid daily order: around and around I run. I grow dizzy but refuse to stop. I have become a slave to my running. I run because to stop means to die.

In letters I complain about my inability to think anymore. Being condemned to be around people you have nothing further to learn from is an oppressive, soul-crushing punishment. But I must not let this show; outwardly, we listen to the radio, discuss the news, tell jokes, and prepare for holidays.

As in years past, it was far from easy to prepare for Passover in prison, but I decided to try my utmost. A month earlier, the flu went around, and not knowing what else to do the wardens gave each prisoner a small onion

– a traditional folk remedy. Inmates who had gone months without seeing a fresh vegetable ate their onions with great appetite, choking back tears as they did so. But I decided to let my onion sprout, and to use the sprouts for the Passover bitter herbs, the maror. I placed my onion in a pan with water and left it on the windowsill. My cellmates scoffed at my gardening attempt, but I ignored them and thought about what else I'd need for the seder. I turned to Hillel for help. "Have you gone mad?" he said. "Even on the outside I never did a seder." So I continued the preparations on my own.

Fortunately, I had saved a postcard from Israel depicting an eighteenth-century seder plate from Germany exhibited at the Israel Museum. This proved invaluable in helping me reconstruct the seder; without it I would never have remembered what was required. As for the traditional four cups of wine, I used the raisins my father had given me even before I was sent to labor camp. I would use two raisins every Shabbat for Kiddush, pronouncing on them the blessing, "Blessed art thou, O God, King of the universe, Who has created the fruit of the vine." After nine years of imprisonment, I still had a couple of handfuls left. I had also carefully saved up the spoonfuls of sugar we were allotted daily, and now had an entire bag of it.

Now I was ready to make wine. I put raisins, sugar, and water into a water bottle, and hid it under my bunk, next to the wall that housed a heating pipe. I wasn't certain that the experiment would work, or that it wouldn't be discovered in one of the periodic searches. If they had found the water bottle they would accuse me of alcoholism, which was about the last thing I needed.

At about that time, during one of our visits to the yard, I noticed a small green shoot sprouting up through the asphalt of the adjacent yard. I took it as a small symbol of delicate freedom triumphing over smothering tyranny, but also, and more pragmatically, as something I could use for the karpas portion of the seder, if other prisoners didn't pluck it first.

For the Passover shank bone, I'd use a cube of meat soup that had been secretly brought to me from Israel years earlier. For the egg – a symbol of mourning our inability to bring the Passover sacrifices in the Temple – I'd use some egg powder given to me by Ida Nudel. Also, prisoners were allowed to receive a package of food, up to a kilo, once every half year. The refuseniks from Moscow timed their deliveries so that the matzah would arrive just before Passover. The method worked this year, too.

On the night before Passover, I lit a match and performed the traditional search for chametz. "You're wasting your time," my cellmates said. "We ate every last scrap this morning. There's nothing to find."

Then I rushed to the yard where I'd seen the small green shoot, explaining to the guard that I needed it for a special herbal remedy. This left only the seder plate itself. I asked a guard for a copy of *Pravda*. When the shifts changed, he asked me to return it. I claimed I'd not yet finished reading it, and that I'd give it to the next shift. I cut a circle out of this Communist rag and along its edge wrote the names of the seder objects, and hid the whole thing under a blanket.

Once more I suggested to Hillel that we do a seder together. "I've already told you," he said, "it's not possible." Then, much to his surprise, I showed him the *Pravda* seder plate. "But there's no wine," he protested. "We can't put on a seder without the four cups." I kneeled down and took the water bottle from its hiding place beneath my bunk. Hillel opened it and took a whiff. It was wine! So we sat down, together with our Russian cellmate, to begin: "This is the bread of affliction our forefathers ate in the land of Egypt. All who are hungry, come and eat…" It was a wonderful feeling to celebrate the holiday of freedom, even in the heart of a Soviet prison. "It's the first time in my life," Hillel marveled, "that I'm taking part in a proper seder. I've been thinking how tragic that Jews in the Soviet Union today can celebrate Passover – the most widely observed of our holidays – only in prison."

Early the next morning, guards ordered Hillel to pack up: much to my disappointment, he was being suddenly transferred to another prison, but I had no idea where. Only several months later did I have the chance to find out. It happened that Sharansky was in the adjacent yard, and I asked him in a whisper if he knew Hillel's whereabouts. "Yes," he said, "my mother came on a visit recently, and told me that all of your friends from Operation Wedding have been released." My joy knew no bounds. Perhaps because of our seder, God saw fit to liberate them. I imagined their triumphal arrivals in Israel, and how enthusiastically they must have been greeted.

The seder had indirectly helped me too, for when Hillel got to Israel, my sister came to him to ask, with some trepidation, about how I was. Was I terribly miserable?

"He's not miserable in the slightest," he replied. "Not long ago he even put on a wonderful Passover seder for us." This encouraged my family considerably; now they knew that my spirit had not been broken, that I was fighting for my spiritual liberty even in prison.

But all of this I only learned much later. At the time, I could only guess about Hillel's fate. I wanted so much to believe that happiness was still possible, that even after the heart has almost withered in one's chest, there is still a chance of life. But I told Gena that I didn't think Hillel had been released.

A man must always be prepared for the worst if he is to avoid deflated hopes. But even as I spoke, other words raced through my head: "Could he really be free?"

We contacted prisoners in other cells who also believed Hillel had been released. This became a certainty two weeks letter, when we received letters from Ida Nudel, Natasha Rosenstein, and Natalia Khassina, which implied that others had been released too. In honor of Hillel's release, I prepared a festive meal for Gena and me.

As for my own prospects for freedom, however, I suppressed any hopes, fearing disappointment. I resumed my studies and my daily routine, and gave no more thought to the possibility of my own release. Nor did I need such thoughts. I was prepared to serve out my term. At the same time, it's not easy to live without hope or faith. I still believed in God and His hidden ways.

My cellmate Gena was having a harder time, even though he was only in his second year in prison. Not much interested in study or reading, he would lie in bed for days on end, scratching his head, pacing with a vacant look in his eyes. He had checked out, and possibly even gone insane. I would lift my head from a book to find him making gestures with his hands behind my head. "What's with you?" I'd ask gently. "Why don't you read a book?"

"Everything's okay," he would say with his idiotic smile, "everything's okay."

But in fact nothing was okay. Gena's hopes for a quick release had been dashed, and he was desperate for an outlet. "Yosef, I have jaundice," he told me on Shabbat morning after he had tossed and turned all night. "It's an infectious disease. I'll probably be admitted to a hospital, and if they can't cure it, I'll be released." Indeed, his skin had turned yellowish, his eyes had reddened, and he began to breathe with difficulty. I called a medic, who checked Gena's vitals. "Nothing serious, for now," he pronounced. "I'll come back tomorrow." Gena stayed in bed for the next several hours, then leaped up, raced around the cell, stopped to pray against the wall, and then turned to me. "Yosef, God has cured me."

But he was not cured. On Sunday evening I wrote an appeal to the KGB about the letters from Israel that had been withheld for months, and the next morning, as I was praying next to the window, I heard the sound of paper being torn. When I finished praying, I found that my appeal had been shredded into the trash can. I was reminded of the psychological pressure tactics sometimes used to make a prisoner's life so unbearable that he has no alternative but to obey the authorities. I didn't want to believe that Gena was capable of such dirty tactics.

"Gena, why did you do that?"

A friendly smile. "What's the matter, Yosef?"

"Why did you tear up my appeal?"

"I didn't."

"Gena, tell me the truth." I hugged him in a fraternal way, but he recoiled.

"What's with you, Yosef?" And then he went about his merry way, humming to himself as though nothing at all had happened.

Tears of pity welled up in my eyes; I felt ashamed for this young man. It hardly mattered whether he had been compelled to pretend madness, or put on this act of his own volition, or even really was out of his mind. I couldn't remain in a cell with him. Although transfers are generally not permitted, I felt I had to act. In this realm, I had no reservations; I acted without hesitation. Though I had very little confidence in Soviet law, I drew up a request to be transferred "for the sake of keeping order." Though it might have helped my case, I included no reasoning to the request, since in that case the request might be deemed an act of "informing" on my cellmate and might be used against him.

Just then a ringing of bells to announce an inspection. A guard comes in carrying a list of prisoners. "Two prisoners in the cell," I reported. He marked the list and walked out, but before the door could close behind him I stepped out to hand him my transfer request. Leaving a cell without authorization was considered an escape attempt, and in such cases guards may use live fire. Three guards tackled me, and tried to drag me back through the door. I resisted, desperately clutching at the bars in the corridor.

"There's no point in resisting," they said. "We're putting you into another cell." Exactly what I had hoped for, in other words. When they locked me into cell 16, free from Gena's crazed looks and the degradations of cell 19, I felt elated, even though I knew punishment awaited. If only I could escape from prison this way. I began to sing aloud: "David, the king of Israel, lives!"

The feeling turned out to be infectious. Balakhonov, upon hearing I'd been moved, decided it was a prelude to my release. (Hillel had been put in this very cell before his release, and his bedding was still here.) "Yosef," Balakhonov called to me, "tell people in the West that that they're giving us pills to weaken our willpower." He shouldn't have done this. Shouting across a corridor meant certain punishment. If I answered, I'd be caught. If I didn't answer, he'd continue shouting until he got caught. "Calm down, Vlodya, they're not taking me to Geneva just yet." I whispered, but the guard outside had heard me. "Mendelevich! Punishment." My mood wasn't dampened.

The deputy head of the prison, Nikolayev, who usually played the "good cop," came by for a chat. "What is this, Mendelevich? You couldn't wait until we looked into your transfer request?"

"No, I couldn't wait."

"Well, you'll have plenty of time for thinking it over. For resisting guards, unauthorized exit from the cell, and talking with other prisoners, I'm giving you ten days in solitary."

"I'm ready for it."

I had prepared by wearing thick socks and long underwear. The solitary cells in the basement for political prisoners were rather roomy: three-by-two meters, with a bed that folded up onto the wall. Truth be told, after the day's excitements, I was looking forward to being alone.

But almost immediately I began to be troubled by thoughts of Gena, and the case began to seem more than a run-of-the-mill failure. Many other Jewish prisoners, after all, had befriended this innocent young man, even if he had started to behave strangely lately. When he had been in solitary, Hillel Butman had shared bread with him, taught him some Hebrew, and given him a Hebrew dictionary. Gena had also shared a cell with Sharansky, who had given him some photographs as a gift. In fact, Gena had been sent to solitary after demanding that Sharansky be transferred to a cell with other Jewish inmates. But I had failed him. Moreover, to see an innocent young man reduced to depravity, his human dignity stripped away, is a terrible thing to behold. It affected my ability to appreciate the goodness in man, an ability that is vital to one's powers of resistance in prison. (Years later, after the fall of the Iron Curtain, Gena visited Jerusalem. In the new Russia, he had become a businessman, apparently with ties to the mafia. I didn't mention his behavior in prison.)

As these dark thoughts crowded in on me, my legs felt leaden, and my left arm felt as though it were being stabbed by hundreds of needles. My chest pressed in on me. I couldn't understand what was going on, but I instinctively felt that I had to resist with all my powers, that I had to move. I began pacing the cell, then running, leaping from side to side until I was bathed in sweat. The physical effort shunted aside my bad thoughts, and more pleasant fantasies began to take their place: visions of being freed, of reuniting with friends. I painted in more and more details, until the visions grew more vivid and realistic, and for the first time in a very long time I forgot that I was in prison.

In the past, I would stop myself at this point; the unleashed imagination can be an extremely dangerous thing. But now, with all my energies sapped, my dreams of freedom were the only thread connecting me to my redemption. I remember thinking that one day I might pay dearly for the imaginative freedom I allowed myself, but for the moment the medicine worked.

The bedtime ritual: unclasp and lower the bunk from the wall, put a mug under my head, socks on my hands, a sleeve over my head, and a handkerchief over my face so that my breath doesn't chill my face. The hard part is falling asleep, which means not thinking about prison. I imagine a flock of white sheep herded by a black dog. Doesn't work. A camel stepping through the desert in front of a stand of palm trees. Nope. Now I'm submerging myself in a mikvah's warm purifying waters: once, twice, thrice…

I awake at dawn to the chirping of a sparrow, an hour before wake-up call, but the noise of a prison stirring has already begun. Large crates of black bread and salted fish wrapped in paper are being brought in through the distribution hall. The door slot opens and I watch the guard take my bread from the crate, fascinated by the sight of all those loaves. Will I ever be able to buy as much bread as I want?

"Take your boiling water."

"I'm taking it, I'm taking it. Can I have more later?"

"Fine. Knock on the door and I'll come with more."

A pleasant guard, for a change. I sit on the narrow bench bolted to the table and hold the mug with both hands, letting it warm my hands – and my heart. As I let the first sip revive me, I think about what a wonderful thing water is. But I should hurry if I want more. I gulp down the rest and rush to the door, knock, and wait. Steps in the corridor. A strange voice.

"What do you want?"

"Any hot water left?"

"You already got yours. That's enough."

Too bad. I was late, and the day shift had arrived. It's impossible to get anything from these people. I return to the bench and turn my loaf of bread around in my hands, admiring its brown crust peeling away to reveal the bread within. I doze off like that, on the bench. Sleeping in a sitting position is allowed – they may harass you but not punish you for it. I wake myself up to say the Shacharit prayers, which by now I remember almost by heart. I take my time, singing the words, sometimes inventing melodies to accompany the prayers into the heavens before parachuting back to earth. Not wishing to let it go, I extend the prayer for hours. I live within it.

With prayers over, I wash my hands, break the bread crust, and tear away the soft interior. It's a good thing one isn't supposed to eat before the morning prayers; this way, I'll have more bread left for the afternoon. With the help of a splinter of wood I had found in the cell, I cut off the best part of the loaf to save for Shabbat, and slice the rest thinly. I eat yesterday's stale bread with a bit of today's fresh bread so that I always have something stored up, and also so I don't know exactly how much I ate. This affords me a small sense of freedom.

In fact, I set myself the goal of freeing myself from my dependence on my jailers. They give me 450 grams a day, but I find I don't need it all, and decide that by the time my stay in solitary is up, I will have saved up one day's ration of bread. After several days, I discover that I can store up two days' rations, or even three – which will mean leaving solitary with 1350 grams. An unwritten prison law dictates that a prisoner does not eat bread in his final day in solitary, since he is about to return to his cell, where presumably the food is better. The last day's portion is usually left for the next prisoner to occupy your cell. On my first day in solitary, I found the bread from the previous occupant, but it was so stale and moldy as to be inedible. I wrap my own slices in newspaper and squirrel them away (storing bread for the next day is prohibited).

The newspaper is the English-language *Moscow Times* (I hid it in one of my shoes), which I read aloud and then translate into Hebrew. I know that I must not neglect practicing for even a single day. As the saying goes, "If you forget a language for a single day, it will forget you for two." I read an article on "the construction of housing units in the Soviet Union." I talk to myself in Hebrew, embroidering the subject: "The housing shortage can be explained by large-scale urbanization. Whereas this process took shape in Europe fifty years ago, in Russia most people still live in rural areas."

The cell's "toilet" is a bucket, on the rim of which I have draped some rags so that I can squat on it more comfortably. At least I am alone; no one rushes me. But somehow, the morning hot water arrives every morning just when I'm on this "toilet." A guard slides open the door slot and shouts at me. "Well, do you want your hot water or not?" I very much do want my hot water; it's my primary source of warmth, after all. And lest you think this is a country of barbarians, I can report that we are also given a cup of tap water for washing up. I use it to wash my hands before saying the Hamotzi blessing over the bread.

I've been speaking of bread as though it were a monolithic thing, but in fact it could be white or brown, whole wheat or rye, dense or light, overbaked or half-baked, the crusts coal-black or bark-brown. This gives me the illusion of plenitude, and also offers a diversion: every day I review my store, like a rich lord counting his treasure. It comforts me to know that at any moment I can retrieve something from it.

Today I get a small piece of salted fish: I eat half of it, with the bones, and leave the rest for Shabbat. Yesterday we were given soup consisting of water, two pieces of cabbage, and some potato. At least there's no danger of it being *treif*. I saved the potato for Shabbat, and one piece of cabbage for today, so now I have the luxury of a fish and cabbage sandwich. The next course is salted rusks, which I wash down with hot water, thanking the Almighty for His beneficence.

A prisoner who thinks about nothing but food will soon go mad. As I eat, I think about other things – about the meaning of mortal life, about how a man who wanted to go to Israel ended up in the cellar of a stinking prison thousands of kilometers from Jerusalem.

I have one more way to pass the time down here: guessing the time for the afternoon prayers. Without natural light, I cannot tell the difference between 2:00 p.m. and 5:00 p.m. Once in a while I can hear a distant radio, and I know that the guards change shifts at 4:00 p.m. After prayers, the monotony becomes more oppressive. All I can do is mark off the passing of another day on the wall.

The cursed heaviness of limbs comes back like a wave of paralysis. After five years of prison, your body begins to wear down, and I notice more symptoms with every passing day. On Friday night, after a long prayer and satisfying meal, I begin to whirl in dance. Years later, I would dance for three hours straight at my wedding in Jerusalem. Guests asked where I had learned to dance like that. In solitary confinement at Chistopol prison, I said, where I danced not from joy but from despair. As I dance around the cell, a vision of Jerusalem – rebuilt and renewed and radiant – flits before my eyes. As I whirl faster and faster, the steps becoming leaps, the cement floor begins to come apart, and I think only of breaking out into freedom.

"Mendelevich! No more dancing!"

I stop. "But I'm celebrating today."

"Celebrating what?"

"My friends have been released. You remember Butman? He's in Jerusalem!"

"So why haven't they released you?"

That's the question I've contemplated least of all. The Soviet authorities do not obey any logic.

"Just look at this fellow," the guard tells his colleagues. "These Jews – you punish them and they're actually happy!"

A day before I'm due to be released from solitary confinement, KGB lieutenant Galkin pays me a visit. "No matter what you do, we're not putting you with Sharansky. You can pull your little stunt a thousand times and it won't help."

The next day, I was led out of solitary. The guards pretended not to notice the two portions of bread I was carrying, and took me to the cell of the Armenian nationalist Razmik Zagrobian. Razmik was a charming, quiet, reflective man, but his Soviet education had implanted a streak of cold rationalism in him. He denied everything, including morality itself, even as he believed in high ideals. He treated me respectfully, and our first months together were pleasant enough. For the first time, we managed to bribe the prisoner who distributed food for an extra ration of bread by hiding some tobacco in the trash bin that he took out every morning. The bread was for Razmik, who was sickly and thin.

To relieve his chronic headaches, Razmik would stand on his head, yoga-style, for hours on end. Once he was convinced of something, he couldn't be persuaded otherwise.

"Yosef, I don't feel well," he would say, his legs up in the air.

"It's because you're standing on your head."

"No, this helps my headaches."

He had another fixation: he claimed that I was suppressing my belief in my imminent release. Even had he been right, there would be nothing wrong in it. Sometimes I believed my release was imminent, sometimes not – but I didn't brood about it. His aim was to "expose" me, and show that my hope was baseless. Every radio report on the stalled Salt-2 arms negotiations would send him into raptures. "It's all over. The Soviets will never reach an agreement with the Americans."

It seemed to me that he unconsciously envied me, which would have been natural. Who wouldn't envy a cellmate whose case drew worldwide attention, especially if you yourself are utterly unknown and feel yourself to be dispensable? Despite my efforts to avoid the subject, Razmik returned to it, like a man compulsively picking at a scab.

Things got worse on this score after Sharansky was granted a visit from his mother. The day after the visit, I was able to talk to him through the wall separating our exercise yards. As Razmik exercised in the center of the yard, keeping a lookout for the guard above, I leaned on the wall as Sharansky relayed what he had learned. "Altman, Khnokh, Penson, and Zalmanson have been pardoned. Kuznetsov and Dymshits were exchanged for Soviet spies as part of the arms reduction deal between Carter and Brezhnev. Apparently Brezhnev promised that if the US Senate ratifies Salt-2, he would release you, me, Ida Nudel, Fedorov, and Marchenko. The Senate is expected to ratify the agreement on November 25." At this point, Razmik signaled that the guard was turning our way, and we had to cut short the conversation.

On November 12, 1979, as he passed our cell, Sharansky dropped a note in the trash bin outside the door. When I came back from the yard, I took in the bin and found it. "On October 13, all political prisoners are declaring a strike to stop the practice of stealing our letters." I was not pleased. It was bad timing. The day before had been Yom Kippur, and now we were supposed to fast again? Was there justification for it?

That evening, however, I changed my mind after overhearing a conversation between Sharansky and Misha Kazakhov. The two men's cells were on two sides of the corridor, and they sometimes shouted to one another in English. Sharansky was twice thrown into solitary for it. Misha had been on a hunger strike for eleven months so far, during which he had been beaten, tortured, force-fed, and (despite his severely weakened condition) put into solitary confinement. I repeatedly contacted him through covert channels to try to persuade him that ending the strike was a matter of self-preservation, but he held firm. "I will continue my strike as long as they don't send the forty-page letter I wrote to my mother on December 15, 1978."

The conversation between Sharansky and Misha that evening went like this:

"Will you end your strike if we support you?"

"I'll end it on condition the authorities give me their word that I will receive medical treatment and be given the food parcels that my mother sends."

Since our own strike would persuade Misha to end his suicidal mission, I decided to take part, even though the strike would take place over the Sukkot holiday. My demand was simple: to receive all the letters sent to me from my stepmother and sisters in Israel.

For reasons of health, Razmik decided not to join the strike. From the outset of my strike, I sensed he would make trouble. He told me he suffered from having to eat in my presence. Instead of starving in peace and quiet, therefore, I had to comfort *him*. Despite the great quantities of pills he was swallowing daily, he continued to contort his face and whine. When he ate, I would turn my back on him.

"Yosef, there's enough here for two. If you'd like, I'll secretly give you some and no one would have to know."

"No, I've declared a hunger strike."

"But no one would see. Do you really have to be honest vis-à-vis the guards?"

"No, but I want to be honest with myself."

He was sorely disappointed by his failure to tempt me to trick both the world and myself, but I knew very well what giving in would mean: I would take it as permission to give up in other ways. It was a dangerous slippery slope. In the meantime, I'd become so used to hunger that my outward behavior was indistinguishable from that of prisoners who were not fasting. Medics came to check up on me several times, but even before the strike I was so thin that there wasn't much left for them to examine. (Years later it would turn out that I had suffered in prison from a stomach ulcer.) When my muscles cramped in the exercise yard, I forced myself to keep jogging. The medics would look down on me from the guard tower above the yards. "The eighth day of his strike, and he's running. Where does he get the energy?"

The truth was that I had an abundance of energy, but it was not of the physical sort. I simply knew that any change in my prison routine would make things even harder, so I kept on going. On the eighth day of the strike, I was given five letters from Israel; ten letters on the ninth day; and another eight on the tenth. I also got letters from Natasha Rosenstein and Ida Nudel. I figured that if I kept this up for a year, I would get all the letters that had been sent to me. But life is more important than letters, and much to the wardens' relief I decided to put an end to my strike, as did Kazakhov and others, many of whom had achieved little or nothing. Sharansky received some postcards from Moscow.

In the meantime, the Americans were protesting the buildup of Soviet troop levels in Cuba, and the ratification of Salt-2 had bogged down. I lost my peace of mind. In light of the report from Sharansky's mother, and in light of optimism in the Soviet press that the arms control agreement was all but signed, I had started to see my release as an increasingly realistic possibility. When this hope now melted away before my eyes, it came as a heavy blow. Such is the fate of hopes hung not on divine agency but on the vagaries of Salt-2.

I had by now also lost most of my interest in studying. What was the point? My mind had been depleted by a decade of imprisonment. I continued studying, but with nothing like the determination or enthusiasm I had exuded earlier. More and more frequently I would have to interrupt myself to shake off the leaden feeling that threatened to overcome me. At such times, our cell resembled a circus ring or insane asylum. Razmik would be doing 150 push-ups and then stand on his head. I would do a series of ten squats, another series of jumps in between squats, then lie on my back and madly pump my legs as though riding a bicycle, and finally fifteen minutes of grueling running in place. This allowed us to hang on until evening, but only barely.

Meanwhile, our tobacco deal with the guard who distributed food was discovered, and he was replaced with someone who wouldn't be bribed. Razmik began to show signs of malnutrition, but when I offered him a portion of my bread he refused. "You deserve no less than me. And anyway, I don't want anything from you." One way or another, I felt I had to find a solution for him. One breakfast-time, making sure no other guards were in the corridor, I offered the man on the other side of the door-slot an American pen in exchange for an additional 150 grams of bread a day. He snatched the pen, and pushed a thick piece of bread through. When I offered it to my cellmate, however, he once more declined. "I don't need bread. If you want it, eat it yourself." At this he sank into a sulking silence that lasted for the next two or three days. I didn't understand it, and that Shabbat I tried to open a conversation with him. "Razmik, I feel as though I'm being put on trial without knowing the charges, and without the possibility of defending myself. Frankly, it's hard to take. I must know why you're giving me the silent treatment. I don't know what I've done, but I do know that I've always tried to treat you well."

"That's just it," he blurted out, like Balaam's ass suddenly speaking. "You've always been good to me. You like acting nice and earning gratitude."

"But what does this have to do with the extra bread?"

"You've been oppressing me for months, wanting to show that you're strong, and I'm weak, that I don't have the willpower to control my hunger. That's why you invented this business with the extra bread rations."

I could hardly believe my ears. How was it a form of cruelty to have shared my bread with him? Why in the beginning did he eat it? Maybe now that he imagined his dignity had overcome his hunger – as befitting a true revolutionary – he preferred to forget his earlier weakness?

All this began to stir up dark thoughts about the malevolence concealed in the human heart. In almost every case of sharing a cell, I would discover that beneath the outwardly good relations with my cellmate, a sinister undercurrent had all the while been more or less unconsciously flowing in the opposite direction, and only at some later stage would it burst forth. When it inevitably did, it often washed away the good dimensions of the relationship we had been building. I felt that this dark impulse sooner or later would have overcome a man who had no religious faith.

I requested transfer to another cell, and was taken to a tiny corner room. I expected to feel the same sense of liberation and relief I'd felt after I had moved out of Gena's cell, but it seems my nerves had been stretched too taut to feel even that.

Next I requested food that had been prepared without meat. Such rations were available in the prison; in fact that's what was given to prisoners in solitary. "I cannot order that you be given inferior food," the warden replied. "The prosecutor would reprimand me for such a thing. The food you've requested is given as a punishment to prisoners in solitary. We must give you the food prison procedures require; whether you eat it is your business, not ours. If you wish, you can appeal to the medical staff, and if they see no reason to object I can order the changes in your menu." That is exactly what I did, and after several days I began getting vegetarian soup, consisting of a slice of potato, two pieces of cabbage, onion, and a bay leaf. It was the first time in a long while I had eaten vegetables, and somehow this small success revived me a bit. I resumed reading Bialik's *Book of Legends*, studying Hebrew, and even exercising, and this is how I expected to pass my final five months in prison.

But it was not to be. I was once again transferred, this time to a narrow cell holding two other prisoners: a Latvian nationalist named Maigunis, and Ogurtzov of the All-Russian Social-Christian Union for the Liberation of the People. Acting almost automatically, I announced a hunger strike and demanded to be taken to a one-man cell. I could not bear the thought of another round of petty conflict with cellmates. On the third day of my strike, doctors made the determination that continuing would irreparably harm my health.

As I've mentioned, when it came to its Prisoners of Zion, the Soviet regime inflicted suffering, but did not murder. In the end, therefore, I was taken to a one-man cell, which officially had the status of a "clinic." Viktory. Once there, upon ending the strike, I asked for a cup of warm water. The moment I sipped it, a spasm seized my throat, spreading from there to my legs and left arm. One more "victory" like this, and I would be dead.

Life at the clinic is monotonous: wake-up, breakfast, walk in the yard, studies. By five o'clock every evening, life has stopped. Letters have already been distributed, the *Pravda* read, a meager dinner consumed. This is the hardest time in the prisoner's day. The whole day you anticipate something:

you might get a good letter, or hear on the radio about some Israeli success in some field or other. But after 5:00, when there's nothing more to look forward to, you live in a kind of half-dead hopelessness.

On the other side of a wall, my neighboring inmate was the son of General Shuhevich, who in the 1950s had commanded the Ukrainian Independence Army, a guerilla force that fought against Russian occupation until the sixties. Shuhevich Jr. had the habit of calling me on Shabbat through the toilet pipes. He was quite ill; everything hurt. He was then forty-two, and had been in prison since the age of fifteen. I empathized with him; I, too, was hurting all over: my head felt dizzy, my heart ached, my legs would get bloated in the morning and develop yellowish spots. A doctor inspected my legs and nodded. It appears he had to write a reply to a complaint issued to the health ministry by Natasha Rosenstein. He jotted down the standard answer: "Mendelevich is healthy."

In fact, Mendelevich was barely alive. I suffered from acute insomnia, which meant that even at night I wasn't free from the prison. I would lie with my eyes open, hour after hour until dawn; when I got up I tried to trick myself into believing I had slept. But the trick failed. The world looked strangely flat and one-dimensional; nothing excited my interest.

People have often asked me: was torture practiced in Soviet prisons? When you can no longer stand yourself, when the world arouses in you nothing but disgust – is that not a form of torture?

And yet I always place God before me and remind myself that I have a people and a homeland. Chaim Drori writes from Israel: "Believe me, this is a wonderful country. It's worth living for." And so I soldier on. I study, pray, and issue requests, among them that my family from Israel be permitted to visit me. This is turned down. "We have no diplomatic ties with Israel." Natasha Rosenstein travels to Chistopol to see me, but is turned away. "Cousins are not considered relatives." The Rosensteins have been trying to emigrate to Israel for eight years, yet the authorities, when they grant exit visas to Jews at all, grant them precisely to those not going to Israel.

I now have four months left of my prison sentence, and Sharansky has three. His imprisonment has been far from easy. His cellmate is a fifty-year-old Lithuanian nationalist named Viktor Piatkus. From my exercise yard, I overhear their conversations.

"Viktor, you're always trying to tell me what to do. Who gave you the right to treat me like a child?"

"Well, the fact of the matter is that I have vast experience in life generally and in prison life in particular, and you still don't understand how to behave here."

"I'd appreciate it if you kept your views to yourself from now on."

I knock on the fence between the yards, summoning Sharansky over.

"Anatoly, how can you stand that man's chutzpah? Demand a transfer!"

"I don't think the authorities need to be dealing now with squabbles between political prisoners."

"And for that you're willing to tolerate him?"

"I don't have too long to go now."

Several days later, Sharansky and I met face to face for the first time. Snow had accumulated all night, and prisoners weren't given shovels to clear it, so it was impossible to use the exercise yards. Sharansky therefore asked to be taken back to his cell. At that very moment, I was taken out to the yard. He was still there. I immediately recognized his face from a photograph Ida Nudel had sent me in 1975. His appearance had changed. His cheekbones stuck out sharply from his ashen face. Only his eyes still shone with kindness.

"Anatoly!" I cried.

"Yosef!"

We embraced. The momentarily confused guards realized their mistake and tore us apart. We were not punished, since it was the guards' "fault." But they couldn't cut off our contact completely. Each day, as I was led past Sharansky's cell, I greeted him under my breath with a "Shalom," as though I were talking to the guard. "What did you say?" the guard asked.

"Nothing, nothing."

There was also a crack in the door to my yard, and I would wait for Sharansky to pass by on the other side. "Shalom, I got some letters from Israel today."

"I've received nothing for a month now."

At this point the guard would intervene.

I discovered that Sharansky's cell was opposite mine, and that sometimes, if we spoke softly enough, the guards wouldn't hear. But it was better to sing to each other. On Friday nights, after Kiddush and a meal, I would sing to dispel the loneliness, and using a sing-song voice would communicate with Sharansky.

"Do you hear me?" I would sing.

"Yes, Yosef, I hear you."

"Shabbat shalom, Anatoly."

"Shabbat shalom," came his lilting reply.

Hearing this, I felt the angels of Shabbat descend and dispel the loneliness.

Once, rather than singing the usual Shabbat greeting, Sharansky's voice was flat. "My father died the day before last."

A hard blow. For days afterward, I find no rest. How could I help? What could I do to support him, console him? I write the Kaddish on a slip of paper, and role it inside thicker paper into a pea-sized pellet. The next day in the yard, I tap on the fence and tell Sharansky to expect a delivery. When the guard above us momentarily turns his back, I throw the pellet up, but it bounces off the wiring above and falls back. The guard turns back, but it is snowing, and he doesn't notice the fallen pellet. The moment he isn't looking, I pick it up and launch it again, once more without success. You need a sniper's accuracy to get it through the netting of wires. The half hour is up, and I'm taken back to the cell feeling like an utter failure. I can't even help a friend.

The following day I tie the note to a string attached to the inside of a ballpoint pen, which I then try to push through a tiny hole between the fence and the ground. But before Sharansky can find the hole from the other side, our time is up. Another failure.

On the third day, I again try the throwing method, and on the second attempt the pellet goes through. "It arrived!" Sharansky says. There's no sweeter word to a prisoner's ears. Now he can say Kaddish for his father.

"Yosef, could you write for me a copy of Psalm 27? Avital recommended that I read it every day." I do so, and succeed in throwing it to him over the yard wall. It strengthens me to help a friend whose predicament is perhaps even worse than mine. On Shabbat, we sing to each other again.

"What are you doing today?" I chant.

"I'm reading the Haggadah, which is helping me learn Hebrew. I already know all the verses from Psalms in it, and I'm inspired by the heroism of the author of the Psalms, King David."

What a wonderful man, this Sharansky, I think. I sing to him in reply: "King David lives!"

"Mendelevich, stop talking with other prisoners," a guard barks.

"I'm not talking, I'm singing."

"No singing allowed."

A short time later, Sharansky's three-year prison sentence was up, and he was sent to a labor camp in the Urals. I had two months left, and one more challenge to meet. I was transferred to the cell of Vlodya Balakhonov, Igor Ogurtzov, and Maigunis – not easy men to get along with. Maigunis was due to be released in two months, and was planning to meet Andrei Sakharov and then to try to leave the country. Ogurtzov was illiterate, and had nothing to do all day but recline on his bed motionless.

Balakhonov, more alert than the other two, used to declare that he was not a Russian but a citizen of the world. By now his theory had changed: as a Russian, he felt the duty to warn the world of the Russian threat to mankind, and the only way to address the threat was to dismantle the Russian Empire and to let Russians live only in those territories they held when they became a distinct nation in the fifteenth century. This theory was anathema to both Ogurtzov, who gloried in the greatness of Russia, and Maigunis. Each of the three took me aside at some point or another to declare his abiding hatred of the other two, and each told me that the moment I'd be sent back to camp, they'd petition to be transferred out of the cell.

My cellmates attributed my optimism to my hope for an early release – a hope that had some grounding in reality. How they envied me. Balakhonov told me every day that he had no doubts concerning my early release. But that's not what I prayed for. When I turned to God, I asked Him to lead me on the path to faith, to help me stay true to myself, and – despite all evidence to the contrary – to preserve the love of my fellow man.

· · · · ·

First thing in the morning, I rush to get in line for the toilet and sink. My cellmates have lately been similarly hurrying to take care of their personal hygiene before breakfast. Moments after wake-up call, Vlodya fills the metal basin and washes his feet. Maigunis leaps off the top bunk to try to be the first to the toilet. Ogurtzov launches into his yoga routine, trying hard to keep a dignified expression on his face and not show the strain. All this is taking place in an area of two meters square – the area left open after four bunks, a table, a toilet, and a sink are accounted for. It is impossible not to accidentally bump into a cellmate or step on his foot. Taking care of your needs and being considerate of your cellmates are thus incompatible goals, and tension builds up very quickly. Why, for instance, must Vlodya wash his feet in cold water every morning? It only makes him cough and sneeze for the rest of the day. Yet he adamantly refuses to reconsider, just as he adamantly demands that the air vent be kept open at all times. Otherwise, he insists, he feels suffocated. Maigunis, however, suffers from earaches, and the draft from the ventilation only makes matters worse. But instead of saying something, he simply wraps his head in a towel. Lately, he has started to smoke again, and Igor can't stand the smoke. He has three years left to serve of his fifteen-year sentence, and wants to keep healthy. But keeping healthy in prison is next to impossible.

Vlodya, meanwhile, like nearly everyone (including me), suffers from hemorrhoids. But unlike him, I could never pull down my pants in front of everyone and soak my backside in the water basin. The rest of us try to ignore his daily soak. We have long ago abandoned the convention that dictates that using the toilet is best done in a stall with a door. Here there is no stall, and no door, and anyone can see you suffering on the pot. "Suffering" is exactly the right word for it, both because you're at the center of the cell's attention (or so at least it seems to you) and because you feel hurried. We have running water only at certain hours, and if you miss the morning window of opportunity you have to hold it in until evening. As a result, most prisoners suffer from hemorrhoids and chronic constipation.

I aim to get up first to wash up and pray. In this Tatar wasteland, it's impossible to determine the direction of Jerusalem, so I pray toward the window. For this reason, I always ask for a bunk by the window; otherwise I'd have to ask permission from the prisoner who sleeps next to the window, and would be very lucky if he agreed. The sight of my praying usually arouses the guards' ire. "What are you doing over there next to the window? Planning an escape? Hey, you, come to the door at once." Obviously this isn't very conducive to feeling close to God, and my attempts to transcend my environment – the shouts of the guard, the grunts of Vlodya's exercise routine – aren't working very well. Soon Igor, too, approaches the window, crosses himself, and begins to pray.

As soon as I finish, a new problem crops up. I'm trapped between the window and the bunk, and don't want to disturb Igor's prayer. But it's so crowded that one prisoner cannot move without causing all the others to shift places. My solution is to sit on the floor reading Bialik's anthology until Igor is done.

Then the moment we've all been waiting for. Sounds of door-slots sliding open come from across the hall. The prisoner's trained ear picks up and interprets the slightest noise. If we hear one of the slots slide shut more quickly than usual, it means the prisoner has refused food, and has declared a hunger strike. In such cases, I put my ear to the door, waiting for the guard to pick up the internal phone and report. I strain to hear the cell number. Sure enough, it is cell 18, which holds Gena. I wonder what has happened. He's usually reluctant to strike. We're sure to find out later.

In the meantime, it's our turn, and we all wait to see what kind of bread we'll get. Its quality is often the subject of vehement argument.

"The bread today tastes unusually good," Vlodya says.

"Not at all, Vladimir Fyodorovich," Igor counters. "Very ordinary bread. They've just added potato."

The distribution of bread among us is a sensitive matter. The eyes of a hungry man scrutinize each piece trying to discern which may be slightly larger than another. We stick to a careful order: the first piece we get through the door slot goes to Vlodya, the second to Igor, the third to me. We each place our slices on the table. Vlodya looks intently at his, measures it against Igor's with a ruler, concludes that the latter has received fifty grams more than the others, and begins to saw off the excess with a piece of string. In the interests of fairness, every few days we switch the order of distribution. But each of us knows, of course, that such sophisticated methods cannot address the fundamental problem: hunger. The distribution fills a kind of ceremonial function, unconsciously compensating for our meager portions.

Today, however, Vlodya can bear it no longer. When the door clicks open for morning inspection, rather than reporting the number of prisoners in the cell, he screams so loudly that the entire corridor echoes with his rage. "I'm starving! I demand enough bread to meet our minimal needs. At the Nuremburg trials, the Nazis were charged with giving their prisoners insufficient food, and you're giving us even less!" The sergeant's face remains impassive. He knows we are hungry, but rules are rules. He cannot give out more than is specified in the rules. The door slams shut behind him.

The bread games continue. I maintain that actually the bread is sufficient, but that because it is strictly rationed and limited we feel that it's not enough. After the Exodus, the people of Israel received manna from heaven, but because it was rationed, they felt resentful. On the strength of this theory, I began to eat even less than the daily bread I was allotted: that way I'd become less dependent on the prison authorities, and earn another small sliver of freedom.

But what to do with the bread I saved in this way? I could dry it out and make rusks, but then what would I do with the rusks? I could give them to Vlodya. Although the memory of Razmik's resentment was still fresh, I couldn't bear watching Vlodya suffer. Once he hadn't managed to get dressed in time to be taken out to the yard, and got six days in solitary confinement in return. To protest the punishment, he refused to eat or drink during those days. When he returned to our cell, he looked like a walking corpse. Only his eyes were still alive. "Look, boys, I'm still here!" He began a traditional Russian folk dance, apparently to show us that his hunger strike hadn't broken him.

After a few leaps, however, he collapsed. We picked him up and carried him to his bunk.

"Boys, do you know what I dreamed about during my strike? In Geneva, where I used to work, there was a small café where we would get a roll and a cup of coffee..." We didn't have such delights, of course, but I did prepare a nutritious meal for him. Vlodya had brought some dried fish from his previous cell, and I soaked these in water, pulled them apart, and mixed them with breadcrumbs. Vlodya was pleased. "Yosef, you're a real chef. You should have worked in a restaurant." Only he could have praised my "cooking" with such enthusiasm.

When the slot opened at lunchtime, we again had an agreed order of who would stick his bowl out first. Looking through the slot, we watched the ladling hungrily. "Stir it up before you ladle it out! Ladle it from the bottom! Why have you given me the watery part from the top?" This seemed to us like a matter of life and death. We brought the bowls to the table and checked our portions. One got a potato, another just cabbage. Vlodya added to his soup the rusks I'd given him together with a half liter of water to make it look like more.

God save me from having to ever again witness the deterioration of a human being, the degeneration of a creature made in the image of God.

$\bullet\ \bullet\ \bullet\ \bullet\ \bullet$

Passover arrives again, my last in prison. (I couldn't know at the time that I'd spend my next Passover in Hebron.) This time I am preparing for an exodus of my own, since I'm to be transferred in a few days.

By now I had long practice with preparing for the holiday in prison. I had a half kilo of matzah I'd received in a package – my main staple for the next eight days. I tell my cellmates that they can have my bread, explaining that it is forbidden to me. Once more, the night before the holiday I conduct the ritual search for chametz under the bewildered stares of my cellmates. They fail to understand that it is only the faith in my tradition that sustains me. Ten years of imprisonment have not shaken my trust in God, my belief in the goodness of people, or the steadfast focus on my aim to live in Israel.

"Yosef, when you get to Israel you'll be a national hero."

"Not at all, Vlodya. We have some three million heroes. That's precisely the source of our strength."

My transfer came swiftly. I was given an hour to prepare as an officer stood in the cell monitoring my movements. Vlodya managed to slip me a note by putting it in some jam. "Have a little before you go," he said. I scooped out some jam with the note, and hid it in my mouth.

Then I was locked in an empty room while my belongings were searched. When I was brought into the search room, I saw my Israeli postcards and photos scattered about. My writings had been confiscated and burned as "suspicious material."

"I protest this confiscation."

"It's your right to lodge a protest."

At that moment some bills were discovered between the pages of a book.

"This will be given to the state."

"But it's my money."

"You're forbidden to have money."

They also confiscated a photo of Jerusalem's landscape showing the Temple Mount. "Religious content. Forbidden."

"I protest the confiscation of postcards showing views of Israel. I received them legitimately."

"Enough of such insolence. Gather your stuff. No more chatting."

As I'm taken out through the prison gates, I realize that even after three years holed up inside I now take no pleasure in the gloomy landscape of low shrubbery and muddied snow. My guard is chewing on a white bread sandwich with eggs and onion – mocking my hunger, mocking the fact that it's been years since I've seen real white bread or eggs.

It is a long journey. The ice on the Volga has thawed, so rather than take us on foot over the river to Kazan, they drive us around the river in prison vans. Six hours in a sealed compartment. The other prisoners pass the time chatting.

"Since they brought the political prisoners," says one, "our lives have become easier. No more beatings, and the food has improved." (Three-quarters of Chistopol inmates were political prisoners.)

"Yes, the authorities seem afraid of them. The 'politicals' write complaints about every little thing."

"Just look what goes on in other prisons: torture, beatings, ten-day stints in solitary…"

It seems we "politicals" were relatively fortunate.

At the Bugulma prison in Tatarstan, I felt ill, and doubting that I could stand the journey, I requested a medical check. Upon hearing that I wanted to go to Israel, the young doctor, a Komsomol member, began to spew forth all manner of anti-Israel nonsense he'd picked up from the Soviet press. I stayed silent. I had come for treatment, not for an argument. "Israel and world Jewry seek to exploit the Arab and conquer his ancestral lands…"

Finally, my patience snapped. I could manage without medicine. "Everything you've said is complete nonsense, and it's of no interest to me. If you'd like, I could tell you things that aren't reported in your newspapers." An hour-long seminar on Jewish history ensued, after which I rose to my feet. "I came to ask for medicine, and we've ended up in an argument. Be that as it may. I can manage without your pills."

"No, no. That won't be necessary. I'll examine you, and write you a prescription." And indeed he gave me a prescription for vitamins and other pills, and listed me for additional rations to stem my malnutrition. I never got the additional rations, because that very night we were taken back to the vans to continue our journey, but the memory of that doctor who was willing to listen to the truth has stuck in my mind. Was it the fault of ordinary Soviet citizens that they were spoon-fed propaganda and falsehood?

All told, the journey took three weeks, stopping nearly each day at a new prison, each time getting searched again, each time the guards making some snide comment about my postcards from Israel. Each time I must try to appease their brutal rage.

"What are 'human rights' anyway?" a young soldier asks me earnestly in the transport train. "They say that in the Soviet Union they don't exist, but I don't see why I need such rights. I take a girl to the movies, and then we, you know… Well, what more so-called 'human rights' do I need?"

I refrained from replying. I'd had more than enough of propaganda during this trip. Once I found myself giving a lecture to an attentive audience of prisoners and guards both. Everything went well until I got to the Bolshevik takeover, at which point the entire train car erupted. "Don't you dare criticize our holy Lenin," the criminals shouted. I couldn't fathom how this idol worship meshed with daily reality: these men, of all people, should know that reality better than most. They see the giant Soviet prisons, each the size of a town. They build massive infrastructure projects with their own sweat and blood, only to read in the papers that they were built by idealistic Komsomol youth. The criminal prisoners know all of this, and yet they persist in their irrational support of the regime.

"When you get to the West," one of them tells me, "tell them how they mistreat us. I was once in a cell with three others. One fell ill, and we called for a doctor. He never came. We started banging on the door. The guards gassed us, and when we were about to pass out they burst in and beat us with iron bars, dragged us outside, and threw us into a snowy yard. Two days later, they came and found two dead, and a third paralyzed for life. They're putting me on trial for organizing a 'rebellion,' and will probably sentence me to death."

Another inmate pipes up: "I was serving as a paratrooper when China attacked North Vietnam, and my unit was assigned to aid the Vietnamese. They stationed us in the snow and gave us one meal a day, and when we went to headquarters to demand better conditions they charged us all with mutiny. Our labor camp, near Murmansk, manufactured spare parts for military vehicles. The food had worms; the guards beat us and abused us. When a few brave prisoners tried to burn down the camp, the army was called in and shot anyone attempting to escape. The rest of us are now being tried for inciting an uprising."

They told me these things in the hope that someone in the West would hear about their terrible plights, but after they told their stories they usually calmed down and went back to talking about vodka and women, and I got the impression that this wallowing was a kind of daily cathartic ritual for them.

· · · · ·

The train reaches its destination at midnight. Most prisoners are asleep on the floor of their cells. As a political prisoner, I am in my own small cell. The familiar anxiety: where are we? The infamous Berezniki camps in the Urals? Or further, in Siberia? I have managed to hang on to a map, and know that we have been travelling in the direction of Chusovoy, and sure enough it turns out we have arrived in the old familiar Perm 36. I catch myself thinking of it in a certain sense as "home." I'll be interested to see which members of the camp staff are still there.

The immense apparatus that is Gulag 81 functions flawlessly. Each group is taken off the train and herded to its respective camp. My turn comes, and I jump off the train with my two bags into snowy darkness. The guards exchange comments about me. "A political. Should have been executed a long time ago." "Yeah, my brother was killed serving in Afghanistan, and this guy is still roaming the earth."

The camp commandant Major Zhuravkov himself greets me. Our reunion brings me no joy. He and his men know my points of vulnerability: Shabbat, books, keeping kosher. I would have preferred being sent to a new camp. But what can I do?

I'm dragged through a grungy square toward a prisoner transport car. Alone. Always alone. These ten years have taught me not to put my trust in anyone, and not to expect help. Man is the social animal, they say, but camp affords no society. Every man to himself, every man to his suffering. "Love your fellow man as yourself" simply does not exist here. Love must be directed at a particular person. My need to love – and be loved – is something indefinable, like an inexplicable anxiety. One day it comes to me: "I want to love." But there's no one here to love. I dream about finding in the camp a Benjamin, whose soul could intertwine with that of his brother Yosef.

I'm sealed into a car's metal compartment, and instinctively curl up into a ball as we bounce violently over the rough Ural roads. There's no use in trying to hang onto the bench to avoid getting banged up; the only thing to do is to imagine that I am Yosef, the son of our forefather Jacob, swaying on camel-back at the head of a long desert caravan.

At last we reach Kuchino. The camp is larger than when I left it. A wooden barracks has been replaced with a two-story stone guard tower. The empire is expanding. Prisoners have taken to calling the place Kochinwald, after the Nazi concentration camp Buchenwald. Here there is no extermination, just the slow, systematic murder of a man's personality, faith, loyalty, and capacity for love.

The guards – many of whom were still in school when I was last here – look at me with curiosity. "Look, a 'dangerous state criminal.'" Behold the still-wandering son of Moshe and Chaya.

As before, I'm put in solitary quarantine, ostensibly for medical reasons but in fact in order to break down the new arrival's will and self-control. Though it is the dead of night, the prisoners try to gather any crumb of information. I hear Lyosha Safronov from cell 2. "Who's there?"

Prisoner camaraderie trumps the fear of getting caught talking to another inmate. "Yosef Mendelevich, just arrived from Chistopol prison."

"Shalom, Yosef!"

"Another word and you'll be punished," Captain Bellov says.

Another search of my belongings. Having learned that searches drag on longer the more emotion your face betrays, I feign a look of indifference as the guards rob me before my very eyes. Indeed they have robbed me of thousands of days of my life. They have robbed part of the humanity in me.

One day you may chance across a man in Jerusalem who looks like any other, except that his heart is darkened with memories of interrogations, searches, solitary confinements, and humiliations. Merciful God – how is it possible to bear it?

Meanwhile, Captain Bellov continues the search. "Hebrew books: forbidden. Postcards from Israel: forbidden. Warm clothes: a violation of camp dress code." I manage to save a Jewish calendar and the enameled mug my father had given me in 1971.

The next morning, the distribution of breakfast rations is accompanied by the sound of argument about our pathetic portions: thirty grams of grits, two hundred of bread, and fifteen grams of sugar. The heavy door to my cell clangs open and someone hands me a bowl, his fingers dipping into the muddy mash. "Why so meager?" I ask. "The others have it even worse," he said. This is Misha Chaporenko, who in 1941 murdered six Jews at a flour mill near Czernowitz. Here in camp he has befriended both the Jews and the wardens.

After breakfast, I succeed in contacting the other prisoners being held here: Sergei Kovalyov, Marinovich (a member of the Kiev branch of the human rights movement), and Lyosha Safronov. All three have declared a hunger strike with the goal of being transferred from the camp to a prison, where they believe they will have better conditions and less harassment from the guards. Each man and his own choice, I suppose.

"Yosef," Lyosha calls out, "Vadim wants to talk with you."

"Who's Vadim?"

"He'll tell you himself."

I go to the toilet, and hear a muffled voice. "Shalom. I'm Jewish. I've been imprisoned since 1979 for planning to flee to Israel." It turns out this naïve boy had intended to hijack a plane in order to demand the release of Sharansky, Ida Nudel, and Vladimir Slepak. "Yosef, do you know Hebrew?"

"Yes, and when we meet we can study together. Speaking of which, why don't you have a Hebrew name?"

"Find one for me!"

After some thought, I give him the name Dan. He likes it.

The next day I spot him through a hole in the door: a tall, sturdy fellow of about twenty, with a boyish face. He has been sentenced to thirteen years, but from now on we'll be together, and nothing will frighten us. Dan and Yosef: two sons of Jacob.

· · · · ·

One afternoon I'm instructed to gather my belongings and prepare to be admitted into the camp. Once more I'm concerned that my remaining Hebrew books and postcards will be confiscated, but this time I'm helped by the characteristic incompetence of the local authorities. At 4:00 p.m., Major Chukaynov got the order to transfer me into the camp, and the general assembly is scheduled for 4:30, so his search is rushed and cursory. "Were these books published in the Soviet Union?" he asked.

"Of course." I lie, without batting an eyelid.

Next, my postcards arouse great curiosity. The guards have never seen anything like them. Like a chirping bird, I cheerfully go on at length about them and where they came from. At this rate, I could have smuggled in a submachine gun. At the last moment, however, Chukaynov gets suspicious. "Leave us the books," he says, "and we'll look into the matter. You can have them back during the next shift." The head of the next shift is Captain Rak, my old nemesis, and I know he won't let me take anything. But having no alternative, I enter the camp with only the belongings I've been permitted to take with me.

After a three-year absence, I'm back, but no one awaits me. All of my friends are already in Israel. They did at least leave me a parting gift. At the Perm transit station, I notice something carved into the bunk in cell 87: "Altman, Zalmanson. Iyar, 5739 (1979)." They had written this the year before, on their way to freedom, though at the time they didn't know where they were headed. "Yosef Mendelevich," I add below their inscription. "Next year in Jerusalem."

Returning to a place that once vibrated with a shared life with my friends saddens me. Veteran prisoners, men who have been here for fifteen or twenty years, bombard me with questions. "We thought you had been released. Why are you back? Have they forgotten you?" The questions make me uncomfortable. In their eyes, I'm an utterly forgettable, inessential man, someone left behind. I myself see things differently: I wonder not why I haven't been released, but why Sharansky, Nudel, and Yosef Begun have not been freed.

It turns out that there are a couple of other Jews in camp: Leonid Ludman and Vladimir Sverdlin. The former is a tall engineer from Leningrad, about forty years old. He had attempted to smuggle out articles critical of the Soviet state, and had applied for an exit visa for Israel. The foreigner who had agreed to smuggle out Ludman's essays was caught at customs. The articles were found to contain the name of a military device on which Ludman had worked, and he was sentenced to twelve years for "revealing state secrets."

He takes me aside. The swampy land is spongy underfoot. "As an Israeli citizen, I welcome your arrival. I must tell you something secret. I must ask you to listen, but not to understand. They can read minds. But you can think in Hebrew. They cannot understand our language." He looks at me for my reaction, but I stay silent. I've learned the importance of silence. "The People's Republic of China has conferred on me an award for excellence for a new discovery. I discovered that the KGB uses radio waves to monitor our thoughts." His face contorts. "Those bastards have implanted a radio receiver in my upper jaw, and they can cause me to suffer hellish pains with their broadcasts. Right now, as a punishment for talking with you, their broadcasts are giving me diarrhea. But I cannot remain silent about this. It's my national duty." He looked at me again. "So what do you say?"

"I'll consider what you have said."

He looked crestfallen at my tepid reply. Later I learned that there was a raging debate in camp as to whether Ludman was mad, or merely pretending to be. Both were reasonable, but either way, it was clear that he found his imprisonment too hard to bear. He would wander around aimlessly, with a dull look in his eyes. He wouldn't read or write. I myself made no determination about him, except that I would stay away from him. If he had let himself deteriorate like this, one couldn't expect him to adhere to ethical principles.

A day later, he stopped me on a path. "I'm surprised that you're keeping your distance," he said. "We're the only Israelis here, after all." Did he really imagine that after our conversation the day before I'd want to befriend him? And yet many others did befriend him to hear about the latest secret developments in "Soviet weaponized radio." It's free entertainment.

I have other worries. I wait until Captain Rak's shift is up, and I approach the head of the next shift, Captain Lyaponov. "Major Chukaynov left some of my belongings here after they were searched and said I could have them back during the next shift," I say.

"Why should I do his work for him?" Lyaponov retorts.

With ten years of experience, I can see quite clearly what will happen next. At the end of his shift, Lyaponov will report that Chukaynov isn't doing his job, which was to complete the search. Chukaynov will come to me, his face reddened with vodka. "Why did you lie? I didn't fob off the search onto another shift. Take your damn bag!" And this is how I will get all my books back, and will be able to continue my studies in the Torah and in Bialik's *Book of Legends*.

When he finished his hunger strike, I arranged for Dan to get extra portions of food. The young man had a voracious appetite; he would gulp down two bowls of porridge and ask for more. Fortunately, we could get more from the cook, who had taken a liking to political prisoners.

Dan studied Hebrew from a beginner's book Mark Dymshits had left for Lyosha Safronov. I had used the same book – by Shlomo Kodesh, the grandfather of the ulpan movement – in Riga in 1965. Dan was coming along fine, but was frustrated by his slow progress. He still carried traces of the bohemian life he had enjoyed in Leningrad; he would strum his guitar, and sip tea with an ex-KGB lieutenant named Gregorian. When Gregorian's father was arrested for illegal trade in potatoes, the son had offered his services to the military attaché of the American embassy in Moscow. He spied, with considerable success, for three years, until he was caught and sentenced to fifteen years.

The other former KGB man in camp was Sverdlin, who had been one of the outstanding cadets in the KGB academy in Moscow. There he was groomed for a position in the ideological division of the agency. He was engaged to the daughter of Rozhkov, a member of the Communist Party central committee and a close friend of Brezhnev. But someone at the academy wrote to the rector accusing Sverdlin of homosexuality. When the false charge was relayed to the central committee, Sverdlin quit the academy in disgust, enrolled in law school, and harbored an abiding hatred for the KGB. In the course of attempting to contact American espionage agents, he met an Iraqi who had come to study in the USSR, through whom he hoped to meet the American military attaché. He promised he had valuable information for the Americans. A meeting was set up, but the only people who showed up were KGB agents. It turns out that the Iraqi had been an undercover KGB agent. Sverdlin was slapped with eight years in prison.

The story sounded far-fetched, but one glance at this imposingly tall man with an obstinate lower lip was enough to convince you that he was more than capable of such adventures. It had been more than a decade since he had left the KGB; he was no longer privy to any special secrets. But thanks to his vivid descriptions, I got another view into the inquisitional methods of the Party apparatus.

In the inordinately suspicious camp atmosphere, few doubted that both Sverdlin and Gregorian were collaborating with the KGB. Moreover, each of them was sure that the other was an informant. Gregorian suspected Sverdlin of watching him, and Sverdlin suspected Gregorian of monitoring *him*.

Without the aid of Zinovy Karsyevsky, I would have been hard pressed to know the truth. Zinovy had taken part in the struggle for Ukrainian independence back in 1944. He was arrested the next year and imprisoned for several years. When he got out, he founded the Ukrainian National Front, and this got him arrested again in 1965, when he was sentenced to fifteen years. As was then the Soviet fashion, he was sent to a psychiatric institution in Kazan in 1971, where he was held until 1979. He was declared mentally ill, and sent to the Carpathian Mountains in the Ukraine. There he founded a Helsinki Watch committee (most of these committees had been disbanded in 1977 with the arrests of Orlov, Ginzburg, and Sharansky). At this point, the KGB remembered that Zinovy had eight months more to serve, and had sent him to camp the month before I arrived.

I sometimes felt that Zinovy had been brought to camp especially for me, since were it not for him I would have had no one to consult or draw support from. He was an authority in several areas: the Second World War, partisan warfare, prison, underground resistance, and psychiatric wards. Through all these experiences, he had salvaged his good sense, his simplicity, and his sense of humor. Between prisons, he had managed to complete his university studies.

He had also managed to return to the political fray. Zinovy felt that the struggle for Ukrainian independence must be fought by itself, independently of the so-called Russian "democrats." He believed in the Creator, and fully identified with the Jews' return to independence and our struggle to return to our homeland. As for the various "struggles" and "campaigns" in camp, he understood that they often served merely to give relief to certain personal issues: rage, the lust for power, etc. "It is not the idea of democracy but the demon who animates these struggles," he would say. Such a clear-headed approach was extremely valuable to me. I myself had reached the conclusion after ten years in prison that not every "struggle" is carried out for ideological motives, but I wouldn't have expressed this opinion openly. By articulating it in the way he did, Zinovy freed me from the feelings of guilt that often accompanied my reluctance to storm the barricades, so to speak.

I was never much interested in struggle for its own sake. My struggle at the moment was simply to learn Hebrew. I arranged it so that Dan and I would be sent to work paving a new asphalt path in the camp courtyard. This way, while hauling around construction materials, we could be together most of the day. Like parched earth, he thirstily absorbed everything I shared about Judaism. He began to cover his head with a cap at all times, to avoid pork, and to cease working on Shabbat. We didn't mind spending our evenings loading and unloading truckfuls of coal and cement if it meant being able to take off Saturdays.

After my friends were released, even the authorities seemed to regard my imminent release as a realistic possibility and they backed off accordingly. But this changed when they saw Dan slipping away from their grasp.

"Mendelevich," Zhuravkov said, "Vadim Ehrenburg will not be going to Israel."

"He will."

"I must warn you not to influence him with your Zionist propaganda."

"There's no propaganda involved – just Hebrew lessons."

I also began tutoring Sverdlin and Ludman. None of them had celebrated a Jewish holiday, so for Rosh Hashanah I decided to gather the best treats I could find and put together a festive holiday meal. I wasn't familiar with the customs unique to Rosh Hashanah, but I at least wanted to create something of the holiday spirit. I put a photo of Jerusalem and Mount Zion on the table together with several Rosh Hashanah greetings I had received over the years. In honor of the holiday I put on the white undershirt that my father had sent to me in the Leningrad prison in 1970. I recited the blessings for all the dishes, and talked about the necessity for Jews to remain united even in the remote reaches of the Urals.

I had high hopes that if Ludman saw that he had loyal friends he would stop his ravings, but things turned out differently. On seeing my attempts to give the handful of Jews in the camp a semblance of unity, he took the liberty of gossiping about Sverdlin in an attempt to sow seeds of suspicion about him. He also called Dan a liar and collaborator. Dan believed Sverdlin to be a collaborator, but didn't know what to think about Ludman. In short, the mutual backbiting undercut my attempts at forging some sense of unity even before they began. To my great surprise, I also discovered that each of the three competed with the others for my friendship and company.

In order to salvage matters, I decided to involve my friends in a common cause: berry picking. Before I was sent from camp to prison, I hadn't paid much botanical heed to trees, but by now I knew that they could be a good nutritional source. In this respect, Perm 36 was well appointed. On one side of the camp's main avenue grew a stand of trees, some with red berries. Using a long stick with a nail on the end, I could pull branches toward me and reach the ripest clusters. I picked several kilograms this way and boiled them with sugar to make a jam for Shabbat. One tree, however, gave me no rest. It was the most attractive of the camp trees, and bore the plumpest berries, but it also happened to stand next to the entrance to camp headquarters, so no one dared touch it. I proposed a joint venture to Jonas Simokitis, a Lithuanian who was

serving ten years for attempting to flee abroad. I brought over some scaffold-
ing normally used to make repairs. I climbed the tree, and Jonas clambered up
the scaffold. Working quickly, as if we were on our own plantation, I bent the
branches with my stick, and Jonas picked the berries.

As luck would have it, the dastardly Lieutenant Chodinov, his splotched
face bearing signs of excessive drinking, spotted us. For a moment, he stood
beneath the tree hesitating whether he should declare our vigilante picking
impermissible. To distract him, I began rambling on about how wonderful the
tree was, and what excellent berries it produced – the cure for all the world's
diseases. He stood there for a few moments, and turned to leave. Other prisoners, interpreting this as tacit consent, came to ask us for our berries. Members
of the camp elite – the cook, the storeroom manager, the work supervisor –
each got a cluster.

For the Sukkot holiday, we were less lucky. We had gathered in "the Lenin
room," so named because it was the place prisoners were supposed to pore
over Lenin's writings. No one did so, of course; prisoners used the room as a
place to have their tea and chat. As we were sitting down, a prisoner named
Potyomin came in. He had served the Gestapo as a translator, and after the war
had studied German at university. He was always complaining that in being
sent to labor camp he had been separated from his friends, most of whom
had been Polizei and former Nazi collaborators. Once in a while he would
be taken to testify in some trial or another, and shortly thereafter we would
read in the papers about the death sentence that had been handed down in
the case. Between trials, he would make his living by informing. And now
this old bespectacled man was creeping toward us in the Lenin room, where
he sat down in a corner to read. We had no wish to celebrate in his presence.
Ludman, the boldest among us, turned to face him. "Maybe you should leave,
comrade."

"I'll just sit here quietly," Potyomin said. "You're not disturbing me."

"You fascist bastard. We're not disturbing you, but you're disturbing us!
Get out of here while you still can."

Potyomin left, but was soon replaced by guards who charged Ludman and
Ehrenburg with "desertion to the enemy camp." The next morning, Ludman
was sent to the camp's internal prison for six months, and because he refused
to work there, this turned into a year. Dan "only" got fifteen days in solitary
confinement, though this had nothing to do with Sukkot. The week before,
he had clambered up to the roof of the sawmill to catch a pigeon for Shabbat.
When I explained to him that none of us knew how to kill a bird in a kosher

manner, he came down, but by then the guards had already seen him. It was for that incident that he was now punished.

While in solitary, Dan put on two pairs of underwear to keep warm. Captain Rak, catching him, made him strip off all his underwear entirely, and Sergeant Rotenko punched him several times in the kidneys in order to teach him to obey Soviet law. This caused Dan to fly into a rage, and he got an additional ten days.

With Dan in solitary, I offered Hebrew lessons – and a shoulder to cry on – to Vlodya Sverdlin. After being brought to camp, he had approached one of the leaders of the Ukrainian underground with an offer to help start an anti-Soviet underground in camp. This was taken as a KGB provocation, and the Ukrainian instructed ten prisoners to complain to the KGB that Sverdlin was inciting them. Zinovy and I discussed the matter with Lyosha Safronov, who had himself taken on a leadership role in camp.

"But, Lyosha, if Sverdlin is in fact not working with the KGB, it will turn out that you've informed on an innocent fellow prisoner."

"And if he is a KGB man?"

"Then what is accomplished in ratting him out to the KGB? You could have simply told him you'd have nothing further to do with him."

"My intuition tells me he's an agent."

"Can we afford to rely on intuitions rather than on facts?"

But Lyosha was certain that Sverdlin was collaborating with the KGB, and it seemed to me that Sverdlin's Jewish appearance contributed to that certainty. After other prisoners turned their backs on him, Sverdlin began to be cultivated by a young and talented Armenian named Parpoyir Ayrikian, and together they began to bribe one of the factory supervisors to secretly bring them food and letters. They were discovered, and put on trial. Ayrikian and the supervisor were found guilty, and Sverdlin was let off. Did this mean that Zinovy and I had been mistaken about him? Did Sverdlin really have KGB ties?

In Sverdlin's previous camp, he had come to know Sharansky, who according to Sverdlin told him the details of his trial and asked his legal advice. This didn't ring true to me. Why would Sharansky share such things with Sverdlin?

In the meantime, the authorities were trying to cut off our communication with the adjacent camp 35. We had been using the services of two guards, nicknamed the German and the Cockroach, who in exchange for money would get letters out. To get the money to pay them off, we arranged for our families to send a food package to us via the German that would include a box of American cigarettes we could sell for four hundred rubles. The German brought the package, but something was missing. He had stolen the cigarettes for himself. Not long after, a search was conducted and the food that had arrived in the package was confiscated on the grounds that it was not food that was sold in the canteen and therefore was prohibited.

In short, the authorities had decided to clamp down. Yet not everyone accepted the new state of affairs. Lyosha, who was then in solitary, was determined to report the theft of the cigarettes to the commandant. The rest of us argued that doing so would be counterproductive. The whole exchange was conducted through notes that Lyosha smuggled to us at five rubles a pop through a guard nicknamed the Bug.

Meanwhile, Dan was looking for ways to smuggle a report of his trial to the West. He negotiated with a camp driver and with the German, but nothing came of it. Finally, he said to me, "I'm going to pay the Bug to smuggle out my report." I asked him to let me think about whether that was the most prudent thing to do. As I was thinking it over, however, Dan impatiently gave over the documents. Something told me that this was a rash thing to do, but the deed was done. The very next day, Dan was sent to the camp prison for six months on charges of "disobedience." There was no hint of the real reason. Let the man think he had fooled the authorities.

· · · · ·

I usually kept my Hebrew books overnight in a storeroom; it was searched less often than the barracks. But one day I left them in my room and returned from work to the discovery that my bags had been searched and my books removed. I went straight to Zhuravkov and demanded them back.

"Since they're in Hebrew," he said, "we'll have to send them off to translators to be checked. Besides which, they weren't published in the Soviet Union. We noticed that the binding isn't original."

I'd had the books for eight years; the authorities had finally figured out my trick. I reiterated my demand that they be returned.

"You have used them to spread Zionist propaganda." That explained everything. This hadn't been a random search.

I wandered around not knowing what to do. Ten years of this had utterly exhausted me. But I still had to take care of Dan, to pass him some food. I headed back to the storeroom to get some biscuits for him. Captain Rak and Sergeant Rotenko were waiting for me there, apparently searching for my other books. I had prepared for such an eventuality by putting my suitcase and backpack in one place, and my bag of books in another. The two men searched the suitcase and backpack and found nothing illegal. Just as they were turning to leave, Rotenko's eyes fell on the second bag.

"Is that yours too?"

"It is."

"Then why did you try to conceal it from us?"

My heart filled with the adrenalin of battle in a way I hadn't felt for years. They took the *Book of Legends*, the poems of Bialik, my grammar books, and histories. At least the Torah, to which I had affixed the title page of a Soviet-published book of Yiddish poems, passed and would stay with me.

I was ready to declare a hunger strike – even of a month or two. I had promised myself to fast that year between Rosh Hashanah and Yom Kippur, but I took pity on myself and told myself that I fasted quite enough even without such pledges. Perhaps it was for breaking my pledge that I was now being punished, or for not studying the *Book of Legends* diligently enough, or for failing to take sufficient care of Dan. I felt I had failed him by not strenuously enough opposing his decision to hand over his trial documents to the Bug. I had failed the biblical injunction "Do not stand idly by the blood of your neighbors." But I knew that after I began my strike, I would be sent to the camp prison where I could support Dan more closely.

I consulted Zinovy. "I understand that you need to do this," he said. "It's important to take a stand now so that the authorities don't feel they can arbitrarily confiscate books from Jews later. When you leave camp, Dan will find it difficult on that score. In the meantime, since you have the energy, you should use it." I told him that if I were still striking in a hundred days, he should make sure that the other political prisoners would ask me to stop in order to save my health. Their request would allow me to finish the hunger strike in a dignified way. Of course, I could stop at any time, if I saw fit to do so.

The only thing that remained was to alert those outside the camp. I waited for a reply from friends in Moscow that would confirm they had received my message.

Zinovy suggested that I demand the return of all my books. I had doubts about this, since it was clear to me that they would likely never give them all back. "But you must believe that you'll get them all back," Zinovy insisted. Ultimately, I did believe it, and the belief strengthened my conviction.

In the meantime Kovalyov had been released from camp prison and faced a dilemma: would he go to work? On the one hand, he had declared a hunger strike in the first place because of his demand to be sent to a prison rather than to work. On the other, how could he resume his strike now that he was gravely weakened – and noticeably aged – by his ten months in the internal prison?

In a number of conversations with Zinovy about the matter, I came to the view that Kovalyov's strike had been set to fail from the outset, since its principal motivation was despair. He would have been wiser to abandon the strike earlier; weakening yourself to that degree benefits no one except the authorities.

When I saw Kovalyov just after his release, it appeared he himself knew that he had to end the strike, but couldn't bring himself to do so. Very early on the morning that he was expected to return to work, I roused the camp's most well-regarded prisoners and took them to a meeting with Kovalyov behind the bathhouse. I proposed that the elite of the political prisoners of Perm 36 would formally call for him to go back to work so that he could save face. We had no right to come to a decision like that on behalf of others, of course, but if it could help matters, why not try?

I accompanied him to the factory entrance to ensure he didn't get cold feet and change his mind. The problem was that my expectations of him in effect matched those of the authorities. Did I not fear that we would be accused of wishing to help the authorities? I felt, however, that sometimes one simply could not stand by while witnessing suffering; in certain cases, one must step in and help. After Kovalyov's release and return to work, Marinovich and Safronov were also let back into the camp, and they too resumed work. Sometimes retreat requires more wisdom, decisiveness, and courage than continuing a futile fight. All three listened to reason and went back to work, and all three were transferred to a prison a month later, just as they had wanted.

By then, I had received the awaited confirmation from Moscow, acknowledging that they had received my notification that I was about to declare a hunger strike. The signal came in the form of a postcard with a portrait of Lenin. This had been our code. Now I could begin. (This happened a year to the day before my wedding in Jerusalem.)

The simplest way to begin was to refuse to go to the factory. The first day, a guard found me in the barracks. "Why aren't you at work?"

"I'm on a hunger strike."

"I don't know anything about this. You're not on my list. Go to work."

My job at the time was to unload coils of metal wire from delivery trucks (each coil weighed in at about sixty kilos) and haul them to the factory, where I would load them onto the axle of a machine that emitted a deafening screech and belched up clouds of fine metal dust. After a night of doing this at a fast pace, on no food, I collapsed onto my bunk. Since I wanted to be put into solitary for my hunger strike, and not for refusal to work, I worked like this every night for a week, despite the hunger, until my temples throbbed and my hands trembled and I finally sank to my knees on the concrete floor in utter exhaustion.

For seven days, the camp authorities took the conventional approach, ignoring my strike entirely. When Zhuravkov made an appearance in the factory, he avoided me. On the eighth day, when I was simply too weak to go to work, Rak and Rotenko came to the barracks and ordered me to gather my things. My bag had long since been packed, after careful deliberation about which books to take. Since I could expect to be searched, I couldn't risk taking along my remaining Hebrew books, so I had packed a textbook on the history of Asia (published in the USSR) and my Russian-Hebrew dictionary in which I had concealed my "amulet": chapter 34 of the book of Exodus, read on Shemini Atzeret, in which Moses receives the second set of stone tablets at Sinai (just as I wanted to get back my Torah from the Soviet guards). I had heard that in 1975, at the Vladimir prison, Berg-Rabinovich, who kept this same chapter hidden, had his copy confiscated, and got it back only after a month-long hunger strike.

The transfer into a solitary confinement cell is by now a familiar routine; if there is a newness this time it is in my quiet and deep confidence in my eventual victory. There ensue the routines of a hunger strike: the pointless attempts to persuade me to eat, and above all, the joy in it, the pleasant tension of engaging in a struggle during which not a single moment goes to waste. Every moment, in fact, is dedicated to faith, to Israel, and to my friend.

I make contact with Dan almost right away through the toilet pipes. "Dan, how are you occupying yourself?"

"I mostly lie around reading."

"What about Hebrew?"

"They've taken my Hebrew textbook."

"I declared a hunger strike to demand the return of all the books they confiscated from me."

"I'll join you!"

I've already planned my daily schedule: morning prayers, exercises to prevent my muscles from atrophying, and then work. This involves putting together a Hebrew dictionary of the most commonly used two thousand words, writing a curriculum for studying Hebrew grammar, and finally, writing a textbook complete with passages, exercises, and even illustrations. All of this is intended for Dan, though who knows if we'll ever see one another again. In the afternoon I nap, then get back to the pedagogical work, designing a course in Jewish history beginning with Abraham.

But how do I get all of this to Dan? Despite the frigid winter, I summon the will each day to venture out into the four-by-four meter exercise yard. I ask for a shovel, and clear the accumulated snow into piles, one of which is just under the guard booth. This corner is a "dead spot"; the angle is such that the guard cannot see it. Each time I go out, I wrap some teaching material in plastic, and pace the yard, watching the guard booth from the corner of my eye. At the right moment, my hand flashes out of my pocket like an unsheathed sword and deposits the package in a hole I've prepared in the snow pile. On my way back to the cell, I hastily smooth over the hole, leaving a red string to mark the spot. Next it is Dan's turn to visit the yard. The next half hour seems much longer to me, but finally he returns to his cell escorted by guards. As he passes my cell, he lets a single word escape his clenched teeth. "*B'seder.*" How impatiently I have been waiting for that word.

In the evening, as the shifts change, I quiz him on verb conjugations and try to encourage him to study harder. This is done entirely in Hebrew, with a man who until recently knew only a single word in that language: *Yisrael.*

There are other times, however, when I don't feel like doing a thing except brood. And what do I brood about? That's exactly what has bothered me for all my years of imprisonment: my tendency to stare into space. For a long time, I tried to suppress these moments of daydreaming and brooding and reflection, until I understood that such moments can afford some of life's most sublime pleasures, after which you can joyfully return to the world.

But the world I find myself in is a hostile place. On the twentieth day of my strike, the commandant, the "doctor," and some guards barge into my cell. Force-feedings are normally conducted in the second week of a strike, but they've apparently tried to postpone it as much as possible in the hopes that I'd break first. The guards easily overpower me, shove a rubber tube down my throat, and pour into it a liter of murky liquid. Zhuravkov, who came to enjoy the show, is apparently nauseated by the spectacle and leaves the room clutching his chest. When it's over, I collapse onto the bunk, my throat and stomach in wretched pain. This process repeats itself every five or seven days.

Sometime in the first month of my strike, Fyodorov shows up. "We know that you've timed your strike to coincide with the Madrid conference (a follow-up to the then decade-old Helsinki Accords). It is therefore a political gesture." It seems that he is expressing a widespread view within the KGB. My aim is to prove that the strike is aimed at nothing more than getting my books back, and my next week is spent trying to prove this to local authorities. I send complaints to all echelons to insist that the confiscation of my books was entirely unprovoked on my part, and that the commandant not only does not want to solve the problem but has refused even to meet with me.

Meanwhile, my sister Rivka Drori, a mother of three, put everything on hold and traveled to Madrid. In the US, Glenn Richter and David Stahl rallied on my behalf (their activities on my behalf over the years are far too numerous to count). The American-Canadian Jewish philanthropist Edgar Bronfman, president of the World Jewish Congress, met with the Soviet ambassador to the US Anatoly Dobrynin in an effort to negotiate my release. (The new Reagan administration was a riddle to the Soviets, and the Russians were interested in finding points of contact.)

At the same time, Natasha Rosenstein inquired about me to Major Zhuravkov. The reply: "The aforementioned prisoner has left the camp and his whereabouts are unknown." When this reply was publicized, it caused a wave of anxiety. Katya Seroussi, a young Paris-born Tunisian Jew living in Jerusalem (and my future wife), cried all night upon hearing the news. She had been one of the heads of a youth movement for Soviet Jewry, and had followed my case for years. Thousands rallied in Jerusalem to demand my release.

On the fiftieth day of my strike, Zhuravkov himself appeared. "We have no desire to see your strike drag on for any longer," he said. "People in the West are making too much of a fuss about you."

I had won. I was given back a letter from Israel, my textbooks on Hebrew and Jewish history, and my map of Israel. I demanded and was given permission to see Dan. We embraced, and I handed him the Hebrew textbook, urging him to study.

When I got out, my friends greeted me. They had expected me to be taken out dead, and asked in amazement how I had emerged victorious. "Jews from across the world helped me," I said. "Yes," they answered, "we know that you Jews always come to one another's aid."

I continued the strike another week, demanding a promise signed by the commandant that I would receive medical care and food supplements after I left solitary confinement. Against my advice, Dan relied on verbal pledges and ended his strike. "If you're eating, you must be healthy," he was told, and he was kept in the internal prison.

I was transferred to the camp clinic, where I was held in total isolation and under strict warnings not to contact other prisoners. The conditions weren't bad, but the sudden pivot from the daily battle of wills to utter rest threw me into depression. To keep my spirits up, I began to hatch plans for continuing the hunger strike.

After illegally contacting my friends in camp, I was discharged from the clinic, and put back to the wire coils and the terrible industrial noise and dust of the factory.

A young prisoner named Ivanov, who had recently been transferred from camp 35, had news of Sharansky, who apparently was the only political prisoner left in a camp crawling with criminals, former Polizei members, and informants. Sharansky was too short to reach the electric switches on the huge lathe where he had been assigned to work. A special stand was built for him; the main thing was to keep him working. Some of the pieces of machinery he had to operate weighed thirty or forty kilos. The authorities had it in for him, and used any excuse to make his life even more intolerable. At the end of 1980, he had been sent to clean up the "death zone" near the camp fence where anyone who moves is shot. On Chanukah, he was caught lighting candles, and at that point he realized the authorities wouldn't let him be and that he had to take a stand. He launched a strike to demand the confiscated candles back. This landed him in solitary confinement, where his stay was repeatedly extended.

Such was the bleak news from camp 35, where a number of prisoners had been sent to prison after a full year in solitary. I began thinking about how I might reach camp 35 to be with Sharansky and encourage him. I knew only too well how emotionally difficult the first years of labor camp could be.

In the meantime, a young, intelligent soldier who had been sentenced to seven years for having contacted foreign espionage agencies (in reality his attempts were in all probability nothing more than child's play) arrived in camp. I thought I detected in him something almost imperceptibly non-Russian. "Sasha," I said one day, "I hope you won't mind an indiscrete question."

Guessing the question, he smiled. "Yes, I'm Jewish on my mother's side. A KGB man instructed me not to tell you because you're a Zionist." Despite the warning, he drew close to me, and I sensed I would have a new student.

· · · · ·

As I was at work on February 10, 1981, I was abruptly approached by two KGB officers and ordered to pack my things and leave. Yet another transfer? I was curious to know where I would be taken next. I am shown a watch and some money. "These are yours. You can get them later." This is puzzling; a prisoner is forbidden to have money.

Escorted by KGB officers and a giant guard dog, I am taken by jeep that night to a train. After an overnight journey, I'm parked in a prison for a day, and at nightfall transferred to a plane, where I'm surrounded by special guards. I try to make conversation with them.

"I noticed as we passed through town that there is no food in the store windows."

"Store windows are for advertising. We don't need to resort to advertising."

Then I start lecturing them about Zionism, and soon get so passionate that they would have had no trouble sticking me with a second round in prison had they wished to do so. When we land, I realize we're in Moscow. I'm taken to the KGB prison, the deathly and desolate Lefortovo, where I had spent time after my arrest, and put into a cell with an arms dealer who has every mark of working for the KGB. I send a message to the warden that I will declare a hunger strike unless I'm informed as to the reason of my secret transfer to Lefortovo.

His reply: "I don't know."

"In that case, send me back."

"I will request instructions in the matter," he says.

I fear that those on the "outside" who helped get out the information about my hunger strike over the winter have been caught, and that this is the reason I am here. Or was it an even more serious provocation?

I count the days. On February 22, the twenty-sixth Communist Party congress is set to begin. I realize that if I'm not released in the next several days, by February 18, the situation must be very grave. I'm almost unbearably anxious, but I try to get a grip and remain outwardly calm.

As I finish my prayers on the morning of February 18, contemplating how the widespread assimilation of eastern European Jewry over the last century could possibly be a part of the divine plan, the door opens and I'm ordered out with my belongings. I ask whether I should take my blanket. (If so, I would know I'm being transferred to another cell. If not, I might be headed for release.) I am told to take it. But when I step into the corridor, another guard says: "Why are you taking your blanket, you idiot?" His words sound lovely to my ears.

Blanketless, I'm taken up to the third-floor office of the warden, with polished furniture and rugs – luxury the likes of which I haven't laid eyes on in eleven years. On a table near the door I see an open suitcase holding a suit and jacket. Behind it several somber, expressionless men in civilian clothes are sitting motionless. One of them gets to his feet: "In the name of Supreme Soviet of the Soviet Union, I hereby declare that you have been deprived of your Soviet citizenship due to behavior unworthy of a Soviet citizen, and that you will therefore be deported immediately."

"Thank God!"

"What are you so happy about? Solzhenitsyn wept when we expelled him."

"Solzhenitsyn you banished from his homeland. Me you're banishing *to* my homeland."

"No more talking. Sign here. The form says that eight hundred rubles have been taken from your funds to buy clothing for you."

"These rags cost that much?"

"The balance of your money, another eight hundred rubles, cannot be given to you. The banks are closed."

"I demand my money." I say this merely to register that I will not allow them to rob me without a response from me, but I know that I'll get none of it back.

Then another search, during which they confiscate everything, including photos and my father's letters. "I'm not going anywhere until I get it all back," I say.

"We're not asking you if you'd like to go. We're kicking you out by force."

Wearing my new clothes and a grey hat, I'm bundled into a car, and we're escorted through the city by an entourage of motorcycle cops, as though we were a presidential motorcade. And just like that, in a single night, Yosef is liberated from Pharaoh's prison and becomes a free man. I feel more keenly than ever that our lives – and the life of our people – are made of miraculous stuff.

At the airport, the car abruptly stops and turns around. Are we returning to the prison? No, I am told we're going straight to the plane, and I'm warned not to try to talk with anyone. Before boarding, I notice the colonel who was head of Jewish affairs at the KGB. I know that he is releasing me against his will, and it occurs to me that when your enemy is in retreat, you ought to pursue him.

"Listen, Colonel. You arrested me for trying to fly to Israel, and now you yourself are buying me a ticket out. I know that you've allowed some three hundred thousand Jews to leave the Soviet Union. But many more are left, and I'm telling you that if you don't let all of them go, the regime will collapse." I surprised myself. I had threatened him, but was still in his hands.

His answer surprised me even more. It seems he belonged to a new generation that would in the next few years usher in reforms and democratization. He became serious. "That might be true. We hadn't imagined the strength of your willpower and determination."

I asked myself whether I could take any credit. I am but a simple man. It was not my will but the will of God that His people should be freed from Russian exile.

After a three-hour flight, we land in Vienna. "Comrade Mendelevich," the pilot announces, "Israel Singer is waiting for you." I'm the first off the ramp. I'm greeted by Israel Singer of the World Jewish Congress, as well as the Israeli ambassador to Austria, a representative of Edgar Bronfman, and representatives of the Jewish Agency, not to mention a throng of journalists – a great celebratory tumult. And yet in my heart there lurks a certain emptiness.

At last I am free.

· · · · ·

I recover in a building that has been rented out for Soviet Jewish immigrants. When Singer was asked to go to Vienna on a special mission related to the Mendelevich case, he consulted the Lubavitcher Rebbe in New York. "Bring him a tallit and tefillin," the Rebbe said. So it is that when the ambassador is stymied by my request to put on tefillin, Singer announces that on the advice he once received from the Rebbe, he has brought a pair especially for me.

Now I ask Singer to teach me how to put on the tefillin, and for the first time in my thirty-three years of life, I wrap myself in the sacred phylacteries.

"Yosef, where will you go?"

I'm dumbfounded by the question. "To Israel, of course."

"Well, many Soviet Jews, including many in this very building, prefer to go to America."

"I want to talk to them." It wasn't that I wanted to convince them, but I did want them at least to understand their decision.

We gather in the dining room, a well-lit hall that could not fail to impress a former prisoner. Each of us is served a plate of chicken and potatoes that could alone feed ten prisoners. "I want to tell you my story," I begin. "When we decided to hijack a plane, we dreamed that Jews would be allowed to go to Israel. For this dream we and many others were sent to prison. There we were sustained by the thought that every day we suffered there was the cost we were willing to pay for another Jew to be set free. Those who decide to make their lives elsewhere than in the Jewish homeland harm our struggle and undermine the strength of those who are still imprisoned." Applause. Calls of "bravo." But I would have traded all the applause for bringing even one member of my audience that day with me to Israel.

On the flight from Vienna to Tel Aviv, the El Al pilots invited me into the cockpit for my first glimpse of the country. I felt profound pain, like a long-starved man who is suddenly given a feast, but is unable to eat. The Soviet regime had robbed me of the ability to feel, to enjoy this great moment of homecoming and give it its due.

At the same time, I am overwhelmed upon arrival. My stepmother, Rivka, Eva, Chaim. I must shut my eyes for fear of being blinded, reign in my feelings for fear that my heart might burst. This transition into a new world is indescribable. Minister David Levy hands me an immigration certificate. I feel like a soldier returning in triumph from a combat mission. Thousands of friends and well-wishers greet me. Forgive me, I feel like saying, for not being able to talk with each of you, to answer all your questions. Forgive me for not knowing how to be happy. You are not greeting me alone. Together with you, I am greeting the great day of exodus, the day of divine wonders.

I dreamed of arriving in Jerusalem quietly, of walking to the Western Wall on foot. For now I do not have the chance to be alone with my thoughts. Soon enough, my land, I will come to you and converse with you alone and be close to you. I will yet come to you, my Judean Hills.

For now, I rush to the Western Wall, back to the place from which we were first exiled from God's city, to herald the news of its sons' return.

O God of Abraham, Isaac, and Jacob, bring back Your people Israel from the four corners of the earth to your city Jerusalem, soon may it be rebuilt.

Epilogue

Twenty-five years after publishing this book in Russian and Hebrew, I sit in my home in Jerusalem composing an epilogue for its appearance in English. By Israeli standards, we might call the book a best seller. In various public appearances over the years, I have spoken about the book – and my life – before hundreds of thousands of people, each time reliving my experiences and feeling moved anew.

Not infrequently, strangers on the street or in a bus – old and young alike – stop me to say how much the book has meant to them. People who had been gravely ill have drawn encouragement and strength from my story. *Ba'alei teshuvah* and homemakers from Meah She'arim to Bnei Brak have been strengthened in their love of Torah by reading it. Each points to a particular passage that they found especially affecting. Sometimes, having myself forgotten that passage, I am surprised. And then I remind myself: this is not just a book, but a soul baring, the revelation of a Jewish spirit connected to God. Just as the Torah has seventy facets or dimensions, so too does the Jewish soul, which, after all, is itself "a portion of God on high."

Much to my surprise, some readers also praise the book's literary style. Yet I've never claimed to be a professional writer. I merely recorded my experiences. If the resulting book came out felicitously, it is due not to any literary talent (for I have none) but to the fact that my life has been one extended miracle. And so, page after page, I relate the wondrous and miraculous events that have visited themselves upon me – wonder upon wonder, miracle upon miracle. I do not know by what merit God has graced me with this chain of wonders. I merely thank Him that this wellspring of deliverance has befallen me, and that He has given me the eyes to see, to remember, and to record the divine miracles that accompany us daily.

There is perhaps one further miracle: that I have treated every experience as a challenge to confront and as a test to withstand. And I have withstood.

· · · · ·

In the years since my book first appeared, many have asked me why I did not publish the book in English. I was aware of the expense involved in such an undertaking, and was afraid too of the appearance of vanity in seeking to be published in foreign languages. So I would answer: I have faith that one day the book will become urgently necessary to American Jews, and when that day arrives, matters will take care of themselves and – without need for my own initiative – the book will see the light of day in English.

And so it was. On the thirtieth anniversary of my miraculous release from Soviet prison, the telephone rang. On the other end of the line was a distinguished woman who, along with many other devoted Jews in America, had led the Soviet Jewry movement.

In those days, the movement had gone under the banner "Let my people go." Clearly, this wasn't an exact quote from Exodus. It referred of course to the demand God – through Moses – made of Pharaoh: "Let my people go, so that they may worship Me." Now I heard the voice on the line from America complete the verse. "Yosef, why not publish your book in English? Your story is critical for Jews on this side of the ocean. You can't imagine the disastrous toll assimilation is taking on Jewish communities here."

"Pam," I replied, "I've waited for this call for thirty years. Now I know the time has come – and not just in America. Across the globe it has become painfully clear that true redemption can be achieved only with the addition of the second part of the verse: 'so that they may worship Me.'"

· · · · ·

Let me call your attention to an easily overlooked passage at the beginning of the book. You may remember that as I recalled my childhood, I described how evil men imprisoned my dear father for a crime he had not committed. The world seemed to be upside down; all that had once been secure no longer seemed so. No justice, no one to rely on. Who could save us from disaster? I didn't even know that soon my mother would leave us forever. Yet darkness and oblivion encroached upon me.

My entire life I've carried within me the image of a miserable and frightened Jewish family facing a large, menacing court building where my father was to be sentenced, a family powerless to save our loved one from a terrible fate. To save him, and to save us.

And then an unexpected cry rose from my heart: "Please, O God, save us!" I was frightened by my own cry. What was happening to me? To whom was I appealing?

Looking back, I now understand that for the first time in my life I was praying. But how? No one had taught me of our merciful Father in heaven who possesses the power of salvation. On the contrary, I had been taught that there was no God. But the pure soul of a child somehow knew: there was indeed Someone who could save us.

So that is what happened: God revealed Himself to me, and I have followed Him all the days of my life since. Perhaps that first feeble prayer, so full of weeping and pleading, was primitive: "Save my father and I will follow You." Perhaps nothing more might have come of it than a weepy, frightened child who in a time of crisis recognized that a great force existed that held the power of salvation.

Fortunately, however, something else happened. That first moment of connection within a child's soul gave birth instead to an ever-intensifying faith. Only five years after that initial encounter with God, I found myself working as an activist in an underground movement dedicated to the reinvigoration of Russian Jews. And ten years later I had already become a brave warrior, weapon in hand, in the struggle to redeem the people of Israel.

· · · · ·

Before our fateful arrest at the airport, I told my friends, "There is no meaning in the life of a slave who cannot be true to himself."

We were arrested and sentenced. We did not panic, nor weep, nor beg our oppressors for mercy; we did not betray our people. Miraculously, the people of Israel, together with good people the world over, stayed the hand that had malevolently been raised against us, and we were spared.

In my view, the trial and sentencing were but the beginning of the story. A man can discover deep within himself spiritual strength and momentary transcendence. But it is a different matter to withstand the monotonies of imprisonment day in and day out for years at a time.

I must confess that my eleven years in prison were not at all grey and wearying. Each day brought a new discovery, a new joy. Appearances were to the contrary: an onlooker who saw me would have pronounced me miserable. Indeed, what joy could be left to a starving slave laborer in the freezing expanses of Siberia?

And yet I experienced it differently. For starters, I was accompanied by the knowledge that every day we sat in prison brought more Jews from exile to freedom. No less important, however, I experienced each day as another miraculous step towards coming close to God. Even in prison, I knew how not to be a slave. I knew that a slave is not one who is physically hemmed in by bars, but one who is controlled by external forces that consume him and rob him of his life and from which he cannot escape.

I remember the fifty-day hunger strike I staged near the end of my imprisonment as a demand to be permitted to study Torah. I consciously aimed not to indulge in self-pity, not to falter, but to carry on normally: prayer, exercise, and covert conversations with the student in the next cell. One day, I was in solitary confinement, doing nothing. I no longer felt like I had to do anything in order to sense His closeness. That sense of closeness granted me the renewed vigor I needed to prevail. One man versus all the forces of evil. That is the secret of inner fortitude.

Thirty years later, I'm living the life of a free man in Israel. As everyone knows, the life of a free man possesses at least as many difficult challenges as the life of a prisoner or slave.

Someone who called to urge me to publish this book accurately observed: "The value of your book lies in the fact that you have so faithfully and consistently continued to live the life you began all those years ago." He was right. If I were to honestly ask myself, "Are those values you believed in – the people of Israel, the land of Israel, and the Torah of Israel – still significant for you?" I would answer, "Yes, yes, yes!" Not only have I not veered from the path on which I originally set out, but I have progressed along it. I have studied a great deal of Torah, and, aware of how much I do not know, I wish to learn much more. I have endeavored to act for the good of the Jewish people here in Israel, and wish to do so much more. It is for this reason that I feel privileged to address Jews all over the world.

I know only too well how difficult it can be to endure life when things seem grey and depressing, when our sense of hope and meaning is lost. I too nearly reached the point of such despair. Yet I found a way to elude my weaknesses, to find myself, and to be as my Creator wishes me to be: strong and joyful. And thus I call to the readers of this book: follow me towards a life of joyful purpose and meaning.

About the Author

Yosef Mendelevich was born in Riga, Latvia, in 1947. When he was ten years old, his father was arrested on trumped-up charges and sentenced to five years in prison, provoking the young Yosef's first prayers. By age sixteen he was engaged in the underground struggle for Jewish rights in the Soviet Union. When he founded an underground Jewish organization, he began to study Torah clandestinely and to observe Jewish law, and was among the first in the Soviet Union to return to Jewish observance and faith. At age twenty-two, he was arrested during an attempt to hijack a Soviet plane to make aliyah to Israel. He was sentenced to fifteen years imprisonment. In 1971, the sentence was reduced to twelve years, which he served under the most difficult conditions in the brutal Soviet gulag. During his time in the gulag he stood trial once more for observing Jewish commandments in prison, and endured a fifty-six-day hunger strike to effect the return of his Jewish books. With the help of the efforts of world Jewry, he was released from the gulag in 1981. Since then he has lived in Israel, where he served in the IDF and earned his rabbinic ordination as well as a master's degree in Jewish history, and currently teaches at Jerusalem's Machon Meir Yeshiva. He is married with seven children and many grandchildren.

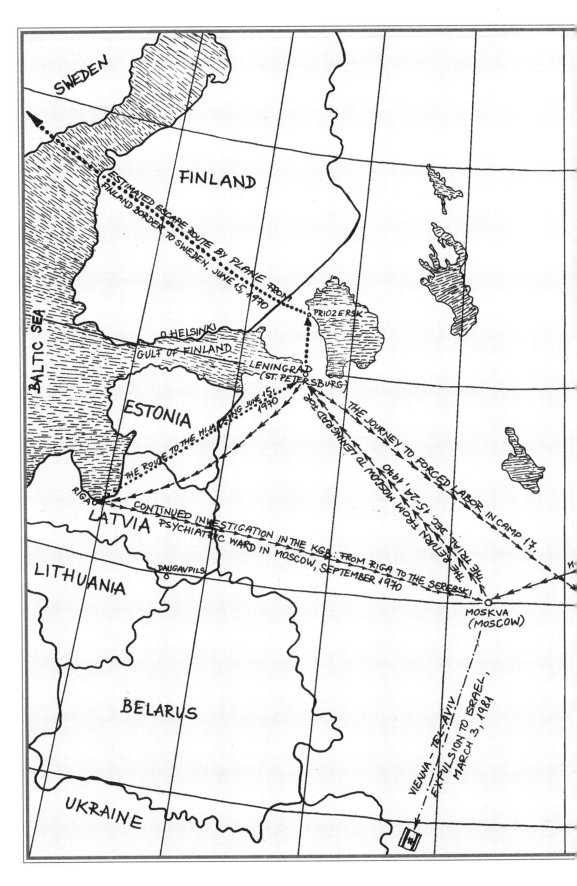